3 0132 0206313

D1492606

CALENDAR PIGS

CALENDAR PIGS

Written and illustrated by
Georgina Jack

Northumberland County Council	
3 0132 02063134 2	
Askews & Holts	Jun-2011
JF	£17.99

Book Guild Publishing
Sussex, England

First published in Great Britain in 2011 by
The Book Guild Ltd
Pavilion View
19 New Road
Brighton, BN1 1UF

Typeset in Palatino by
Ellipsis Books Limited, Glasgow

Printed in Spain under the supervision of MRM Graphics Ltd, Winslow, Bucks

A catalogue record for this book is available from The British Library.

ISBN 978 1 84624 567 1

To my mother and my husband, Ron,
for their unfailing love and support.

Acknowledgements

To Jessica Latham for modelling Emma in the illustrations.

To my niece, Ann Eggleston, for all her help.

List of Illustrations

Chapter 1

The Edge of the World

'Thorny Edge!' shouted the conductor, apparently convinced that his half dozen passengers were deaf, and again 'Thorny Edge!' loudly and importantly, as if announcing the metropolis of the north.

Obediently we sprang from our seats. Yet, as if to remove all doubt from our minds that we had reached our destination, the officious conductor turned and added, 'There's your stop. Right there,' indicating with a jerk of his thumb a metal pole, striped black and white, which had long since lost identification and was leaning at a curious angle.

As the rickety red bus slowed and shuddered to a halt, I peered through the dusty window and thought I had journeyed to the moon. Ahead stretched Sourhope Valley, a craggy wilderness, reminding me in its eerie emptiness of some imagined lunar landscape illustrated in a science fiction book. The valley was so bare and empty that I could see a road winding all the way through it, twisting and turning like a long silver snake until it reached the distant hills and disappeared. My heart sank. This was no holiday resort. I stared at the bleak valley and could not have been more disappointed.

'We're not really getting off here, are we?' I asked anxiously. 'There's nothing here.'

'Yes, Emma, we've arrived at last,' said my mother, busily collecting luggage, surprisingly most of it mine, a fact that I had previously noted and puzzled over.

'But Mum, this isn't a proper place,' I protested, convinced that some dreadful mistake had been made. 'It's empty. I think everybody's left.'

'It's Thorny Edge anyway,' she answered cheerfully. 'Come along, children.'

So at this sorry excuse for a bus stop we alighted, my mother getting off first to help me down the steep steps, aided by an impatient push from my brothers, David, aged thirteen and Neal, aged eleven. I would have been best pleased if they had stayed on the bus because they always teased me unmercifully, but they leapt from the steps like frogs from a pond, landing beside me on the grass verge. They were followed more sedately by two other passengers, who moved off in the wake of the bus as it rattled on its way to the terminus. One was a slightly built man with a skin like a wrinkled old wash leather, who turned out later to be the village postman, and he tipped his cap and grunted as he passed.

'Oh aye,' he said grudgingly, as if obliged to say something in the presence of strangers, for such folk were rare in Thorny Edge.

'Good evening,' replied my mother pleasantly.

'Aye?' he said, with an odd questioning lilt to his voice, sounding surprised that she thought so, but not prepared to commit himself to an opinion.

'You haven't noticed an old Morris car waiting around here, have you?' she asked hopefully.

'No, but then Ah hevn't been lookin' fer one,' he pointed out, and vanished into a nearby cottage, as stony-faced as its owner.

The second passenger was even less inclined to be sociable and kept her eyes deliberately averted. Her face suggested a life fraught with troubles, not the least of which was an enormous goitre forcing her head to one side and causing me to think that something had a stranglehold on her neck. I tried not to stare, but my attention had already been captured by the rough wooden box the woman carried and the intriguing noises coming out of the air holes in the top – sometimes a shuffle, sometimes a slither, and sometimes a sort of snort that made us all look at each other in alarm. The woman had carried the box all the way from Shiretown, and as it plainly contained something alive and kicking, she had cradled it carefully, her gnarled hands clutching the lid and constantly checking the knots in the string. The boys gazed at the box with eyes like saucers, and I could contain my curiosity no longer.

'Mum, what's in her box?' I asked.

'Shush, Emma. I don't know, but keep your voice down or she'll hear you.'

There was, however, no need to worry on that score because the woman's attention was engaged elsewhere. She and her companion in the box had been met by a hatchet-faced man, driving a horse that looked on its last legs and a cart that belonged in a museum. His own appearance was so shabby that I was tempted to ask if he had stolen his clothes from a scarecrow, and he seemed somehow welded into the scruffy cart. He didn't move to help the woman aboard, and not a word was exchanged between them as he whisked her away, leaving only a cloud of dust behind.

Then we were alone. Squinting against the setting sun, I studied the winding road ahead, hoping to see my uncle who should have been there to meet us. I had forgotten what he looked like but I could see no uncles fitting any description, and he wasn't on his way to meet us, since I could tell at a glance that the road was empty as there were no hedges or bushes interrupting the view. The fields were enclosed by dry stone walls in a patchwork of stark stripes, and the few trees that survived were bent like jagged question marks away from the prevailing wind. Apart from the slight movement of grazing cattle, nothing stirred. The air was as silent as in a ghost town, and so still that when a cat, intent on its evening stroll, leapt from a gateway, everyone started in surprise.

'What sort of place is this anyway?' I asked, bemused by the strangeness of it all, so unlike home with its busy streets and gossiping neighbours, and the sense of something going on all the time. I had heard the conductor shout 'Thorny Edge!' Indeed, I had been deafened by it. And now I put two and two together and made five.

'Is this the edge of the world?' I asked.

'No, of course not, pet. It's west Northumberland. I know it's wild, but you'll soon get used to it. Then you'll like it. I think it's lovely. It's what I'd call majestic.'

'But it looks bare. Just like the edge of the world,' I insisted.

'Don't be silly,' said David scathingly. 'You can't remember, but we've been here before, and as you can see, nobody fell off, because we're still all here.'

Neal joined in, looking scornfully down at me in his superior way.

'You're stupid, you are. There's no such thing as the edge of the world. The world's round. Everybody knows that. Everybody except you, Miss Stupid.'

They moved towards me, laughing at me, but just then my mother intervened. Reluctantly she had decided to move on, and she picked up her handbag and the heavy suitcase and began to organize everyone into action.

'Come along, children. Behave yourselves. We have enough problems. I think we'll have to walk.'

'Isn't Uncle Matt coming?' I asked disappointedly.

'Well it doesn't look like it. Perhaps he's run out of petrol. Farmers can only claim a small wartime allowance, but I'm surprised he hasn't brought the horse and cart, or just come himself. He has his faults but he's a considerate man. Though mind you, he's always late. Your aunt Dot says he'll be late for his own funeral.'

We crossed the road and set off, my mother struggling with the suitcase, me carrying a small case full of odds and ends such as toothbrushes and socks, and the boys swinging a leather bag between them, with scant regard for the safety of its contents – the homemade pies, cakes, buns, and rolled baked herrings, tasty contributions to the communal larder. But we had only walked a few yards when we heard the distant drone of a car engine and we paused, watching the hilly road ahead. From far away a buzzing brown dot kept appearing and disappearing like a wandering bee as it bounced over the rough road, and as it drew near it gradually took on the shape of an old car.

Eventually this car reached the opposite bank and meandered slowly down until it came close to a ford in the river. There it seemed to hesitate before decisively gathering momentum, swooshing through the water with reckless abandon, its front wheels spraying waves as if it were a speedboat. Once out of the water, however, it struggled to recover from the swim, coughing and spluttering against the steep gradient, and finally choking to a halt. We crowded round the suffering vehicle and a pleasant face peered out at us through a yellowing windscreen, a smiling face flashing big square teeth and surveying us with shrewd blue eyes.

'Uncle Matt! Uncle Matt!' shouted the boys, carelessly dropping the bag, and at this he opened the car door and emerged, grinning sheepishly. After tipping his cap politely he greeted each of us in turn, starting with my mother.

'Hello, Ellie. How are you?' he asked, showing concern. 'Have you heard any news of John yet?' but she shook her head sadly. The John he referred to was my father, who was away fighting in the war, later to be called the Second World War, and had been reported missing in France. Uncle Matt patted her shoulder sympathetically and then moved on to the boys.

'Hello, David. Hello there, Neal. By heck you've both grown. You sure have,' he said, ruffling their thick black hair, his hand lingering enviously as he remembered the days when he had been the proud possessor of just such a glossy mop.

At last he turned to me, his blue eyes twinkling, and I had the strange impression that for some reason I was special to him, that he had saved the best till last, like the walnut crowning a chocolate cake. As I looked at his shiny shoes, buffed to the glow of polished jet, and his smart dandy-like outfit, I could not help comparing him with the scruffy and unpleasant man in the horse and cart. Yet he had been on time, collecting his wife and her companion in the box, and by contrast my new-found uncle had plainly taken too long titivating his appearance. I felt a little wary of him, but suddenly he knelt down and gave me a cuddle.

'Here she is. Hello, Emma. By, but you're a bonny lass and no mistake,' he said, to my surprise and shy satisfaction.

'What kept you, Uncle Matt?' I asked, and he laughed and stood up.

'The pesky car did, Emma,' he replied. 'She just wouldn't start.' And as he lifted the luggage into the car boot he apologized profusely for his lateness.

'I'm sorry, Ellie. Real sorry. Couldn't get her going until the last minute. Tried all day. I tightened things, and tinkered with things – you know how you do – but sometimes she can be an awkward beggar. And I'm no mechanic. I'll have to get Bill at Coldstone Mea to take a look at her engine before you go home. I'm afraid I lost me temper after a bit. Gave the blighter couple of kicks. Didn't do any good though. Only hurt my toe as it happened. And the trouble is I should've been in the hayfield, so Dot's furious. Says I should've tried to start the car yesterday, and she's right of course. She's always right, is Dot. She'll tell you so herself. Tells me often enough. By heck she does.'

He continued chattering while opening the car doors, and after we took our seats he started turning the car around, a manoeuvre that was no simple three-point turn but involved noisy grinding of gears and frantic yanking of the handbrake, as the car shot backwards, stopping just short of the ditch, and then jerked forward, speeding across the road towards the steep bank opposite. A little tassel dangling from the rear window blind danced about wildly, and there was an ominous clanking sound as the exhaust thumped against the under-side of the car. But our driver remained unruffled.

'Hold on to your hats!' he advised. 'She's in one of her pesky awkward moods. Blast her!' And he wrenched the handbrake again with grim determination.

For a while we see-sawed frenetically to and fro, but finally we were facing the ford once more and after a neck-jerking lurch progressed steadily towards it. But once again Uncle Matt treated the river as a challenge, letting the car hurtle into the water until it splashed so high that the windscreen wipers had to work overtime. The car didn't seem to enjoy its bath, because it whined all the way up the next hill, juddering as if it might stop at any moment. Only Uncle Matt appeared unconcerned. Adopting a sort of kick-and-hope philos-ophy, he kept jabbing his foot on the brake pedal to dry the brakes out, and then slamming hard down on the accelerator to encourage the car to keep going.

'Onward and upward!' he cried again and again as he rocked back and forth in his seat, urging the car forward. 'Onward and upward!' until at last we reached level ground. Then he sat back, calling cheer-fully over his shoulder as we passed an isolated grey building, 'By the way, Emma, there's the school on your left. What do you think of it?'

'It looks a bit quaint,' I said, noticing the tall chimneys and the gabled roof with its small bell tower. 'And it's funny that the windows aren't protected against bombs by sticky tape, like all the schools back home.'

'Nobody drops bombs up here, Emma. It would serve no purpose,' he said complacently, and though I was too polite to agree that there was nothing in Sourhope worth bombing, I understood that bombs would be wasted in such a wilderness.

What I did not understand was why he had singled me out for an opinion on the school, and why, as we passed it, the boys kept sniggering and casting knowing glances from me to the school and back again until I felt uneasy. Then we turned right to face the valley once more, and our destination was pointed out to us – High Windlestraw Farm, far in the distance where fields met fells.

'That looks a million miles away,' I said critically. 'Who'd want to live right up there? I know I wouldn't.' Again I was met with sniggers and significant glances.

The road dropped and then climbed steeply up through a quarry, over a rough track that Uncle Matt told us was called Slate Bank. Here the car ran slower and slower until he braked for a moment, letting the engine idle.

'Sorry about this, folks,' he said, 'but I need you to get out. I'll keep her going while you all push, hard as you can. We'll have her up the hill in no time.'

It occurred to me that his was by far the easier task, but we willingly gathered at the back of the car and pushed with all our might and with some difficulty, because the car was heavy and Slate Bank so steep that it felt vertical to the feet, like walking up a down escalator. The surface was strewn with sharp slivers of stone from the quarry looming over us, slivers that shifted and scattered under my flimsy sandals, and it was a relief when we reached the bank top and paused for a moment, breathless and panting, looking at the valley below. All was desolate. Beside us two empty cottages leant against a disused chapel as if seeking shelter, and a ruined house sat halfway up the hill ahead. Paradoxically it seemed that the higher we climbed the less there was to see. Even the houses dotted here and there seemed to want to be invisible, all lying low and presenting a granite grey front to the world, like ancient relics from the past. The smoke from chimneys was the only sign of occupation, for we had met no one, seen no one, since leaving Thorny Edge. Then suddenly I noticed a bigger farmhouse, close at hand but screened by a rare clump of trees, and in the driveway the horse and cart that had left us at the bus stop. I tugged at my mother's sleeve and pointed.

'Oooh, look! That's where that weird woman lives. The one with the box.'

'Yes, that's right,' said my mother, adding as she climbed into the car, 'we saw those neighbours of yours at the bus stop, Matt.'

'Oh, the Downleys,' he said disapprovingly. 'She's all right, but he's a queer cove. Treats his wife shamefully. Straps her into a cart to pull the milk cans. Uses her like a cart horse.'

'I think he looks like the Devil,' observed David, and for once I agreed with him.

'Yes, they're strange people up here, aren't they?' I said. 'Not very friendly.'

'Well you'll be just as strange yourself soon,' said Neal, with a faint smirk.

'No I won't,' I said. 'Why should I?'

'That's for me to know and you to find out. You just will. That's all.'

'I will not,' I said indignantly. 'I certainly won't. Will I, Mum?'

'No, of course not, Emma. He's just teasing. Take no notice. And you, Neal, you watch what you say.'

The car chugged slowly up the last slope, and then for the first time ran smoothly down to the house. On the road a black and white dog stood wagging his tail in anticipation of our arrival, and as soon as Uncle Matt emerged from the car the collie leapt at him affectionately, swirling round his legs, darting over his feet, tripping him up, and generally getting in his way. He ignored all Uncle Matt's impatient commands, and somehow avoided the hefty kicks aimed in his direction, adroitly swerving out of reach. As one by one we climbed out of the car he repeated his tricks for each of us, wagging his tail in an ecstasy of welcome, planting his paws on the boys' chests, and then licking my face with slobbering gusto.

'Stop that, Split!' shouted my uncle. 'Come on out of it, stupid dog. Here, Split!'

'That's an unusual name, Uncle Matt. Why do you call him Split?' I asked shyly.

'Oh, you can see for yourself,' he said with a wry smile. 'He has a split personality. He's schizophrenic, he is. A law unto himself. We discovered that early on, like. You think he's goin' to do as bidden, but he generally does the opposite. Don't know why I keep him on, unless mebbe it's for laughs.'

Carrying the luggage, he strode down the stone steps and we all followed eagerly, approaching the farmhouse from the side. It was set well below the road, the roof at the back sloping almost to the ground and growing moss and houseleeks on its corners. From the front, the house and attached byre presented a severe aspect, plain as a pikestaff, but the side entrance through the yard made up for that with a rare burst of colour. I stopped, spellbound, gazing at a rockery alive with violas, a dazzling display of painted faces of every hue from the palest cream to the deepest blue, and all nodding like an appreciative audience in time to the musical sound of the garden spring below. The spring, which had been led from the fell to supply fresh water for the house, gurgled from a narrow pipe, tinkled over stones into a small trough, and cascaded to the pebbles below, jingling like sleigh bells.

Accustomed as I was to simply turning on a tap, this unusual source of water fascinated me, but the boys were more interested in the rowan tree in the garden wall. It was a tree that seemed designed to be climbed, so easy was its access, so obligingly situated its branches. It looked as if it had grown out of the wall, elbowing loose stones aside as the bole expanded, and now it dominated the yard. But though the branches hung laden with bunches of scarlet berries, not a berry stained the pristine paving stones beneath. It was as if the tree had been warned that Aunt Dot would tolerate no such liberty, because everything everywhere was as neat as a new pin.

Uncle Matt led us through the side door and over three mats, laid out like stepping stones – one outside, one inside, and one to be on the safe side. For in the matter of footwear, as in so many matters, Aunt Dot was inflexible, insisting that shoes were wiped three times and most meticulously, and we soon became used to her screams of 'Feet! Feet!' whenever we approached either door. But for now, with us being new there and him being well schooled in her strict ways, my uncle gave us a lesson on navigating the three mats. He pushed the luggage into the kitchen, and turned towards us, holding up his flat hand in a cautionary gesture, as if preventing a stampede indoors.

'Wipe your feet!' he warned, and proceeded to demonstrate, moving nimbly from mat to mat, shuffling his shoes back and forth, up and down, rapidly and with abandon, as if dancing an Irish jig.

We could not even begin to emulate his fancy footwork, but we did our humble best, jigging our feet with more energy than skill while he watched us with a critical eye.

'You mean like this, Uncle Matt?' asked Neal, laughing as he gave a spirited performance on the first mat in which his feet hardly touched the ground.

9

But our uncle frowned and shook his head.

'No, definitely not,' he said reprovingly. 'You're tryin' to fly over it, and that won't do for your aunt Dot. My meanin' is, it won't do at all.'

Then he favoured us with an encore, sweeping his feet over the third mat in a thorough wiping motion that left no doubt of his serious intention. I half expected him to round off the proceedings with a spirited shriek, but soon realized that he would never let himself go to that extent in the hallowed precincts of Aunt Dot's kitchen. The atmosphere in there had a sobering effect on all of us, and a hush fell as we stole reverently over the flagstoned floor, scrubbed so clean that it seemed a sacrilege to walk on it.

In awed silence and in single file we passed by a bench supporting buckets of fresh water, and a pine table displaying a batch of brown loaves, somewhat stumpy and misshapen, but freshly baked and giving off a wonderful aroma. Ahead a larder door stood open, revealing five sad-looking hams suspended from hooks, together with eggs in trays, sufficient for a fortnight of Easters. Jugs of milk ranged from cow-fresh to almost curdled, and there was also a small hoard of tinned fruit, rarely obtainable in wartime, which Aunt Dot enjoyed counting but never opened, always saving them for a rainy day.

A planked door on the left opened to the living room, which we entered, huddling together like sheep, waiting to be acknowledged. This room was also spacious but spartan, though warm enough from the heat being thrown from an open fire in an ugly black range. An oblong table covered with a snowy cloth occupied the centre, surrounded by six ladder-back chairs, standing stiff and straight like sentinels guarding the condiments and cutlery. A grandfather clock and an unadorned sideboard backed flatly against the far wall as if trying to be inconspicuous, and the rest of the furniture consisted only of chairs – a small rocking chair, a carved corner chair, and two armchairs, lumpy and squashy.

It soon dawned on me that there were no other reception rooms. Apart from the two bedrooms, that was the house and that was all of it, the rest of the building housing only animals. The one exception was the bathroom, if such it could be called. It was a small primitive stone hut at the bottom of the garden, a lavatory furnished with a broad wooden seat out of which two companionable holes had been cut. It was known as 'the netty', and looked as if it was not the most convenient of conveniences, especially on icy winter nights.

Aunt Dot, who was much smaller than I expected, had her back to us as she busily stirred a big black pan on the open fire. She now put her spoon down and turned, head tilted and eyes piercingly curious, looking us over in her pert, bird-like way. Then she smoothed her hair, patted her apron, and stepped forward to greet us. I expected hugs all round and a special welcome for her sister, whom she had not seen for some years, but she held back, standing as woodenly as the ladder-back chairs. She smiled, a bright brittle smile, but remained rigid and tense, as if operating on a tight spring mechanism, over-wound and ready to snap if not handled carefully.

'Ah, there you are at last. I'd just about given you up,' she said, her tone implying that we were deliberately late, and my mother looked disappointed at such a greeting.

'It's been a long journey,' she pointed out, sinking thankfully into an armchair.

'Yes, you'll be glad of a bite to eat,' said Aunt Dot briskly, 'but what a pity you didn't get here sooner. I've made a few broth but they've thickened up a bit and the potatoes have gone mushy. Still, I've done my best and everything's ready, so eat up. Did you all give your feet a good wipe?'

In a few minutes we were seated at the table consuming a bowl of steaming broth with mushy potatoes. The broth was fortified with barley, no favourite of mine, and was thick enough to stand a spoon upright, and I soon discovered that as it had thickened it had caught on the bottom of the pan. I stirred up floating black particles and detected a slightly burnt taste, but no one commented, and Aunt Dot's challenging expression discouraged criticism. In addition to the burnt taste, however, or perhaps to disguise it, the broth, like my aunt, was distinctly peppery. Knowing nothing then of her volatile nature or that she was very touchy about her cooking, I pointed at the offending dish and opened my mouth to expose its several short-comings.

'This broth's . . .' I began, and Aunt Dot visibly stiffened, but my mother, who seemed to be expecting just such an outburst from me, shook her head slightly and finished my sentence.

'Very tasty, isn't it, Emma?' she said, giving me a meaningful glance.

I took the hint, though my words were even more difficult to swallow than the broth. But we were all hungry, and Aunt Dot's culinary disaster, the first of many, was eventually dispatched, even to second helpings in the case of my two undiscerning hungry brothers.

11

Then iced buns were unpacked, and Aunt Dot produced ginger biscuits from what appeared to be a surprisingly unlimited supply in a cupboard beside the fireplace, and I had the impression from the proud way she served them with a little flourish that she regarded them as a rare treat, that she treasured them and collected them the way some people collect works of art.

'Now we'll all have a nice cup of tea,' she said brightly. 'What would we do without a nice cup of tea?' And we sat talking and drinking a seemingly endless quantity of the brew until Uncle Matt departed into the byre. Then Aunt Dot fastened her cold grey eyes on me and began to ask personal questions, interrogating me until I felt uncomfortable, and even, in an odd way, guilty.

'So tell me honestly, Emma. Honestly mind! Are you well behaved?' She asked this as if she were enquiring into the training of a dog or a horse. 'I mean – always a good girl?'

'Well – I do – try,' I answered, embarrassed.

'And do you help around the house? With little jobs and so on?'

'If Mum wants me to,' I said truthfully, conscious of how seldom my mother called upon me to do so.

'But you *are* useful? You *have* been brought up useful?'

'She's only eight, Dot,' my mother reminded her, rather anxiously, I thought.

'Can't start too soon to be useful,' persisted Aunt Dot. 'Too many layabouts nowadays doing nothing but take up space.'

I shifted uncomfortably in my seat, and as usual my mother came to my rescue.

'She's the best little girl in the world,' she said, smiling reassuringly, and at that I took the opportunity to remove myself from the conversation.

If I had doubts about my uncle's nature, I was beginning to have many more regarding my aunt, and I found myself resenting her questions. Besides, I was keenly aware that my brothers were not being cross-questioned at all. So I moved away to the window, curling up on the wide window sill. Though I didn't suspect it then, that window sill would become my refuge, and I would spend many a lonely hour behind its concealing curtains. But now dusk was descending on the valley, intensifying the atmosphere of mystery and isolation. I stared at the hills opposite where only one house light glimmered, and at the dene, known as Todd Tingate's Dene, though no one could tell me why. Beyond the dene stood Todd Tingate's farmhouse, now derelict, and beyond that swept vast tracts of moorland, circling the Northumbrian hills.

'It really is a wilderness,' I murmured, half to myself, 'just a wilderness. I bet it's terrible up here in winter, when you have snow and ice. I bet it's like the North Pole.'

'Well, you'll soon find out,' said David smartly.

'Whatever do you mean?'

'Nothing. You'll soon know.'

I suddenly shivered, conscious of a chill down the spine, but was unable to account for it, except that I sensed there was something wrong, some worrying change or threat to my peace of mind, hidden only from me.

'Mum, what's going on? What does he mean?' I asked in trembling tones.

'Oh, nothing, Emma. Take no notice, pet. He's only making mischief. Now come and sit by me on the rocking chair. You'll like that. See what your aunt Dot's doing? She's lighting the oil lamp. We can't press a light switch up here, you know.'

Once again she gave the boys a warning look, this time so stern that it discouraged them from further comments for the rest of the week, thereby lulling me into a false sense of security and making the blow, when it finally came, even more devastating. For they understood the real reason for this visit. They knew what I did not – not yet. They knew that the purpose of the long journey to Sourhope was to leave me behind, without my mother, the very centre of my world, for the duration of the war.

Chapter 2

Making Hay While the Sun Shines

Aunt Dot suited her name down to the very 't' at its end, serving as
it did as a description of her size and shape. For she had been created
dainty in almost every particular, as dainty and fragile as a doll, with
two notable exceptions – her hair and her character. It happened that
by a curious quirk of fate all that daintiness had been crowned by a
shock of strong red hair, vigorous and unruly, and as she had a natural
aversion to anything unruly, she kept it under control by means of
a long black bootlace. This she tied severely at the front and tightly
in a bow at the back where her hair fell in a sober pageboy style,
firmly restrained.

The colour she could not control and it glowed gloriously red like
hot embers in a fire, reflecting her fiery temperament, because to
describe her character as forceful would be to understate the case.
She may have been a dot, but every steely inch of her four-foot-eleven

figure radiated determination, and apart from the 't' in her name she hated anything about her to be crossed. She always insisted upon her own way, sweeping aside all obstacles, and she had married a mild-mannered man who, as long as he was not personally inconvenienced, indulged her every whim, allowing her to rule the roost, or at least to believe that she did, so that she became steadily more and more obdurate. I once saw her pinned against the barn wall by an escaped bull, eyeball to eyeball with it, and such was her strength of will that in the end it was the bull that blinked and backed away. Indeed, woe betide anyone who stood in her way or attempted to thwart her purpose.

It was not surprising, therefore, given her iron will, that straight after breakfast on the following morning we were all put to work. Uncle Matt had been dispatched early to collect the horse, Sandy – so called because of his colour – and harness him to the hay-rake. While the rest of us had been eating breakfast, a simple meal of brown bread and home-made butter, Aunt Dot had pirouetted impatiently round the table, eager to put her plans into effect for making hay while the sun shone. The boys enjoyed healthy appetites which, given time, might have extended to three or even four slices, but Aunt Dot was having none of that, clicking her tongue irritably, and removing first the butter from the table and then the bread.

'My goodness!' she had exclaimed inhospitably. 'I'd rather keep you two for a week than a fortnight. Come on, now, boys. Enough's enough!'

And shortly afterwards, and almost without knowing how it happened, we found ourselves spirited outside and lined up in the front meadow, reluctant volunteers for hayfield duty. Any lingering thoughts we might have entertained of investigating the delights of the farm, or exploring the neighbourhood, or simply enjoying our holiday were soon dispelled. We were each supplied with a hand rake and were given a brief demonstration on how to use it to turn the newly mown hay, already dry on top, to let the damp underside face the sun.

'Your uncle Matt should be back at any minute,' Aunt Dot promised. 'He'll take over when he comes with the hay-rake.'

'Then can we play?' I enquired hopefully.

'No, Emma. Then I'll find a different little job for you.'

But time passed without a sign of my uncle, and my mother became increasingly curious, finally unable to resist asking the question that was on everyone's mind.

15

'Dot, where on earth is Matt? Wherever can he be?'

'Oh, he's in the top lot, catching the horse. It takes time, you know, but he won't be long. I'm sure he'll be here at any minute,' said Aunt Dot defensively.

She pursed her lips, discouraging further discussion on the subject, and we gradually settled down, speaking of other matters as if my uncle and the horse were not expected, turning the hay pretty well in unison and working together quite contentedly in the warm sun. The novelty of the task somehow made it easier for me and my brothers, transforming work into play, though Aunt Dot appeared distracted, and seemingly driven by a need to work faster than any of us, including her, were able to. As she worked she glanced repeatedly at the sky, making the same comments again and again about the excellence of the weather, but in a superstitious way, as if she thought it might change if she stopped continually singing its praises.

'Such a lovely day! Really lovely! We're so lucky. But we have to take full advantage of good weather like this. It's most unusual to have such a long fine spell. Good weather that lasts, I mean – that's the thing. And we must get on while it's here. That we must. It's just perfect hay weather. Perfect.'

I found her obsession with the weather strange at the time, but later I understood why she set such store by a fine day. I was to discover that the sun seldom showed its face for long in those cold hills, more often than not hiding away as if reluctant to waste warmth and radiance on such a bleak landscape. Yet on the rare occasions when it did shine, everything looked better, with the sharp contours softened by a shimmering haze. Even the farm looked different, more homely than plain. And that first day itself could only be described as beautiful – the sky azure blue and the sun steadfastly brilliant, lending the hayfield an idyllic aspect.

A soft breeze ruffling the hay wafted seeds and spicy dust into the air, giving off an earthy smell, warm and sweet; while high overhead a skylark sang, soaring and sinking with the easy motion of a yo-yo, warbling to us as it rose and fell. At our feet fieldmice scattered, sprinting from the threatening rakes, trailing long tails which the farm dog chased but never caught; instead bounding back to trip over our feet, jumping the rakes and panting for applause. I had been given the smallest rake but it was still too long for little me, so the dog's antics compounded my incompetence. There was no denying that he got in the way, and Aunt Dot kept edging him aside with her rake and pointing a commanding finger at the middle distance, ordering him to 'Go!' and to 'Sit!' and to 'Stay!' Any sensible dog would have had the wit to obey, especially as her prods in his ribs became ever more forceful. But Split regarded her commands as teasing gambits, part of the fun, and gazed at her with puppy-like devotion, redoubling his efforts to perform acrobatic tricks.

He had been with Uncle Matt, and at first Aunt Dot took his reappearance as a sign that his master was on his way too, but two hours passed and still there was no sign of him. Then at last he arrived, hot and bothered, red in the face from heat and exertion, and conspicuously alone, lacking a horse of any description. All he had in tow was a bucket that squeaked and rattled, announcing his approach, as did his muttered oaths, which we could distinguish from some distance away. He was like the prologue before a play, setting the scene for us by his moans and groans, and Aunt Dot sighed, suspended work, and waited, leaning impatiently on her rake and regarding him with mild irritation, much as she did the fieldmice.

He had taken a bucket of crushed oats to tempt the horse to follow him; sadly underestimating the animal's intelligence, for no work-shy horse would leave the lush grass of a verdant pasture for a handful of dry oats. What puzzled Uncle Matt was that sometimes the ruse worked, but only if Sandy felt in the mood to cooperate. Like everyone else on my uncle's farm – like Aunt Dot and the dog, like the goats and the geese, even the moles and rabbits – Sandy pleased himself. At one point he had stuck his head in the bucket, raising hope, but after a quick nibble he had bolted, galloping round the field as if favourite for the Derby. It was ironic, as my mother later remarked, that the racehorses Uncle Matt backed rarely ran fast enough to win, but Sandy managed to outstrip every farm horse in the district, too fast to catch.

'What happened, Matt?' asked my aunt, adding bitterly, 'As if I didn't know.' He looked as sheepish as his entire flock of Swaledales.

'A horse! A horse! My kingdom for a horse!' muttered David, and both boys sniggered, so that Uncle Matt, who did not quite catch what was said, shot a suspicious glance at them.

'Yes, why haven't you caught the horse, Uncle Matt?' I asked innocently.

''Cos it ran faster than me,' he answered tetchily, flinging his arms in a despairing gesture. 'That huh-horse!' he cried, choking on the word. 'That blasted animal! He's more like an eel than a horse. By heck, he's a slippery customer! He was off like greased lightnin' whenever I got near. It's not my fault. It isn't, Dot. I'd like to cut his pesky legs off. That I would!'

'It would certainly stop him running away,' quipped Neal. But Uncle Matt was in no temper to see humour in the situation, and he advanced threateningly.

'I'll cut your pesky little legs off too in a minute,' he shouted, and Neal retreated, returning to rake hay as if his life depended on it.

Split had already made himself scarce. As soon as he heard his master's voice, he sensed that after his recent dereliction of duty he would not be popular, and retired to a safe distance, hiding behind a pile of hay. There he attempted to become invisible, a difficult task for a black and white collie in a hayfield, but he rose to the challenge, or rather sank to it, flattening every part of his anatomy, even to his laid-back ears and tail tucked under. Only his bright eyes remained alert, ready for further retreat, and if necessary to relinquish the field. Meanwhile, Aunt Dot attempted to bring the haymakers to order.

'Well, this won't do. It simply won't. We can't laze around here all day, wasting time. We must get on while this lovely weather holds. Now Matt, you go back and have another try at catching Sandy. I'm sure you'll manage this time. What a pity you didn't take a handful of cowcake. Try that when you go again. Sometimes he likes it for a change. And hurry, Matt! Hurry! We'll keep things ticking over here.'

She sounded like an officer rallying flagging troops and I noticed that even the rake at her side was standing to attention. We all leapt into action, resuming our work, all of us except Uncle Matt, who mopped his forehead, slowly and thoughtfully, and then stood scratching his arm, mulling over the situation in his mind. Many men, when faced with the prospect of returning to the chase of a rebellious horse on a steaming hot day, of pursuing flying hooves and avoiding flying clods and cowpats, would have sought an excuse. Uncle Matt was one of those men. He had no intention on that sticky, enervating afternoon of renewing acquaintance with the back end of a horse. But experience had taught him to keep his intentions to himself, and in his dealings with Aunt Dot to proceed with caution, feeling his way carefully to that moment of suppressed triumph when she made the decision that he had led her to. So he now nodded in agreement.

'Right. All right. I'll do that, Dot. I'll be off straight away. Right now, in fact.'

'Good,' she said, without raising her eyes from the rake.

'Right then. I'll go. My meanin' is, if that's what you really want.'

'It is. We'll get on much faster with the horse.'

He grimaced dubiously. 'Of course, but there you have it, Dot. First catch your horse. It's not that easy. It's dashed difficult. You have him in your reach and before you can say "Gotcha!" he's gone and out of reach. He's like a flash of lightnin' – like that flyin' horse – Pegasus, I think it was. If I didn't know better I'd swear the blighter had wings.'

Aunt Dot paused for a moment and regarded him as one might a petulant child.

'Now listen to me, Matt. It's quite simple – you have to let him know who's boss.'

'I think he knows,' he replied ruefully, 'and it isn't me.'

'Nonsense. Sometimes you catch him quite easily. Now go and get him.'

'But it all takes time, Dot. It's a job in itself. I could have a lot of work done down here while I'm up there wastin' time.'

'But that's the whole point of having a horse, Matt – to save time. It's absurd. That lazy horse idles the day away while we do all the work.'

'Yes, you're right, Dot. Right as ever. Never wrong. All things bein' equal, like. But just look what you've achieved without the horse. It's a true sayin' that many hands make light work. You've all done wonders, and what have I achieved today? Absolutely nothin'. It occurs to me that if I'd been helpin' here instead of runnin' a long-distance handicap against Sandy, why, we'd have this field half finished.'

Aunt Dot felt some sympathy for this reasoning but once she had set her mind on a course of action, right or wrong, she would not be diverted.

'We'll get on faster with the horse,' she insisted.

'Oh yes, once I've nabbed him and led him to the stack yard and harnessed him and yoked him into the hay-rake. That's if I can catch him at all, of course.'

She frowned, and he appeared to give in. 'Anyway,' he said, 'I'll have another try, as you suggest. I'll be off now. Wasted enough time today.' Then he added with a touch of sarcasm, 'If I'm not back before dark, send out a search party.'

He began to walk away, but hesitated, half turning as if struck by a sudden thought.

'Unless,' he said, producing his trump card and staking everything on it, 'unless you'd like me to brew you a pot of tea before I go? You must be ready for a cup after all your hard work. You certainly deserve one. All of you. Tea hits the spot on a day like today. It's so refreshin'. But no. Mebbe it's too soon. I'm guessin' it's only about half past twelve. A bit early. Yes of course. It's a daft idea – *tea*. A silly notion, *tea*. It's just such thirsty weather that *tea* comes to mind, and I just thought you might be ready for a cup. But you're right. It's better to catch the horse first. Definitely. There's no hurry for *tea*.'

He had thrown the suggestion casually over his shoulder as if of no consequence, though carefully repeating and emphasizing the hypnotic word 'tea'. And now he ambled off up the meadow while Aunt Dot stared at his slowly trudging back. She stood motionless and I had the idea that some sort of psychological struggle was going on within her. Tea was her Achilles' heel, and whenever she found herself within reaching distance of a kettle she automatically filled it and brewed up. For her to work more than two hours without that essential boost to her system was practically unprecedented, and the dreamy look that always came into her eyes at its mere mention softened her expression and with it her resolve.

'Stop!' she shouted, and Uncle Matt, who had been expecting the call, turned and endeavoured to look surprised.

'Yes, Dot? Somethin' you want?'

'I've been thinking,' she said, 'as you say, it's a hot day, and I suppose everyone's thirsty. I know I am. And now's as good a time as any for a break. Tell you what – I've an idea. You take over here and I'll go and make us all some tea and a bite to eat. If it's half twelve it's lunchtime.'

'But what about the horse?'

'Oh, just leave him for the present.'

'Really? Do you think so, Dot?' he asked ingenuously, his heart lifting. 'Well, all right. You know best. You're the boss. You know that. Now, are you quite sure?'

Without a word she handed him her rake and strode up the field, her red hair swinging jauntily from side to side as she made short work of the distance to the front door. I had been witnessing an object lesson in handling Aunt Dot, and I should have been taking due notice, perhaps even jotting down notes. But at that point I had no idea that I would soon be needing all the help I could get in dealing with her. Since first meeting them, I had rather assumed that my aunt had Uncle Matt under her foot, like a fourth doormat. 'Uncle Matt the doormat' was a phrase that irreverently popped into my head more than once, though I never dared voice it. But now I saw him in a different light, and just as it was in his relationship with the horse, it was difficult to decide who was the boss. He had undoubtedly won that round with Dot, with a complete turnabout, and it struck me that he was as wily as a fox, and that no one, not even Aunt Dot, would walk all over him.

Meanwhile, my mother also downed tools and followed my aunt into the house, and in a little while they returned carrying a rug and two big baskets containing sundry cups and plates, two big billycans of tea, bread and butter, and a selection of my mother's pies, both savoury and sweet. Gratefully, we all sat on the rug or the warm grass eating an alfresco lunch in what had now become a convivial atmosphere, a special occasion. For everyone had what he or she wanted. Aunt Dot remained indisputably in charge, taking full credit for the feast and drinking tea as if it might go out of fashion. Yet Uncle Matt had procured for himself an afternoon that promised to be much more agreeable and less energetic than his morning had been. We all enjoyed the treat of a picnic in the hay, and as for the horse, he had the whole day off.

Only the dog was left out of it. Only he suffered, because the necessity of distancing himself from Uncle Matt automatically also distanced him from the pies. Normally he would have whined and begged for his share, but now he dared not show his face, even though the subtle smell drifting over the field, especially the tasty whiff of meat pies, set his sensitive canine nose twitching. He was hungry, and that tantalizing smell only made things worse. He spent some time gnawing a splinter of old sheep's horn that he had unearthed while burrowing under the hay, but it tasted stale and dry. Then he lay there snapping his jaws ravenously at various beetles and grasshoppers, and eyeing with more than casual interest a passing frog, but eventually his nose took over, leading him towards the meat pies. He advanced tentatively and spasmodically, like a soldier on tactical manoeuvres, keeping his body low and darting in short runs punctuated with sudden stops, when he froze still as a statue. Making stealthy but steady progress, he crawled first left, then right, uncertain of his reception but ready in his hunger to risk all, even a threat to his legs, for a slice of pie. Sadly, by the time his complicated manoeuvres were finished, so were the pies, but Uncle Matt, now happy as a sandboy, gathered up the scraps, folded them between two slices of bread, and to show there was no ill feeling, threw them at the disappointed dog's front paws.

'There you are, you villainous pesky dog!' he said good-humouredly, and while Split made short work of the sandwich, he wiped his buttery hands on his trousers.

Then we all helped to clear away the picnic and recommenced raking. By evening the hay in the front meadow had all been turned and when the midges began to bite we gladly took refuge in the farm-house. Uncle Matt whistled for Split and departed to round up the cows for milking, while Aunt Dot partook of a fresh pot of tea and followed him to officiate in the cooler house. Tiny as she was, she ably carried away the heavy pails of milk and, straining every sinew, lifted them high to pour the warm liquid into a metal cooling tank above the sterilizer. We watched, fascinated, as the milk oozed through the holes and trickled in a frothy fountain down over the tubes of cold water and through a strainer into the ten-gallon churn that was nearly as tall as I was. Meanwhile, my mother busied herself making the evening meal and afterwards we all sat round the table happily discussing the various exciting excursions that might entertain us the following day. It was an academic discussion as it turned out, because Aunt Dot had already decided for us.

'It's all settled,' she said briskly. 'Weather permitting, it's Todd Tingate's tomorrow. There's hay waiting there for attention.'

I had my excuse at the ready.

'I'd like to help you, Aunt Dot,' I said politely, 'but my hands are all blistered from the rake.'

'That's all right, Emma. We won't be raking tomorrow. We'll be forking and stacking,' she said, then added, as if bestowing privi-leges on us, 'and you can all help. I can find a nice little job for each of you. There's a lot to do. Don't worry – you won't be bored.'

'But my hands are sore and my legs are all scratched and bitten,' I protested.

'Well, Emma, maybe they'll be better tomorrow. We'll dab them with glycerine. It stings a bit but you're a brave girl aren't you? You'll need to be, living up here.'

In time I would know never to oppose Aunt Dot's wishes, nor cross her in any way, but I had been brought up in a household where my opinions held some weight. If not always adopted, they were at least considered, and I yet had much to learn. So, rashly appointing myself spokesman for the rest, I piped up on everyone's behalf, 'But Aunt Dot, we're supposed to be on holiday. I want to play tomorrow.' And for once, my brothers murmured in agreement.

She turned on me with cold grey eyes, her gaze concentrated in a stare such as a gorgon might have used to turn someone to stone. Then she smiled – a strangely disturbing smile.

'Now listen to me,' she snapped. 'You *can* play. You can play in the hay. You can build pikes. It's just like building sand castles, only more use.'

And so the week's holiday passed in work. Aunt Dot kept a weather eye on the barometer, and as long as it registered fair she acted the martinet – issuing orders, giving no quarter, and dismissing all appeals out of hand. We raked and forked, carried and flattened, shaping the dried hay into small mounds, or kyles as Uncle Matt called them; then into tall pikes, and finally into a huge stack, from the top of which I peered down on the world like a dwarf from a giant's shoulder.

Fortunately, after that first day, Sandy's mood changed and thereafter, for some reason, he allowed himself to be caught without much effort and yoked into the hay-rake and then into the flat bogey, obligingly pulling one or the other all day. At times he carried us too, as he plodded to and fro from field to stack yard, for after a pike had been tied with chains and wound onto the bogey, we children climbed up and were borne aloft on its crown. There we sat, cushioned by hay, swaying as stately as maharajahs on elephants, a dangerous perch, but we soon learnt to balance. Then we looked forward to a faster ride back, hanging on for dear life as the bogey rattled over bumps and we slid about on its slippery bed.

Towards the end of the week, however, progress was halted for a while; this time, though, it was not Sandy but Split who put a hold on proceedings. Despite being directed to keep behind the bogey, and given several instructive reminders from Uncle Matt's boot, he took it into his head to dart in front of the horse, causing the startled animal to rear in alarm and bolt for the gate. We clung on desperately as he careered towards the opening, so narrow that normally he had to be steered carefully through. Uncle Matt stared after him aghast, and then began to run, shouting at the top of his voice, 'Whoa, boy! Whoa, Sandy! Whoa there! Whoa!'

We never knew whether Sandy heard him or if it was some instinct that caused him to stop, but he came to a halt suddenly, abruptly, and just too late. We felt a sharp jolt as the bogey hit the gatepost, jack-knifed, and hurtled us pell-mell off the rear end. Luckily we suffered little hurt other than scrapes and scratches, but the bogey and the gatepost were less fortunate. Both sustained damage and work was suspended. Uncle Matt swore long and volubly. Then he steadied the horse, loosened him from the shafts, and in a futile but understandable gesture set off in angry pursuit of the dog, yelling after him as he ran, 'Come here, boy! Here boy! So I can strangle you. Come here now. So I can cut your pesky legs off. Here, Split, here! You cretinous collie! You useless lump of rubbish! Come here to me!'

Split managed to resist this threatening invitation, rapidly making himself scarce, and all we saw of him for the rest of the afternoon was a pair of pricked up ears far away in the distance. When Uncle Matt returned to inspect the damage he discovered that all the metal parts, such as the old iron wheels, were fortunately intact, but that a vital bolt had bent, piercing the bogey and splintering its surface, and that the gatepost had snapped off near the bottom. Still uttering threats at the missing dog, he set off in search of a suitable piece of wood to mend the bogey with, on the way collecting a saw, a hammer and nails. Then, muttering the occasional curse and with a soothing cigarette dangling from his lips, he commenced the repair. But he soon realized that he needed a drill, and after a moment's thought decided to borrow one from John Phillip's farm, Nettlehead. Curiously, once he had made that decision, he perked up. His temper improved, and he began to whistle through his teeth, making the cheerful noise of a boiling kettle, a harbinger of good things to come.

Nettlehead was a bastle house, a sort of fortified farmhouse, not the nearest household to High Windlestraw, but invariably the one he headed to first for help. It was obvious, even to me, that Aunt Dot suspected him of having a soft spot for Mrs Phillip, the local beauty, and certainly when it came to borrowing from Nettlehead he dropped his usual cavalier approach. In general he tended to borrow a tool on the basis of a semi-permanent loan, so that the lender risked losing both itself and friend, as Shakespeare would have put it. But when it came to Mrs Phillip, he was punctiliously prompt. He liked having an excuse to avail himself of another visit, and so the drill he was borrowing from the Phillips to repair the bogey would be taken back that very day.

While my brothers and I played in the hayfield, Aunt Dot and my mother spread the wet grass left behind by the pikes. Aunt Dot timed the duration of Uncle Matt's absence to fetch the drill and was visibly irritated by the faraway look in his eyes when he eventually returned, at least in body if not in spirit. The drill in his hand, a smile on his lips, and a flush of excitement on his cheeks, he was eager to impart his news. He had found Mrs Phillip in the hayfield, keeping cool in silk pyjamas, and that vision had plainly made a lasting impression on him. As he mentioned maybe twenty times, to Aunt Dot's manifest annoyance, Mrs Phillip had looked most attractive, a very comely sight, in fact.

'She was workin' in the hay, Dot. Wearin' silk pyjamas. I mean to say, Dot, silk eh? What do you think of that? Pink they were. No – I tell a lie – I would say more of a peachy colour. Yes, definitely, peach. I saw her close to, like,' he said musingly, and Aunt Dot directed one of her stony stares at him.

'Well good for you, Matt! So that's what took you so long. You've been sightseeing.'

'But silk pyjamas are just the ticket, Dot. Just the thing.'

'Just the thing for what?' she enquired with a sharp look. 'Sliding out of bed?'

'No, she was tellin' me, Dot. She explained that they're cool, you see, bein' silk, like. For workin' in hot weather. They're a good idea, Dot. A very good idea. Definitely.'

'Oh, you think so, do you?' she asked, in deceptively pleasant tones.

'I do, Dot. I definitely do,' he persisted recklessly. 'You should get some. You really should.'

'So that's what you think, is it? That's your considered opinion? That I should buy expensive silk pyjamas to strut around the hayfield in?'

'Well, my meanin' is, Dot, they look lovely on Mrs Phillip and I'm sure they'd suit you too.'

Lithe as a willow wand she bent down, and a second later a carefully aimed clod of earth winged its way in his direction, causing him to duck just in time.

'I know what your meaning is, Matt Wheatley,' she said, flashing him one of her looks that could kill, 'so just get your mind off silk pyjamas and onto fixing that bogey as fast as you can. You can leave the gatepost till tomorrow morning. Get up nice and early. And by the way, when I can afford pink frippery, you'll be the first to know.'

'Fair enough,' he said, deflated, his enthusiasm for silk pyjamas slightly dampened. 'I just mentioned it, an' that. A bloke can mention an idea, can't he? My meanin' is, it's a free country, isn't it? Leastways until Adolph Hitler gets here.'

He retreated, disgruntled, but, inspired by the anticipation of a return visit to Nettlehead, where the vision that was Mrs Phillip might still be decorating the hayfield, he set to with a will and soon had the bogey back in commission.

By the end of the week most of the hay had been gathered, putting even Aunt Dot into a good mood, so much so that on the last full day of the holiday she relented, giving us the day off.

'All right,' she said, smiling her wintry smile. 'Off you go. You can play today.'

I regarded her suspiciously. 'Do you mean – play in the hay building pikes, Aunt Dot?'

'Oh no. Today you can do what you like. There'll be bread and treacle on the table at twelve if you're hungry, and after that you can please yourselves.'

Delightedly we ran wild and free around the farm. We tunnelled through the hay in the barn, leapt like cheetahs from the wall to the meadow, climbed the rowan tree, chased each other over the fell, and played hide and seek behind the big grey boulders. In the afternoon, fortified by treacle and bread, we followed the stream down through the dene to the burn, where we found a natural swimming pool, overhung with willows on both sides so that the branches intermingled in a lacy sylvan tunnel. The boys had taken swimming trunks, intending only to paddle, but in that pool of slowly swirling water, deep and dark, cool and magical, they could duck and dive in the company of zigzagging green dragonflies, and swim in competition with speckled silver trout. Not yet able to swim, and wary lest the boys pushed me in, I sat some distance downstream on a bank of meadowsweet and wiggled my toes contentedly in the shallow water. It was pretty there by the burn, unlike most of Sourhope, which seemed to me to live up to its name. I shared the bank with tiny blue butterflies and little pop-eyed lizards basking on stones. Dozens of wild bees buzzed on the opposite bank, and wagtails bobbed like bathers in and out of the water.

It had been, I thought, a surprisingly pleasant day, all the more surprising because the boys had included me in their play. Contrary to my usual experience, I had not been mocked or mimicked, or tripped or tied up, or tormented in any way. They had not harassed me or pulled my hair, or undone my belt, or fired pellets at my legs, or tried any of their habitual tricks. In fact, they had been unexpectedly kind, and when they found a field mushroom as big as a tea plate and perfectly formed, they handed it to me to carry proudly to the house. I was a little disconcerted at this unaccustomed attention, and though gratified, I felt strangely uneasy.

In late afternoon the midges descended, attracted by the water. Then other bothersome insects pestered and persisted until we were driven back to the farm, pursued all the way by clouds of black flies, some big, some minute, but all buzzing maddeningly round our heads. As we fled we passed a bank covered in a mass of globe flowers, pale gold and full blown like cream puffs, and I risked more midge bites to pick a bunch as a parting gift for Aunt Dot. I could never have anticipated how unappreciative she would be, or that she would tell me through disapprovingly pursed lips that 'I never clutter up my clean house with smelly, messy, insect-ridden flowers, least of all wild ones that are nothing but weeds'.

Nor could I have known that the globe flowers, once picked, would last little longer than my present happiness, and that the parting when it came would not be the one I expected, and would almost break my heart.

Chapter 3

Betrayal

That evening when we returned tired and happy to the house, we found a visitor installed in the living room, a burly and genial Northumbrian, filling an armchair with his ample proportions and the air around him with tobacco smoke. He had a face like a full moon and a figure that proved he was no stranger to suet puddings, popular fare in those parts, often rolled between layers of leeks. Bill Batey, who farmed at Coldstone Mea, ranked among those select few whom Uncle Matt considered as friends. From time to time they shared farm machinery, helped each other in emergencies, or simply called on one another for a good gossip. But on this occasion Bill had been summoned to tinker with the car, to make sure that it could be relied upon to start on the following day.

Compared with Uncle Matt, who barely knew his carburettor from his big end, Bill shone as a mechanical genius, and having twiddled and fine-tuned the engine till it sparked instantly into life, even when Uncle Matt started it, he naturally assumed he would be welcome to stay for supper. A cruelly memorable evening ensued, the details of which became emblazoned on my mind, not because of the presence of Bill Batey, though he dropped a hint or two as to my imminent fate, but because I began the evening secure in the blissful euphoria of a carefree childhood, and ended it feeling lost – bewildered and betrayed. Bill rose from the armchair as we entered, and after introductions were made all round, he sat up at the table, uninvited but ready to tackle whatever was put in front of him. Nor did he stand on ceremony, but instead confidently addressed Aunt Dot as she bustled about, setting out cutlery.

'Ah'll be havin' a bite ta eat if yer askin', Dot,' he said, winking at me as if I would appreciate his presumption.

Aunt Dot hesitated. Having extended hospitality to a full house for a whole week, she had almost exhausted her resources of food and energy, and for an instant looked a little dismayed. But after reflecting that he had just done the household a favour, and that all things eventually come to an end, even the constant caring for guests, she grimly accepted the situation of having seven for supper, gritted her teeth, and got on with it.

'Make yourself at home,' she said unnecessarily, since Bill's elbows were already resting on the table as he toyed optimistically with a knife.

Then, after a moment's thought she pulled on her wellingtons, dashed out to the garden, and returned carrying a trug full of prime plump onions. These she peeled, sliced, peppered generously, and boiled in an enormous black pan on the fire, adding knobs of butter when the liquid began to boil, then served accompanied by a big plate of bread. It was basic cooking, not exactly food fit for a king, but despite her heavy hand with the pepper pot, we all found this simple fare unexpectedly appetizing.

'Ah do like a nice bit o' boiled onion,' stated Bill more than once, and proved the point by demolishing several helpings. 'Now that's what Ah call a right tasty bite,' he said appreciatively, every time he emptied his plate and she obligingly refilled it.

Aunt Dot had set the table automatically and without due thought as to what was appropriate for what she was serving, but Bill only used one utensil – his knife. He steered the onions onto the knife with the aid of a chunk of bread, then slurped them into his ever-open mouth. Like the leafy sea dragon of Australia, which, having no teeth, ingeniously sucks in its food, he sucked, slurped and swallowed in one easy motion, following every mouthful of onion with juicy bread, and noisily smacking his lips. I watched him, fascinated, as he flicked the onions home with the practised air of an Italian gourmet eating spaghetti. And conscious of my interest, he kept winking at me as if we knew each other well and shared a special secret.

Whatever that secret was, I thought, it was certainly not the art of eating onions, for whereas he controlled his with ease, mine flew all over the plate. They were as difficult to tame as Uncle Matt's horse; just as slippery and elusive, falling off my fork with a splash, slithering away like snakes in wet grass, and trickling buttery juices embarrassingly down my chin. But on studying Bill, I realized where I was going wrong, the fork being the main problem. Bill, a self-confessed onion addict, had dispensed with that useless utensil for a reason, I now realized, and he was demonstrating the correct technique. So I put down my fork, grasped my knife firmly, and reached for a chunk of bread.

'No, Emma,' said my mother quietly, shaking her head.

'But Bill uses his knife,' I protested.

'You'll cut your tongue off, pet.'

'Good idea,' said Neal, 'Let her do it, Mum. That *would* be an improvement.'

'Bill hasn't cut his tongue off,' I argued and, as if on cue, with a deft thrust of his knife and a timely flick of his tongue, he secured a straggle of escaping onion into his mouth and pointed the contentious knife at me.

'Ah but – Ah've had plenty o' practice. Plenty,' he said proudly. 'And Ah can see that you, lass, haven't had any. Noo think o' that.'

He winked again and grimaced as if we were fellow conspirators, defying convention, but just then Aunt Dot intervened, settling the issue by handing me a soup spoon and the boys the same. Then, since she believed that everyone should have the benefit of her opinion whether they wanted it or not, she turned back to Bill, gave him a sarcastic little smile and spoke loudly and with a touch of condescension.

'Yes, I will say you're a dab hand with a knife. You have a good aim, a steady hand, and a fearless wrist action. You perform at the table like a sword swallower.'

'Kind of tha ta say so, Dot,' he answered, unabashed by this public slur on his table manners. 'As Ah've mebbe mentioned, it takes a lot o' practice.'

And practice had plainly made perfect, for he not only wielded the knife safely and skilfully, but managed to keep up a steady stream of small talk at the same time, so just as the knife flashed and sparkled to and fro, so the conversation also scintillated. And when the pan had been declared well and truly empty and his plate cleared of onions for the last time, he took more bread to mop up the juices, making sure that not a single drop missed his attention and that he left the plate as clean as on the day it was made, maybe even cleaner.

'By, that was a tasty bit o' onion,' he reminded us, and added, greatly understating the case, 'Ah'm partial ta a bit o' boiled onion, like.'

Then he leant back, unbuttoned his waistcoat to allow his portly stomach room for expansion, and relaxed, ready to resume the social chit-chat. To my surprise he turned to me, putting on spectacles the better to see me, scratching his stubbly chin reflectively, and regarding me with cautious amusement as one might a playful kitten.

'Aye then, so you're Emma,' he said with a wink, as if he had been expecting to meet someone of that name and now had time to identify her. 'Well, little Goldilocks, how'd ya like yer new home, eh? How'd ya like livin' up here?'

I hesitated, my face screwed up in thought. I had no wish to hurt anyone's feelings and on the whole I had enjoyed the holiday. But I knew in my heart that I was ready for home, for friends and familiar things, for favourite places and life as I had always known it, and suddenly my words came tumbling out, tripping over each other in one long breathless sentence. And as they tumbled, pride took over.

'It's very nice in a way, and I've enjoyed my stay, thank you, but there's not much here and it's really very dull, not at all like home, 'cos we have shops you see, and buses and trains, an' – an' – we have an ice-cream parlour, and a fish an' chip shop and two cinemas, and we have cinder toffee, and a man who comes round the doors selling ginger beer and sarsaparilla, and I love sarsaparilla, an' – an' – we have a bluebell wood, and a park with swings and a banana slide, an' – an'– an air-raid shelter in the garden to play in, and friends to play with, and oh, lots of people, really nice people, an' – an' – everything.'

He held up his hands as if surrendering and leant back, laughing heartily.

'Stop! Stop right there! You win. Ah'll have ta give in. We've nothin' like that up here. We canna compete with all that excitement. No, not in Sourhope. Not at all. It's that quiet up here at times that ya can hear the grass grow. Shiretown's the nearest for shops and traffic, but even then ya'd be short on swings and banana slides. All we have is cattle and sheep. Oh aye, we hev a canny few sheep an' no mistake. And plenty o' onions an' all, as well as the knack of doin' them justice. I reckon that's something ya'll learn when ya've lived here a bit.'

'Yes, perhaps I would if I stayed here,' I pointed out politely, 'but you know we're going home tomorrow.'

He looked puzzled, glancing quizzically at Aunt Dot, and she shook her head and waved a warning finger as if to silence him. Then she briskly cleared away the plates and delved into the cupboard in search of ginger biscuits.

'How about a nice cup of tea?' she suggested, changing the subject. 'What would we all do without a nice cup of tea?'

I noticed that she always offered a *nice* cup of tea, as if some people might prefer the alternative, but we all accepted with alacrity, having discovered the deep thirst that follows the hearty consumption of onions. Several cups later, Bill burped loudly and with gusto. Then he pushed his chair back to stretch his legs, put away his spectacles, took out his pipe and fiddled about with a tobacco pouch. And for the rest of his visit the pipe dangled from the corner of his mouth as he puffed and talked simultaneously, steadily enveloping the room in a spicy smoky haze, which Aunt Dot could barely tolerate.

Nevertheless, both aunt and uncle hung on his every word. Isolated as they were from society at large, especially Aunt Dot, who rarely left the farm, they were eager to hear his gossip, but for the most part the talk flowed over my head, the names of people and places sounding alien and outlandish. I listened without much interest as he described how Joe Pigg had lost his job at the lead mine, how Robson Reed o' Byrehope had won first prize for a roan heifer, how Feg the coalman had taken on the grave digging, and how Sarah Jane o' the Clay Hole had given birth to twins. After every item of news he blew billowing clouds of smoke around him, filling our lungs too until we choked and discreetly drew back.

Meanwhile, he himself became shrouded in a haze of fumes, a mysterious figure holding forth through it, now inhaling with a sucking sound, now making 'put-putting' noises as his teeth gripped the pipe and he searched his memory for more tittle-tattle. It was only when he mentioned, as if of little consequence, that Mad Mary was on the march again that I pricked up my ears. Thankfully I knew nothing then of the part that Mad Mary would play in my life, but always eager to satisfy my curiosity, I was about to ask why she was called mad, and where she marched, and when. But before I could, he moved on to a different tale.

'Oh, and Willie o' the Bogs got lost in the Elf Holes. It took the lads that volunteered two hours ta find him, but he was lucky. He could have been a goner.'

And now I did prick up my ears.

'Excuse me, Mister – er – Bill. Did you say Elf Holes?'

'Aye, that's right, Emma. The Elf Holes.'

'Is that where the elves live?'

It was a foolish question, but after all I was only eight, and very credulous and imaginative. However, my scathing brothers instantly barracked and mocked me until I felt totally humiliated. Only Bill took my part, removing his pipe from his mouth to punctuate the air with it as he spoke.

'Ah but – ya never know, lads. Always keep an open mind on everything, even elves' he advised, though I saw that he had a twinkle in his eyes.

And it was this twinkle that drew my attention to the fact that his eyes were odd in colour, with one blue iris and one brown, and only matched in the centre, where tawny flecks streaked away from the pupils. This phenomenon was new to me, and at the first awareness of it I was disconcerted, reluctant to look at him directly. It was, however, difficult to avoid his gaze, and I decided to focus on the brown eye, which seemed warmer and kindlier, though I noticed that it was always the blue one that winked. Then he bent towards me, speaking close to my ear, his breath thick with onion-flavoured tobacco. Though careful not to give offence, I shrank back a little.

'It's like this, Emma,' he said. 'Nobody kens what lies behind the name Elf Holes. But it's a fact that them's ancient caves underneath. A fair labyrinth of tunnels. And Willie swears he found a great chamber, and when he struck a match the walls were hung with multi-coloured stones that sparkled like diamonds.'

'Ooooh, I'd like to see those,' I said, being fond of sparkly things.

'By no!' he answered sharply. 'Keep away from there. Just mind how long it took us ta find Willie. Besides,' he added with a sly grin, 'the elves might get ya.'

He winked again, the blue eye operating once more, leaving me confused as to what was true and what false, though I was perfectly prepared to believe that this wild place harboured all manner of weird and supernatural beings. But was he just having a joke at my expense? Then he repeated his warning, sounding serious enough.

'Noo, keep away from there, Emma. Keep well away.'

I stared at him, bemused, wondering why this odd man with his odd eyes had such a short memory. He'd clearly already forgotten what I'd just told him.

'I will,' I promised, 'and anyway, as I said, I'm going home tomorrow.'

He looked down at me as my chair rocked to and fro in front of him, and his expression changed to one of deep sadness, as if the sight of my earnest little face had brought some tragedy home to him. His eyes, both the blue one and the brown one, filled with tears, and he suddenly reached across and patted my head in a kindly fashion.

'Poor little soul,' he murmured, 'poor bairn. It's too bad. Too bad ta bear.'

Then he turned away, leaving me disconcerted once more. He put his pipe down, took out a grimy handkerchief, for which he had found a variety of uses when mending the car, and after wiping his eyes and leaving a smudge of grease over the brown one, gave his nose a good blow, long and loud, like a trumpeting elephant. And curiously, by doing so, he started a fashion, because my mother then also reached for a handkerchief, dabbing at her eyes and nose, and Uncle Matt rubbed his moist eyes with the cuff of his shirt sleeve.

There followed a lull in the conversation during which everyone avoided my gaze and looked uncomfortable, and I felt unaccountably distressed. Had I missed something? Had I said something wrong? Whatever was the matter? Then Uncle Matt broke the silence, changing the subject to talk of war, and when my mother recovered her composure she joined in, describing the air raids, and the bombings and blackouts.

'And then there's the everlasting queues,' she said. 'You queue for hours for some little extra, something to supplement the rations, anything at all. I know you're all on rations too up here, but we rarely sit down to bacon and eggs as you do, and we haven't had chicken for dinner since last Christmas, and then it was an old boiler. I often have to make meat and potato pie without the meat, and the weekly butter ration's so small you could eat it at one meal. Growing children need nourishment, so I often do without. You're lucky that life hasn't changed so much in the north. You're hardly touched by the war.'

Bill bristled a little, waving his reinstated pipe.

'Ho'd on a minute. That's not so. Not altogether, like. Our eldest son's away fightin' in the war, and he's sair missed round the farm and a big worry for-by.'

My mother sympathized, and he went on to talk of life before the war, of old days and old ways, staying until Aunt Dot rose and cleared the table, when he thanked her for his onion supper, reminding us all how tasty it had been, and patted my head again in passing.

'Mind the elves don't get ya,' he said, then dug deep in his pockets for his cap and departed.

Uncle Matt followed to see him off and then catch up with the evening chores, and the rest of us sat around the fire discussing the day's events.

'It's been a grand day, Aunt Dot,' said David, grinning bashfully, like someone rehearsing a part and embarrassed by the acting of it.

'Yes, a super day,' agreed Neal. 'That pool was magic!'

'Yeah, magic,' repeated David, 'I never expected anything like that. The water was as deep as anything. I wish I could swim there again. I wish we didn't have to go home.'

Aunt Dot looked gratified.

'Well, it's nice to know you've enjoyed yourselves, boys. It's a pity I had to work you so hard, but up here work has to come first.'

'Oh, I didn't mind,' Neal assured her. 'In a way I enjoyed making hay, especially the bogey rides. I just wish we could stay longer. In fact, we'd like to stay for good.'

'Would you indeed? Well, what a pity you can't. But as you know, there's only one bed besides that temporary shakedown you boys have been using. Of course – one of you could stay if you like.'

'Me, I'll stay,' volunteered Neal.

'No, I asked first,' cried David.

'No, me!'

'No, I'm the eldest.'

Then they both began shouting in unison, 'Me, me, me, me,' developing an insistent rhythm, louder and louder, each trying to drown the other out, until the noise became impossible to ignore. I had been only half listening, while gazing peacefully into the fire, imagining that I could see tiny black dragons breathing tongues of flame through the peaty smoke. The day had been long and busy for an eight-year-old, and I felt very sleepy. But David nudged my arm as if including me in their game, and not to be outdone, I joined in the clamour, scarcely knowing what I clamoured for.

'Me, me, me, me,' I cried, turning the noisy duet into a noisier trio.

A minute later I realized that the boys had stopped shouting and had lapsed into silence, that mine was now a lone voice and the so-called game was abruptly curtailed. My last little cry hung plaintively in the air the way the sound of a bell goes on reverberating for a time after the tolling has ceased. Suddenly four faces closely surrounded mine, staring with such intensity that I felt hemmed in and oppressed. Somehow all the heads seemed to have grown disproportionately huge and grotesque, as in a distorting mirror at a funfair.

35

Uneasily I glanced at their expressions, Aunt Dot's watchful and intent, the boys' registering a strange sort of triumph, my mother's showing abject misery. The faces blurred as fear gripped me and tears started in my eyes. Then suddenly I was startled as Aunt Dot moved closer still and kissed me, just a quick peck on the cheek, but a kiss all the same, for the first and only time in her life.

'All right then. That's decided,' she said, moving away, now business-like again. 'You can stay, Emma. It'll be a nice change to have a girl about the place, as long as you behave yourself, of course. And you can help me with little jobs around the house. That's grand. And now it's all settled, would anyone like a nice cup of tea?'

Taken aback, I tried to retract.

'Oh no, Aunt Dot. Not me. I didn't really mean it. I can't stay, thank you all the same. I'm not old enough. I have to go home with my mum. I can't stay. Can I, Mum?' But to my surprise and horror, she sat with eyes averted, hanging her head, and replied tonelessly as if the matter were now out of her hands, a dreadful deed done.

'Yes, you can if you want to, Emma. You'll be safer here. Just until the war's over.'

I did *not* want to. I knew that with every fibre of my being. I felt terrified at the thought. But somehow I had been tricked and now I appeared to be trapped. Pride would not allow me to beg in front of the boys who watched my every move, and besides, my mother's attitude puzzled and hurt me. I felt bewildered by the swift turn of events, too confusing for someone of my tender years to take in. Until now my mother had wrapped me in an atmosphere of love and security. In fact, I had always secretly believed that she loved me best. But here she was, practically giving me away as if I were of no account, as easily discarded as yesterday's newspaper. I searched my mind for a solution. Had I brought this misery on myself? I wondered. Had I really screamed to stay here – away from my mother – separated from everyone and everything I loved – left behind in this outlandish place?

Helpless, I turned an imploring gaze on her, hoping that she would, as usual, come to my rescue, but she avoided my eyes, sitting for a time with her head in her hands. Indescribably hurt and bewildered, I withdrew into myself, becoming silent and morose, unable to turn my mind to anything else. Nor was there further discussion on the matter. My mother instead now concentrated on packing clothes – not mine, I noticed in despair – and I was put to bed, my makeshift sleeping arrangement consisting of the two armchairs in the living room pushed together, with a folded blanket tucking me in. No one offered me any further explanation or comfort, and when the rest of the household retired upstairs I cried and cried into my pillow, eventually falling into a troubled sleep.

But with the eternal optimism of youth I awoke feeling better, confident in the daylight that the evening's events had been a dream, or a joke, or some kind of cruel game. I knew with certainty in my heart of hearts that my mother would not, could not ever leave me. At any rate, I refused to believe it possible. After breakfast we all climbed into the car, all but Aunt Dot, who waved us off from the roadside, smiling her bright little smile till we were out of sight. Then we chugged slowly down the road, so erratically that I marvelled at the accuracy with which Uncle Matt managed to hit every hump and pothole in its rough surface, and my mother, usually the epitome of patience but this morning plainly on edge, began to show her irritation. She kept goading him to put on a spurt, but the trouble was that he would insist on talking. He went on incessantly, taking an unwarranted interest in the scenery and showing no sense of urgency at all. Though we passengers were all subdued, he was as chirpy as a cricket, taking his eyes off the road and at least one hand off the wheel to point out and comment upon everything and everyone we passed.

'That's Emmerson Reed's place,' he said, indicating with a leisurely wave the farm beside Slate Bank. 'See that? He's still in the thick of haymakin'. My meanin' is, I've beaten him this year. He's usually finished first, but this time I've won easily.'

My mother refrained from reminding him of the help we had given all week. She was too busy clinging to the window handle as the car lurched towards the quarry wall, only straightening up in the nick of time to avoid hitting it.

'That'll be Dick Charlton collectin' eggs,' he said, as he sighted a lorry turning along a farm track. 'I dare bet he makes a bonny penny from that business, but you'd never know it. He's as tight as old Scrooge.' And the car, following his gaze, wandered onto the left verge, bumped and jerked over the grassy mounds, and flung us sideways so that my mother grabbed the handbrake to save herself and lowered it quickly as the car juddered and slowed.

When she regained her balance and looked up, hat askew, it was to see a sheep on the road – an old sheep, half-witted and stationary, staring at our car, mesmerized.

'Oooh, Matt! Look out!' she cried. 'Mind the blooming sheep!'

The car veered sharply to the right, and to the boys' amusement threw us all in that direction, as we skirted and narrowly missed the petrified sheep, deafening it with a prolonged blast on the horn, and putting the creature to crazy flight. Undaunted and eager to absolve himself from blame, Uncle Matt turned round to look at the skittering sheep, now almost a dot on the horizon, and momentarily lost control of the car.

'Whatever next?' he demanded, frantically twisting the steering wheel to get back on the road. 'It's a good job I've got my wits about me! You should be grateful for my quick thinkin'. That'll be Tom Caygill's sheep. They're always gettin' out. He's useless at mendin' his dykes. What I say is, look after your dykes and your dykes'll look after you. Definitely.'

'Never mind the dykes, Matt,' cried my mother, steadying the wheel herself. 'Please! Just keep your eyes on the road and your hands on the wheel, preferably two hands in the quarter to three position, not one at twelve o'clock.'

'I don't follow that,' he said, glancing at his watch, 'I only make it ten to nine.'

'Forget it, Matt. Just drive. Just do your best. But hurry!'

'No, Ellie, fair dos. Point taken. You're quite right,' he said, agreeably, scratching his nose thoughtfully as he spoke. 'Eyes on the wheel, hands on the road. No, t'other way round. Nowadays you need to take every care. There's so many daft drivers about. You'll not find many as good as me. By no means. Of course I've been drivin' for years. And I bet you'll be surprised to hear I've never passed a drivin' test. Never even taken one. Never needed to. Never had a lesson neither. Just took to drivin' like a duck to water. I reckon I'm what you call "a natural".'

'A natural what?' enquired my mother, with more than a touch of harshness.

'Why, a natural driver, of course. Like some people are born with a silver spoon in their mouth, so in a manner of speakin' I was born with a steerin' wheel in my hand. Oh, see that horse and cart ahead? That belongs to Harrison Maughan. He must be deliverin' cattle feed to the Coulsons. It's not delivery day but they get special treatment. Always pay cash on the nail.'

My mother sighed deeply and took another look at her watch, murmuring, 'I wonder, Matt, can you get past him? Safely, that is. We don't want any accidents. Don't want to end up in the ditch.'

'No bother,' he declared, overtaking with his foot hard down on the accelerator, so hard that the car seemed to tilt sideways on two wheels as we screeched past, missing the ditch by a few blades of grass, and so startling the horse that it whinnied and reared like a bucking bronco.

Instinctively we all flinched and cowered down, protecting heads and arms in a futile defensive gesture, fully expecting the horse's hooves to crash through the windows as the car swerved recklessly, cutting in front of the animal's flailing forelegs.

'Ooooh, Matt!' shrieked my mother, holding on to her hat as her gloves and handbag were propelled to the floor. 'For heaven's sake! Careful, Matt! Careful!'

We thought our end had come and crouched low, trembling with fear. Then suddenly and miraculously the car steadied and we found ourselves on course again. One by one we cautiously lifted our heads, all visibly shaken, and turned to look through the rear window at the now wildly cantering horse. My mother shuffled back in her seat and breathed deeply. We three also sank back in relief, though still glancing round, still wary of the flying horse that might catch us up. Only Uncle Matt seemed unaware of the consternation he had caused, both in and out of the car. He turned sharp left at the school, away from the runaway horse, and resumed his customary speed of twenty miles an hour, his attention soon diverted by an incident of passing interest.

'Just look at that!' he said, carelessly taking a hand off the wheel to gesture at a blue-uniformed figure labouring uphill on his bicycle. 'Well, I'll be a monkey's uncle! If that isn't our postie! By heck, he's not half late today!' And with that, he acknowledged the postman with a well-meaning honk on the horn, causing the surprised cyclist to wobble perilously, zigzagging across the road. 'Hah! That sure livened him up,' he said, grinning, 'and he needs to look lively. He's good and late this mornin'.'

'So are we, Matt! So are we!' cried my mother, still shaken to the core by the near collision with the horse, and now totally exasperated. 'If we ever get to the bus stop in one piece it'll be just in time to miss the bus.'

And indeed the bus drew alongside within seconds of our leaving the car. The luggage went on board first, then my brothers climbed on and my mother bent towards me – not to pick me up or help me onto the bus as I fervently hoped, but to give me a big hug, tight as tight, and a kiss on the top of the head. Then suddenly, and without looking back, she was gone.

I stared in disbelief as the bus rumbled noisily off – big, battered and bright red. I could see the boys waving and grinning through the back window, but not a sign of my adored mother. Then I began to run after it, and in a blur glimpsed my brothers at the window, mocking my plight. I ran faster and faster, my frantic legs pedalling the air with the momentum of a hamster treading a wheel, running and running in blind panic, and behind me I could hear my uncle's footsteps running after me.

'No, Emma!' I heard him shouting. 'No, girl, no! It's no use! Stop, Emma! Stop!' But still I went on running, convinced that I could catch the bus, that the driver would see me reflected in his mirror and slow down to wait for me.

Surely, I thought, even now I could be saved. Then the bus gathered speed, swayed and clunked as it rounded the bend, and disappeared. It was all over. And only then did I give up. Only then did I stop running. I stood breathless and trembling in the middle of the road, a strange sound pounding in my ears, my world crumbling around me. It was, after all, no dream, no joke, no game. My mother had really gone, leaving me all alone. I sobbed uncontrollably until I knew my heart was broken and would probably never mend, sobbed with an abandon that I never indulged in again, because in that moment I lost my innocent trust in adults and my childish faith in my own worth and began, at the tender age of eight, the painful process of growing up.

In the midst of my sobs I felt Uncle Matt pick me up and carry me off the road. I was vaguely aware that he was doing his clumsy best to comfort me. Awkwardly at first, and then with growing confidence he uttered a stream of consoling words, making countless promises that he could never keep of wondrous things that he could never afford. He stopped short of promising me the moon, but only just. And none of it made the slightest difference. I wanted nothing in the world but my mother, and only when he mentioned her name did I calm down a fraction and take notice.

'Did I hear you say she's coming back?' I gasped between sobs. 'She really is?'

'There, there, Emma. She is. Definitely. Yes, she is. There now.'

'You're sure, Uncle Matt? You're really sure? She's coming back for me?'

'Sure as eggs is eggs,' he said, comfortingly, but I no longer trusted anyone.

'Cross your heart and hope to die,' I demanded.

'Fair enough,' he said, obligingly going through the motions.

'When, Uncle Matt? When is she coming? Is it soon?'

'Quite soon. She's comin' in October. Definitely. You have my word on that. And meantime she'll be writin' to you, an' that.'

'Will the war be over then?'

'Well now, if I knew that, Emma, I'd be wearin' gold earrings and carryin' a crystal ball. But she's comin' anyhow.'

'October's a long time away,' I said forlornly. 'It's practically forever.'

'Oh no, Emma, it'll be here in a flash. Here before you know it.'

'And she's coming for me then?'

'Yes. Well, that's if you still want to go. My meanin' is, you might like it here and settle down, like. I've always wanted a daughter, a bonny little girl like you. But if you don't care for life up here, then you don't have to stay. There now.'

'And I can go home in October. For sure?'

'You can that, Emma. I promise. That's if you're desperate to be off and leave me. Now, dry your eyes and we'll have a bit look in the post office. I just need a quick squint at the paper to see which horses are runnin' at Newmarket this afternoon and maybe use the telephone a minute, and then we'll see what can be bought for you. Some liquorice, mebbe, or a jigsaw puzzle, or a comic, or, as it's a special kind o' day – a day when I've gained a daughter – till October anyway – maybe we could manage all three. My meanin' is, surely Mrs Featherstone'll have somethin' to please you.'

He produced a handkerchief that had constantly missed the wash and smelt of cigarettes and hayseeds, and after spitting on it to make it moist, wiped my tear-stained face, spitting and wiping to his satisfaction with a total disregard for hygiene. Then I walked beside him, holding his hand, clinging on tightly like someone drowning who clings to anything that floats.

'You see, Emma,' he explained, replacing the handkerchief in his pocket with the hayseeds, 'you can't introduce yourself to Mrs Featherstone when you've got a dirty face. It gives the wrong impression. Or to her daughter, Olive, either, come to that. She's a comely lass is Olive, whatever your aunt Dot says to the contrary, but don't tell your aunt I said so, mind, or you and me'll fall out before we start. Now, Emma, we'll have some grand times together. I dare bet on it. You're good company and so'm I. I'm very easy to get on with. Ask anybody. Oh yes, we'll get along well. Just till your mother comes, of course. Then we'll have to see what's what.'

A pleasant-faced Olive Featherstone produced a number of treasures to put a temporary end to my tears, though the world still looked loathsome to me and I panicked whenever the thought of my mother flashed into my mind. But in the midst of my despair shone a ray of hope. I only had to hang on until October and I would be with her again. The few weeks till then would be like a holiday – soon over. Meanwhile, Uncle Matt concluded his business and we were invited into the cosy kitchen, where Mrs Featherstone offered us tea and treacle tarts. Plainly Uncle Matt was a favoured customer and he lingered in evident enjoyment, despite Aunt Dot's instructions before we set off to go straight back and be quick about it. Even on our way out he turned at the door and treated the Featherstones to his most engaging smile.

'You couldn't oblige me with a packet or two of ginger snaps, could you, Olive? It'd be much appreciated. My meanin' is, it'll help to keep the peace, an' that.'

He came out whistling, carrying a brown paper bag, and lingering at the gate for a further chat. As I waited I pondered on his flirtatious approach to attractive women – first Mrs Phillip and now Olive Featherstone. At this stage it struck me as incongruous, since to my mind he was not the lady-killer type. By traditional standards he was not handsome, and if pressed for an opinion on his age I could only with certainty have placed him this side of seventy. To me, most adults seemed old, and having glimpsed him on occasion without his perennial cap, revealing only a fringe of hair encircling a tonsured head, the impression of great age was confirmed in my young mind. As it turned out, however, he was only thirty-five, and he benefited from the shortage of young men around.

I was to discover that his habit of chatting up ladies, of flattering them and twinkling his intense blue eyes and flashing his splendid teeth at them, opened many doors and was surprisingly effective in shops, adding a variety of under-the-counter products to our wartime rations. Already it was clear why Aunt Dot had such an ample supply of ginger biscuits in her cupboard. But for now at last we were back in the car, where, by dint of much frenetic wheel turning and yanking of the gear lever, he performed the nine manoeuvres that distinguished his three-point turn from everyone else's. Then, with a friendly wave from Olive and a final kangaroo hop from the car, we set off for High Windlestraw, which, for the time being at least, was to be my new home.

Chapter 4

Goosey, Goosey, Gander

Despite his roguish ways, Uncle Matt was in essence a sympathetic character, but not so Aunt Dot. She was a creature of moods more changeable than the weather; they could alter from hour to hour, so that she seldom stayed in a good mood for long. Born under the sign of Scorpio, she faithfully exhibited its unpredictable traits – sweet as honey one minute, touchy and sharp-tongued the next, demonstrating that she had more in common with a shrew than merely her small size. At times she could be as cold as the Lornhope wind that blew through the valley, winter and summer, chilling our bones. She could be just as sharp, just as bitter, and just as unforgiving; always swift to chide and slow to bless. Setting herself impossibly high standards in everything, especially tidiness and cleanliness, she demanded the same high standards of others, and needless to say, Uncle Matt and I, a farmer and a child, seldom lived up to her unrealistic expectations.

Initially I felt very much at a loss struggling in this strange and strict regime, but gradually, in self-defence, I took to following Uncle Matt's example, learning to be wary, trying to be diplomatic, and stifling spontaneity in all matters involving my aunt. My one aim was to survive as pleasantly as possible until the blessed day of my mother's promised return. And in my painfully uphill struggle to become a junior diplomat, Uncle Matt gave me every help and encouragement.

'That's it, Emma. That's the way, girl,' he said with a wry smile. 'Watch what you do. Careful what you say. You're learnin' fast. A wise head on young shoulders, you might say. Definitely.'

One day I ventured to probe his feelings on the fine and hazardous line that he and I trod daily. We were walking together to Brackenfield on a pleasant balmy evening after escaping from another of Aunt Dot's fractious moods, during which we had both received a severe tongue-lashing. Neither of us had any idea what had induced the sudden onslaught, and I squeezed his arm in sympathy and fellow feeling.

'Uncle Matt, do you mind *very* much about Aunt Dot?' I enquired, fairly confident of his answer, but as usual he surprised me.

'Mind, pet? Mind what?' he asked, genuinely unknowing.

'Well – you know – all the tickings off we get. You know – her quick temper.'

'Oh, that! I never bother my head about that, Emma,' he declared stoutly. 'She doesn't mean it, you know. She just lets off steam. It's water off a duck's back to me, girl. You see, you get used to her harpin' on an' that, and eventually you stop listenin'. After a bit it's like livin' next to traffic – you don't even hear it. Anyway, you can't have everythin' in a woman, now can you, Emma? And your aunt Dot's very special in other ways.'

'Is she?' I asked in undisguised surprise.

'Why, of course she is. It's obvious, isn't it?'

'How exactly do you mean, Uncle Matt?'

'Well – Emma! I'm astonished you need to ask,' he said with a rather fatuous grin, proving himself, as ever, the romantic. 'Think about it, Emma. Just picture your aunt Dot in your mind's eye. Now, honestly speakin', have you ever seen hair like hers? My meanin' is, hair that glorious colour? I dare bet you haven't. It's the colour of a chestnut thoroughbred horse. It's as rich as beech leaves in autumn. Or, tell you what, Emma,' he added, waxing eloquent, 'have you ever seen the settin' sun light up a corn stook?'

'I'm afraid not, Uncle Matt,' I replied, disappointingly truthful.

'Well, there's your very colour. I tell you it's not every day you'll see that particular colour, that precise shade, except mebbe on a film star, and then it's likely out of a bottle. Yes, she's a good looker, your aunt, and no mistake. She's what you call ornamental to a home, especially when she's not twistin' her face. I'm proud of her, Emma, and that's nice. In this life you have to count your blessings. You have to take the rough with the smooth, and be darned grateful for the smooth.'

I pondered at length on this conversation, feeling confused at first, but finally I concluded that the key to the problem surrounding Aunt Dot undoubtedly lay in the red hair. Therein was the solution to the mystery of why Uncle Matt put up with her constant bad temper. It appeared that her particular shade of red possessed qualities akin to witchcraft, and that my uncle tolerated the indignities inflicted upon him, even to the occasional flying missile, for the simple reason that he was under its spell. He was bewitched by it, and after he had revealed his secret I took special notice and observed that he always defended his red-headed wife, always agreed with her – at least to her face – even if he privately held the opposite view and had to find devious ways of changing her mind to suit his.

So I looked at her fiery hair with new interest, and for the first time in my young life began to covet that colour. I hoped that my hair, presently a pale reddish blonde, would deepen and redden as I grew older. Then I too would take on this inexplicable power imbued in the redness, and then perhaps people would pay me more heed; would not desert me quite so easily. From that moment on, therefore, whenever I had the right of a wish – such as on a new moon, or when seeing a rainbow, or prior to blowing out candles on a birthday cake – I gave myself two wishes to include my newly acquired desire for spellbinding red hair. Meanwhile, I took comfort in my alien situation by forcing myself to think positive. I could never forget the deep hurt inflicted on me by being left behind like mislaid luggage, or reconcile myself to the pain of separation from my mother, but having been assured of her return in October, I concentrated on that happy prospect. First, however, I needed to know exactly how long I would have to wait, and to that end I consulted the large calendar on the kitchen wall.

It was a farming calendar, illustrated with photographic portraits of contented pigs, every month a different variety, and every pig a

winner in its own class, all patently benefiting from feeding on a cele-
brated brand of pig meal known as 'Porkers Concentrated Swill
Supplement (Made from a Secret Recipe!)'. The calendar had been
pinned, straight as a plumb line, next to the larder door, too high for
me to view it comfortably. So in order to study it properly I climbed
on the kitchen stool, taking with me my small case of coloured pencils.
My intention was to circle the sad date of my mother's departure
and count from there to her return, but only when poised with the
pencil did I remember that no precise date had been mentioned. Ever
the optimist, I counted to October the first, circling that all-important date, and it was at this juncture, as I leafed through the picture
gallery of fat pigs, that I experienced an irresistible urge to embel-
lish the current portrait of August's porker.

Naturally I knew nothing about pigs, but the calendar provided
information as to the name and characteristics of each breed, and
it appeared that the choice of this particular month, known as the
Tamworth, not only produced good bacon but was well known for
her sterling qualities. Clearly she was an impeccable pig, a cut
above the norm, and she boasted an abundance of red-gold hair,
rather like mine in colour, together with a pleasant face – for a pig,
that is. So, after carefully choosing the appropriate pencils, I began
by drawing a big gold halo over her head and wings sprouting
from her back. Then I coloured the eyes green like mine, adding
long lashes, also like mine, and a tartan ribbon like the one I often
wore, tied to her curly tail. I stepped down to admire the effect,
meticulously straightened the calendar, replaced the stool, and, like
any petty criminal, distanced myself from the scene. Knowing Aunt
Dot's temper, I had no idea what had possessed me to take such
a personal risk. Perhaps I felt like introducing a friendly face to
the cold and impersonal kitchen walls, or perhaps I simply allowed
an urge for self-expression to get the better of me. Suffice to say
that once the wilful deed was done and there was no going back,
my heart began to pound like a steam engine and I shook in my
shoes waiting for the discovery of my wicked deed and its imagined consequences.

But to my relief and surprise, no one commented. Aunt Dot went
about her business for several days with her face tripping her up,
her lips severely pursed, and her eyes avoiding mine, but none of
that was altogether unusual. Then too, on several heart-stopping occasions when we were alone, she turned her basilisk stare on me and

opened her mouth as if to take issue about something, but inexplicably changed her mind. So after a time I breathed more easily again, and, under the misapprehension that I had somehow escaped detection, subsequently adopted the pig calendar as my own, using it not only as an informant, telling me how time was passing, but also as a solace, helping me to pass that time. And despite feeling as unloved as a baby abandoned on a doorstep, I gradually began to settle down at Windlestraw.

I found my new life very strange, but tried to make myself useful both in and out of the farmhouse. Naturally I preferred to be outside with Uncle Matt, away from my prickly little aunt, and under his guidance I soon learnt to care for small animals. When a certain newborn calf suffered unexpected rejection from her mother, I experienced fellow feeling for the poor forlorn creature, and stepped straight into the breach, taking the place of a foster parent. She looked so fragile and defenceless, swaying on her spindly legs, that I dearly wanted to help, and Uncle Matt, who was always eager to reduce his workload, readily agreed.

'Come on then, Emma. If you're that sorry for her you can make yourself useful and feed her. I'll hold her steady, like, and you give her your fingers to suck.'

I offered my hand, rather apprehensively, and was startled to feel her tongue, rough as sandpaper, rasping over my vulnerable fingers.

'Whoooops!' I cried. 'Oooooh! She's nibbled my fingers off! Oooh, Uncle Matt, I think she's swallowed them!'

I panicked, kicking the pail between us, spilling milk over my feet, and snatching my hand away to count the fingers, convinced that at least one would be missing. But there they still were, all present and correct, just wet and a bit red. Uncle Matt shook his head and tut-tutted impatiently.

'Don't be silly now, Emma. You're all right. She won't bite. Definitely not. She can't. You see, she's got no top teeth at the front and the bottom ones are only baby teeth. If you take my meanin', Emma, she's just a baby.'

'But something grated my fingers,' I protested, unconvinced. 'It was like a nutmeg grater. Honestly, Uncle Matt.'

'That's only a bit of roughness on her tongue. She needs that for eatin' grass later on. Cows like to wrap their tongues round long strands of grass and pull. Now try again. Try and teach her how to feed. Let her keep suckin' and lower your hand into the milk. There now – she's takin' milk. See that? Now, Emma, that's it. That's your job till she learns to fend for herself. You'll make a grand little land girl. Ever since the war started I've kinda fancied having a land girl helpin' round the place.'

Feeling the calf feed from my hands was an uncanny sensation, but rewarding in that she soon began to thrive. I called her Tiny, though Aunt Dot considered it a daft name for what would one day be 'a great big galumphing cow', as she put it. But Tiny she remained, and because I fed her almost from birth, she adopted me as her mother, following me whenever she could and licking me affectionately whenever she caught me unawares.

So it was that I learnt new skills, whether I wanted to or not. But of all the farm tasks that fell one by one to my lot, my speciality became poultry, and I liked the hens best. I soon noticed their resemblance in many funny little ways to people, and in Sourhope there was a profound shortage of people, the population consisting mainly of sheep. I missed company, particularly in the form of friends of my own age, and spent many a lonely hour scanning the unpromising countryside for a possible glimpse of even the most distant figure. That intense loneliness drew me to befriend the companionable hens, and I observed their antics as I swung to and fro on the wicket gate by the henhouse.

I began to talk to them, chattering hours at a time, pouring my troubles into their minute ears. They answered in a different language, of course, though they had a lot to say for themselves, being especially sociable at feeding time, when my echoing call of 'Cluck, cluck!' summoned them to the trough. They were attentive listeners, too, tilting their heads sideways and drawing their necks back as if in thought, giving the flattering appearance of hanging on my every word, so that I had the impression they understood everything I said, and decided to test this theory by consulting my oracle, Uncle Matt.

'Those hens look as wise as owls at times, Uncle Matt,' I said. 'Tell me, are they really as clever as they seem?'

'Clever? Them hens? That's a laugh!' he exclaimed, scathingly. 'You can see for yourself they've got tiny brains. No room in them pinheads for much in the way of a brain, Emma. My meanin' is, nothing much stirs upstairs in them. They're birds, aren't they? And you've heard of the expression 'birdbrain'? Well, they've got 'em.'

His answer disappointed me, though I thought no less of my

hens. Indeed, I rarely thought of them as hens at all, so strongly did they remind me of little old ladies as they strutted round the enclosure, puffing their chests out and turning their heads from side to side, blinking their button eyes, or sauntering pensively, lifting one leg in the air and pausing, curling their claws like ladies treading in something unpleasant. Proud of their fine feathers and fretful if any were lost, they paraded their finery sedately unless disturbed by Split, who had a nasty habit of ruffling their feathers with a well-intentioned barking leap, as if to instil some discipline into their aimless lives. At that they broke into a frenzied bow-legged waddle, or winged into clumsy flight, squawking and screeching as they scattered. But once in the henhouse, sitting on the nest, they behaved with the utmost decorum, folding their feathers over their feet and shuffling into position, like modest women arranging the drape of their dresses so as to cover their knees. There they guarded their privacy, even from me, and cackled with satisfaction when they laid an egg. They were peace itself except for the cockerel, who roused the neighbourhood at dawn with his arrogant cock-a-doodle-doo.

One day while chatting of this and that to Uncle Matt I inadvisably disclosed my profound thoughts on the subject of hens, and he looked quizzically at me, pushing up the peak of his cap to scratch his head with a used matchstick. Economical by nature, he always kept a few spent matches in the box, devising a number of handy uses for them, everything from toothpicks and chewing sticks to manicure aids and probes for itchy ears.

'Hens? Old ladies?' he queried, regarding me with some perplexity as he scratched extensively all round the cap brim, though careful to keep the cap on throughout. 'And how do you make that out then, Emma?'

'Well, you know. It's the way they walk, the way they move, all their funny little ways. They're just like old ladies. Don't you think so, Uncle Matt?'

He stared at my eager face as if I had taken leave of my senses and shook his head, nonplussed but reluctant to disappoint.

'Maybe so and maybe not, Emma. I'll say this – you sure have a powerful imagination. But you see, I'm just a plain simple soul myself, and to me hens are hens and old ladies are old ladies, and that's the way of it the wide world over. But take my advice, pet, and don't mention that notion of yours to your aunt Dot. She wouldn't understand. Definitely not. She might think you're likenin' her to an old hen, and believe me, that wouldn't do. Wouldn't do at all.'

The thought had never occurred to me, though she was bird-like in many ways, but I heeded the warning and kept any further fanciful notions to myself. I might have been discouraged altogether by this rebuff, had not a speckled hen, known to me as Gertie, caught my eye, closed one of hers, and winked. So I continued to keep a watchful eye on the hens, especially the precocious Gertie, and it was at this juncture that Uncle Matt took advantage of my rapport with them to unload from himself an unpleasant task, palming it off on me. He began his negotiations by using flattery, paying me what he said was a well-deserved tribute.

'By, Emma, pet, you're not half good with them hens. You do a grand job. You do, Emma. Yes, a grand job. You're a little expert already. You've taken to the hens like a duck to water.'

'Thank you, Uncle Matt. I like the hens,' I said, my face glowing with pride.

'Tell you what, Emma,' he suggested, as if to reward my efforts, 'I think you deserve promotion. I think I'll put you in charge of the geese an' all.'

Horrified, I stood stock-still, regarding him incredulously.

'Oh no, Uncle Matt! Not . . . the geese!' I quavered.

'You'll manage just fine,' he said, as though the decision had already been made.

'Oh no! Please no! Not the geese, Uncle Matt! They're as big as me. And ever so fierce! Scary as anything! I try to keep out of their way.'

'Oh, nonsense, you'll be all right. I dare bet you will. Ten to one you'll have them eatin' out of your hand in no time. You've got the knack, as they say. Definitely. You sure have, pet. How'd you like to be Keeper of the Geese, eh?'

'I wouldn't really, if you don't mind, Uncle Matt. Honestly, I'd much rather not.'

'In fact, you could be Keeper of all the Poultry. That's a grand title for you, Emma. Head Poultry Keeper. What a great idea! And why not? After all, the situation's vacant. Save me advertisin', an' that. How'd you like it, eh? What do you think?'

Put like that, it seemed ungracious to refuse, especially as his bright eyes were riveted expectantly on my face, but though flattered, I knew that this new position was a dubious one, more punishment than promotion. I gazed fearfully at him and in a panic put forward my final pathetic defence, my last-resort resistance.

'But, Uncle Matt, I'm only little. I'm only eight.'

'I know, and it's amazin', Emma. You'll have to keep remindin' me, 'cos you're that good at everythin' that I'm inclined to forget.'

His blue eyes twinkled and he smiled proudly at me, so proudly that somehow there seemed nothing to do but accept.

I soon found, however, that the grandiose titles carried no remuneration or advantage of any kind, but the disadvantages were legion. The geese were a different proposition entirely from the hens – both domestic birds, but otherwise chalk and cheese. Whereas the hens fluttered harmlessly round my feet, the geese extended their long, sinuous necks like ostriches, meeting me eye to eye. And whereas the hens were all for a peaceful life, the geese proved war-like, always ready for a fight, and not only aggressive, but deafening with it, especially when in full cry. Only pride kept me from opting out of the ordeal, for such it was. I approached the geese at my peril and fed them in self-defence. They were given a mixture of tit-bits to supplement their diet of grass, and when they heard the clank of the metal bucket and saw me cowering behind it, they advanced in a body, uttering loud, guttural cries, like a marauding tribe of white warriors on the attack. Webbed feet pounded the ground, long necks stretched threateningly forward, and gaping beaks opened in a fanfare of honks. Like the coward I was, I backed away, throwing food at them, scooping up big handfuls and flinging them wide to deflect the assault, retreating till the bucket was empty, when I ran for my life.

Once the hay had been harvested, the militant geese took occupation of the front meadow, fiercely defending it from invasion. But they were not averse, if opportunity presented itself, to extending their own frontiers even further. Should the bottom gate be left open, as sometimes happened, they wandered as geese will, heading for pastures new, and in particular for the pasture belonging to the farmer opposite, where the grass was always greener, there being no resident geese to crop it. These escapes occurred quite often, causing Uncle Matt to threaten to cut their little legs off – a stratagem which, while solving one problem, would have created others, especially for the geese – and they caused the farmer whose land it was, Ned Hutchinson, to become increasingly irate, and to leap about on his hillside like a wild man, furiously waving his stick and shaking his fist.

Despite being lumbered with the pretentious title of Head Poultry Keeper, I had no control over the escapees' wandering ways – or, indeed, over their wayward personalities. But I often helped Uncle Matt to bring them home, and very angry he was on those time-wasting occasions. Then one day the whole sorry situation came to a head. We noticed the white gaggle gourmandizing as usual in Hutchinson's field, and as usual set off to retrieve the runaways, when to our amazement we saw Mr Hutchinson appropriating them as if they were his own. Brandishing his stick, and followed by three slinking dogs, he marched down the pasture, and instead of chasing the geese back home, herded them up to his stack yard. For a minute Uncle Matt stared, eyes popping and mouth open, while his face took on a rich purple hue. Then he started like a warhorse, snorting and treading the ground impatiently.

'The blighter's stealin' my geese!' he cried. 'See that, Emma? See that? He is. He's snafflin' them. He can't do that! He's workin' a flanker, but I'll have 'im. That I will! I'll have the law on 'im. I'll cut his thievin' legs off. Come on, Emma!' And so saying, he waved his stick in imitation of his counterpart, as if he envisaged a duel of sticks at three paces, and strode down the meadow, shouting for me to follow.

I did so without enthusiasm, having little confidence in my ability to serve as the rearguard, but in any case he strode up the opposite field with such furious purpose that he reached Hutchinson's stack yard well ahead of me. Sensing excitement in the air, Split bounded at his heels, but I, I'm somewhat ashamed to admit, hung back, in no hurry to join the fray. For fray there was, a noisy altercation, which I could hear taking place behind the haystack as I waited at a safe distance. Uncle Matt was demanding the return of his errant geese, while Ned Hutchinson claimed they now belonged to him, possession being nine-tenths of the law. Split, despite being outnumbered by the resident dogs, recklessly engaged them in a frantic skirmish, and the geese, deprived of their late lunch, honked irritably in the background. Almost drowned out by the rising clamour, Uncle Matt could just be heard appealing to Ned's better nature.

'But they're not your geese, man. They're *my* geese. You can't just snatch them. Surely you can see that? My meanin' is, Ned, they're mine! Now, just be sensible and give them back. I promise, Ned, you'll not hear another word from me.'

'Hoots, no! Not a chance! Ah'll be dashed if Ah will,' came the uncompromising reply, whereupon my uncle began to show signs of losing his temper.

'Don't be stupid, man! Now Ned, give over! They're *my* geese! You can't keep *my* geese. You must know that. Be reasonable.'

'That's the whole point,' argued Ned. 'Ah *do* keep your geese. They feed here all the time. They feed here, so they might as well bide here.'

'So that's your game!' shouted Uncle Matt. 'Don't give me that malarkey. I've had my eyes opened with you all right. You're nothin' but a pesky thief!'

'Oh yeah?' said Ned, a fan of gangster films.

'Yeah! For two pins I'd wallop you one!'

'Aye? You and whose army?'

There followed worrying sounds of a scuffle, with harsh words bandied back and forth and the noise of blows struck and cries of pain, so that I edged anxiously forward. Then the dogs joined in, barking like a discordant canine choir. And when, some tense minutes later, Uncle Matt emerged, victorious, driving his rebellious brood before him, I noticed that he had acquired not only his geese, but also a bruised eye and a bloody nose. I carried the stick while he nursed his nose, and between us we shooed the geese home, the gabbling gaggle wobbling their indignant heads in a jerky rocking motion.

Generally, when driven en masse they goose-stepped smartly together, but now they strayed and straggled like a defeated army deprived of its rations. They grumbled all the way back, angered by the interruptions to their afternoon graze, and disgruntled by Split's attempts to keep them in line. But their grumbles were as nothing compared with those of Uncle Matt when he reached the house and recounted every detail of the campaign again and again to Aunt Dot, while she bathed his bruised eye with warm water.

'Well, anyway, Dot, that's it,' he said finally. 'That's the last straw. Say what you like, but I'm sick to death of them geese. They're always boltin'. Always on the run. Somethin' has got to be done. I'd like to cut their ruddy little legs off. That I would.'

'Good idea,' she answered, calmly applying the warm cloth to the affected area. 'We'll have roast goose twice a week till Christmas. Of course you'll be eating your profits, but maybe you've secretly come into money?'

An uneasy silence followed, during which he took the cloth from her, lowering his face over the basin, while she refilled the kettle. Then, after a few moments, he raised his head, looking inspired.

'I've got it. Tell you what I'll do. I'll round up the lot of them and find the ringleader. I'll have an identity parade. Make an example of the culprit, and that'll teach them all a lesson.'

My aunt laughed loudly and merrily, a rare occurrence, and I too thought the suggestion a joke. For who can tell one white goose from another? Or extract a confession from a goose? Or teach a silly goose new tricks? But to our amazement he put his plan into operation, and as Aunt Dot and I had shown scepticism, he huffily enlisted the help of Split, without whose special skills he could have rounded them up in half the time. As it was, the selection process became lengthy and arduous, as fraught as a beauty contest, but in the end he picked out a goose that he thought led the rest and manoeuvred her apart, leaving her in a small pen intended for sheep.

'There! That'll larn ya,' he said to the surprised goose with evident satisfaction. 'You'll not be leadin' me a pesky dance again.'

Shocked and concerned, I pleaded for the goose, since she could not speak for herself and seemed so helpless, just scurrying round the prison pen, honking hysterically, searching for her companions, who wisely kept away. Though I never cared for geese as a species, I felt sorry for her. I guessed that she had taken the blame for no better reason than that she alone had a distinguishing feature: a dark feather under one eye lent her face a droopy aspect, a slight suggestion of villainy, but only if you were looking for it. Try as I might, however, I could not convince my intractable uncle that this ugly goose was in any way a swan, in any way redeemable.

'But it's not her fault, Uncle Matt. Honestly. They're all to blame.'

'It's somebody's fault, Emma, and I'm positive she's the one,' he replied doggedly.

'She can't help her face, Uncle Matt. None of us can.'

'Ah but, Emma, she has a villainous face. She's got the evil eye. She's the culprit, all right. Odds on she is. I'm never wrong about a face. Yes, for my money, she's definitely the one. I'm certain sure of it.'

It soon became evident that the poor goose was doomed and I waited in some trepidation for the much-vaunted ceremony of cutting off the legs, but as usual Uncle Matt was bluffing. After several thoughtful cigarettes smoked on the perimeter of her pen, staring fixedly as she waddled in circles and honked with the frequency of a child's new bicycle horn, he announced his intention of selling her at Shiretown market, and insisted that I went along for the ride.

'We'll have a grand time, Emma,' he promised, 'just you and me, pet. A grand day out. The two of us. Not a word to you know who, but we'll make a day of it – a bite of dinner and everythin', but on the sly, like.'

'And who will you sell the goose to, Uncle Matt?'

'Dunno, Emma,' he replied, pensively. 'Anybody that wants one, or maybe some fool that doesn't know he wants one yet but'll find out soon enough – to his cost, I might add. She may be a bad lot an' that, but I'll not let her go cheap.'

'And when will we take her?' I asked, still in two minds about the proposed expedition.

'Next week, Emma. Next market day. So that's settled then. It's a date, Emma. Definitely.'

Chapter 5

Cloth Caps and Corduroys

Accordingly, early the following Tuesday morning Uncle Matt thrust the goose into a sack, she protesting with all her raucous and feather flying might, he just as fiercely determined. It was quite a fight, and one which could have gone either way, but at last she was safely secured inside the sack and, once shrouded from daylight, she settled down, becoming subdued and quiet – ominously quiet. We set off late to catch the bus, a long and hurried walk before us, and Uncle Matt with a heavy goose to carry, but luckily we managed to hitch a lift on a cattle feed lorry for part of the way and arrived in good time, only to find a queue already formed beside a red telephone box. It was the one bright landmark in austere Thorny Edge, and as such, also served to indicate the bus stop for Shiretown.

The people in this animated group, conversing in a strange dialect peppered with rolling 'R' sounds, were a motley assortment of some seven or eight locals – tantamount to a crowd in Thorny Edge. Uncle Matt plainly recognized everyone and engaged easily and eagerly in social chit-chat, combined with friendly handshaking, cap tweaking and cigarette sharing. His own cigarette packet was reluctant to leave his pocket, and so he profited more than the others from this rather one-sided exchange. The day being fine, the time passed pleasantly, with a lively interchange of gossip and neighbourly banter. A ruddy-complexioned farmer, blatantly curious, took an intrusive interest in Uncle Matt's affairs and was fended off in a subtle but masterly fashion.

'What's tha got in yon sack then?' began the red-faced farmer.

'Oh – this and that – you know,' replied my uncle cagily.

'Oh aye? It'll be a canny weight then.'

'Yes, you're right at that.'

'And how did tha come by that bonny black eye?'

'Oh – er – walked into the byre door in the dark,' replied Uncle Matt, without batting an eye – either the uninjured one or the bruised one in question.

The rest of the queue, accepting the explanation, murmured and nodded sympathetically, but the ruddy face stared back in disbelief.

'And how *is* tha wife nooadays?' he enquired meaningfully.

'Right as rain, thanks. You see, *she* was nowhere near the byre door,' said Uncle Matt disarmingly.

'Ey-wey,' sighed the man, patently disappointed, and having been discouraged from these searching lines of questioning, he then turned his attention to me, looking me up and down until I blushed with embarrassment.

'Ah see tha's brought a bit lass along. What's tha doin' with that bit bairn?'

'Taking her to Shiretown on the bus,' answered my inscrutable uncle.

'Shiretown, eh? And is tha buyin' or sellin' at the mart then?' He glanced significantly at the sack.

'Yes, that's right,' said my uncle, giving nothing away. Baffled, the man revived his interest in me.

'How'd tha come by that bit bairn?' he persisted, whereupon Uncle Matt vaguely mentioned the war and left it at that, turning to talk to a cross-eyed woman behind. While answering him, she focused on the man in front, causing some confusion.

Apart from this brief show of interest, the goose and I were largely ignored, and kept ourselves to ourselves. The bus was late, and the driver anxious to make up the lost time, so the very second after we climbed aboard it set off again with a jerk, causing us to sit down quickly at the front. I flopped into the window seat, Uncle Matt sat beside me, and the goose – Droopy, as I now thought of her – squatted in the sack on his knee. In a short time we had left the bleak country of Thorny Edge behind and I began to appreciate the rugged beauty of the Northumberland scenery, my only regret being that I would be obliged to get off at Shiretown rather than travel on as I secretly longed to do – all the way home to my mother.

The road passed through pinewoods, then through a small town called Aidensmead, several hamlets, and some sparsely populated stretches of countryside where the occasional isolated bus stop loomed up out of nowhere with no sign of habitation, except for the odd lonely figure patiently waiting. Sometimes people got off the bus en route, but on the whole we picked up passengers going to market, most of whom carried bags or boxes, while some sported walking sticks or fancy canes with handles carved from wood or bone into the shapes of animal heads. With the bus almost full and fewer stops now for pick-ups, we rattled along at a faster rate, the engine noisy and the air pungent with the smell of diesel fumes. The conductor moved to the rear to collect fares and the passengers all settled down, talking quietly amongst themselves. The goose stayed peaceful, either lulled into contentment by the motion of the bus or snoozing, bemused into thinking that day had turned into night. Uncle Matt nodded at the gently undulating sack and winked, nudging me with his elbow.

'Goosey, goosey, gander, eh? That's it isn't it, Emma, eh?'

'Poor goose. Taken from her family and friends,' I answered sadly.

'Whither shall I wander, eh?' he continued, smirking. 'Well she won't be wanderin' to that blighter Hutchinson's again. She's off to goodness knows where.'

'Poor Droopy,' I said. 'Taken from everyone and everything familiar to her. I know what that's like, Uncle Matt, and it's really hard.'

'Serve her right,' he answered unfeelingly. 'My meanin' is, Emma, she should've thought of that. She should've behaved herself. But I reckon she was always up to no good. The leader of the pack. I tell you, I don't like that wicked look in her eye. I definitely don't.'

'But you've got a black eye yourself now, Uncle Matt. Doesn't that make you see things differently?'

'Not a bit!' he declared vehemently. 'Not a jot! In fact, how I got it makes me see more clearly, and the way I see it is that she's got the evil eye. She's a bad influence over the other pesky rascals. Now here, Emma, cop hold of the sack for a jiffy, while I find my cigarettes.'

He deposited the goose sack, which I found decidedly heavy, on my small lap, and commenced a search of his jacket pockets, shortly producing a packet of cigarettes and a box of matches. But no sooner had he lit up and sat back, comfortably relaxed, than someone behind us tapped him on the shoulder and sniffed loudly. We both turned, confronting a woman with a seemingly naturally miserable expression, and about whom everything appeared to be long and thin – not only her figure but also her face, of which every single feature seemed elongated. She had a long, thin nose that sniffed involuntarily, a pointed, prominent chin, slanted squinty eyes, and a thin pinched mouth tightened by wrinkles into a disapproving line.

'I'm afraid cigarette smoke doesn't agree with me,' said the censorious mouth, expanding like an elastic band into a downward curve, and then contracting back to its straight line.

Uncle Matt treated her to his most sympathetic smile.

'Oh, that's a shame. A terrible affliction,' he said guilelessly. 'I'm real sorry to hear about that. Fortunately I'm not affected at all by smoke. Doesn't bother me in the least. Now me, I just love to smoke. Never happier than when I'm enjoyin' a good cigarette, like this one.' And as if to prove the point, he replaced the noxious weed between his lips and puffed contentedly.

She sniffed indignantly and tapped him again.

'No, you don't understand. What I mean is – you can't smoke.'

He raised his eyebrows, patently surprised.

'I assure you, madam, that I can. I've been doin' it for years.'

'But what I mean is you mustn't. It'll upset me if you do.'

Uncle Matt pondered for a moment, cigarette lowered, the pleasurable act of smoking briefly suspended, and it crossed my mind that had the complainant been even a moderately pretty woman he would have been easily converted to her viewpoint. At times he could be as chivalrous as the next man, maybe even more so. But she was not the slightest bit pretty and this was not one of those times.

'And it'll upset *me* if I don't. My meanin' is, I'm dyin' for a smoke, and I'm not about to waste a perfectly good opportunity and a perfectly good cigarette. As it happens, I haven't smoked a Capstan in years. This pesky war, you know. And I've just managed to cadge this one – a rare treat in these days of deprivation, as I'm sure you'll appreciate.'

The lantern-jawed woman gave a disdainful sniff and prodded her husband into action, insisting that he defend her, stand up for her rights.

'Tell him, Arthur. I won't have it! You tell him I won't have it.'

'She says she won't have it,' declared the husband, a meek little man reminiscent of a character on a seaside postcard, as short and round as she was long and thin.

He then commenced a lengthy protest, to which Uncle Matt made no reply but went on smoking, while she, brandishing a rolled umbrella, added weight to her husband's arguments by repeating everything he said. Uncle Matt's expression was one of acute boredom, and as if to incite an explosive situation further, he began to sing a popular song to himself, slowly, only pausing to inhale at intervals, and softly crooning the lyric, 'When a lovely flame dies, smoke gets in your eyes', a sad and romantic song, but it seemed to make the thin woman all the more enraged. Soothing as his singing might be to the cows in the byre, it acted on her like a red rag to a bull. She grew even more agitated, and despite the proximity of her protruding nose to the offending smoke, her thin face suddenly jutted towards us, projecting forcefully between us until it seemed to be sharpening to the shape of a wedge. Her umbrella constantly hovered over Uncle Matt's recoiling shoulders, threatening to descend on his becapped head – and maybe on my bare head too, I thought, shuffling into the corner and trying to adjust the balance of the goose, who was growing increasingly restless.

It seemed to me that the dispute was rapidly getting out of control, and all for the sake of a cigarette, which he had almost finished anyway. I glanced at my intractable uncle, but his face showed no emotion other than mild irritation at not being allowed to smoke his special cigarette in peace. Clearly there was to be no ground given by either side, and he and the thin woman were by now the focus of everyone else on the bus. Some joined the argument, smokers versus non-smokers, several shouting comments or suggestions. The conductor, registering official disapproval of the ruckus on his bus, adjusted his peaked cap as he prepared to advance down the aisle, and as he did so, the atmosphere suddenly became charged with suspense.

I sat quaking, tightly clutching the sack, which had begun to rock from side to side in an alarming manner. I wondered nervously what would happen next. Would we be put off the bus in the middle of nowhere, stranded, with no transport to take us either to the market or back home, and left to contend with a troublesome goose? Or would the petty disagreement develop into a full-scale fight – Uncle Matt's second fight within a week? Both possibilities were daunting prospects, I thought, not sure which alternative was the worst. Then all at once matters came to a head, literally, because the thin woman, growing careless about wielding her umbrella, accidentally caught Uncle Matt's left ear a glancing blow, knocking his cap askew. Though more startled than hurt by this half-expected assault, he wheeled round in his seat ready to do battle. His cigarette end fell to the floor unheeded, still smoking by itself, and I quivered in fright. But whether the dispute would indeed have worsened or somehow been amicably resolved we never knew, because the issue became irrelevant due to the intervention of a third party – the goose!

Suddenly, like a fury, she burst out of the sack and exploded into the air, rocketing upwards, dusty and indignant, surveying the assembled faces. Nor did she like what she saw because, with surprising venom that took everyone's breath away, she issued hiss after hiss, loudly and savagely, as her head stretched out towards the startled passengers.

'Hsssssss! Hssssssss!' she went, over the cowering heads of the couple behind.

Her elastic neck, seemingly about twenty feet long by now, extended through the air and then revolved from side to side, twisting with the menace of a cobra emerging from a basket, preparing to strike. She hissed through her gaping beak as only an angry goose can hiss, and suddenly she ceased to be an inert presence occupying a sack and became a vociferous and assertive force, filling the bus with manifest fear. In ordinary circumstances most of the passengers would have been familiar with the sight of a goose waddling around a field or a farmyard, and would not have turned a hair at a honk or a hiss, but in the close confines of a crowded bus the effect was sensational. A vicious goose materializing unexpectedly and apparently out of thin air conjured up disturbing thoughts, even the horror of a grotesque apparition. It was the surprise element that so startled and shocked everyone, causing general hysteria and mayhem.

Pandemonium broke loose. There was a mass movement away from the front seats to the back of the bus. Men cried out. Women screamed. A child burst into tears and whimpered piteously. The thin woman with the umbrella promptly fainted, and her slender and unresisting form was dragged without ceremony between the seats, her feet trailing, by her husband and a helper, the red-faced farmer with the enquiring mind. The conductor, who happened to have his back turned to the gyrating goose, found himself pushed aside in the resulting stampede, and hit his head on the luggage rack. Groaning in pain, he sank to the floor to join the thin woman and her umbrella, thereby forming an obstacle in the aisle which the fleeing passengers had to climb over.

Meanwhile Uncle Matt leapt into action. Sometimes I considered him slow in thought, word, and deed, but when he was fast he was very fast, and now he moved faster than the speed of light. Like a flash he snatched the goose, who was still rising like a phoenix from the ashes, then he retracted the aerial neck, forced down the hissing head, knotted the top of the hessian sack, and after a quick fumble in his pockets, produced some string, which he used to reinforce the knot. Though smothered by the sack, the goose gave a last defiant hiss before subsiding, and Uncle Matt, having just, like a magician, accomplished the vanishing trick, sat facing the front, looking serene and composed amid the chaos. I was speechless, lost in admiration of his cool nerve in a crisis. Then the driver, up to this point apparently oblivious of the proceedings, decided it was time to investigate the noise behind him. Bringing the bus to a standstill, he turned round, peering past the partition separating him from the passengers.

'What's up, Harry?' he shouted irritably. 'What's all the commotion? What the heck's going on?'

Uncle Matt looked nonchalantly behind him. I looked too. There were at least ten people on the back seat, which should only have seated five. Other double seats near the back held three or four. The passengers all seemed stupefied, and the conductor, although he had picked himself up from the floor, kept rubbing his head in a dazed way. No one answered the driver's question and, already behind schedule, he was keen to get on.

'Keep yer noise down, the lot of ya!' he shouted. 'In all my years as a driver I've never heard such a rumpus! And Harry, sort them out, will ya? Yer've got far too many at the back. Get them moved.'

With that, the bus pulled away, and the conductor tried to deal with the congestion, urging passengers forward. But no one would budge. Then he threatened to put people off the bus and a pale, sickly looking youth objected, pointing an accusing finger at Uncle Matt.

'But that man's got a nasty snake-thing. A great horrible hissing snake. I'm not sitting anywhere near him. Not me! Not if you paid me!'

Still clutching his head, the conductor moved bravely towards Uncle Matt, but stopped short of his seat for a moment, dithering in the aisle before coming alongside him. He peered suspiciously at the sack.

'*Have* you got a snake? 'Cos if so, you'll have to get off. Snakes aren't allowed on this route.'

Uncle Matt turned to face him, plainly offended.

'Me? Do you mean *me*? You're askin' me if I've got a snake? Do I look like somebody who travels with snakes?'

'I dunno,' said the conductor dubiously. 'But you look to me like a troublemaker. You've got a black eye for a start.'

'Well, Harry,' sighed my uncle. 'It *is* Harry, isn't it? Well, I can assure you, I've never travelled with a snake. Except mebbe a two-legged one, unbeknownst.'

Harry turned to look intently at me, as if more likely to elicit the truth from an eight-year-old child.

'What's he got in the sack, lass?'

'A goose,' I admitted timidly, whereupon Harry rounded irritably on my uncle.

'What do you want to bring a goose on a bus for? Causing a disturbance!'

'And why not?' my uncle demanded indignantly. 'How else would I take a goose to market in these difficult days of petrol shortage? I can't fly there on her back, can I? I tell you, I wish I had as many pounds as times I've taken geese on buses. And not a bit of bother until now! I've never had such a vexin' journey. There's been no peace at all. And for what? My meanin' is, what harm's my little goose doin'? She's not takin' up a seat, is she? She's not botherin' anybody, is she? She's all tied up and safe as houses, less trouble than some of your daft passengers. They're the troublemakers, not me. What a carry-on about nothin'!'

'You're sure it's a goose?'

'Sure I'm sure. Definitely sure. Would you care for a closer look?'

'No, no. That's all right. Don't trouble yourself. I'll take your word for it,' said Harry, backing away. Resuming his official manner, he added, 'But just keep the thing under control. Just – watch it. That's all.'

He returned to the back of the bus and again attempted to move passengers to the front, again meeting with resistance. Eventually there was a gradual reluctant drift forward, but a gap still remained between us and the other passengers. It was as if they suspected that we had contracted a highly infectious disease, and even those who had boarded the bus after the goose incident somehow took the hint and kept their distance.

All was quiet now on the goose front, but only Uncle Matt appeared completely relaxed.

'Well, well, Emma, my pet, what a to-do, eh?' he murmured gleefully. 'That was a bit of a lark, wasn't it, girl? I mean, Emma, would you credit it? Grown people frightened of an inoffensive goose! But it proves I'm right. She has the evil eye sure enough. Oh yes. Anyway, pet, I'll pass her back to you for a bit. It's time for that interrupted smoke. That last precious ciggie was wasted, and there's plenty of room behind us now. I see that Mrs Spindle-shanks and her hubby have moved away. So I dare say there'll be no objections. In fact, I dare bet my shirt on it.'

He lit another cigarette and, as anticipated, no one objected this time. The most likely objector, the thin woman, was by now well removed from the smoke, lifted by her long-suffering husband into the middle of the back seat. There she sat bolt upright, eyes slightly glazed, clutching her umbrella in front of her for dear life, like a weapon defending her against all comers. Others seated near her also remained on their guard. Indeed, such was the repellent power of my uncle's sack that when we reached Shiretown the entire busload of passengers hung back, allowing us to disembark at our leisure before anyone else. And when we then headed for a small café on the front street, usually a popular venue after the long bus ride, no one showed any inclination to follow us. Not that being ostracized troubled Uncle Matt one jot.

'Tea and toast for two, I think. Don't you, Emma?' he suggested blithely. 'That'd go down a fair treat.' As he strolled along, gently swinging the goose sack as if rocking a baby, he sang a few refrains of 'Tea for two and two for tea', shaking his versatile matchbox in a rhythmic accompaniment, like castanets.

'But what about Droopy, Uncle Matt?' I asked.

'She doesn't care much for tea and toast,' he said, grinning broadly. 'Now I see they've got a notice saying "No Dogs Allowed", but as it happens, Emma, there's no mention of geese. So with a bit of luck we can hide her under the table and hope she keeps her beak shut. After our cuppa we'll set about disposin' of her.'

All went well in the café, with tea and toast greatly enjoyed, until the goose became bored and developed an urge to contribute to the low murmur of sedate café conversation by giving an occasional honk, so that Uncle Matt had to keep coughing to mask the sound. Then she shuffled her way, still inside the sack, towards a table leg and, leaning against it, tilted the table slightly. It was as if we were holding a séance and the summoned spirit was manifesting its arrival. Crockery began to slide dangerously and a teaspoon fell from its saucer and clinked to the floor. In a trice Uncle Matt bent down, scrabbling about under the table to adjust Droopy's position. Then, casting etiquette to the wind, he placed his elbows firmly on the table, holding everything steady. But the damage had been done and our waitress had been alerted to the strange goings on. After a tersely whispered conference with another waitress, she began to haunt our table like the spirit we appeared to be summoning. Neglecting other diners, she hovered over us, watching us with deep suspicion and surreptitiously trying to peep under the limp oilcloth draped over our table. Fortunately we had both finished our toast and Uncle Matt had poured his third cup of tea before she made her mind up to approach.

'There's no dogs allowed,' she said primly, pointing at the notice.

'No dogs, eh?' said my uncle, showing interest. 'Quite right as well. I mean to say – dogs in a café! The very idea. I should think not indeed!'

'Even in sacks,' she proceeded, indicating the concealing tablecloth.

'Oh, *we* haven't got a dog. Did you think we had a dog then? No, definitely not. No dog.'

'Nor cats neither.'

'Don't have a cat neither.'

'You've got some kind of animal in that sack. I know you have,' she insisted, and as if to confirm her opinion, the goose gave three consecutive honks.

'Well, all right then, I have. But it's only a little goose.'

'Don't be silly.' she said superciliously. 'Nobody brings a goose into a café.'

'*I* do,' replied Uncle Matt proudly.

'Well there's no geese allowed either.'

'Oh? Is that so? Fair enough. But mind you, there's no notice to that effect,' he pointed out legalistically, and the goose honked in agreement.

He tried to resume sipping his tea, but a certain constraint had settled on the entire café, an anticipatory hush, making our position untenable. The waitress buzzed round our table like an annoying wasp, and the café clientele sat watching and listening with rapt attention as if we had been specifically engaged at no extra charge to act as the cabaret. In the end we were not exactly thrown out of the café, but were embarrassed into leaving. The indignant waitress kept dashing between us, clearing the table until there remained only the cup that Uncle Matt held in his hand, unable to put it down because his saucer had vanished. Several times she tried to snatch it from his grasp, but it was a battle of wills which he was determined to win and he held the cup fast until he had downed the last drop. Then, at length, he rose with as much dignity as he could muster, and while I cringed in mortification he led the way out with a nonchalant air, casually swinging the protesting sack. Not for him the silent ignominious retreat. He paused in the doorway, addressing his captive audience as if taking his final curtain call, determined to have the last word.

'I'll tell you one thing,' he proclaimed in loud, ringing tones, 'it'll be a long time before I bring my goose in here again for a cup of tea.'

And on that note we left, while behind us the café instantly erupted into noisy chatter, the remaining customers becoming as convivial as they had previously been shocked into silence. Then we proceeded to the busy precincts of the mart, where farmers continually came and went all morning, and there we hung around for some time, vainly trying to find an unsuspecting customer to take Droopy off our hands. There was little demand for a single goose, and at first we had no success, because wary farmers who knew my uncle well were more than a match for him and made sure they avoided eye contact. But after a while he spotted a young farmer – greener than grass, my uncle described him as – and swooped on him like a hawk on a rabbit. As I listened to the ensuing sales patter I realized that the young man, who began by being adamant that he wanted nothing to do with any goose, of any shape, size or description, had as much chance of escaping his fate as the goose had, maybe even less, because she was the more experienced escapee. Gradually his resistance was worn down, and finally, in the hope of clinching the deal, Uncle Matt untied the string, revealing Droopy's startled head.

'Just look at those distinctive markings,' he said, pointing with pride at the dark eye feathers. 'That's a touch of class, that is. I'll tell you somethin' – free, gratis, and for nothin' – and it's this: you're lookin' at a top-notch goose there. Look at the size of her! You'll never see a better. I tell you, I wouldn't be partin' with this goose, not at any price, but I need the money.' He gestured with some embarrassment at his black eye. 'You understand my problem. Only temporary, of course – the coppers'll start flowing in again before you know it – but for now my need for a bob or two's urgent.'

'But I don't want a goose!' insisted the young man, 'I don't keep geese. I've never liked them. Vicious, noisy things.'

He attempted to back away, but Uncle Matt laid a restraining hand on his arm.

'You'll like this one. Who wouldn't? As you can see, I've had a bit of trouble,' he said, again indicating his black eye, 'and there'll be more of these comin' my way unless I cash in some of me assets fast. That's why your goose is goin' so cheap. But I expect you'd guessed that already. You look like an intelligent chap, with an eye for a bargain. My only comfort is that she'll be goin' to a good home. I know she will, 'cos you've got a kind face.'

And so it was that in a comparatively short time the deal was clinched. The bemused young man had, I noticed, developed the air of hunted prey, and he parted with the asking price without a quibble. After the customary spit and handshake to seal the bargain, Uncle Matt gave him back the traditional lucky penny and I said goodbye to Droopy – from a safe distance, of course. I tried not to let my thoughts dwell on her likely fate, but ever since she had been singled out as leader of the pack I had been unable to visualize her in any position other than upside down on a serving platter, surrounded by roast potatoes and parsnips. I felt very sorry for her, squatting dejectedly in that inhospitable sack, with the young man staring at her, his face crumpled in helpless bewilderment. There was a brief moment when she turned a mournful eye on me, and so I waved back and made a wish that her new owner would grow fond of her and keep her as a pet. Then the young man bent over to tie the sack and she honked aggressively in his ear, sadly lessening the likelihood of her acquiring that status. Uncle Matt, however, suffered no concerns for her future prospects. Brushing right hand against left in a done-and-dusted gesture, he dismissed an unpleasant episode from his mind and smiled contentedly, taking my hand.

'We got a dashed good price there, Emma. More than I ever expected.

Though mebbe I should've charged him sixpence extra for the sack.'

'But he couldn't have carried the goose without the sack, Uncle Matt.'

'Exactly, pet. That's what you call a seller's market. A good chance missed. It's not like me to let a business opportunity slip, but there we are. Can't win 'em all.' And with the goose money tucked in the pocket next to his heart and a fresh spring in his step, he led the way into the mart itself.

Traditionally, the mart functioned as an essentially male province, an arena where men wearing cloth caps and corduroys rubbed shoulders with other men wearing trilby hats and cavalry twills, all competing in the business of buying and selling sheep and cattle. They encircled a ring of sawdust into which frightened animals were driven, sliding and stumbling, goaded by an attendant wielding a stout stick, and startled by a barking commentary from the auctioneer. Around the ring, wooden seats rose in tiers like the seats in the coliseum, and there we sat and watched the auction, Uncle Matt having no intention of buying anything, but only being there to keep abreast of market values, while I was shyly aware of being regarded by the other occupants as something of a curiosity.

I found myself overwhelmed by the sheer scale of everything – by the great width of the bench seats and the big beefy farmers sitting on them or standing blocking my view, by the sonorous chant of the auctioneer bellowing repetitively in my ear, by the resonant blare of protests as animals were prodded nervously through the sawdust, by the throat-catching pungency of the all-pervasive smell. Everything combined to make me feel very small and insignificant, like a Lilliputian child among giants. And, intriguingly, the sale proceeded as if by magic. None of the bidders appeared to make a sound or sign, and yet the auctioneer shouted out bids and the animals ended up sold. I queried this phenomenon with Uncle Matt and he discreetly pointed out bidders.

'Over there, Emma. See that bloke seems to be twitchin'? And that one at the ringside winkin'? Now, over that way, him in the tartan scarf, he's pullin' his ear, and t'other way, him in the green cap, he keeps raisin' his eyebrows. Now mind what you do, Emma. Don't scratch your nose, pet, in case you buy somethin' we don't want.'

I sat rigidly, terrified to move in case I bought one of the big brown cows spattered with manure that held the ring, and it came as a relief when the auction neared its close and Uncle Matt suggested a bite to eat. I leapt to my feet with alacrity, but as we were leaving, passing the metal enclosures and picking our way carefully over the recently hosed cobbles that now ran with liquid manure, I noticed a black and white calf, beautifully marked. She stood alone, shivering and snivelling from a head cold, and her dark, soulful eyes seemed to beckon to me, imploring me to take her away. My heart went out to the poor lonely calf, separated like me from her mother, and I stood still, refusing to budge, pleading with Uncle Matt to buy her.

'No, Emma. Definitely not, girl. She's a Friesian,' he said, tugging at my arm, 'I don't keep Friesians. Shorthorns are best for up our way.'

'Oh *please*, Uncle Matt. I'll help. I know how – I fed Tiny.'

'No, Emma! She's a bit femmer, I'd say. Delicate I mean. In fact, fair dead on her feet.'

'She just needs looking after, Uncle Matt. She's lovely really.'

'Yes, she's not a bad looker, I'll grant you that. In fact, she's a bit of a bobby-dazzler. But we don't need another calf right now, and up Sourhope way we all keep shorthorns. Besides, I don't know what your aunt Dot would say.'

'Oh please, Uncle Matt. We can't leave her. It would be too awful. Too cruel.'

He swivelled his cap thoughtfully, studying the calf.

'All right, Emma. Tell you what we'll do. We'll see if she's goin' cheap. Mind you, I'm not promisin' anythin', but sometimes at the end of a sale you get a bargain.'

We retraced our steps, but this time positioned ourselves at the barrier round the ring, where I had to stand on tiptoe in order to see even a little of the action. But when the calf came in, looking fragile and sorry for herself, Uncle Matt piped up loudly.

'That's the sickliest creature I've seen all year,' he asserted. 'It's a disgrace to sell her in that condition. She'll be lucky to last the night.'

He went on in that vein till the bidding was under way and then, with a surreptitious wiggle of the thumb, he bid for her; without much opposition, she was knocked down to him. We paid the bill at the office and arranged transport, and then, with a light heart and a healthy appetite, I followed him to a side-street restaurant for lunch.

'I'm ever so glad you bought the calf, Uncle Matt,' I said excitedly as we walked along, and he glanced down at me, pulling a glum face.

'I'm not too sure that I am, Emma. She was cheap enough, like, but I just hope she's not dead by mornin'. And goodness knows what your aunt Dot'll have to say about a Friesian. She'll probably be real cut up about it, and I'll reap the benefit. She's dead set against all foreigners.'

'Shall we call her Patch, Uncle Matt?'

'No, pet, not Patch. That's more for a dog or a cat. It lacks the dignity of a handsome cow. She's too bonny for that name. Have another think.'

'I will. I'll think of something to suit her perfectly,' I said as we stopped at our destination, a shabby door in a narrow side street.

And putting that decision on hold, we stepped inside the restaurant, which turned out to be a fancy name for a fish and chip shop with tables, the dining area consisting of wooden cubicles back to back with trestle tables fastened to the floor. A hot, steamy atmosphere met us at the door and a long queue led to the counter. At first Uncle Matt's face fell as he glanced at the line of people and then at his watch, but fortunately we recognized some familiar faces. There, queuing stoically, stood several passengers from the morning's bus, including the nervous youth, and they were only too pleased to give way to Uncle Matt, even without his sack. Indeed, as they hustled him to the front of the queue, they continued to watch him uneasily, rearing away whenever he went near his pockets, as if he might produce something scary and snake-like. The menu consisted purely of battered fish, chips, and mushy peas, liberally sprinkled with salt and vinegar, and washed down with something chosen from a selection of lurid-coloured bottles containing variously flavoured fizzy drinks. To me the meal was delicious, but sadly it could not be lingered over in the way it deserved to be because my aunt had provided a comprehensive shopping list and we had as yet purchased none of her specified items. We both knew that to return home without every item on the list ticked and present would be to court disaster.

Our first call was to the Co-op, where I watched when we paid for the groceries, as a little metal cylinder containing our money flew on a wire tramway up to the office; when it came back down to the counter, as if by magic, it now contained the receipt and change. At this shop Uncle Matt acquired a cardboard box, and we then dashed round what was clearly a familiar route to him until the box was full, its varied contents including a puzzle book and two comics for me.

Shiretown sprawled on a hill in a maze of sloping streets and old stone buildings, and our final purchase was hastily chosen after a steep climb up a narrow side street to an ancient ironmonger's. The shop was dark and poky, smelling of creosote and carbolic, and it was packed from floor to ceiling with everything anyone could ever want in the way of tools, utensils, and commodities, from axes to zinc buckets. Here, with a certain grim satisfaction, Uncle Matt bought a strong catch and a padlock, together with a hefty chain, to reinforce the message he had delivered to the geese by making an example of Droopy. Then came a frantic rush for the bus, in which, curiously, the only seats still available were at the front.

So ended my first trip to Shiretown, which had been unexpectedly eventful, every bit the grand day out that Uncle Matt had promised, though he could not have foreseen its rich diversity. Happily, there were to be other similar excursions to come, because although he pretended otherwise, my uncle set little store by education and, even after I started school, he kept me off whenever he fancied my company on one of his jaunts. He always wrote the same graphic note to excuse my absence: 'Emma was sick to her stomach after her supper last night. Definitely.' This regular letter did nothing for my aunt's already dubious reputation as a cook. From time to time I enjoyed our subsequent trips to the market, but none surpassed or even equalled that first outing, in which the goose was undoubtedly the star turn, but Uncle Matt came a close second.

On that occasion we arrived home at teatime and met with a mixed reception from Aunt Dot. Initially there were moments of accusation and acrimony because, just as Uncle Matt had jumped to unfair conclusions regarding the goose being a bad influence, so Aunt Dot was inclined to blame me for leading him astray in the matter of the calf. She liked to make the decisions on buying stock, and was less than enthusiastic at exchanging a perfectly healthy goose for a sickly motherless calf, and a Friesian at that. Besides, she had had a difficult day, yet again retrieving the wayward geese from Hutchinson's field, and thus proving beyond doubt that Droopy was not the ringleader; as I thought from the very start, she had been wrongly convicted. Clearly the whole gaggle suffered from wanderlust, and at Aunt Dot's insistence, even before he could have his tea, Uncle Matt had to take his new lock and chain to the bottom gate and try to make it goose-proof.

By early evening, however, all was well. The calf was delivered to the farm at just after seven, and as soon as Aunt Dot laid eyes on her she calmed down, for there was no denying the appeal of the fetching little Friesian. And years later, my aunt and uncle had cause to thank me. I called the calf Beauty, taking the hint from something Uncle Matt had said, and she turned out to be just that – a real beauty, the best cow they ever had, and all her offspring were almost as good.

Chapter 6

A Close Shave

In September I started school, much against my will. Up until then I had enjoyed discovering everything education had to offer me, but now, as the dreaded day drew near, I grew increasingly apprehensive, fraught with nameless fears, mainly about my fellow pupils. Ever since arriving in Sourhope I had been trying to adapt to an unaccustomed lifestyle among unfamiliar people. I did my utmost to fit in to this new life, so foreign to me, but hard as I tried, I remained a mystified outsider. There was no doubt about it – to me, the locals were strange.

I wondered at their quaint habits and curious customs, that included chewing matchsticks and eating onions from a knife; and at the way they carried grotesque sticks, or sinister boxes containing mysterious creatures, or sacks that had a life of their own and moved by themselves. Then, too, I found it difficult to understand their peculiar dialect, especially when the accent was strong, and I was completely baffled by the secret signals they used when buying cattle at the mart. During my comparatively short stay I had so far encountered several weird individuals, including one who appeared to be missing a neck, one who looked like the Devil, one with eyes whose colours didn't match, and one with the longest face I had ever seen and an unnerving habit of beating people about the head with a rolled umbrella.

All in all, there was nothing there to inspire confidence in my fellow man – or, indeed, woman – and if the adults were strange, I saw no reason to suppose that their children would be otherwise. While I did not exactly *expect* them to have two heads or a tail or some other such abnormality, I would not have ruled out the possibility. And the more I anticipated my first day at school, the more my imagination ran riot, until I felt as reluctant to leave the farm as one of Uncle Matt's lambs being led to the slaughter. Then there was the journey there and back to contend with. To my consternation, I heard Aunt Dot mention that I would have to walk to school by myself, and I remembered the road only too well. I had walked it once or twice with Uncle Matt and it was the longest and steepest I had ever encountered, except for roads in disturbing dreams that keep on lengthening. This one was a tortuous road, shadowy in its twists and turns, allowing practically anything to lurk hidden, lying in wait to pounce on me. And surely, I thought, on dark days it would be a nightmare road. But when I approached Aunt Dot about this she showed no sympathy, summarily dismissing all such fears and fancies.

'Nonsense!' she said sharply. 'Stop making such a fuss! It's just a road like any other, and you've walked it before so you know it well. You'll manage, and I've no time for mollycoddling. Heaven knows, I've too much to do as it is!'

I said nothing more just then, knowing that it was no use pleading with her, that it would only make her cross, but I could not stop thinking of the ordeal in store. So on the evening before my first day, feeling restless and uneasy, I sought comfort and reassurance from Uncle Matt as he sat milking in the byre. I noticed that he always wore his cap back to front for milking, and wondered if his intention was to confuse the cows as to whether he was coming or going.

'Uncle Matt, couldn't *you* take me to school? Please, Uncle Matt,' I enquired, fastening him with large, imploring eyes.

'Yes, of course, Emma,' he said, raising my hopes. 'Oh yes, definitely. I intend to, pet. I thought you knew. I'll be takin' you all right. Tomorrow, that is. Get you properly settled in, an' that. Hand you over to the headmaster, and tell him what a clever girl you are. We've got to get you off to a good start, now haven't we, pet?'

'I know, but what I mean is, couldn't you take me every day? It's a long walk. It's millions of miles, and you see, I'm only eight.'

'Oh no, no, Emma, not every day. Sorry, pet, but it can't be done. For a start it's the busiest time of day on a farm. And the top and bottom of it is, Emma, your aunt can't cope with it all on her own. As it is we'll have to be up at the crack of dawn tomorrow so that I can take you the first time.'

'Please, Uncle Matt! *Please!*'

He turned towards me, his cap tilted at a rakish angle against the cow.

'I'm sorry, pet, but I just can't. Haven't the time, and haven't the petrol. It's the war, you see. Those rotten Nazis. But don't worry,

Emma. You'll be all right. You'll be just fine. You will now, definitely. So don't worry.'

But I did worry, and went on gazing at him with beseeching eyes, willing him to take notice. He had, however, turned his face away from me, burying his nose in the cow's stomach, so in desperation and in a small voice that could hardly be heard over the champing of cows I finally confessed the extent of the fear that obsessed me.

'I'm frightened, Uncle Matt. Really frightened. Scared stiff in fact.'

'What's that you say, Emma? Did you say *frightened*?' he asked, sounding surprised, having forgotten, if he had ever known, how it feels to be eight years old and away from home for the first time, facing the unknown. 'Well, I must say I'm astonished, Emma. I had you down for a real brave girl. A little lion, in fact. You know, Emma, when we took our goose for a ride on the bus and it shot out of the sack like a jack-in-the-box, you were the only one besides me that wasn't feared of it.'

'I was the only one who knew for sure it was a goose, Uncle Matt. And anyway, she was pointing her beak away from me.'

'Well, there's no reason to be frightened now either. It'll all work out. You'll see. In fact, when I come to think of it, you might cadge a lift on the milk lorry. There now. You'll enjoy the ride.'

At that I brightened a little, but again he disappointed me.

'Course it depends what time Joe comes. If he's on time he'll give you a lift, no bother. But my meanin' is, if he's late you won't half have to run for it. Can't rely on him, you see. Kind enough bloke. Salt of the earth. But a terrible time-keeper is Joe.'

Then, as if to preclude further discussion on the subject, he suddenly burst into song, serenading the cow he was milking, who happened to be called Daisy, with two rounds of 'Daisy, Daisy, Give Me Your Answer Do', and following that with his usual repertoire of old favourites that featured regularly in his milking-time concerts. He claimed that he sang to increase the milk yield, that the gullible cows were lulled by a good tune into giving generously. But I suspected that he simply liked singing and enjoyed the sound of his own voice. In the seclusion of the byre he entertained a captive audience, uninterrupted except for the occasional moo from a musical cow joining in, and he sang full-throatedly, giving the songs his all.

The sound of his pleasant tenor voice filled the byre, but for once it failed to find an appreciative listener in me. I felt utterly dejected, and stood silent and doleful, gazing around me at the depressing scene. In front of my tearful eyes a row of cows presented their muddy tails, hanging like bedraggled tassels, tempting me to pull one. But I resisted. I had seen how cows could kick without warning, and with a wallop like a maddened mule, and I had no intention of offering myself as target practice. I kept well back, but was careful not to position myself too near the small byre, for in its murky depths rats' eyes glowed from the cowcake bins, flickering on and off like distant torches in a dark tunnel. And when it came to rats, my sympathies lay with the Pied Piper of Hamlyn, who had sensibly drowned the lot. Outside the open door, rain drizzled miserably, matching my mood, and clouds of midges floated in a flimsy haze, waiting for a victim to plague.

The very air was stifling to me, heavy with the mingling smells unique to old byres, a pungent odour of fusty hay, manure, disinfectant and damp animals. Even the dog smelled damp, stale as a sweaty sock, as he nuzzled my arm, sensing my distress, whimpering sympathetically. He always showed his caring side by thrusting his nose into my hand, in the mistaken belief that it would make me feel better, and this unsolicited but well-meant gesture sometimes came out of the blue as a shock. It was disconcerting to say the least – one minute standing there lost in a lone reverie, and the next grasping a long, wet nose. But I stroked his wet head anyway, grateful for concern from any quarter. At that troubled moment I desperately wanted my mother. I wanted her cheerful smile and comforting arms and the familiar sights and smells of home. I longed to feel safe and loved once more, and despite my determination to keep my feelings to myself, tears flowed and would not be restrained. They rolled steadily down, dripping and drizzling like the rain, until my eyes felt brimful and my face as wet as the dog's. For want of a handkerchief I wiped my eyes on my hand and my hand on my dress lest Uncle Matt should notice, but I needn't have worried, for his attention was otherwise engaged.

He had just finished a lengthy version of his favourite song, 'I Think that I Shall Never See a Poem Lovely as a Tree' – not that the song started life as a lengthy one, but it turned out that way, because he dramatically elongated 'po-oh-oh-em', trilled a lot every time the word 'tree' cropped up, and kept repeating himself in striving for perfection. He left a modest interval between songs, as if for imaginary applause, and whenever I glanced at him he had his eyes riveted on the pail as he squirted milk rhythmically into the centre and watched with an almost child-like wonder as the white ripples widened and whirled. When he had finished he pulled the pail away to safety, sat back, and examined my miserable little face intently.

'Well now, Emma, you're very quiet. Not like you at all. You seem a bit down in the dumps, I'd say. What's up, pet? You're not still worryin' about school, are you? Haven't I told you, you'll be all right? You'll show 'em. All of 'em. In fact, Ah dare bet on it. I dare bet you'll be top of the class. My meanin' is – you'll be top right enough. In my opinion you're a real clever girl. There now.'

I smiled faintly, and sought further reassurance.

'Uncle Matt – this headmaster – can you tell me something about him? I mean, what he's like?' I silently willed him to give a good report, and he thought for a moment, scratching his forehead with his thumbnail, pushing up his cap where the band felt tight.

'Well, he's kinda square shaped,' he said at length. 'I mean short and stocky, like. Built like a barn door. I've noticed him at the Cornmill show, 'cos he wins all the prizes. He's a great gardener. No doubt about it. They say that when it comes to horticulture he really knows his onions.'

'He likes onions, does he, Uncle Matt?' I asked, wondering if he ate them from his knife.

'Likes them? He's passionate about 'em. Absolutely potty about 'em. They say that what he doesn't know about onions isn't worth knowin'. Grows 'em as big as your head. In fact as big as *my* head, and mine feels too big for my cap in this sultry heat.'

I felt puzzled. So far these confidences had given me a curious insight into the headmaster's character, but I still needed to know more of him.

'And what else, Uncle Matt?'

'Oh – carrots, leeks, cabbages – you name it, he grows it.'

'No, I mean what else can you tell me about him? What sort of person is he?'

'We-e-ell now, I've heard he's deaf. Deaf as a post, so they reckon. And strict. A bit strict, like, but fair all the same.'

'What do you mean by strict, Uncle Matt?' I asked nervously, the word having an ominous ring.

'Well, you know, Emma – you know – he makes his pupils jump to it and keeps them on their toes, an' that,' he explained, and I stared at him, disconcerted.

'It's not a ballet school, is it, Uncle Matt?'

'No, no. Don't be daft, pet. It's what's called an elementary school.'

'Then why does he do that? Keep them on their toes and make them jump?'

'Well, that's the way he likes 'em. He's a stickler for discipline, so I've heard. Stands no nonsense you see, Emma. In fact folks reckon he has a cat-o'-nine-tails for them that gets out of hand.' And then, seeing my horrified expression, he added hastily, 'But mebbbe that's not true. Probably not. Why no! It can't be. Definitely not. Likely it's just a false rumour.'

I had never heard of a cat-o'-nine-tails, but shuddered at the sound of it.

'What is it?' I asked fearfully.

'What's what?'

'The cat thing – what you said – with the nine tails.'

But he began to bluster and retract.

'Oh, it's nothing, Emma. Don't you worry your pretty little head about that. I shouldn't have mentioned it. Just forget it. I'm sure that even if he has one, which he most likely hasn't, he'd never use it on a nice little girl like you.'

I was about to enquire further, but just then a cow down the line shook her head, vigorously rattling her tethering chains and mooing mournfully as if tired of waiting, impatient to get the business of being milked over and done with. Obligingly, and with the sprightly step of one who is keen to escape, Uncle Matt bounded into the cooler house, emptied the full pail into the cooler tank, returned and moved his stool beside the fretful cow. I followed him and tried again.

'What exactly does he do with this queer cat, Uncle Matt?'

'Do? Cat? Not a thing, Emma. Forget it. It's nothin'.'

'But just tell me. Tell me about it. Please!'

He had, however, regretted letting the cat out of the bag, so to speak. He became tight-lipped and evasive, curling up like a tortoise retreating into its shell, determinedly withdrawn. He kept his face turned away from me into the cow's rump, and his whole attitude was now one of non-cooperation. The more I persisted, the more obdurate he became, answering me only once more and in a tone of finality.

'It's nothin', Emma. Nothin', nothin', nothin'! Definitely now – nothin'! You understand me, Emma? Nothin'!' Then he lowered his voice and, glancing around cautiously, added, 'But don't mention it to your aunt Dot. Now mind, Emma – not a word!'

I had gone to the byre hoping to be reassured but came out feeling just the opposite. I spent the night tossing and turning, tormented by thoughts of the cat-o'-nine-tails, imagining how it would look – maybe like a normal cat but larger of course, with longer claws, sharper teeth, and slanted luminous eyes; and the nine tails would be raised and rigid, fanning like peacock feathers before it sprang. The next morning, after a meagre breakfast of sugar on bread, a wartime delicacy, I sat clutching my lunchbox and pencil case, tired and terrified, resolving to do nothing that might incur this weird headmaster's displeasure. It seemed that he was endowed with more than his fair share of peculiarities, but I would pretend not to notice. I would ignore his square shape, speak up so that he could hear me, and show keen interest if he mentioned onions. And I would try my best, though greatly in need of practice, to stand on my toes if required. I would begin as I meant to go on, by being a model pupil.

Sadly, however, I began by being late for school, thanks to my friend and mentor, Uncle Matt. I now experienced once again his propensity to be late – late by nature and late by habit. Should he ever find himself in danger of having time to spare he would fritter it away until it all ran out, leaving him with his habitual last-minute rush. And on this occasion he felt he needed to make a good impression. He wanted to look just right, and his standard of sartorial elegance necessitated a shave, a complete change of clothes, and polishing his best shoes till they reflected the sky.

After the milking at dawn, therefore, came the shave, and as he made his elaborate preparations I became more and more agitated. Already alarm bells were ringing in my brain, because I had witnessed this ritual before – and it *was* a ritual – solemn, ceremonial, and worst of all, lengthy. There being no bathroom in the house, he set up his shaving tackle on the wide living-room window sill, where maximum light fell on his face. He propped up the mirror and formally arranged his toiletries just as a priest might place symbolic artefacts on an altar in precise order. Next he tied a towel round his neck, like a bib, settled himself comfortably on a low stool, and slowly commenced operations. I waited, heart in mouth, as he stirred the shaving cream in a rhythmical circular motion, with all the meditative concentration of a Renaissance painter mixing colours for yet another masterpiece. Then I moved forward and hovered nervously.

'We haven't much time, Uncle Matt,' I ventured to point out.

'Mmmmm,' he agreed, stirring contentedly, lathering up the foam and applying it liberally to face and neck, then pausing to survey the effect.

'I say, Uncle Matt, it's getting late. There's not much time left.'

'Uh – huh,' came the disappointing response.

Next he took a small razor and, holding his nose to one side, carefully coaxed away the offending whiskers with studied deliberation, cutting a pattern of diagonal stripes through the cream until he looked like a native of a primitive tribe wearing warpaint. I waved at him in the mirror, reminding him that I was there – and waiting.

'I've been thinking, Uncle Matt – I don't want to be late on my first day. Not on my very first day. That looks really bad, don't you think?'

'Hmmmm,' he murmured agreeably, intently studying the reflection of his face once more, and though I had steeled myself for the ordeal ahead, for facing the trials of starting a new school, for being a stranger amongst strangers, I now began to feel my courage ebbing.

'Please, Uncle Matt. Please help me. Please hurry,' I pleaded in a low, tense voice, the muttered supplication sounding almost like a prayer before his gimcrack altar, and he answered amiably but absently.

'Be right with you, Emma, girl. Nearly done, pet.'

He had now finished scraping his chin and had begun to pat his face lovingly with a wet flannel. Normally I could find some entertainment in watching the finer points of his shaving technique, but now I felt very much on edge. Now I knew beyond all shadow of a doubt that we would be late, very late, but I feared a worse fate than that. My frightened young mind had formed an odd idea that I would break all existing records for lateness – the school record, the county record, maybe even the world record. Panic seized me utterly, giving full rein to an overwrought imagination in which I saw myself paraded in disgrace before the whole school, and leading to an extraordinary idea floating from nowhere into my mind that in these outlandish parts of the country they might still tar and feather people for such serious offences.

Meanwhile, my uncle calmly inspected his face, examining it minutely from all angles for stray hairs, and having found none, gave his reflection a last lingering look of satisfaction, the satisfaction of any great artist on completion of a major work. Then, to my disbelief, he held up the mirror and began to sing to his complacent image in the looking glass, composing his face and contorting his lips as if about to kiss his reflection, while he commenced a tremulous attempt at 'I'll Take You Home Again, Kathleen'. So tense had I become by this time that my patience finally snapped. Uncharacteristically, I threw a tantrum. If he could sing at such a time, I thought, then I could dance, and dance I did, frantically from side to side, waving my arms about and screaming hysterically.

'Uncle Matt! We'll be late! I'm late for school, Uncle Matt. Very late! Late! Late! Late! Do you hear me, Uncle Matt? I'm going to be late on my very first day!'

He stopped, open-mouthed, put the mirror down, and stared at me reprovingly.

'Hey there, Emma, steady on girl. Calm down, girl. You're all right. What an almighty fuss! What a carry-on,' he protested, plainly aggrieved.

But at least he stood up, and at that I breathed a sigh of relief. And a minute later I breathed another, as Aunt Dot came to my rescue. She dashed into the room at her usual steady sprint, set down the bucket she carried, and paused briefly, appraising the situation in her inimitable quick way. Her little head rotated like a human periscope from the clock face that appeared to me to be racing, to my troubled face, to Uncle Matt's slightly guilty face, and back to the clock. Then she moved into action, chivvying him remorselessly, and though I nearly always took my uncle's side, for once I was on hers and very grateful for her intervention.

'Hurry up, Matt! Come on now, hurry! You're well behind the clock,' she began. 'Hurry, hurry!' was her constant cry as she helped him to get ready.

Demonstrating the energy and skill of a hyperactive valet, she went to work, polishing his shoes, fastening his tie, holding his jacket, brushing his trousers, straightening his collar, and finally fetching his handkerchief, car keys, and the indispensable cap. And still she found breath to urge him on, giving me the impression that she had done this before and often. Her rallying cry of 'Hurry, Matt, hurry!' resounded throughout her urgent ministrations, and only occasionally did Uncle Matt dare to protest at being so unceremoniously manhandled.

'I'm hurryin', aren't I? Can't you see I'm hurryin'?' he protested – a feeble protest which she ignored as she would a whisper in the wind.

'Hurry!' she shrieked, pushing him through the door. 'Hurry now,' she repeated as she followed us across the yard. 'Hur – ry, hur – ry,' she called after us, sounding like an echo in the Swiss mountains.

And then we were off, literally in leaps and bounds, because Uncle Matt ground his gears and forgot to lower the handbrake and blamed Aunt Dot for distracting him, and the car lurched forward with a jerk, shuddering and juddering. Then it steadied and started again, commencing the long descent to school, a slow one because, like my uncle that morning, the car seemed to be suffering from acceleration problems. I agonized every inch of the way, mentally willing the vehicle forward, and yet at the same time dreading its arrival.

'Can't this car go any faster, Uncle Matt?' I enquired, tactfully blaming the tool rather than the workman.

'It's not a racin' car, Emma,' he said huffily. 'Just an old Morris.'

'Is that the car's name? Morris?'

'Cars don't have names, Emma. That's the make. She's a Morris. A Morris Cowley.'

'How do you know it's a she, Uncle Matt? Surely Morris Cowley's a man's name?'

'Well, you see, Emma, cars are like ships – they're all called "she". Maybe that's why they're so dashed awkward at times. Temperamental, you might say. Like women.'

'I only ask because the man next door to us at home used to call his car Tin Lizzie – after his wife, he told me.'

'I guess she must've been an old banger,' commented Uncle Matt ambiguously.

'Anyway, Uncle Matt, we'll call this one Morris. It sort of suits the name,' I said decisively, and for the rest of the journey I allowed him to concentrate on his driving while I tried out my own methods of propelling the car forward.

Now that I knew the car's name I felt sure that this inside information would give me some influence over its performance, and with my face averted I whispered constantly into the brown leather upholstery, urging the engine to go faster. Yet still I dreaded arriving, and when we did finally do so, all was as I feared – all was silent. The school bell had long since ceased ringing and the strident sound of the morning hymn had raised the roof and died away. Prayers had been mumbled and announcements announced. These everyday procedures were already forgotten, and lessons, doubtless soon to be forgotten too, were now in progress. As we made our way tentatively through the iron gates, Uncle Matt holding my hand to give himself courage, the school exhibited that deserted air, that deep awesome silence that causes you to walk on tiptoe and speak in whispers.

But we were not alone after all. Halfway across the yard we heard footsteps pounding behind us, and turned to see another late-comer, a boy of about thirteen, who was so colourful that our initial instinct was to shade our eyes. Nature had given him a flying start by bestowing him with bright orange hair and vivid freckles like spots on a toadstool, but his clothes added to the effect, suggesting that he wore whatever mismatched garments his elders and betters discarded. These hand-me-downs he wore with panache, and he might have carried the whole thing off had it not been for his garish pullover, a garment knitted in a bizarre Fair Isle pattern from multi-coloured scraps of wool, giving every appearance of being the product of a colour-blind knitter. Like Joseph's coat of many colours, it incorporated every shade of the spectrum, and left a dazzling impression on all who beheld it.

The boy grinned broadly at us and, colourful to the last, revealed a curve of yellow teeth, which stirred in me vague memories of a banana I had been given before the war, before this exotic fruit vanished from greengrocers' shelves. Yet, curiously, I felt relieved at the sight of him, initially because he had only the one head and apparently no tail and (apart from resembling a walking rainbow) no visible abnormalities, which boded well for the rest of the inmates. But then I realized that he was even later than I was, and if the record for lateness had indeed been broken, the honour or dishonour now belonged to him, letting me off the hook. Perhaps after all, I thought optimistically, I would escape being tarred and feathered. But oddly, he seemed equally pleased to see us, attaching himself like a limpet to Uncle Matt.

'Hello, mister. Ah'll show ya the way, mister,' he said, all eagerness to oblige. 'Ya'll be wantin' ta see the headmaster. Ah'll take ya to 'im. Follow me, mister.'

He led us into school through a shabby brown door which looked as if many feet had moodily kicked its ageing paintwork, and then along a dingy corridor, the walls half-tiled in mottled institutional green, glossy and garish, and the wooden floor worn and smelling strongly of chalk dust and powdered disinfectant. Halfway down the corridor he stopped outside a sombre oak door, which he declared to be the headmaster's study, and there we waited in some trepidation, Uncle Matt looking almost as jittery as I felt. The door displayed a fancy brass plate on which the title 'HEAD TEACHER' had been engraved in elegant lettering, but constant fingering and occasional polishing had worn away the central letters, leaving only 'HE   EACHER', a phonetic message that did nothing for my peace of mind. I read it compulsively over and over, several times out loud, and the more I read it the more deeply sinister it seemed. 'HE EACHER – HE EAT CHER – HE EAT YER,' I mouthed to myself, trying out the various versions, and wondering uneasily if the elegantly engraved 'HE' referred to the headmaster or the mysterious CAT.

'Stay there, mister, and don't move,' said the colourful boy, and with an oddly proprietorial air, indicated a specific spot on the floor where he wanted us to stand. 'This is his room, like, but he'll be in the classroom right now. Ah'll just let 'm know yer here. His name's Clout, by the way. Clout by name and clout by nature.'

He grimaced at me, providing a brief but sickly glimpse of custard-coloured teeth. Then he braced himself, visibly straightening his shoulders, and after taking a deep breath, marched purposefully into the classroom ahead, clearly the main room as it boasted a double door, which he left slightly open. Uncle Matt shuffled uneasily on the spot, twiddling with his cap, rummaging in his pocket for cigarettes which he dared not smoke, and clicking his tongue impatiently, while I went on reading over and over again the engraved warning on the study door.

There is something about a headmaster's study which, even when we reach maturity, still intimidates, causing the heart to flutter and the knees to tremble. We were both experiencing those symptoms, but Uncle Matt had another reason for feeling ill at ease. Etiquette demanded that he remove his cap on entering the school premises, thus putting him at a severe disadvantage, his cap being vital to his composure, almost part of his head, like an organic growth. So the embarrassment of baring his baldness for public view always made him feel cruelly exposed and vulnerable.

We presumed that the boy had to wait to attract the headmaster's attention, because silence reigned for a few minutes. Then came an ear-piercing yell that made me jump and caused Uncle Matt to leap convulsively and let out a sharp shriek as if launching into an eight-some reel. Evidently the yell had been torn from the headmaster on his first glimpse of the flashy pullover – understandably, I thought, because although a miracle of wartime economy, it was a pullover that was difficult to contemplate at close range without the benefit of dark glasses. And the yell, which drowned out the boy's opening remarks, was swiftly followed by an angry roar.

84

'*What* the devil? What . . . ? What the . . . ? What do you think you've come as, boy? It's not fancy dress today. You gaudy clown! How dare you come to school looking like a patchwork quilt?'

'But, sir . . .' began the boy, and got no further.

'And what time of day do you call this, eh? You have the confounded nerve to trail in here, well and truly late, and done up like a clippie mat! I don't know how you dare show your face! The school day's half over!'

Any hopes I had entertained of encountering a kindly headmaster who put more emphasis on the solid virtues I felt that I possessed in abundance than on superficial details such as punctuality, were instantly dispelled. And now I listened with something of a vested interest to the way the boy handled the situation, hoping to imitate his strategy.

'But, sir, I had ta sarra the hens,' he explained, dispelling another hope, as he spoke a language unintelligible to me.

'Do what, boy?' shouted the headmaster. Speak English, stupid boy!'

'Sarra the hens, sir! Ah mean – *feed* 'em.'

'Well say so, boy! And don't you dare shout at me. I'm not deaf!'

Nervously I reminded myself that when my time came I must try to pitch my voice carefully, not too loud and not too soft, a tricky task, but clearly necessary. I had no previous experience of head-masters, but this one sounded terrifying, his voice like thunder and his manner formidable, worse than my wildest imaginings. And then there was his secret weapon, still as yet concealed from me – *The Cat*.

'Whatever you do to your hens, boy, do it in your own time,' growled the headmaster, 'and get yourself here before the bell. I have my eye on you, Gormley, or I would have if I weren't blinded by that pullover. Tell you what, gormless Gormley, that pullover's enough to frighten your hens to death. And speaking of birds, I want you here with the larks tomorrow, or you'll answer for it. As for today's punishment, let's make it quick. Step this way if you please, Master Gormley.'

As far as I could tell, Gormley's feet seemed to be stepping the other way, dodging about like an evasive boxer, and all the while he protested loudly, now putting forward a second excuse – one that made it clear to me why he had been so pleased to see us.

'But, sir. No, listen, sir. Ah wasn't all that late, sir. Not at first, like.

But then Ah had ta look after yer visitors, sir. That's why Ah'm a bit later. But Ah didn't mind, and there's no need ta thank me, sir.'

'Thank you, indeed!' exclaimed Mr Clout, affronted.

'Not at all, sir. Only too glad ta help,' said Gormley.

'What? You impudent boy! What are you burbling about? What visitors? I haven't any visitors. Don't you try to bamboozle me, Gormley, you – flashy maypole! Save your stories for bedtime.'

'But ya have, sir. Two visitors. Honest, sir. Ah left them outside yer room. They're waitin' there, sir.'

'*Wh-oo-oo?* You garish oaf! *Who* is waiting?' demanded Mr Clout, and after a moment's thought, Gormley came up with a telling answer, pulling no punches.

'Sir – a canny little girl and a short man, bald as a coot.'

Uncle Matt winced visibly, his morale hitting zero, and I squeezed his hand in sympathy. Then we heard the *clump, clump* of heavy feet on a wooden floor, and suddenly a disconcertingly hairy head thrust itself through the door opening and peered curiously at us.

'*Yes?*' it enquired in a loud, peevish tone.

But Uncle Matt, still recovering from the double shock to his system – first of the leap into space, when the headmaster yelled, and then of the blow to his self-esteem at the boy's description of him – found himself incapable of speech, and could only point silently at me.

'Ah! I see. I understand. Be with you in a tick,' said the door-framed head, and vanished.

We heard the *clump, clump* of feet again, and then the distinct sound of a clip round the ear, then another, followed by squeals of pain as Mr Clout dealt summarily with Gormley. As I would learn later, Mr Clout was not one to defer punishment until passion cooled and reason prevailed. 'Strike while the temper is hot' was his motto, and he lived by it. He now issued instructions, rumbling like thunder at the class, all of whom were sensibly silent except for a snivelling Gormley.

'Copy out pages eighty-nine to ninety-four in your very best hand-writing,' he boomed, scribbling the numbers on the blackboard. 'And draw all the diagrams. Neatly, mind you. Very, very, neatly. That exercise should be a rare treat for you, more than you deserve. It concerns the foxglove, Digitalis purpurea, a poisonous but most beguiling plant, and should keep you busy till I return. But woe betide you if it does not. I tell you, heads will roll if there's any fooling about while I'm out. Remember now, I'm just next door.'

Once more the footsteps clumped towards us, as I shivered in anticipation and Uncle Matt cleared his throat noisily in preparation for acting out his role of conscientious guardian. But this time the classroom door was flung open, and before it was banged shut again, in a flurry of flapping tweeds the headmaster was with us, impatiently pushing open the door to his study and ushering us inside.

Chapter 7

Cat and Mouse

It was a small room, little more than a cupboard really, and it seemed to grow smaller once Mr Clout had squeezed in beside us. For though short in stature he carried considerable bulk, which, as Uncle Matt had described earlier, had settled itself into a square shape, as broad as it was long. I had resolved to ignore this aspect of him, but found myself fascinated by it, and also by his extraordinary hairiness, the like of which I had never seen outside a zoo. This hairiness began with his clothes, his Harris tweed suit and mohair waistcoat, but by no means ended there. For his hands grew stubbly hairs like bristles on a scrubbing brush, and his face sprouted hair so profusely that I wondered why Uncle Matt had taken such pains in shaving to impress a headmaster who was distinguished, if for nothing else, by a superfluity of whiskers. These whiskers were rampant, almost concealing his features, so that he looked for all the world like a koala bear – fluffy and cuddly on the surface, but with more than a hint of hidden menace.

Not a word had been said to prepare me for this bizarre bush of hair that he hid behind, and I felt distinctly aggrieved that my uncle, in issuing a full description of Mr Clout's peculiarities, had made no mention of this outstanding one, which now came as something of a shock. I could only assume that the omission was down to envy, but I could not resist pointing it out in a tactless stage whisper, which unfortunately came out louder than intended, startling me as well as my uncle.

'You never mentioned "hairy", Uncle Matt. Just "square", not "hairy". You never said.'

'Shush!' he hissed sharply, still clearly intimidated. There being little room for manoeuvre in the cramped study, he made way for Mr Clout's ample proportions by backing into the far corner, inadvertently sweeping me along in his wake.

Meanwhile, grunting from the effort, Mr Clout heaved himself behind the kneehole desk which almost filled the room, and into the waiting chair, which groaned in protest at his weight.

'Clout!' he barked by way of introduction, with a curt nod at my uncle, who started nervously, dropped his cap, picked it up and dusted it on his sleeve, then diffidently nodded back.

'Please. Sit down,' said the headmaster, indicating the only other chair, and so my uncle sat, folding his precious cap over one knee, while I stood beside him as close as I could manage.

I rather fancied sitting on his other knee, keeping the cap company, but suspected that Mr Clout would disapprove.

'Well now, good morning, Mr – er?' he said, raising his bushy eyebrows enquiringly.

'Wheatley,' muttered my uncle almost inaudibly.

'Ah – Weakling. Yes, Weakling,' said Mr Clout, writing the name on his memo pad and nodding as if he considered it appropriate.

'No, Wheat-t-t-ley!' shouted Uncle Matt, in his agitation putting in three ts and spitting them out so forcibly that a drop of saliva dribbled down his chin, but still failing to penetrate Mr Clout's ear, or else only reaching the deaf one.

'Quite so. I know. I *know*,' answered the Headmaster in the weary tone of one dealing with a particularly dull pupil. 'That's what I said – *Weakling*. I assure you that I can remember your name very clearly. Besides, I have a note of it here. In black and white, as it were. And what can't speak can't lie,' he added triumphantly.

He took a pencil and underlined the name on the memo pad, then turned it round and with a flourish presented it to us, thrusting it forward insistently, as if urging us to read, mark, and inwardly digest. Taken aback, Uncle Matt opened his mouth, gawped for a moment, and then closed it, while I silently applauded this prudent decision.

'You're very late,' said Mr Clout, changing the subject and addressing us both as guilty pupils, 'but I suppose you don't know any better. I, on the other hand, set great store by punctuality, and of course by rights I should be teaching now. I always like to begin the term with the best subject – Nature Study, that is – my aim being to inspire the young rascals.'

'Is that so? Nature Study, eh? Well, well, fancy that! Nature Study,' burbled my uncle, trying to sound inspired, and Mr Clout eyed him narrowly before turning his gimlet gaze on me.

'I take it this young lady wishes to join us at St Simon's?'

I wanted to deny any such wish and make a run for it, the door, so near and yet so far, having suddenly developed a magnetic attraction. But I resisted its pull, bravely nodding assent, while Uncle Matt answered for me, giving my name and particulars, none of which vital information appeared to register fully with Mr Clout. Indeed, from then on it seemed that he either misheard or misinterpreted most of Uncle Matt's intentions, because at times my bumbling uncle talked too much and at others too little. But he had promised to do his best for me, acting *in loco parentis* as it were, and I trusted him implicitly, especially as he seemed at first to strike just the right note, outlining the standard of my intellect and abilities with fulsome praise.

'Emma's very bright,' he said smugly. 'My meanin' is, she's real clever. Brainy, that is. Even quicker than me in some respects,' he added, smirking as if there were no higher praise. 'And she's only eight – but ahead of her years, so I've been told.'

'Good, good. That's very good. Most promising,' answered Mr Clout, visibly softening his attitude.

He rubbed his hairy hands together, producing a crackling sound that reminded me of a faulty electric fire we once had at home, and, thus encouraged, Uncle Matt warmed to his theme.

'In fact, she's that clever that I dare bet she'll pass for the grammar school if she's still here when the time comes, like.'

Mr Clout's eyes gleamed as he envisaged his first success in twenty years, and he squirmed contentedly in his chair, which creaked and groaned noisily under the strain.

'*Really?* You really think she's that good, Mr Weakling?'

'Definitely! Oh yes, definitely.'

Mr Clout leaned back in the long-suffering chair and thoughtfully combed his tangled beard with his fingers.

'To be honest, Mr Weakling, I must confess that we haven't gained many passes – or indeed any – for Shiretown Grammar for – well, quite some time. Not our fault, of course. I blame the examiners. Do you know that these days they put no value at all on Nature Study? That's a very short-sighted policy in my opinion.'

Uncle Matt smiled sympathetically. Though he winced every time he was addressed as Mr Weakling, he now felt more at ease, back to his usual ebullient self. In his opinion the interview was going well, thanks to the splendid way he was handling things with the headmaster.

'Is that so, Mr Clout? Well, you can't fail with our Emma. She's what you call outstandin'. She's just so good! Not only quick but imaginative. She has an amazin' imagination. It runs riot! And she gets such outlandish ideas. You wouldn't believe the weird things she comes up with. You should hear the way she talks to the hens – as if they were people! I tell you, my mind boggles. Definitely. I'm flabbergasted at her fanciful notions. In fact, sometimes I think she's in a world of her own.'

He had gone too far. I guessed as much when Mr Clout's expression, which had been verging on the friendly, changed to one of disapproval, and in a displeased gesture he swept his hand repeatedly over his face, causing the hairs round his eyes and mouth, which had been upstanding, to droop dismally down.

'Oh dear, not good, Mr Weakling. No, no, dear me, no,' he said, dismayed, looking like a koala bear suddenly deprived of his eucalyptus. 'Very *imaginative*, you say? *Fanciful*, you say? These are *not* traits that I like to discover in my pupils. Nor do I allow such traits to develop, Mr Weakling. I flatter myself I know how to deal with fanciful notions. I soon put a stop to outlandish ideas. I don't encourage any airy-fairy, whimsy-whamsy fiddle-faddle in my school. No sir! Conformity is the keynote here, coupled with common sense, of course – good, solid, down-to-earth common sense. Personally, I would add to that two other attributes – a love of nature and a certain dexterity in wielding a trowel – but these extra accomplishments are merely icing on the academic cake.'

He began to describe the principles on which the school was founded, extolling its virtues in extravagant terms, which, even at the tender age of eight, I found difficult to believe. He sprawled in his capacious chair, spreading himself until he overlapped, and leaning back so heavily that the chair squeaked and wheezed under the stress. It occurred to me as a passing thought that there were four voices in that interview, and so far the chair had had more to say than me. Mr Clout now sat relaxed, his waiting class forgotten. He solemnly stroked his straggly beard and pontificated at length, as headmasters are prone to do, while we inattentively allowed our thoughts to wander. I had no idea where Uncle Matt's thoughts went, but he gradually developed a glazed look, and as for me, I found two diversions. I spent a few fascinating minutes watching the way Mr Clout's whiskers ruffled and rippled like feathers in a breeze as he spoke; then I set myself the task of discovering the whereabouts of *The Cat*.

I could see no sign of feline occupation, not even a hair or a saucer of milk. No box. No basket. No cage. No suitable container. And no space for a cupboard. In fact, nothing. It was all very perplexing. But after some thought I concluded that the terrible cat-monster must be kept in the classroom. That made sense, I reflected with a shudder, as it would then be ready for action. Meanwhile, the dreary voice droned on and on in the dull monotone of the long-term deaf, the sound gradually becoming soporific, like a repetitive tune played on two notes. Then suddenly there was silence, and I noticed Mr Clout's beady eyes studying me from behind shaggy brows. I started nervously as he leant forward and his voice rapped out like a machine gun.

'Recite the alphabet!'

But recovering quickly, I did so with alacrity and accuracy.

'Right! Let me hear your nine times table.'

In nervous haste I delivered it without drawing breath. Then he pointed a hairy finger at me, like an accusing gorilla.

'Now!' he said, pausing dramatically, as if about to confound me with an important and difficult task. 'Name three wild flowers.'

In trepidation I said the first thing that came into my head, and that was the names of the wayside flowers of home.

'Dandelion, daisy, daffodil, sir.'

'You're stuck on the letter D, girl,' he bellowed. 'And D is for dunce. Remember that. Besides, you've chosen such common flowers when there are hundreds of truly wonderful wild flowers out there – the fragrant orchid, Gymnadenia conopsea, to name but one. Tut-tut, girl. Dear me. But never mind. Another chance, eh? Name three British birds.'

Once again the thought of my real home was, as ever, paramount.

'Sparrow, starling, seagull, sir.'

And again he was unimpressed.

'Now you're stuck on the letter S, girl. S is for stupid. Remember that. You won't see many of those boring domestic birds round here. No indeed, you have a rare treat in store, because from curlew to wagtail, our birds are better. They're wilder and more beautiful. Our birds are special. Yes, girl, very special!'

My sense of justice, always strong, now rose to the surface as I rashly tried to defend myself.

'But, sir, I got them all right. Six out of six, sir.'

He frowned darkly, his hairy eyebrows meeting in the middle, closing over his glowering eyes like torn curtains.

'Got them all right, sir,' he repeated, imitating my childish tones.

'Got them all right, indeed! What good is that, girl, when your answers are so trite, so ordinary? We must widen your horizons. Broaden your biological vocabulary. I hold Nature Study in the highest esteem. To me it's the most important subject in the curriculum. And I suspect, young lady, that your knowledge of this extensive field is very limited.'

I had to agree with him there. My primary school had chiefly concentrated on the 'three Rs', to the undoubted neglect of other subjects. This was my first real brush with Biology, evidently the most important subject of all, and I was ashamed of my ignorance. Mr Clout had soon spotted that shortcoming, and I decided that it might be wiser to admit my other shortcomings too and start with a clean slate.

'There's something else, sir,' I confessed. 'I don't know much about onions.' Then, seeing how startled he looked, I added hastily, 'But I'm willing to learn.'

He inserted his little finger into his ear and shook his head as if he had been swimming and water was lodged near the drum.

'I could have sworn you said – did you – say – "onions"?' he asked hesitantly.

'Yes, sir.'

'What about them, girl?'

'I know nothing about them, sir.'

'And you – er – want to?'

'Oh *yes*, sir.'

He took a thoughtful tug at his moustache and spoke soothingly.

'Onions, eh? Well, that's a first. But there again, why not? A harmless enough ambition. Onions, yes. Good. We'll have to try you out in the vegetable plot. You'll learn all about onions there. You'll like it. It's behind the wall. Out of the wind.'

I had the feeling that he was humouring me, and it came as no surprise when he began tidying his desk and shuffling papers as if winding up the meeting.

'Well, Mr Weakling, I think that's all I need to know, and now I really must return to my class. Unless you have any further questions?' My uncle, who had been sitting as still and quiet as a hibernating dormouse, suddenly came to life – rather to my regret, as he instantly introduced a jarring note.

'As a matter of fact, Mr Clout, I have,' he answered dreamily. 'I was just wonderin' – that picture on the wall behind you – I don't half fancy it. Would you consider sellin' it to me?' Then he added, as if conferring a favour, 'I dare give you half a crown for it.'

Mr Clout's eyebrows shot up in astonishment, arching like hairy caterpillars on the move. He half turned as if to refresh his memory of the picture in question, a Victorian watercolour of an idyllic pastoral scene. It portrayed an impression, frozen in time, of an Arcadian farm, featuring a picturesque farmhouse surrounded by perfect animals – well-groomed horses, superior cows and cuddlesome sheep, all looking their elegant Sunday best, without a trace of dirt or manure in sight. Impeccable hens and model ducks posed by a pond, and pretty girls frolicked in the hay, surrounded by a lush and fertile landscape. The whole faultless scene represented the very antithesis of farming life in Sourhope, certainly of farming life as Uncle Matt knew it, which probably explained why it affected him so power-fully. Perhaps in some primitive superstitious way he believed that if he could capture this fantasy painting of an ideal farm he would one day achieve it in reality. But whatever the reason, he acted like a man possessed, apparently having forgotten my very existence. He was conscious only of the painting, and he had to have it. As if in a trance, he took out a cigarette, tapped it purposefully on a matchbox, and then when I nudged him in the ribs, tucked it behind his ear, all without moving his eyes from the painting.

'Half a crown,' he said again.

'It's not for sale,' replied Mr Clout, abruptly shattering his dream.

'But I dare give you half a crown for it,' persisted my uncle, his tone implying that such a munificent offer should be snapped up in case it was withdrawn.

'I've told you, it's not for sale.'

'I know it's not for sale,' agreed my uncle reasonably. 'My meanin' is, I can see there's no "For Sale" sign on it, but just supposin' you were willin' to sell, I dare give you half a crown for it. Two shillin's and sixpence. There now.'

I could hardly believe my horrified ears. My future educational prospects were at stake, yet my imprudent uncle thought fit to prac-tise the bargaining techniques he employed at the mart! As for Mr Clout, he could barely conceal his indignation. He struggled for an utterance, and then, speaking slowly and distinctly as if addressing the dunce of the class, he determined to remove all possible doubt or misunderstanding.

'How can I put this, Mr Weakling? It – is – not – for – sale!'

'Go on then, three shillin's,' sighed Uncle Matt, with an air of resignation.

'Mr Weakling,' said Mr Clout austerely, 'you should be one of those spivs one reads about nowadays, who sneaks about with a suitcase, buying and selling on the black market.'

'Several people have told me that,' said Uncle Matt, flattered. 'Now, we have three shillin's on the table. That's three bob to you. What do you say?'

'No! I say no!'

'All right, but you drive a hard bargain. Three and six it is then,' said my uncle, reluctantly conceding to a shrewder operator. 'Can't say fairer than that, but it's my final offer.'

Mr Clout rose threateningly from his chair, whereupon the leather cushion, relieved of its burden, relaxed with a deep sigh. He leant forward, arching his fingers on the desk, and snorted in exasperation.

'Mr Weakling! How many times do I have to tell you? Once and for all, the picture is not for sale. It isn't even mine to sell. It belongs to the school, and is the property of the education authority.'

At that, Uncle Matt brightened. He hitched his chair and leaned forward eagerly.

'Is that so? Well I dare give them half a crown,' he declared, now dealing with a new client and adjusting the price back to the original offer. 'I dare bet they'll be interested too. Maybe you could contact them on my behalf? Pass my offer on, eh? I dare bet ten to one they'll be interested. There might even be a backhander in it.'

Mr Clout literally bristled and, whipping out a pristine white handkerchief from his top pocket, mopped the perspiration from his forehead. He had his own old-fashioned ideas of how a parent should behave towards a headmaster, and Uncle Matt did not conform to them.

'Mr Weakling, I must have told you a thousand times that the picture is not for sale. That is my final word. Now, may we drop the subject? Please!'

Then, almost in desperation, he turned to me.

'Have you any questions, young lady? Before we go. I must get back to my class. I've been missing far too long.'

I did have a question, a question that had been burning in my brain and trembling on my lips throughout the entire interview. I knew with absolute certainty that I should not ask it. All instincts told me to keep quiet, especially since Uncle Matt had reduced the headmaster to a state that was, to say the least, overwrought. But now that this opportunity had presented itself I was sorely tempted. Hard as I tried, I could not resist. I had to know. So, casting aside all my carefully made resolutions, I blurted it out.

Sir, where do you keep your cat?'

He sat down heavily and the chair emitted a loud groan.

'My c – cat?'

'Yes, sir, your cat. *The* cat. You know – *The Cat,*' said I, nodding significantly.

He stared at me, stupefied, with the bewildered air of one who unaccountably finds himself rubbing shoulders with the inmates of a lunatic asylum. Then he frowned, his brain struggling to make sense of the question, and absently tweaked the shorter hairs of his moustache as if encouraging them to grow long like the rest. At length his face cleared as he mistakenly thought he understood.

'Oh! You must mean Tiddles! Someone's told you we have a kitten. Dear me, child! What an extraordinary question! Is that the best you can do on your first day in a new school? You arrive late, disrupting an important lesson, and then have the unmitigated gall to enquire blithely about my cat! Tut-tut, girl. What a poor show! Tiddles is at home with my wife, of course. And look here, young lady, where I keep my cat, and whether I have a cat, and indeed any other aspect of my private life are no concern of yours. Is that quite clear?'

'Yes, sir,' I murmured deferentially, instantly subdued and mortified.

He looked confused, as well he might. Uncle Matt looked confused too, as well he might. And I felt confused, more confused than both of them put together, and on two counts. First, the name 'Tiddles' did not conjure up the savage deformed beast I had been led to expect; and second, it was a mystery to me why Mr Clout kept his cat at home. I had been given to understand that it administered punishment, swooping like a targeted missile on offending pupils. But it could hardly swoop effectively if he had to go home first and fetch it. And again I found him staring at me, looking from me to my uncle in what could only be described as a disparaging manner, almost as if we were two of the spivs he despised, trying to sell him parachute silk. Plainly, he had formed a poor opinion of the pair of us, and I felt embarrassed and humiliated both on my own behalf and on that of Uncle Matt, who himself showed no shame. And now Mr Clout sat running his fingers distractedly through his hair till it stood away from his face, resembling in its startling spikiness something in the nature of an old flue brush.

'The question is,' he said, fingering his whiskers thoughtfully while appraising my small person with frank distaste, as he would a rabbit nibbling his prize radishes, 'what to do with you. Yes, what to do? That's the problem. You're only eight and undoubtedly puny. Not like our robust farming stock. They're all big girls in the senior class. Yes, all big girls and boys compared with you.'

He demonstrated their size, waving his hairy hands in great circular sweeps until he knocked over a pencil pot, and I began to fear I had entered a school of giants. I had of course seen the boy, Gormley, and he was only marginally bigger than average, but for all I knew he could be the smallest, like the runt of the litter. And just then I could feel myself shrinking further, cut down to size by humiliation. It seemed to me that I was being assessed unfairly, not as a potential pupil but more as a specimen of livestock. I might have been the sickly calf we bought at the mart, rejected by informed opinion before even entering the ring. The only insult not yet inflicted was a prod in the rump with a stout stick, and perhaps that would come later. I turned to Uncle Matt, my guardian and protector, confident that he would support me.

'Uncle Matt, say something,' I whispered insistently, tugging at his sleeve.

For a split second he removed his eyes from the picture and surveyed me in a kindly fashion.

'You shouldn't have asked that daft question about the cat,' he said sadly, laying the blame squarely at my door, and my heart sank down to my short white socks.

An uncertain smile flickered over his face as he gazed into my pleading eyes. Then he turned back to the picture, and I suspected that he was weighing up which was the best option – on the one hand, standing up for me and ensuring my best interests; on the other, the remote possibility of acquiring the picture he coveted so much. And I knew I had lost when he winked sheepishly, thoughtfully scratched his ultra smooth chin, and spoke in a tone tinged with regret.

'Well, she is a bit little, like,' he said apologetically, as if I should have known better. 'My meanin' is, small for her size.'

'Quite so!' cried Mr Clout triumphantly, drumming his fingers on the desk. '"Little" is the operative word, Mr Weakling. The *mot juste*, if I may say so. Alas, little in all respects, including intelligence. Quite frankly, we often find incomers a bit backward in some ways. For a start, this young lady has no knowledge of Nature Study whatsoever. Now I know she's not entirely without hope, not without a spark of any kind. She does have her interests – onions and cats to name but two, though if I may say so, there are other things in life. So all in all, Mr Weakling, and taking the broad view, I've decided to put her in the infant class – that's Miss Speedwell's class – the child can't do much harm there. We'll see how she gets on, and in the unlikely event that I've misplaced her, we can always move her at a later date.'

Once again my heart sank, right down to my small-sized sandals, and, summoning all my courage, I spoke up indignantly, determined as a last resort to defend myself.

'Oh, but you know I'm not an infant. I'm no baby. I'm eight, and I was doing well in my old school.'

Deafness must have been catching, because neither gentleman showed a sign of having heard me, and again I turned hopefully to Uncle Matt for help, but he skilfully avoided my gaze. He just sat there, attempting to look profound and nodding his head like an articulated toy dog in a car window. It never occurred to him to risk annoying Mr Clout by defending me, or indeed to stand up for the insulted incomers in general, of whom he himself was a prime example. So when the headmaster rose, precipitating grateful squeaks from the chair, and with as much hauteur as he could muster gestured meaningfully towards the door, Uncle Matt, almost grovelling, also lurched to his feet, eager to escape. As if he and Clout were now bosom friends, the pair shook hands warmly, but only briefly as it happened, because the headmaster rapidly removed his as if handling a hot potato.

'Well, bye then, Mr Clout,' chirruped my two-faced uncle. 'Don't forget to pass my offer on for the picture. My meanin' is, start negotiations at half a crown, but between you and me and the gatepost, I'll go to three and nine. I've really enjoyed our little chat. It's been grand meetin' you. I never thought we'd get on so well, like. It's been a real interestin' experience.'

'Quite a memorable experience for me too, I assure you,' answered Mr Clout, in what I took to be a sarcastic tone, but Uncle Matt seemed unaware of it.

'Cheerio, Emma,' he said, grinning rather shamefacedly. 'You'll be all right. And remember what I said. Remember now – you'll be top of the class.'

And with that he removed the cigarette from behind his ear, donned his cap, and backed out respectfully, as if leaving royalty. For some reason quite beyond my childish comprehension, he departed with a jaunty air, the air of a man who has done a good job and deserves credit. Furthermore, he disappeared with a speed that earlier that morning I would not have thought possible. He had behaved more like a mouse than a man, shamelessly kowtowing to Mr Clout, and for a while my faith in him was shattered. My unimpressed head-master had dubbed him 'Mr Weakling' and it seemed to me that he had got it right.

Despite everything, however, the termination of that long and dreadful interview came as a great relief to me, and Mr Clout also seemed glad it was over, glad to stretch his legs and have the chance to vent his feelings in some way: as he heaved himself round the desk, he apparently forgot my presence and aimed several petulant kicks at the mahogany veneer. First he kicked the drawer fronts, and then the side panels, and he appeared to feel better for the exercise. But in a minute or two he had collected himself, and with unseemly haste ushered me out of the door and into the small classroom, thus sealing my fate.

As it happened, however, I soon ceased to resent his decision to place me in the infant class. Young as I was, I realized that it was entirely Uncle Matt's fault and that when he had made his untimely excursion into art dealing, he had lost all credibility as a responsible guardian. However, he had inadvertently rescued me from the scary prospect of Mr Clout's class. And besides, I instantly liked the look of Miss Speedwell, an attractive, fresh-faced young woman with a warm disposition and the high ideals peculiar to the inexperienced teacher. Mr Clout handed me over with a short and inaccurate intro-duction.

'This is – er – Emily – something or other,' he said, thrusting me forward by the shoulders, glad to be rid of me, clearly regarding me as a potential troublemaker, a future Gormley. 'She's one of the Weaklings,' he muttered, adding under his breath, 'in more ways than one.'

'Hello there. Nice to meet you. Come with me,' said Miss Speedwell, smiling reassuringly as she took my hand. 'Now, where would you like to sit? Perhaps you'd like a desk to yourself till you get to know everyone? How about this one? It should suit you.'

The desks were constructed in pairs and she led me to one of an empty pair at the back, a small oak desk, liberally splashed with ink blots, scribbled with thoughts – none uplifting – and carved with the initials of ages. The integral seat of slippery smoothness joined the desk by means of iron supports fixing both to the floor, thereby elim-inating the customary classroom noise of scraping chairs. It was wonderful to sit down at last and rest my weary legs. I had been standing for some considerable time, and what with the anxiety and the tension and disappointment and one thing and another, I felt tired. The room was pleasantly quiet after the hustle and bustle that had beset me all morning. Apart from the sound of Miss Speedwell's soft and kindly voice, peace reigned. She handed me a well-worn copy of *The Wind in the Willows*, instructing me gently to enjoy the pictures and read what I could until she had time to attend to me. It was a favourite book, one which I had read many times, so I opened it at random, laid it flat on the desk, and surreptitiously looked to right and left.

The class consisted of ten pupils, including me. There were three five-year-olds who had just started that morning, two tearful, one asleep; and five six-year-olds were engaged in infantile activities. One was sucking her thumb, one was picking his nose, one was sliding from side to side along the seat, one was scribbling in big aimless circles, and one was furtively tying the long ringlets of the girl in front to the upright bar of her backrest. A fellow eight-year-old, a backward boy, presently occupied Miss Speedwell's attention, as he struggled unsuccessfully to master the multiplication of tuppence ha'penny by three.

Slowly I began to relax, allowing myself to reflect calmly on recent events, and gradually becoming more settled in my mind, more accepting and less upset. After a time I felt strangely content. The clock had not yet struck ten and yet already so much had happened in all sorts of ways that the day stretched ahead like a lifetime. Since first thing that morning my amiable uncle had given me a really hard time, setting my nerves on edge. I had begun by being terrified by the nightmares he had inspired about the cat-o'-nine-tails, then was driven to distraction by the shaving ritual, stressed out of my wits by the interminable drive to school, and totally humiliated at my interview with the headmaster. Finally I had been dismissed out of hand as a puny imbecile and placed in the baby class.

Altogether it had undoubtedly been a traumatic start to a school day for a child of eight, and yet to my surprise I found I bore Uncle Matt no ill will. I believed that on the whole he meant well, and besides, he had been right about one thing – I would have no trouble being top of the class.

Chapter 8

The Mole Man Cometh

What with starting school and all the other novel experiences of my new life, it was some time before September's pig portrait benefited from the expertise of my coloured pencils. When I had a spare moment to climb on the kitchen stool and study this latest pig, I found that it was a Lincolnshire Curly Coat, and a boar at that. He was bulky with big ears and as hairy as his name implied, so I had no hesitation in identifying him as Mr Clout, headmaster of St Simon's; and with a few deft strokes of my pencils here and there – squaring off curves and adding shaggy eyebrows, moustache and beard – the task of perfecting the likeness was the work of seconds.

This porcine image cheered me, because I felt that here on the farm at least, Mr Clout was in my power, with roles reversed and tables turned, as it were. I never passed the boar without sticking my tongue out at him, and when nobody was around I went further, giving him a good prod with the brass toasting fork that hung by its crowing-cockerel handle at the side of the kitchen range. With its sharp prongs I attacked all the vital organs of the boar's anatomy, and though this amateur attempt at witchcraft had no effect on Mr Clout as far as I knew, it did on me, making me feel slightly less afraid of him and more reconciled to my new school.

Meanwhile, Miss Speedwell and I got along like lamb and salad. We instantly liked each other and quickly grew to respect each other's intellect. I became her slave, fetching and carrying as willingly as a well-trained retriever. All day long I trotted to and fro, delivering and collecting books, pens and pencils, and filling the ceramic ink pots that slotted like pegs in the back ledge of the desks. I had to replenish these pots quite often because they were so tempting to mischievous infant fingers, and Billy Reed in particular had a nasty habit of pouring a potful of ink down the neck of any unlucky neighbour taken unawares.

Sometimes I cleaned the big revolving blackboard, a dangerous task, as it tended to swing back with a sudden clunk, catching me out, but I soon mastered its tricky action, covering myself in glory and chalk dust. And in return for these small services, Miss Speedwell allowed me special privileges. After I had finished the set work, which literally seemed like child's play to me, she let me draw or read, my two favourite pastimes. I read avidly, borrowing the books that lined the walls of her classroom, constituting the school library. This privilege was the most important of all, encapsulating my idea of heaven, but running a close second was that of sanctuary – being allowed to stay indoors at playtimes. Others might have regarded that as a punishment, but not me, because it meant that I avoided something I feared almost as much as I did Mr Clout – constant confrontation with the senior pupils, who turned out to be just as he had boasted – all big, alarmingly big. Of course it only took a few days for Miss Speedwell to realize that I was misplaced in the infant class, and that realization threw me into instant panic, because by then I knew where I was well off, and I had become doggedly determined to stay there.

'This work is much too easy for you, Emma,' she said firmly, at the end of the first week. 'I must have a word with Mr Clout.'

'Oh no. *Please* miss, no. *Please* don't, miss.'

'But I must, Emma. It isn't right to hold you back.'

'Please, miss, just let me stay in your class and I'll work ever so hard. I like being with you.'

She hesitated, her kind face doubtful and disturbed.

'Well, I'll be sorry to lose you too, Emma. Of course I will. But you're clearly in the wrong class. In fact, I suspect you'll more than hold your own next door.'

'But, miss, Mr Clout hates me. And what about – *The Cat?*'

'Cat? Which cat, Emma?' she asked, bemused.

'Why, Mr Clout's cat with the tails and everything. I'm terrified of it.'

'Oh, you mean the cat-o'-nine-tails? Well, Emma, I don't think you of all people need worry about that. How on earth did you hear about that? He's had the thing for years, but he hardly uses it nowadays. Only very rarely, as far as I know.'

I should have been reassured by this statement, imparting as it did two items of good news – first, that the headmaster had taken to sparing the cat and spoiling the child; and second, that the said cat had been around a long time. It must be old – senile even –

not at all the fighting force I had imagined, the fury that haunted my dreams. Yet on the other hand, Miss Speedwell had confirmed the existence of the punitive cat, and that was enough for me. I still felt terrified of both the bewhiskered occupants of the big room – of Mr Clout and his sinister cat. And consequently the mental tussle to stay with Miss Speedwell lasted all day, she conscientiously determined to do her duty by moving me next door, and I equally determined to stay put. Desperate straits call for desperate measures, and I tried every ploy I could think of to wear down her resolve. I begged and pleaded whenever I could, followed her every move with big reproachful eyes, and finally imitated my fellow infants by squeezing out a few tears and whining with unashamed piteousness.

'But, miss, they're all so big in there, and after all – I'm only eight.'

'Well, all right,' she conceded at last. 'We'll let it go for the present. I know you miss your mother and feel strange here. I know that life is hard for you just now, so we'll let things slide for a while. But I must find you more advanced work. You must move on somehow, Emma.'

And so for a time I felt secure. My pleasant routine resumed and I settled down at St Simon's, working happily with Miss Speedwell. I even enjoyed the journey there, despite earlier foreboding. Although there were days, as Uncle Matt had foretold, when I had to run like the wind and still arrived late, most days the milk lorry came in time to give me a lift – while Joe collected the Windlestraw milk, he left the engine running and the big cab door open ready for me to hop in.

'Up you go, bonny lass,' he called when he saw me waiting, and I climbed up into the cab as nimbly as a performing monkey, high onto the passenger seat, with a bird's eye view of the valley.

We clanged and clanked down the road, bumping over its rough surface while the milk cans swayed and rattled in the back, empties crashing into full, with Joe and I shouting our conversation over the double din – the metallic clatter from the back and the noisy engine throb at the front. We seldom saw anyone except for the postman, Mr Sparke, who pedalled past us most mornings on his bike, straining up the steep hills and whizzing down them, his yellow cape streaming behind like a bright kite in full flight. He gave a precarious salute as he passed, swerving a little when he left hold of the handlebars, and Joe always answered with a friendly honk

on the horn. We stopped at only five farms on the school route –
High Carts Bog, Low Carts Bog, Carrshield, Low Windlestraw, and
Coldstone Mea. And at each stop Joe leapt to the ground, looked
back, and, as if he meant it, shouted up to me, 'Now, bonny lass,
you look after the lorry.' As the engine rumbled idly, belching out
exhaust fumes, I tried not to think what would happen if the handbrake failed to hold.

Then he would vanish from sight and I could hear him heaving
the full cans onto the back of the lorry and hurling the empties onto
the milk stands. At every collection point except High Nether, the
cans always stood ready; at this one farm, however, we often had to
wait while Mrs Downley, the sad-eyed woman with the goitre, struggled to drag her cans up to the road. Harnessed like a horse, she had
to pull her heavy load uphill on a small cart, and Joe always willingly dashed down to help her, taking the brunt of the burden and
cursing her husband's cruel indifference and laziness.

Joe was handsome in a dark-eyed, rosy-cheeked way, and he
soon became my hero. I loved the lorry ride, which never lost its
excitement and always seemed over too soon. Perched aloft on a
cushion smelling of oil and petrol, with the harsh, insistent noise
reverberating around me, I easily imagined myself part of a
powerful machine, thundering to the rescue of the world by
providing much-needed milk. Every trip was a successful mission,
and if I happened to be a little late for school on occasion, the
understanding Miss Speedwell turned a blind eye. Of course, on
the return journey I had to walk, whatever the weather, but I soon
learnt to abandon the rough meandering road at Fern Cottage and
take a direct route across the fields. This shorter route changed
with the seasons, and despite the sparse vegetation and scarcity of
trees, autumn brought colour of a sort, altering the upland grasses
to pale gold and the thistle heads to silver. Later, the silky thistle-
down drifted on the air, scattering seeds like silver confetti through
the fields. The moors beyond had already been transformed to a
purple carpet of heather, fringed by russet ferns, and the larch tree
that dominated Todd Tingate's dene turned a vivid orange before
shedding its circle of needles.

To my surprise, though frighteningly alone for an eight-year-old,
I seldom felt scared or lonely, partly because the valley lay open to
the skies, hiding few secret places, and partly because the wild landscape had begun to cast its spell over me, inspiring exhilaration rather

than fear. Besides, for an inquisitive child there was always some-thing new to see on the way – maybe migrating birds gathering on walls, or shy rabbits showing glimpses of powder-puff tails. I trod warily, keeping a sharp lookout, often encountering small creatures going about their business. It might be a hedgehog snuffling through weeds, or a stoat or weasel – too fast to be identified – darting past like a streak of chocolate and cream. I began to enjoy being close to nature and to the vast sky which had never seemed as close as it did in those bleak hills.

Already I had learnt a great deal that would have gladdened the heart of my nature-loving headmaster. Yet I lived in fear of being found out knowing anything about anything. And curiously, just as I began to be drawn towards nature in a peaceful way, Uncle Matt moved in the opposite direction. I knew he was a man of many parts, and as autumn advanced he assumed the role of hunter. For a time no wild thing, whether furry or feathered, could feel safe in his vicinity, and his normally mild-mannered and peaceful personality changed overnight to one of aggression. It all started with rumours of a fox in the neighbourhood. When Aunt Dot happened to mention at teatime that it had killed a nearby farmer's hens, Uncle Matt bristled, fingers twitching for his gun.

'A fox, eh? I'll soon fix him, don't you fret!' he declared, glaring fiercely round the table as if he expected to see the sly creature sitting there, spreading his bushy tail like a napkin and tucking in to corned beef and cabbage.

I could not help smiling at his ferocious expression, all the more incongruous as he sat relaxed with his cap removed and his braces slipped off his shoulders to dangle casually round his waist. But he pointed an accusing fork at me, liberally distributing corned beef over the tablecloth, to my aunt's evident annoyance.

'You don't think I'll catch him, do you, Emma? But I will. Definitely. By heck I will! A dirty fox! A scavengin' fox! I'll get 'im! I'll have 'im, never fear!'

'I've read that a fox is a bonny animal, Uncle Matt,' I said, coming to the creature's defence. 'He has a lovely coat and he's very clever.'

'Bonny? Lovely? Nothin' of the kind!' he snorted in disgust. 'He's a filthy scavenger. My meanin' is, he's vermin. As for being clever, well let me tell you, girl, he won't dodge me. By heck he won't! I tell you, I'll have 'im! I'll shoot his ruddy little legs off.'

So for several weeks he strode the fields and hills with a gun at the ready like a trigger-happy cowboy, and often took me along with him. But somehow we always returned empty-handed and never even caught sight of the fox. Once or twice, however, he went off hunting on his own and then it was quite a different story. He returned with the spoils of victory, swaggering like the hunter home from the hills, and carrying an impressive haul of game birds, mainly grouse, but also partridge and pheasant. Without a word he hung them from a hook by the byre door, their splendid feathers drooping forlornly down the wall and their eyes still open. To all appearances Aunt Dot accepted these rare offerings as a tribute to his keen eye and steady aim, but I had a sneaking suspicion, having witnessed his performance as a marksman and also that as a wheeler-dealer – a skill for which he was justly famed throughout three counties – that it would more likely be the latter talent that brought home the birds.

These game birds were undoubtedly a thing of beauty, but as it turned out, they were not a joy for ever. Uncle Matt insisted that they had to be hung for several days, though to my knowledge they had done nothing to deserve hanging – in fact, they had done nothing wrong at all. And Aunt Dot complained that she had never cooked game birds before and had no idea what to do with them. In retrospect, it seemed to me that she might just as well have given them a decent burial, because in any case she cremated them, and by the time the burnt offerings arrived on the plate they looked so wizened and dry that it was hard to remember what species they were, let alone their former glory.

But of all the wild creatures my uncle hunted, the one that obsessed him most was the humble mole. He declared total war on that elusive farm pest, attacking it in a number of ways, ranging in seriousness from sneaking up on it with a heavy spade to savage assault with a variety of deadly weapons. Primarily he used steel traps, which I thought viciously cruel, inflicting as they did a painful end – in both senses. But as it happened, the crafty moles managed to skirt the traps, pushing up hills all around them. Their minute eyes were almost blind, but they could see Uncle Matt coming. And his fury knew no bounds. He leapt on the molehills, digging his heels in like an athlete grounding after a long jump. Then he slammed his spade in the newly riddled soil, expending useless energy flattening it, and shouting at the moles as if they had obligingly gathered under his feet to listen.

'Blast you! I'll cut your pesky legs off! I'll show you! I'll get you! You take this! And that! I know where you live, you pesky beggars!'

Meanwhile the molehills multiplied, as the moles busied themselves extending their homes into an intricate network of subterranean galleries and approaches, diligently discarding the topsoil until the front meadow became more molehill than meadow; and Aunt Dot finally lost patience.

'We'd better have the mole-catcher, Matt,' she said firmly. See to it, and straight away.'

'Nonsense. No need, Dot. No need for that extravagance. A sheer waste of money. I'll catch them myself. I'll get the pesky moles. Just give me a bit more time.'

'Time!' she exclaimed. 'You've had more than enough time. Be realistic, Matt, you'll never catch them. Not in a month of Sundays. And meantime, nothing else gets done. Nothing but chasing moles.'

'I'll catch 'em. Don't you worry,' he insisted, at which she turned cold grey eyes on him and gave a light, sarcastic laugh.

'Let's face it, Matt, you'll only catch them if they surrender; if they suddenly decide to give themselves up and come out quietly with their paws in the air. And even then I guess it would be touch and go. No, just admit defeat, man, and leave it to the expert. We need proper action, and fast.'

'Expert!' he cried. 'Some expert! Expert tea drinker, more like. Last time he drank about three pots of tea.'

'Nothing wrong with that,' said Aunt Dot, who could never regard tea drinking as anything but a virtue.

'Or was it four?' he murmured, counting moodily on his fingers.

'Just get the mole-catcher!' ordered my aunt, in a tone that brooked no argument.

'All right, all right, all right,' he said testily, looking the picture of gloom.

So the word was spread, passed down the dale from ear to ear till it reached the prominent pink ears of Mr Waggott, mole-catcher extraordinaire. And after about a week a letter arrived from him, written on a scrap of torn paper, and looking as if a drunken spider had fallen in an inkpot and then crawled across the surface, accidentally forming words. Aunt Dot kept the letter in a sideboard drawer – for future reference, she said – and I sometimes read it when short of reading material. It said:

Dear Sur,
A will bee ower ta see yoy sum day soon and hev a tock with yoy aboot th MOLES. The prys noo wil hev ta bee one shillin pear acre as Am leevin the plays Am at noo, and goin firther a way.
   Yoors faithfilly,
   B. I. Waggott

'Look at that! Will you just look at that!' shouted Uncle Matt angrily.

He showed it to me, showed it to Aunt Dot, took it back and danced about, waving it in fury, thrusting it in our faces. I tried to pacify him.

'What's the matter, Uncle Matt? What's wrong? Is it the scruffy paper? Or the scribbly writing? Or the poor spelling? What's upset you?'

'Why Emma, *the price* of course! A shillin' an acre! I mean to say – a whole shillin' for every measly acre! I'll never pay that! I can't pay that! No thank you! It's highway robbery. It is, definitely! By heck, Dot! I'll do the job myself. I'll do it today. This very minute. I'll cut their rotten little black legs off if it's the last thing I do. But I'm not payin' a shillin' an acre. Never!'

So off he went, once more to do battle with the moles, to stand alone against an invisible foe, and it soon became evident to me that in the eternal struggle of mole versus man in the form of Uncle Matt, the opponents were unfairly matched, the humble mole being by far the superior force. On the face of it the little moles seemed helpless, their only weapon being powerful front paws, whereas Uncle Matt was armed to the hilt with cyanide, smoke bombs, iron traps, nooses on bent twigs, heavy steel spades and other sharp implements, and, of course, his gun. Yet somehow the moles always won.

This outcome puzzled me, the odds being stacked in favour of my uncle, though secretly my sympathies lay with the downtrodden moles. I liked to think of them fighting back, marshalling their forces in gloomy underground galleries, a brave black-coated band of resistance, blindly manoeuvring to outwit him. I imagined them steering their velvety offspring away from danger to new nests and I silently cheered them on. And, indeed, for a while the moles went on winning. Then one Saturday morning, at Aunt Dot's insistence, B. I. Waggott roared to the rescue on a noisy motorbike, his unkempt appearance taking me by surprise. He was not exactly a knight in shining armour, but more of a bumbling, bedraggled and tea-imbibing tramp.

'Moles, is it?' he enquired slyly, removing his helmet and gauntlets and scratching his greasy hair with grimy fingers. 'Well noo, if it's moles yer afta, Ah'm yer man. Neebody better.'

Uncle Matt snorted sceptically, but led the way to the devastation area.

'As it happens,' my uncle said defiantly, 'it's hardly worth bringin' you all this way. You see, I'm on top of the situation. I've just about got them moles beat. I tell you, I've got them on the run.'

Mr Waggott scratched his head again, casting a professional eye over the front meadow, which had begun to look like a miniature version of an extensive mountain range.

'Aye, Ah can see that,' he agreed. 'They're runnin' reet enough. They're runnin' all ower the shop, man.'

'All right, all right,' said Uncle Matt, firing up, 'let's get on with it then. What do we do first? My meanin' is – how do we start?'

'That's easy,' answered B. I. Waggott. 'We start in the old mole-catcher's tradition, like. It's a tried an' tested method that nivvor fails.'

'What's that then?' asked Uncle Matt, eager to learn.

'Tea,' he said, chortling at Uncle Matt's expression. 'We start with tea. So tell yer missus ta put the kettle on while Ah weigh things up. Afta that long journey Ah'll need tea, an' plenty of it. But not more than three slices o' toast, mind. It's far betta ta work on an empty stomach.'

And after a light breakfast of four cups of tea and three slices of toast, Mr Waggott allowed himself to be led back to the meadow and was persuaded to get down to business in what turned out to be a mysterious process. From my point of view he appeared to do nothing other than Uncle Matt had done in his anti-mole manoeuvres. He dug his holes in the same way and buried things of an unspecified nature in them, apparently using just the same methods. But the intricacies of the procedure must have differed somehow, proving the truth of the old song, 'It Ain't What You Do, It's The Way That You Do It'.

Unlike my uncle, B. I. Waggott had the air of one who achieved things, of being in control and completely in tune with the moles, even privy to their innermost thoughts. Indeed, the first act of his operation was to put his large pink ear to the ground and listen intently, as if he had the mole nests wired for sound. And it occurred to me that in this strategy alone, the size of his ears gave him a natural advantage over Uncle Matt. Then he probed and prodded, thrust and inserted, keeping his back turned to us throughout. And as we moved around, so did he, jealously guarding the tricks of his trade, shielding his activities from view by curving his arms and legs like a crouched crab, and with every move muttering defensively, 'Away noo! Away with ya! Keep away there! Keep yer distance. Be off noo! Trade secrets here. Aye, trade secrets. Oh aye.'

I noticed that some nasty-looking traps entered into the equation, as well as a tin of poisoned worms, but otherwise I learnt nothing of the mystery of the trade. At Uncle Matt's instigation, conveyed by significantly contorted facial expressions and covert gestures, I circumvented the crouched and intently occupied form of the mole-catcher and faced him head-on, hoping to act as informant, or at the very least as a decoy. But he leapt to his feet and waved me away.

'Please may I watch?' I asked innocently but, red with anger, he shook his fist, rattling a lethal-looking spring trap in my face.

'Hadaway from here! Away ya go!' he roared. 'Ah'm not havin' your goggly green eyes watchin' me at work. Stealin' trade secrets! Stealin' me very livelihood from under me very nose! By no! Noo leave me alone with me moles. Nip up-by an' tell the woman o' the hoose ta put the kettle on. Be off with ya!'

Nor did Uncle Matt learn anything to his advantage himself, though he tried hard, giving himself a crick in the neck from craning it in a vain attempt to see how he could save himself a shilling an acre in future. As for me, as I distanced myself, defeated in my attempt to act as a detective, I entertained mixed feelings with regard to the moles. Common sense told me that they had to go, but being fond of *The Wind in the Willows*, I could never regard the sympathetic mole as an arch enemy. One man's mole, however, is another man's poison, and it was with great satisfaction that B. I. Waggott finally rose and surveyed his fatal handiwork, stretching himself and patting his chest triumphantly.

'That should do ya. As good a job as ivvor was, that is. And deservin' of a nice fresh pot o' tea,' he said, with a toothless grin. Hastily collecting his box of tricks, as my aunt called it, he swaggered off to the house to supervise his favourite ceremony – the boiling of the kettle.

He called back at the farm about a week later to collect his traps, further depleting my aunt's stock of tea, and it struck me then in my childish innocence that despite all the arguments before his initial visit, B. I. Waggott had been an all-round success, finding favour for his skills with both aunt and uncle. I heard Uncle Matt remark that he had never seen anyone earn a shilling an acre so fast, and then heard Aunt Dot agree that it was the same with tea – that you had to marvel at anyone who could drain so many cups in such record time.

As for the moles, they simply vanished, for the time being at least, and we never knew why B. I. Waggott's methods worked and my persevering uncle's did not. I mourned the death of the moles, but no such finer feelings troubled Uncle Matt – though, to be fair, he did mourn the loss of his shillings. Flushed with success at the elimination of one pest, for which in time he took the credit, he turned his attention to another – to the timid and inoffensive rabbit, a species of resident that proliferated in Todd Tingate's dene.

One Saturday morning, his thoughts dwelling happily on forthcoming meals of rabbit pie, he took me through the dene to a ridge that was alive with rabbits, scurrying in all directions. He strode towards it eagerly, filled with exhilaration, swinging the gun jauntily and whistling through his teeth, but I followed reluctantly, dragging my feet. My heart was not in the enterprise, because I had once owned a tame rabbit and regarded the creatures as pets rather than pests, certainly not as potential fillings for pies. And my reservations seemed to be shared by Split, though for a different reason. He had been on shooting expeditions before, and had obviously learnt from the experience. Always strong on self-preservation, he therefore followed at a safe distance, joining us willingly enough for the walk, but rather trailing his tail and travelling low, guarding his legs and keeping a wary eye on the gun. As we approached the warrens, Uncle Matt slowed right down, adjusted his cap to a snug fit, and began to move with the stealth of a Red Indian stalking his quarry.

'Shush. Stop your blatherin',' he whispered, 'and creep forward quiet as the grave.'

For once Split took notice and crept like a panther, always wisely remaining at the rear. And as for me, the caution was unnecessary as I had been silently depressed ever since I spied Uncle Matt in the byre furtively making cartridges, and guessed that an attack on the rabbits was imminent. I was horrified at what I saw, not only at the glimpse of his murderous intentions, but also at the alarming preparations: in a dangerous measure of ingrained economy, he was filling old cartridge cases with gunpowder, recklessly fiddling about with powder and shot like a latter-day Guy Fawkes.

And now I could see startled rabbits fleeing in all directions, so much so that I feared Uncle Matt could hardly miss, even with his eyes shut. It seemed to me that if he had been blindfolded and taken a potshot he could hardly have failed to hit a rabbit. But the rabbits put up a spirited defence, flashing warning signals with their white tails, sounding the alarm by thumping the ridge, and finally scrambling harum-scarum for their burrows, diving underground, heels over heads. So there was a sense of urgency about the way Uncle Matt made ready to fire, and with the confident air of a crack shot, he raised his previously primed gun and took careful aim. Split gave a low whine and sank to the ground behind me, licking my legs for comfort, and I clenched my fists nervously. *Oh dear*, I thought, *the poor rabbits, poor innocent creatures*. And closed my eyes.

Seconds later a loud explosion caused me to open them, and I leapt in shock and looked around. There was not a rabbit to be seen, dead or alive. Only a blackened cap lay on the ground and beside it stood Uncle Matt in a haze of smoke, holding half a gun in each hand, both halves smoking, the stock having blown from the double barrel. He stood transfixed, a shimmering ghostly figure with smoke swirling round his bare head.

Split yapped excitedly and began running in circles chasing his tail, as if in relief that he still could, and that all four legs, having been under threat of being blasted away, remained intact. I took an uncertain step forward, staring anxiously at my uncle's hazy figure, and after a moment he slowly turned to face us.

Had he, I wondered, my heart pounding with fear, shot himself in the head? Blown his nose off? I was afraid to look, and yet somehow felt compelled to keep on looking, and at first it was difficult to tell one way or the other. His face was like a mask. Inching closer, however, I saw that he was uninjured but badly blackened and wearing a bemused expression, and that he was trembling from bare head to wellington boots as if in the throes of an electric shock. I waited helplessly as he dusted himself down, picked up his cap and vainly tried to clean it, wiping it on an already blackened sleeve. Then he looked accusingly at the two pieces of gun and tottered unsteadily towards us.

'Yeeee Gox!' he exclaimed unintelligibly, and stood blinking, his teeth and the whites of his eyes gleaming in his blackened face like Al Jolson's when singing a minstrel song.

I took his arm and patted it consolingly, but he started nervously at my touch, and smelt so strongly of smoke that I stepped back a pace.

'Are you all right, Uncle Matt?' I asked – a silly question.

He gave no answer but reeled a little and, reaching for a handkerchief, feebly mopped his black brow, then seeing the colour of the handkerchief, shook his head sadly.

'Well, I'll be blowed!' he cried, his voice shaking.

'You just have been, Uncle Matt,' I pointed out, unwisely as it happened, because my innocent remark touched an exposed nerve, prompting a stream of invective as he railed against anyone and anything remotely connected with the fact that he had almost blown his own head off.

I noticed, however, that he attached no blame to himself, the chief culprit, for trusting home-made cartridges, but instead blamed the gunpowder, and the pesky chap who sold it to him, and the pesky gun for going off like that and giving him a fright. Then he blamed Aunt Dot, whom he suspected of having interfered with the gun when he was out, and the blasted rabbits for not playing fair and standing still till he shot them. He roundly cursed them all, and then cursed life in general, which, in his view, definitely had it in for him, definitely. To relieve his feelings, he aimed a kick at the dog, still circling in pursuit of his own tail, but the wary dog saw it coming and dodged aside, and so he blamed the dog for avoiding the petulant boot. I kept very quiet, hoping to miss my share of the blame, and in a desultory procession we wended our way home. Uncle Matt stumped sullenly ahead, thinking thoughts as dark as his face; I followed, sadly trailing my feet; Split cautiously brought up the rear.

Uncle Matt had lost all semblance of his usual jaunty self. Not only was his appearance bizarre, like an over-zealous chimney sweep, but he also walked erratically, and his hands shook, and he kept muttering strange threats and glaring at the broken gun as if he had secret knowledge that it intended to go off again. After a while he stopped, and to calm his nerves he lit a cigarette, which looked oddly incongruous against his piebald face, like the last glowing ember and puff of smoke in a dying fire.

And more humiliation lay ahead, in the shape of two ladies on the footbridge over the stream. They took one look at him and came to a standstill, barring our access to the bridge. I recognized them as Miss Titchmarsh and her visiting sister, and they instantly dissolved into laughter, hanging over the handrail and pointing at Uncle Matt as if he were a circus clown provided expressly for their amusement. What mainly took them by surprise was not the effect of the explosion but the absence of the habitual cap. They had never seen him without it, and if the unveiling came as a shock to them, it evidently did to Uncle Matt as well, for, ever the gentleman, he automatically raised his hand to tip his cap and then remembered and lowered it, looking rather fatuous.

'Who on earth is it, Phyllis?' said Miss Titchmarsh. 'Who can it be? Could it be . . . ? No, surely not. But . . . it is though. Oh, my goodness it is. It really is. It's Mr Wheatley! Oh my, Mr Wheatley, what a fright you look. Oh dear. Your poor face! So funny! What a mess!'

Uncle Matt was fundamentally a vain man and the laughter wounded his pride. Cut to the quick, he bridled, and instead of waiting to cross the bridge, he waded straight into the water. The stream widened at this point, filling up from the fell to form a shallow pool that flowed down to the burn, and in his haste to escape further ridicule, he plunged wildly through the water, splashing and flapping like a startled duck, and uttering a not dissimilar cry. Split followed, always game for a paddle, but bearing in mind Aunt Dot's reaction if I returned home in wet shoes and socks, I took the conventional route, as soon as the hysterical ladies vacated the bridge. I had to run fast to catch the sodden pair, and when I finally did, I found my uncle seething with righteous indignation, so riled that he scarcely knew what to do with himself.

'What a nerve!' he exclaimed. 'What a ruddy nerve! Fancy commentin' so nastily about my face! As if she had room to talk!'

'She didn't mean it like that. Honestly, Uncle Matt,' I said, trying to placate him.

'She'd no right to make personal remarks,' he retorted. 'Not with a face like hers. Has she looked in the mirror lately? Both of them in fact! They both look as if they should've been runnin' in the St Leger.'

'Oh come on, Uncle Matt. Calm down. You'll be all right once you've had a nice cup of tea and got cleaned up a bit.'

'Yeah! That's just it, Emma. My meanin' is, my face'll clean up, but theirs'll stay the same. So what've they got to laugh about? Just *what*, I'd like to know?'

And when I glanced up at his face, black in colour but blacker still in expression, I knew that someone was in for big trouble, and I guessed it would be the rabbits.

Chapter 9

Of Fascists and Ferrets

Sure enough, on the following market day Uncle Matt returned home carrying a small wooden box. It looked very like the box that had intrigued us all on our journey to Thorny Edge, even to the strong twine strengthening it and the air holes in the top, from which apertures I now detected an unpleasant and pervasive smell. He placed the box on the window sill, untied the string, and with the dramatic air of a conjurer producing a white rabbit from a hat, pulled out a yellowy creature with flickering pink eyes above a matching pink nose that constantly twitched. Naturally I reached out to stroke this curious animal writhing so vigorously in my uncle's hand, but he quickly drew back and shouted.

'No! Don't touch!'

'Why not, Uncle Matt?'

'It'll take your fingers off,' he said proudly. 'It's a killer. It's my new secret weapon – a deadly ferret. A killin' machine. Believe me, Emma, this little yellow terror'll soon fix the rabbits. My meanin' is, girl, from now on we can have as many rabbit pies as we want. We can, Emma, definitely. Think of that, eh? Rabbit pie!'

I noticed that he held the vicious thing by the scruff of the neck as it wriggled and twisted, baring its tiny pointed teeth, sharp as needles. And after this unsettling introduction, during which I squirmed and the ferret squirmed and Uncle Matt cavorted like a doting parent dangling his offspring to be admired, I vowed to myself to avoid the pink-eyed peril like the proverbial plague. He kept this latest addition to his livestock in the small byre, lodging it in a hutch reinforced with bars and several layers of galvanized wire, behind which it spent its days slinking back and forth and watching, always watching. Its predatory pink eyes, more hostile than the rats' eyes, glowed luminously in the dark byre as they focused on all intruders – warily on humans, contemptuously on the dog, and menacingly on the neighbouring rats.

Whenever I passed through the byre I was uncomfortably aware of the pink eyes riveted on me, and I felt they were weighing me up in size and succulence as a potential meal – indeed, as easy meat, I thought with a shudder. I was thankful for the restricting bars and wires, and took an intense dislike to the sneaky snaking creature, which I never thought of as a he or a she, but always as an it, like a supernatural being. Though supposedly domesticated, the ferret seemed to me more savage than anything I had encountered in the wild. So when I overheard Uncle Matt boasting that ferrets belonged to the polecat family, the word 'polecat' caught my attention, and set me wondering whether this unusual breed of cat could be a distant cousin of Mr Clout's sinister cat. That thought raised disturbing questions in my mind as to what specific horror we were harbouring in the dim recesses of the small byre, and I grew increasingly afraid of it. I had no desire to see the repulsive thing in action, killing poor defenceless rabbits, and I determined to have nothing to do with the deadly ferret, or indeed with ferreting activity in any shape or form. The following Saturday, therefore, when, with his mind on rabbit pie, Uncle Matt beckoned me as usual, for once I refused to join him and held back firmly, resisting all attempts to move me. I offered excuse after excuse but he accepted none of them, gradually becoming more and more impatient.

'Now come along, Emma,' he said at length, totally exasperated.

'This just isn't like you. You'll make me late with my deliveries. The Shoemans have recently been collectin' their stuff, but now she wants it delivered, and Mr Shoeman can be a bit funny if you arrive later than expected, like.'

'But, Uncle Matt, I don't want to go rabbiting. I don't like the ferret at all, and I'd just hate to watch the rabbits die.'

'Don't be silly, girl. They're only rabbits. They're ten a penny are rabbits. The ridge is overrun with them and they're nothin' but pests. They just keep on multiplyin', like – well, like rabbits, you might say. And I ask you, what use are rabbits except to eat, eh? My meanin' is, they make a grand pie. Or a stew. Rabbit stew's a winner in my book. Now come along, pet. I need your help. There's milk and eggs to take to Dyke Head and Moss House, and the Shoemans want a few turnips for their sheep as well. It's all to carry, and the gates have to be opened, and I have my ferret to contend with. So put your coat and muffler on and we'll be on our way.'

And off we eventually went, four of us including the dog and the ferret, up the rough road to Dyke Head House – a hard, sharp road, cobbled together with big granite chippings scattered diagonally across two fields. I found it easier to walk on the grass, carrying a small can of milk and a covered basket, while Uncle Matt coped with gates and carried the other milk can and a bag of turnips slung over his shoulder, as well as a small wriggling sack, which he clutched as tightly as if it contained the Crown jewels. It was my first visit to Dyke Head, which stood imposingly on one of the peaks of Sourhope. The house looked larger than others thereabouts and, unlike the rest, was rendered in cement and had been painted white, as had the gates and surrounding fences, so that its outstanding brightness acted as a beacon for the whole valley.

Though insufficient in acreage to be classed as a farm, or even as a smallholding, its splendid appearance caused the tenants, Mr and Mrs Shoeman, as they liked to be known, to consider themselves landed gentry, and to try and lord it over the amused locals. They kept a small flock of Swaledale sheep that to everyone else looked more or less alike, having that certain sameness about them that sheep tend to suffer from. But to the Shoemans they all looked different, each of them possessing a unique personality, and consequently they were all individually named. So it was that Mr Shoeman, without a shred of embarrassment, stood every day at his wicket gate and shouted for his pets by name, calling them in honeyed tones with more affection and respect than he ever showed in addressing his wife. One by one he summoned them to him, fondly, as one would a favourite child; and in precise alphabetical order, a system that made the roll-call easier to remember and ensured that no sheep had her tender feelings hurt.

First he called for Astrakhan, Baa-baa, Bleater, Chops and Cuddles; then Curly, Dinky, Fleecy, Fluffy and Goldie; then Hobbles, Hoofy, Lambzy, Lettie and Loopy; then Mutton, Nibbles, Shanks, Shortie and Woolly. And to his great satisfaction they all came to him, answering to their names and their master's voice. Or so he thought. But what he failed to appreciate was that sheep being sheep, they would have come to him anyway, whatever he called them. They would have come if he had shouted the weather forecast, or the football results, or simply, and perhaps more effectively, if he had rattled his bucket. They would have pandered to his ego by flocking around him just the same, provided he kept up the supply of corn and sheep nuts and occasional turnips, the crunchy supplements to their monotonous diet of grass. Being woolly brained as well as woolly headed, they responded as a mass, and had he engaged the attention of one, the rest by their very nature would have followed. It only took a short time for the locals to assess his shepherding skills and to sum up the situation, and then word travelled up hill and down dale.

'He knows nowt about sheep,' they all agreed, and they were right.

But ignorance can be bliss, and the Shoemans loved their sheep, more than they loved people, and considerably more than they loved each other. Rumours abounded concerning the strange doings at Dyke Head. It was said that the Shoemans treated their sheep like children, titivating them with ribbons and bows in the summer, and in the winter dressing them warmly in jackets and scarves, sometimes even hats. Other rumours, nothing to do with sheep, were also rife. It was said that the Shoemans were Fascists with Nazi connections, and that they were in league with the German owner of a second-hand junk shop in Shiretown, who had had all his windows put out on suspicion of being a spy. Increasingly, the Shoemans became the focus of gossip and speculation, and they incited still more of the same by their insular attitude. Visitors were discouraged, gates kept firmly closed and bolted, and a plethora of notices declaring the premises strictly private threatened trespassers with prosecution, electrocution, and the possibility of becoming dinner for a dangerous guard dog.

I hesitated in some alarm beside the first set of notices.

'Are you sure it's safe to go on, Uncle Matt?'

'Oh yes, Emma, it's safe enough. Leastways safe as anywhere these days.'

'But what about the notices?'

'Oh, take no notice of the notices,' he advised, grinning complacently at his play on words. 'They don't mean a thing, Emma, and I'll tell you for why. Now regardin' number one – prosecution – well, the Shoemans are too publicity shy to prosecute anybody. They'd never draw attention to themselves like that. And regardin' number two – electrocution – well, as you've likely noticed, there's no electricity up here, not for miles, so they'd be hard put to manage that. And as for number three – the guard dog – well, they haven't got a dog of any sort. The plain fact is that they're frightened of dogs, scared out of their wits.'

'Not of Split, Uncle Matt? Surely not! Nobody's frightened of Split!'

'Yes, even Split – and mind you, he has a job just frightenin' the hens. Anyway, Emma, it's all right 'cos they're expectin' me. Not you, of course, but you don't look like a serious threat. And they want their eggs and milk, which,' he added, with an oddly malicious glint in his eye, 'I just hope they enjoy.'

By the time we reached the second gate, which was even more thoroughly adorned with warning notices, my curiosity was aroused.

'So, what's wrong with Mr Shoeman, Uncle Matt? Why doesn't he like visitors? Why don't you like him?'

'I have my reasons, Emma. Though I haven't seen that much of him. He's a bit of a recluse, you might say, so we usually deal with her. But he kinda reminds me of a toad, especially with those bulgin' eyes of his. A big, fat, slimy toad. Except for his Hitler-type moustache. And there's a lot of talk that he's a Nazi. There's no proof yet, but folks think that's why he lives way out here. I mean to say, there's not much of a livin' to be had out of this place. It's not a proper farm, and you don't make your fortune from twenty sheep. So what's he doin' here, eh? And what does he live on? Folks think he's hidin' away and spyin' for Germany.'

'What about Mrs Shoeman then?'

'Well, Emma, I'm not convinced that she *is* Mrs Shoeman. Not certain sure of it. Something tells me they're not married, and I'll explain for why. It's the way he speaks to her. Very nasty it is, and in public as well. Not many wives would stand for that. No way! Wives now,' he said with some emotion, 'wives are inclined to like their say and have the upper hand. No, I think she's a loose woman and no better than she should be.'

'Do you think she knows he's a Nazi? Is she a Nazi too?'

'Now that I couldn't say, Emma, but she's stuck with him despite all, so she must be a sympathizer – the lowest of the low. They both mix with Fascists. Fascists, Nazis – same difference, pet. You'll notice he's got a foreign accent and she hasn't. He says he's Dutch, but folks think he's German. And she's English. No doubt about it. That's why I think she's fast, like.'

First loose, and then fast. It was all very confusing. But by now we were nearing the back entrance to the house, passing through the last white gate, and I was taken aback by the sight of the Shoemans emerging to confront us, and at considerable speed. Mrs Shoeman hovered at the door, but Mr Shoeman ran forward brandishing a gun and bellowing until red in the face.

'Private! Can not you read? Stupid yokels! This is private property! Trespassing, you are! You vandals! Go away! Go! Before I shoot!'

Uncle Matt stood quite still, calling back in a conciliatory tone, 'It's me, Mr Shoeman, only me – Matt Wheatley. I've brought your turnips and eggs. Your wife said you wanted extra eggs this week.'

'Oh Hans, put your silly gun down. For Pete's sake! It's Mr Wheatley from Windlestraw. Nice Mr Wheatley,' said Mrs Shoeman, smiling coquettishly and patting her hair into place, for it was said that whether married or not, she was always on the lookout for a replacement for the boorish Mr Shoeman.

'Oh, it's you, is it?' he snarled. 'And about time, I think.'

He now directed the gun away from Uncle Matt's head, at which he had been carelessly aiming, and turned it on me instead.

'Who is that girl?' he demanded suspiciously, as if I might be the flank of an opposing force, creating a diversion.

'Nobody, Mr Shoeman, just my young niece. Nobody at all,' shouted my uncle, belittling my existence. Then he bent down and deftly exchanged the ferret for the eggs I was carrying, muttering instructions in my ear.

'Take this sack, Emma, and get a good grip at the top. Now, whatever you do, don't let go. Understand? Keep tight hold and stay right there till I get back.' Then he issued similar instructions to Split.

'Sit!' he commanded. 'Sit and stay! Now stay, boy! Stay!' And Split sat, gazing at him with moist, devoted eyes, and wagging a compliant tail.

Uncle Matt picked up the turnips, milk, and eggs, placing Miss Titchmarsh's small special egg box on the grass, and advanced boldly, showing remarkable composure, I thought, in the face of someone who was an armed maniac and possible Nazi. As he walked he talked blithely and non-stop, commenting on the fine weather, the long driveway, the white paintwork, and so on. Split shuffled and whined as he carefully considered his instructions to stay put, then rejected them and followed, wagging his tail warily and drifting round Mrs Shoeman's legs, angling for titbits. The Shoemans both recoiled in distaste, trying to shoo him away, while I, left alone with the hated ferret, put the milk can down and moved nearer to hear what was happening. Uncle Matt faced the couple at the door.

'Mornin', Mrs Shoeman, Mr Shoeman,' he began, while lifting and lowering his cap with the sleight of hand of a magician making an egg disappear.

Mr Shoeman had lowered the gun but continued to eye Uncle Matt malevolently.

'I hope you have not upset my sheep. They do not like the strangers,' he said. 'They run from the strangers and it is not good for them to run. We have the sensitive sheep, especially Curly and Fluffy. They most sensitive are. And Hobbles now, she runs not too well at all.'

'I haven't even seen your sheep,' said Uncle Matt, rather rattled. 'We came up the other way. And after all, you asked me to come. And I'm a busy man. Very busy today, as it happens. But I have brought the soft turnips you ordered for them. And your milk and eggs. They're grand eggs. Fresh as a daisy and every one a brown one.'

He dropped the turnip bag, handed over the milk can, and, folding back the covering tea towel, offered the eggs to Mrs Shoeman, who smiled toothily at him.

'I do think brown eggs have the best taste, don't you, Mr Wheatley?' she said, fluttering her eyelashes as she took the basket.

Mr Shoeman glowered and rounded on her, speaking scathingly.

'And who asks you, Betty? You had better shut up. You vill keep your trap shut! You hear me?'

As chivalrous as ever, Uncle Matt boldly agreed with the lady.

'Matter of fact I do, Mrs Shoeman. I definitely do. Brown's the best colour for eggs all right.' Then he added provocatively, 'I bet there's people in towns who'd sell state secrets for lovely brown eggs like them.'

Mr Shoeman became as gimlet-eyed and fierce as the ferret, and as he outdangered the ferret in that he carried a gun, I held my breath in fear.

'Vot are you meaning by that?' he rasped. 'Just vot do you imply?'

'Only a figure of speech,' said Uncle Matt innocently, and Mrs Shoeman hastily interjected.

'I think, Hans, that Mr Wheatley means people in towns can't buy real eggs nowadays. They have to manage with that awful powdered egg.'

Mr Shoeman rounded on her again.

'And who vants your opinion, Betty? Eh? Eh? No one. That's who. Don't butt in. You always have to do the butting in.'

'Only I do hope, Mr Wheatley,' she continued, undeterred, 'I hope that the milk you've brought this time is creamier than the last can. Some of the milk you've sold us lately has had hardly any cream at all. I don't wish to give offence, Mr Wheatley, as we're such good friends, but some of it's been quite blue – yes, blue.'

For an instant Uncle Matt appeared nonplussed by this frontal attack, but like the proverbial rubber ball, he soon bounced back. It was his proud boast that no townsfolk got the better of him. Townies, as the locals called them, commanded little respect in the valley. To be an incomer was bad enough, and my uncle remained an incomer after ten years in residence. But to be an incomer *and* a townie put a person beyond the pale and fair game even for an incomer. Of course, the Shoemans carried the added stigma of being suspected spies, altogether beneath contempt – but also potentially dangerous, and Uncle Matt now smiled disarmingly and gestured at the milk can.

'Tell you what,' he said winningly, 'you try that and tell me what it's like. You see, some cows give more cream than others. It's as simple as that. If that can's not creamy, I'll try a different cow for you. No bother. Definitely. We aim to please.'

'Oh thank you, Mr Wheatley. Thanks ever so,' she gushed, her eyes shining and her homely countenance blushing with pleasure.

'Don't mention it,' said my uncle graciously.

'Shut up, Betty. For pity's sake shut your mouth,' said Mr Shoeman.

She disappeared indoors to transfer the eggs to a bowl and the milk to a jug, and to seek her purse and a biscuit to rid herself of the dog that kept wrapping itself round her recoiling legs and sniffing appreciatively. The two men continued talking and my uncle moved forward in a conspiratorial manner.

'Don't breathe a word to a soul, mind,' he said confidentially, 'but I could put you in the way of a side of bacon.'

'The bacon?' repeated Mr Shoeman, visibly brightening.

'Yes, bacon. As a special favour, like. From under the counter, as it were. Strictly hush-hush. You know, to go with them eggs.'

Mr Shoeman's podgy face lit up and his eyes bulged in anticipation, like a hungry toad.

'How much?' he asked eagerly.

Hard as I tried, I could not hear the price. I think that even Uncle Matt must have been a touch embarrassed by it, because he just let the cost slip surreptitiously out of his mouth as if it had a will of its own, nothing to do with him. Mr Shoeman gave a tortured cry, followed by what sounded like a Germanic oath, followed by a blunt refusal.

'No! I vill not pay that! Do you think I am mad?' It was a question which, happily, Uncle Matt refrained from answering.

'It's a bargain,' he pointed out, but Shoeman shook his head.

'It is far too much. Much too much. A ridiculous price, I think.'

'It's an absolute snip,' corrected Uncle Matt. 'Where else would you get bacon for that price? Come to that, where would you get bacon at all off the ration? There's a war on you know. Damned Nazis! And a side of bacon'll last you for ages. Weeks and weeks. Lookin' at it that way, it's positively cheap!'

'I vill not pay,' stated Shoeman flatly, his stub moustache twitching in agitation.

'Please yourself,' said Uncle Matt, shrugging his shoulders in an offhand way. 'No skin off my nose. I'm all right for bacon. You're the one without. Believe me, I'm doin' you a favour. I'm sellin' at a loss. I can get twice that price elsewhere.'

'Vell you go and you get it,' advised Shoeman curtly.

The argument continued, growing increasingly heated, until I became concerned for my uncle's safety and began to move back in case a quick getaway was called for. But so engrossed had I been in the lively exchange on the doorstep, that I must have lessened my hold on the sack, and suddenly the ferret leapt out and made a bolt for freedom, slipping to the ground and into a stretch of bracken bordering the fell. At once the enormity of my plight struck me, filling me with horror. I remembered Uncle Matt's pride in his ferret and his big plans for its future. I remembered his pique when previously thwarted in his ambition to eat rabbit pies till the cows came home – the petulance with which he had lashed out at everyone, even Split, who had narrowly avoided a kick in the ribs. I recalled the black expression on his blackened face, reminding me of storm clouds gathering over Lornhope. And I shook in my shoes. But what to do? I had been warned that poisonous snakes lived in the bracken and I dared not venture in. On the other hand, Uncle Matt might return at any moment and, faced with an empty sack instead of a thriving ferret, he might prove more venomous than the snakes. Caught between two evils, I stood rigid with fear – no longer on behalf of the rabbits, but now for myself – fear of snakes, fear of the ferret, and most of all, fear of a furious uncle.

I focused on the ferret as it crawled away, slowly at first, its albino eyes blinded by the light after long days spent in the dark byre, followed by a short sojourn in the dim confines of the sack. If the fronds of the bracken had been spring green and fan-like I would soon have lost sight of it, but they were beginning to turn autumn brown and shrivel like a burnt crisp. I could see the exposed rhizomes, curled and hairy like gorillas' knuckles, and I watched with horrified fascination the teasing glimpses of yellow fur that intermittently appeared then disappeared as the ferret squirmed through them, sniffing for prey. Then all at once it changed direction, heading for the wide open spaces of Black Cleugh Fell, and I panicked, suddenly spurred into action. I stole as stealthily as the snakes themselves, keeping one eye alert for anything that slithered and the other on the ferret. For an awful moment I thought I had lost the troublesome animal, but with a shock I caught sight of it almost at my feet and fidgeting in the undergrowth, its pink nose sniffing the air and its pink eyes flickering. I knew it was now or never, and reached a hand out to take it, but drew back, terrified. I reached out again, withdrew again. The ferret's very aspect repelled me. Its smell sickened me. How could I touch it? Hold it? Then, still hesitating, I heard the crunch of footsteps on gravel, and fear of an angry uncle overcame all other fears. I sprang into action, grabbing the ferret the way he handled it, by the back of the neck, and held on tightly.

The sinewy creature twisted violently in my grasp, snapping its jaws, trying to bite, and I realized that after a taste of freedom, however brief, this fiercely struggling thing would not readily accept captivity again so soon. My small hand could hardly hold it, and for a time the outcome, like the ferret, hung in the balance. Then, with a supreme effort I managed to manoeuvre its hind legs into the sack and dropped the rest in after them, screwing up the thick hessian so that not even air could escape. Just then Uncle Matt appeared round the corner. I stood trembling, flushed and wide-eyed, looking as guilty as a thief caught with the swag. But he saw nothing amiss except for my position, which was different from where he had left me.

'What on earth are you doin' over there, Emma? I've told you and told you, there's lethal snakes in them ferns. You'll know about it if a viper crawls up your leg! Now come out of it, and pass me my ferret.'

With great relief I handed it over, exchanging it for the inoffensive milk can. Then we set off, leaving Dyke Head by a different route, a clay path through a field that led directly down to Todd Tingate's. Like the escaped ferret had done, Uncle Matt proceeded slowly and silently at first, apparently preoccupied with his thoughts. I assumed that he was reviewing his conversation with Mr Shoeman and wondering whether, if he had said this or that, he could have clinched a deal, for he was a man who liked to win every time. As it turned out, however, he had much more on his mind, and was inwardly debating whether profit or patriotism was to be the dominating motive in his dealings with Shoeman, and whether the belligerent foreigner was indeed a Nazi. I too kept quiet, partly because I sensed his introspective mood, and partly because I needed time to recover from my ordeal by ferret.

So we said little until we passed a flock of sheep huddled together in the corner of the field. At first I noticed nothing untoward, but closer scrutiny revealed peculiarly shaped heads, and I saw that they were wearing knitted helmets of some sort tucked round the ears at the sides of their black faces. The helmets reminded me of something. They were of an oddly familiar style and shape. I stopped and stared at them, intrigued and puzzled. Then it dawned on me what I had just recognized, and I shrieked in delight.

'Oooh, look! Uncle Matt, look! Do look at the sheep. They're all wearing tea cosies!'

He too stopped and stared and swore under his breath.

'Blow me!' he said. 'If that doesn't beat all! Those Shoemans are as mad as hatters – sheep hatters, as it happens. They're round the bend, they are. Definitely. More stupid than their stupid sheep!'

He handed me the ferret sack while he lit a cigarette, then took it back and strolled on, smoking in silence, puffing reflectively and blowing leisurely smoke rings until we had almost reached the stile leading from the Shoemans' land. When he spoke, it was in the solemn tones of someone in the confessional.

'I offered the old geezer a side of bacon.'

'I know,' I said.

'He didn't want it.'

'Ah,' I said.

'It's a shame,' he mused, ''cos there's a side hangin' at the back of the larder, left over from last year and lookin' a bit off colour. A bit green, you might say, round the edges. I've been thinkin' we ought to get rid of it, and I can't think of a better customer to take it off our hands.'

'You can't sell him that, Uncle Matt. Not if it's green,' I protested, wrinkling my nose in distaste.

'I can,' he replied pensively, 'but I'll have to drop the price a bit. When it comes to partin' with money, he's not as daft as he looks. Not as green as the bacon.'

'Uncle Matt!' I cried, shocked in spite of myself.

But he had lapsed back into silence, head bent and feet trailing, and we were on our way to Moss House before he felt the urge to confess again.

'You know, Emma, they were the week before last's eggs.'

'No! Really? Uncle *Matt!*'

'The Shoemans won't know the difference, and as the sayin' goes, what you don't know can't hurt you.'

'Well – I suppose not.'

'Though she'd do well to use the cracked ones first,' he added thoughtfully.'

'Oh no! You didn't give her cracked ones?'

'No – well – not many. Just a few, like. And why not? What do you think customers do when they find a few cracked eggs in their batch?'

'Get very cross, Uncle Matt?'

'Yes – I mean no. Make a cake, of course, Emma. They're perfect cake eggs. You see, you've got to crack them anyway for cakes. I fix them up to look nice before handin' them over. A bit of hen dirt hides the cracks, and my meanin' is, she can have a little treat and make cakes.'

'Uncle Matt, do you – by any chance – take the cream off the milk?' I asked, though at heart I knew the answer.

'What me? Skim the milk?' he asked slyly. 'Do I skim the milk? Well, what do you think? Course I do, Emma. We must have our butter, girl. You've seen your aunt Dot makin' butter in that little churn of hers, haven't you? Well, where do you think she gets the cream?'

'I – I didn't think, Uncle Matt.'

'Well, Emma, think on this. Your aunt's not much of a cook, as you know. She does all right considerin', but I've tasted better. You've tasted better, young as you are. So where would we be without a bit of butter on our bread to dunk in our eggs? Now, where? Tell me that, eh?'

'I see what you mean,' I said, bewildered by his flexible code of ethics.

'And by the way,' he remembered, pointing the ferret sack at me, 'don't you dare tell your aunt Dot what I just said about her cookin'. That's between us, or you and me's finished.'

'I won't,' I promised. 'But Uncle Matt, there won't be trouble, will there? Is it all right? I mean, about the milk and eggs and everything?'

'Course it's all right. Definitely it is. You've heard the old sayin', haven't you, Emma? All's fair in trade and war? Well, there you are.'

I could recall no such saying, though something about it had a vaguely familiar ring, and while I tried to pinpoint the true saying in my mind, he resumed his silence, as if mulling over a problem. When he next spoke he seemed a little agitated.

'Anyway, Emma, there's partic'lar circumstances here. You see, I think he's a Nazi,' he said, as if that totally justified his own conduct. 'He claims to be Dutch, but I'm sure he's a Jerry. You should've seen his face when I mentioned state secrets. He looked like a toad caught by the scythe. Now I don't know if *she's* a Nazi, but she's that ugly that she'd pass for one. All in all I have to admit that I'm a bit bothered about the Shoemans and the whole darned business of their milk and eggs.'

'You mean because you give them skimmed and cracked?'

'No, no, not at all. Nothin' like that, Emma. That's fair enough, pet. My problem's whether I should even be talkin' to them. You see, if they're just unpleasant townies it's fair dos to deal with them. But if I knew for sure they were Nazis they'd get nothin' out of me but a phone call to the authorities. So somehow, Emma, but I dunno how, I've got to find out for definite. And I tell you, it'll be a dangerous game. Meantime I play things both ways, and either way I reckon my milk and eggs are too good for them. My bacon is as well, come to that. It's not to be sniffed at – except for the mouldy one at the back. I might sell him that. Scrape it down a bit first.'

'But he didn't want it, Uncle Matt.'

'He will,' he said confidently. 'I dare bet he's thinkin' about it now. But ten to one he'll think of it when she fries them eggs. He'll think of the tasty smell of fryin' bacon and have second thoughts. He'll want it right enough when I bring the price down and let him think it's a bargain. You have to remember, Emma, this is war. I'm sure you agree that we have to find out what he's up to and report him. Those Nazis are tryin' to take over the world. They have to be stopped, by fair means or foul.'

I noticed that I was suddenly included in his plans for catching spies, and I was horrified at the thought. With the memory of a gun pointing at me still fresh in my mind, I was very nervous indeed of Mr Shoeman. To me he was a little mad and very dangerous, more than Mr Clout and the ferret and *The Cat* put together. But I said nothing at the time, and having convinced himself that he had outwitted the Shoemans and at the same time contributed to the war effort, Uncle Matt perked up. He delivered the milk to Moss House with his customary cordiality, and by the time we had retraced our steps to Todd Tingate's and reached the rabbit ridge, he had become all hustle and bustle, preparing to direct the ferret to do its deadly work. He called at the byre where the goats were now housed and collected nets to spread over the rabbit holes, then proceeded purposefully down the ridge, walking with a buoyant air. I made a last-ditch attempt to save the rabbits, but held out little hope.

'Please, Uncle Matt,' I pleaded. 'Don't let that horrible ferret out.' I almost added 'again' but stopped myself just in time. However, he looked like a man who would not be deterred from his purpose.

'But, Emma,' he cried dramatically, waving the nets like battle flags, 'do you see all those rabbit warrens, all those rabbits? They're takin' over the land. They have to be stopped. This is war.'

It was much the same speech he had delivered earlier about a different enemy, and it left me in some confusion as to whether we were being taken over by Nazis or by rabbits, or indeed whether the rabbits were Nazis and maybe also vice versa. The term 'Nazi', though freely bandied about, had never been fully explained to me, but for once I didn't waste time asking questions. I quickly climbed the wall and hid behind it, covering my ears, closing my eyes, trying to detach myself from events on the other side and think only beautiful thoughts. Eventually, however, the sound of Uncle Matt's voice persistently shouting my name penetrated all my defences, and reluctant as I was to face reality, I had to climb back over the wall and contemplate what he and his vicious ferret had done.

I would have preferred to forget the scene of carnage that met my horrified gaze. By himself, Uncle Matt had proved a poor opponent for the rabbits, and on previous hunting trips the only wounds inflicted had been to his cap and his pride. But partnered by the ferret, he became invincible. The hitherto picturesque banks of this gory battle-field were littered with rabbits, some mangled, all dead. And the excitement had even transmitted itself to Split. Normally too lazy to chase rabbits, he now had to be restrained from biting their heads off, to prove himself as much of a warrior as the ferret. In the end there were altogether too many dead rabbits, nearly too many to carry, and I stood my ground and steadfastly refused to touch them. I took the empty basket, the cans and the nets, but not the blood-stained ferret, now safely back in its sack. Uncle Matt coped with that monster and with his bounty of rabbits, which he tied in bunches at either end of an old broom handle, carrying the load across his shoulders like an ancient yoke.

After that, though he often coaxed and cajoled, I categorically refused to go ferreting with him again, choosing instead to stay with Aunt Dot, which in itself was a marked indication of my strength of feeling. Finally he had to accept my decision, but he went anyway, apparently preferring the company of the ferret. He profited from the rabbits in a number of ways – by bartering some, selling some on market days and others at an inflated price to the Shoemans, and of course eating the remainder. For a few weeks he wallowed in rabbits and even helped to cook them. First he indulged in the long-promised rabbit pies, and then in the stews, dispatching plateful after plateful until Aunt Dot declared that she half expected him to hop to the byre and swore she could see his ears growing. He partook heartily of roast rabbit, a firm favourite, and of braised rabbit with mashed potatoes and turnip. He tried rabbit in every conceivable form – sautéed, casseroled, concealed in a suet pudding, and jugged like hare.

He gorged on rabbit till it sickened him, and once he had sickened he lost all interest in the ferret. He stopped taking it out, talked of selling it, and sometimes forgot to feed it. He provided the odd bowl of bread and milk when the spirit moved him, but only grudgingly, as if he had better things to do. His erstwhile constant companion had become an embarrassment, just a nuisance that often went hungry. At times the creature was so hungry that it fell to gnawing the planks that formed the bottom of the hutch and still retained the smell of food. It gnawed persistently, little by little removing splinters, until one night its sharp teeth excavated a hole big enough to allow easy escape. Unable to believe its luck, it waited for an opportunity, and under cover of darkness, it departed, unnoticed by anyone except the rats, one of whom it killed, just for spite, on the way out. Nor was that the end of the ferret story. Long after I had gone to bed that night, and just as Uncle Matt was extinguishing the lamps, we heard a disturbance in the hen-house, where lived about forty hens, including fifteen pullets reared from chicks and ready to start laying any day.

'It's the fox! That pesky fox! I'll have 'im! I'll have his legs off!' he cried, charging about, banging doors and bellowing until sleep became impossible.

Alarmed, I left my warm bed and peered out of the window. I could see Aunt Dot enveloped in one of Uncle Matt's coats, standing beside the back door holding a hurricane lamp high in the air in order to throw light on the path. I could see Uncle Matt's torch bobbing through the darkness as, clad only in pyjamas and wellingtons and clutching a gun, he raced towards the hen-house, looking like a follower of the hunt without a horse, the cry of 'Tally-ho' implicit in his every move. Strangely, however, no sound reached me of any shots being fired. After a while Aunt Dot returned indoors and, thinking the excitement was over, I went back to bed and straight to sleep, but I heard the full horror story from Uncle Matt the following morning.

It appeared that as he drew near the hut he could hear dreadful sounds of flapping wings and terrified squawks, and when he shone his torch inside, it illuminated a heart-rending scene of utter devastation. Only about a dozen hens remained alive and the rest lay dead with their necks bitten. In the midst of them crouched the ferret, interrupted in the pleasure of the kill, dripping blood and feathers from its wicked jaws. Though desperately hungry it had eaten little – just killed and gone on killing for killing's sake, wreaking a terrible revenge for its neglect. Uncle Matt did not even bother raising his gun. He put it aside and closed the door. Then without further ado, in a silent and deadly fury, he snatched the trapped ferret and wrung its neck.

Over the following days some of the slaughtered hens were sold at market, some eaten, some wasted. Meanwhile Uncle Matt brooded bitterly over the creature that he had unthinkingly introduced as a killing machine, until one afternoon in a sudden fit of rage he chopped up the ferret's hutch for firewood. For a time he hated the very sight of the hen-house, and at length he moved the remaining hens and replacement stock to Brackenfield, which, though not such a conven-ient shelter, was a solid stone building, difficult for a predator to penetrate.

I grieved for my feathered friends, my only consolation being that Gertie, the precocious speckled hen, miraculously survived the massacre, living to strut her stuff another day. But I could never bring myself to mourn the passing of the ferret, and I breathed a sigh of relief when I discovered that the hunting season appeared to be over, for Uncle Matt now turned his attention to harmless and peaceful pursuits, such as cutting reeds, digging peat and spreading manure. As for the rabbits, they resumed their carefree family life and went forth and multiplied, trying their utmost to take over the land.

Chapter 10

Like Billy-o

At last the long-desired day arrived and my mother came as promised to take me home – or so I thought. She came with my brothers
in blackberry week, the seasonal name given in those parts for the
last week in October, a traditional holiday from school. Throughout
the month I looked forward to her visit with the intense and seemingly endless anticipation that usually precedes Christmas. The
thought of seeing her again, the thought of going home – these thoughts
woke me every morning and kept me awake at night. I counted the
days. Standing on my sturdy stool, I crossed the dates off the calendar
in fine pencil strokes, scarcely visible, as a prisoner might secretly
scratch the walls of his cell, marking the remaining days of his sentence.
As for the all-important date, which I now knew for sure, I could not
resist drawing a red circle round it, and this shone brightly out of
October's page, signalling a ray of hope as I passed through the

kitchen, confirming the day as a red-letter day. That done, I turned my attention to the monthly pig.

I was sorry to lose September's Curly Coat boar, alias Mr Clout, because of his therapeutic benefits to me, but he had been replaced by a sow known as a Middle White, a fat and superior specimen. She had little piggy eyes and a short snub snout, so squashed that her forehead furrowed behind it, giving her a prim expression and a vacant stare which I undertook to alter. First I drew a bold circle round one of her eyes with a thick-leaded pencil, giving the pig a monocle; then, as no one commented on the improvement, I extended the monocle into spectacles. I had no particular person in mind for the portrait, but when finished I detected a passing resemblance to the boiled-onion-loving Bill Batey's plump and jowly face, so I coloured the eyes behind the spectacles, one blue and one brown, then added a pipe and a cloud of black smoke, and sat an impish elf on the corpulent pink back. The bloated features of October's porker had now become more refined, and the expression changed from vacuous to astute, the face of a pig likely to win prizes for brain as well as brawn, and once again I waited with bated breath for a reaction. But once again, none came.

I thought a great deal about the forthcoming meeting with my mother, living the longed-for moment over and over in my mind. I thought of how pleased we would be to see each other and how she would scoop me up and cuddle me in, and later, of course, take me home. I had no doubt of that happy outcome, because I was, after all, her only daughter and she must want me back, and besides, Uncle Matt had given me his solemn word that it would be so. Night after night, therefore, I reasoned along those lines, as I lay awake happily planning, and often holding a pillow over my head to muffle the insistent splashing of the garden spring below. And so convinced was I that my days at Sourhope were numbered, that I sorted out my few belongings, tidying my clothes, and folding and arranging everything in readiness to pack my suitcase. The night before the great day I could hardly contain myself for excitement, and though it was agreed that Uncle Matt would collect my family while I stayed behind to help Aunt Dot, I did so reluctantly, growing as restless and nervous as Split when he scented a cat and was prevented from following his nose.

Then all of a sudden my mother was there, and just as suddenly things began to go wrong. The often-imagined moment fell as flat as a collapsed soufflé, and the much-anticipated meeting turned out quite the opposite of my expectations, unfortunately spoilt by a silly feeling of constraint on my part. Time had passed, and the easy familiarity of the close relationship I had enjoyed with my mother had been lost. I felt strangely shy, and when I saw my brothers so carefree and content, resentment rose within me. Instead of running into her arms as intended, I merely smiled awkwardly and, with the boys looking on, held back, bashfully keeping my distance, and unwittingly imposing restraint on her. She too hesitated, uncertain as to how best to proceed. She looked pleased to see me, I thought, but generally tired and strained. So at first the conversation limped along in stiff and stilted platitudes.

'And how's my little girl? Are you all right, Emma?'

'Yes thank you,' I said formally. 'Are you all right?'

'Yes, pet.'

'That's good,' I replied stiffly.

'I've really missed you, Emma. The house just isn't the same.'

'I've missed you too,' I said hollowly, conveying nothing of the hurt and heartache that tore me apart every day.

And that was more or less that. Unsatisfactory to say the least. Then there was the dress she had brought for me, which she unpacked after supper and held up for my inspection. It was no ordinary dress, but a dream dress in wartime, a beautiful deep blue check, long-sleeved, warm to the touch, and cut with a circular skirt, a luxury I had long wished for. When I pivoted, as I liked to do, it swung round in a full circle and swirled back as smoothly as a skater's skirt in a fast spin. My mother had saved clothing coupons for the material and made the dress herself, and when she unveiled it I felt in seventh heaven.

'Ooooh!' I cried ecstatically. 'It's the best dress I've ever seen in my life, the best dress in all the world.'

'Good. I'm so glad you like it,' she said. 'Now try it on, and let's see how it fits.'

It fitted perfectly, and I preened and pranced round the room, twirling the skirt like a ballerina, pirouetting in pure joy and wishing I had a mirror to see myself in action. For a while I was on top of the world, close to my mother and wearing my beautiful dress. Then I was struck by a sobering thought and came to a halt in mid-twirl.

'If you've come to take me home, Mum, why did you bother to bring the dress?'

Her face fell and she hesitated, and then sidestepped the question.

'We'll talk about that later, sweetheart. I've only just arrived.'

And instantly my pleasure in the dress diminished. Beautiful as it was, it brought back that cold, unwanted feeling that I had hoped was gone; now it felt almost like a bribe to stay away from home. I stopped preening and twirling, and the more I reflected on the meaning behind the gift, the more the new dress lost its magic, sadly becoming just another dress. Yet still I thought I might be mistaken in my suspicions and tried to stay optimistic, but as the week progressed I heard no mention from my mother of any intention to take me home. Suffering silently from perpetual uncertainty, I kept promising myself that I would ask directly, but somehow I was afraid of the answer. It was an awkward dilemma, so instead I simply pretended that all would be well, and despite my misgivings, tried to sustain hope.

Meanwhile, family relations slowly resumed some semblance of normality. My brothers reverted to their customary mischievous ways, and after a while I gave them a wide berth, attaching myself as usual to Uncle Matt. As it happened, Aunt Dot also responded less favourably to the boys than she had done on their previous visit, when they were at least useful in helping with haymaking. She constantly referred to them as 'hard work' and generally misunderstood their youthful high spirits. In a sort of nebulous way she was fond of them as nephews went, but as nephews went, she seemed to wish they would go. In fact, she gave the odd impression that she regarded boys as a strange species, variously complaining that they ate like vultures, had as many legs as an octopus, made a noise like a barrel-load of monkeys, and left footprints like pet elephants. I had an idea that she would have liked them better if they had learnt to levitate over the kitchen floor or eat biscuits without making crumbs, or if they had taken a vow of silence – or even earned their keep. As it was, she kept thrusting them outside to play.

'Right, boys. Out you go. Play in the fresh air for a while. I can't stand the noise, and besides, you make the house look untidy.'

The weather had turned cold, but she showed no concern, not until they began to create havoc round the farm. They scattered geese, chased heifers, tormented Split, set a trap for me that tripped Uncle Matt instead, and worst of all, untied Billy, head of the goat family. The bothersome business of the liberated goat was a major event involving us all. To the boys it was the highlight of the week, to Aunt Dot it was a major disaster, but it was perhaps best summed up afterwards by Uncle Matt, who described it as a 'right hoo-ha'.

Sometimes the goats at Windlestraw were tethered on long leads at the end of the stack yard, where they could graze the grass verges at the roadside. On the morning when, on a whim, the boys untied Billy, they carried sticks masquerading as rifles and marched him like a regimental mascot round and round the stack yard. But Billy soon tired of this military game. Being adept at breaking loose, he butted the boys aside and took his usual escape route over the garden wall and into the leek bed, leaving ruin in his wake, and sampling anything growing that was green. Uncle Matt emerged from the byre in time to see a white beard floating in mid-air, and for a moment he stood gaping in disbelief, then leapt into action, shaking his fist at the boys and shouting at the goat as if the rebellious animal spoke English and would be persuaded by reason.

'Hey there! Hey you! That's not for you. Come back here! Come out of it. Right now!' he yelled, but the goat went on nibbling delicately at the leeks.

'Ghrrrh! Gerrout of it! Or I'll cut your pesky legs off!' he threatened, as he sped in pursuit to defend his precious vegetables.

It seemed, however, that Billy did not understand English after all. He was making a healthy snack from some small but juicy Brussels sprouts, and proved too quick on his feet for Uncle Matt. Not for nothing are goats renowned for their nimbleness, and the fact that from the boys' viewpoint on the forecourt they cheered every unsuccessful tackle and shouted '*Olé!*' every time the goat eluded seizure only served to exacerbate the situation. The goat seemed encouraged by the audience participation, and Uncle Matt looked unsure as to whether they were cheering him or Billy. He tried to catch hold of the artful dodger by any available part – by tether or tail, by beard or horns, by anything to hand – but all to no avail. And he gradually came to understand in full measure the meaning of the expression 'acting the giddy goat'.

After about ten minutes of dodging and diving, puffing and panting, cursing and swearing, while the goat got the best of it, my uncle had reached the end of his own tether even though he had still failed to reach the goat's, and he was obliged to leave Billy, trampling and sampling to his heart's content, while he went for reinforcements. First he dashed into the washhouse, emerging with assorted weapons – brush, broom, besom, mop, pitchfork, and poss stick. Then he mobilized a squad of helpers, distributing one weapon to each. Aunt Dot was missing, having disappeared into the house to make a midmorning cup of tea, and he followed her in, leaving the front door open and forgetting for once to wipe his feet. She opened her mouth to complain, for she could talk for at least an hour on the subject of dirty feet, but, noticing the way every inch of him registered frustration, and the way he stood, trailing clouds of discontent behind him, she postponed criticism until later.

'Well, Matt, what's getting your goat?' she asked innocently.

He stared at her, stupefied. She had unwittingly gone to the nub of his problem.

'What's gettin' my goat?' he cried. 'I'll tell you what's gettin' my goat. It's *not* gettin' my goat! That's what's gettin' my goat!'

She raised her eyebrows and sniffed disapprovingly.

'Stop drivelling, Matt! I've no patience with tongue-twisters and conundrums and the like. Just get on with it! I'm busy making tea and I'm ready for it. Now, what is it you want?'

'*I'm* tellin' you! Aren't I tellin' you? It's the goat. It's Billy on the rampage. The boys've let him loose and he's in the garden, eatin' everything. We'll have nothin' left to see us through the winter. He needs to be shown who's boss, and I'll not be beat by a goat. But he takes notice of you, Dot. So come on. I have a plan.'

He hustled her outside and handed her the poss stick. Then he took command of the operation, a usurping of authority that she rarely tolerated, but for once she let him have his head. He stationed everybody in position, my brothers armed with broom and besom blocking the exit from stack yard to road, and my mother and I brandishing mop and brush respectively, barring entry to the backyard. Then he and Aunt Dot, wielding pitchfork and poss stick, prepared to tackle the elusive goat. But at the last moment David recklessly reappeared round the corner.

'I strongly fancy swapping for the poss stick, Uncle Matt,' he said. 'Can I exchange the broom for it?'

'Definitely not!' shouted Uncle Matt. 'You would get power crazy with a poss stick. Your Aunt Dot can handle it. She's used to givin' it what for. No, you stick to your broomstick, and with a bit of luck it might fly away and take you and your daft brother with it. Now, get back into position!'

Uncle Matt's plan was a simple one, involving inveigling Billy, by pitchfork and poss stick, out of the garden, round the forecourt, and into the stack yard, where he could be cornered and secured. In itself the plan could not be faulted, but the trouble was that Billy was not privy to the plan. He went on munching the season's last remaining carrot tops, showing no alarm as the armed pair entered the garden, and only mild interest at Uncle Matt's hunting cry of 'Gertcha! Gerrout of it! Out! Out! Out!' punctuated by ever closer threats from the pitchfork. It was only when he caught sight of Aunt Dot's steely eye, and received a hefty blow on the rump from her poss stick, that he lost interest in topping up his intake of greens and hastily fled the garden. And at first he trotted in accordance with the plan through the forecourt and towards the stack yard. Then, for some reason – whether because Neal in his enthusiasm waved the besom too wildly and upset him, or because goats are notoriously wilful and Billy more wilful than most – for whatever reason, he suddenly deviated from the plan and changed direction. Hemmed in on three sides, and beset by noisy people threatening him with long-handled implements, he could only see one clear way of escape, and that was to the left. He turned and charged the low stack-yard wall, taking an Olympian leap over it, but misjudged the distance and landed in the midden below, sinking slowly into its steamy depths.

We watched in awe and wonder as he sailed through the air, white and graceful as a swan, and then sank like a stone into a swamp. The boys found his plight hilarious, but not so Aunt Dot, who looked at them with furious narrowed eyes as if she would love to get her hands on them in some dark and lonely place, the darker and lonelier the better. Nor was Billy amused, because the act of extricating himself from the mire proved difficult. His renowned nimbleness, unbeatable on hard and hilly areas as well as in vegetable beds, clearly did not extend to manure heaps. Slowly he squelched out, struggling to find a foothold, every inch covered with filth. When at last he broke free and shook himself, he just stood there, impassive and subdued, all friskiness gone. Suddenly he was available for the taking, and suddenly no one wanted to take him. Then, with a sigh, Uncle Matt opened the meadow gate and forced himself to the task.

'Yuck! This is a job for kid gloves,' he said, unconscious of the double meaning, and reaching for the tether.

He returned Billy to the family corner and tied him securely to his post, but the other goats would have nothing to do with him, recoiling from the stink of him and retreating as far as their ropes would allow. At the best of times Billy gave off a strong, offensive aroma, sometimes worse than others, but never rose-scented, and surprisingly his family seemed to approve of it. But not so his present overpowering stench, and he became a social outcast, popular only with the halo of flies that circled his head. To restore social relations he had to be hosed down, as did the corner of the stack yard and the route he had taken through it.

'Oh dear me. More work,' complained Aunt Dot, looking daggers at the boys, 'and it's all your fault. What a pity you had to let him loose! And what a pity you can't find anything better to do than get into mischief. Dear heaven! It's dreadful! It's sinful! All this extra work!'

Throughout the afternoon she stormed with a face like thunder from house to byre and back again, speaking to no one, looking through everyone. And for once my usually resilient uncle also sulked. The boys had unleashed one of his nightmares, a footloose and fancy-free Billy, and he vented his rage by taking himself off to the pasture, where he mowed great swathes of reeds with the scythe, swinging the blade with a dangerously vicious action and looking as if he wished the boys were underneath. Trying to pour oil on troubled waters, my mother attached herself first to my aunt and then to my uncle, in a vain attempt to smooth things over, but after a time she lapsed into despair.

'We might have to go home soon, Emma,' she confided.

'How soon?' I asked, with mixed emotions, desperate to keep her with me, but thinking that if she included me in her departure plans, then soon could not be soon enough.

'Sooner than expected,' she answered, leaving me still in doubt.

The atmosphere remained strained all day, with tension building till it could be cut with a knife, till it was as thick and heavy as Aunt Dot's pastry. Even Split was affected by the general mood. Mindful of his legs, he skulked at a distance from the viciously swinging scythe, and his tail, which usually wagged like a metronome, drooped despondently between his legs. There was no sign of tea, and no preparations were being made for supper. Aunt Dot's face remained steadfastly grim, and my mother was about to start packing. But late that evening something happened that changed everything, not only the tense family atmosphere, but also the course of the week. It began with the sound of an aeroplane flying low over the hills, an infrequent circumstance and one that the locals were inclined to ignore, there being no air raids as such up there and little other than sheep for the enemy to bomb. But the boys had learnt to identify the different planes and to distinguish friend from foe.

'It's one of theirs,' said David, listening intently, 'and it's a bomber.'

'Yes, and it's in trouble,' Neal agreed.

We all rushed outside to have a view of the plane, and sure enough, a dark shape was slowly descending towards the horizon, the engine coughing and spluttering.

'I think it's a Dornier,' said Neal confidently.

'No, it's a Heinkel. I bet you anything it's a Heinkel,' asserted David.

They began to argue and then, seeing Aunt Dot's sour expression, automatically subsided. The plane stuttered a little and then stopped. Whining as it fell, it plummeted through the air nose down and crashed onto the hilltop, bursting in a series of explosions into a pillar of flame that lit the sky like a spectacular sunset. For some time we gazed transfixed as the fire raged, steadily turned to a plume of black smoke, and then vanished, as if it had never been, as if nothing had happened. Staring at the fell in astonishment and shock, we could hardly believe that death and destruction could be so swift and leave no apparent trace. The crash became the talking point of the evening, taking everyone's mind off the goat, and diverting Aunt Dot from her 'what a pity' routine. She and my mother made a cottage pie from corned beef, and we were all friends again. The sudden and shocking demonstration of the thin line between life and death seemed to put everything into perspective.

Naturally the boys begged to be taken to see the wrecked enemy plane, and Uncle Matt, who greatly preferred a trip out to catching up with his chores, was easily persuaded of the merit of the idea. So too was Aunt Dot, who elected to stay home and enjoy the peace of a day without us. She packed a picnic, however, and the next day, as soon as farm business would allow, we set off. We tramped for miles over the moors, walking mainly uphill and constantly disturbing red grouse hidden in the heather. They rose abruptly in front of us, whirring with spread wings into startled flight, and startling us in return with their sharp, inhospitable cry, designed to repel invaders.

'Go-bak, go-bak, bak, bak. Bak.' It was a barking call, reminding me of Aunt Dot's strident tones when directing the cows.

I would gladly have taken the birds' advice, because the walk seemed never ending. But the other explorers were determined to press on, Uncle Matt leading the way, whistling cheerfully, and steering us past bogs and swamps and a large dam that attracted the boys like a magnet. I kept my distance from this frighteningly vast expanse of water, but they were keen to return another day and take a swim.

'No way!' said Uncle Matt brusquely. 'Not on your nelly. Just do as you're told for once and keep away. That water's deep and them sides shelve down real sharp. Hear what I'm sayin'? Once you got in I doubt you'd ever get out, and whereas we'd all get a bit of peace, your mother might miss you just a bit.'

We trudged on, and walking on heather proved more difficult than it looked. It was hard going, but I made no complaints. I would have followed my mother to the ends of the earth – which was more or less where we seemed to be headed. Eventually we reached the soaring heights of Lornhope, the summit of which was marked by a tall stone cairn, and sheltering behind it from the wind, we sat eating our sandwiches. It struck me as strange that I had become part of a view I looked at every day, rather like walking into a painting, except that there was nothing there, nothing but heather as far as the eye could see. The boys had been right – there was no edge of the world on this horizon. Hills rolled into more hills, moors into more moors, and the faded heather interspersed with patches of green and brown looked like a soldier's camouflage, as if Mother Nature had disguised the landscape until spring arrived. We had walked all that way to find a wilderness, simply that and nothing more.

'You can see five counties from here,' said Uncle Matt proudly, with the air of one who had personally contrived this feat.

He stood a little apart from us and I ran towards him, eager for a view of a different county, but to use one of his own expressions, if there was any difference they were all alike. The Lornhope wind, icy at any level, at this altitude cut straight through flimsy clothes and froze the blood, and I tried to shelter behind the others. Fortunately we soon came across evidence of the aeroplane, though someone had beaten us to it and removed all the large pieces. A huge hole had been blown in the ground and small metal fragments littered the heather. The boys instantly began collecting souvenirs, amassing metal parts as if they intended reconstructing the plane, and also stuffing their pockets with shrapnel until my mother stopped them.

'I'm not carrying that lot home,' she said, 'and neither are you. We'd need an extra suitcase. Just choose a few pieces, boys. We've enough luggage already.'

I saw my chance and for once I grasped it.

'Yes, and there'll be my clothes to carry this time too,' I pointed out. 'That's more luggage.'

No answer came from anyone, only a snigger from the boys.

'My luggage as well,' I repeated, not to be discouraged.

A look of pain crossed my mother's face. She bent down and gave me a long hug and kissed my cheek, and I clung to her tightly as I should have done when she first arrived. This sudden display of affection, once an everyday occurrence but nowadays a rare treat, sent my spirits soaring like the startled grouse, but in an instant they fell just as steeply, as she sighed and answered in a voice both hesitant and sad.

'Well, pet – maybe not yet – not just yet, Emma. Not this time, but soon, very soon. Maybe next time.'

'Why?' I gasped in anguish. 'I thought you'd come for me. Why can't I go home? Uncle Matt said I could. He promised.' I turned accusingly on my uncle. 'You promised. You crossed your heart and hoped to die and everything.'

'Well I will die, Emma,' he said, justifying his position, 'but hopefully not just yet eh? It's the war to blame, not me. Can't help the war, pet.'

'Yes, you're safer here just now,' said my mother. 'For the time being, at least. You see, no one knows what will happen next. We could be invaded.'

'But why?' I asked again, at a loss to understand, my one coherent thought the knowledge that no matter what, I wanted to be with her. 'The boys are home. Why not me as well?'

'Well, you're just little. You're my baby,' she said, 'and the danger's always there. But it won't be for long, pet. Not long till the war's over.'

I did not, could not comprehend. Only one fact clearly emerged. Once again I was being penalized because I was little. Would I, I wondered, ever be big enough to matter in this bewildering world? Then my mother gave me a final squeeze and stood up, and I curled into myself, chilled and shivering from head to foot, clutching my elbows, clenching my knees, unable at first to move. Despite the recent hug I felt intensely cold and deeply hurt. I had been so sure of myself, so sure that she would take me with her, and now, after all the waiting, after all the joyful anticipation, it was not to be. My own mother had refused to take me back home!

The wind felt even colder and fiercer as we set off for the farm, and with the air of a sleepwalker I trudged after the others, now taking the full brunt of the wind but no longer caring. Behind us the moors turned threatening and dark, reflecting my mood, and a chill mist crept close on our heels, following us down. I kept up with the others, who were hurrying to outstrip it, looking forward to a warm fire and hoping against the odds for a hot meal. And to everyone's surprise, Aunt Dot provided one. She greeted us cheerfully, and we were met by a welcoming smell of stew and dumplings, which she served at once, though I had little appetite for mine. I was already bowed down by the weight of woe, without the extra weight of Aunt Dot's dumplings, which tended to sink like lead and sit heavily on the stomach. I surreptitiously transferred my dumpling to Uncle Matt's plate, and sat silent and inconsolable, toying disinterestedly with the highly peppered stew. Fortunately, Aunt Dot was too busy talking to notice me. She had enjoyed her peaceful day and spent it planning more of the same, working out how to occupy the boys and keep them out of her way.

'I have a nice little job for you two tomorrow,' she said. 'What a pity I didn't think of it sooner. After all, it *is* blackberry week, and tomorrow you boys can pick blackberries. I'm sure your mother won't mind making a nice blackberry pie while I get on with other things.'

'But – there aren't any blackberries around here,' pointed out Neal.

'Oh yes, there are,' said Aunt Dot triumphantly. 'You know that ruined house halfway down the hill next to the Downleys' place? Well, the garden's overgrown, so you'll have to watch out for nettles, but you'll find blackberries galore. We can have two pies, or even jam, depending how many you pick.'

'But the Downleys are those queer people, aren't they?' asked David cautiously. 'The man who looks like the Devil. Don't fancy that much.'

'Me neither,' said Neal. 'I didn't like the look of him.'

'Wouldn't want to cross him, Aunt Dot,' said David.

'Nor me,' said Neal.

I raised my dejected eyes and spoke for the first time since leaving Lornhope.

'I'll go, Aunt Dot. I know Mrs Downley and I'm not frightened. I'll pick your blackberries,' I said, no longer caring what happened to me. But I stung the boys into bravery.

'Oh, it's not that I'm frightened. Not in the least,' declared David.

'Nor me. Not at all,' said Neal, and Aunt Dot smiled happily.

'Good. That's settled then. Blackberry pies tomorrow.'

I suspected that the boys prayed for rain, but the next day dawned bright and still, removing any last-minute excuses. Armed with billy-cans and baskets they reluctantly set off, and I stayed home, frightened of neither Downleys nor devils, but wary of being pushed into nettles. My mother and Aunt Dot busied themselves sorting cupboards, and I curled up on the window sill to read, though without much concentration. From my seat I could see the cairn on Lornhope, reminding me of the moment my mother had refused to take me home, a bitter memory indeed. For a short while, however, all was peaceful, and then suddenly the boys were back, well and truly disturbing that peace. They galloped, shrieking excitedly down the steps, across the yard, and through the kitchen, their empty billycans clashing together as they vied to be first over the threshold, and once again forgot to wipe their feet. Aunt Dot sighed, her only consolation being that at least they were not wearing out her mats.

'What on earth's the matter?' she demanded, and they both began to talk at once.

'A spy! We saw a spy! In the old ruin. Honestly, Aunt Dot, we did. He went into the house.'

'Oh yes? And how did you know he was a spy? Did he say so?'

'We saw him go in, didn't we, Neal? And the funny thing was – the really weird thing was – he went in as a man in uniform and came out a woman.'

'Well, that *is* odd,' she murmured. 'Are you sure that's what happened?'

'Oh yes,' said David. 'We saw him walk down the hill and go in, looking sort of furtive, so we hid in the reeds on the bank and kept watch. When he came out he wore a frock and a fur cape and a woman's hat and everything. But his legs looked peculiar. Sort of bandy and knobbly, and not like a woman's legs.'

'What do you know about women's legs?' enquired Aunt Dot sharply.

'Nothing,' David replied, blushing. 'But they're just different, that's all. Nicely shaped, like Betty Grable's. His were sort of lumpy, and he wobbled about in his high heels.'

'You're not making this story up, are you?' asked Aunt Dot distrustfully, her initial instincts telling her that they had invented the whole thing to annoy her, or to get out of picking fruit, or both.

'But it could happen, Dot,' said my mother. 'He could be a spy. These lonely fells are just the sort of out-of-the-way place a spy would land. He'd be very unlucky to be spotted.'

'Yes, and now we've spotted him, we have to do something,' said Neal, tugging impatiently at Aunt Dot's sleeve. 'We have to tell the police. Straight away.'

With a touch of irritation she dusted his hand from her person.

'Tell the police, Neal? And how do you propose to do that? Where do you think you'll find a policeman round here, eh? On duty in the pasture perhaps? Or catching criminals in the hen-house? Or directing traffic in the byre?'

Neal fell silent, taken aback, but David took up the plea for action.

'But we must do something, Aunt Dot. We can't just let him get away. Can't we phone somebody?'

'Phone somebody? For a spy-catcher you're not very observant. There's no phone in the valley, just the kiosk at Thorny Edge, and by the time you get down there your so-called spy will be long gone.'

The boys stared at her disbelievingly. The suspected spy was the most exciting event they had experienced since the war started. It was the stuff of adventure stories, the stuff of movies. They could, they felt, be famous – heroes even. And there they were, stuck in the wilds without transport or any means of communication. They were helpless, their word doubted and their actions restrained by unhelpful adults. Desperately disappointed, they decided to go back to the old ruin, searching for clues to dispel disbelief, creeping through tufted reed grasses, called sparts, like saboteurs on a secret mission. They found nothing, and after a time remembered to pick blackberries, bringing back almost enough to satisfy even Aunt Dot's exacting standards.

The next morning, however, brought excitement and vindication when the postman arrived. The boys rushed to meet him and returned jubilant, waving a newspaper and whooping and cheering as if they had, after all, caught the spy. A German spy had indeed been caught. He had admitted landing on Sourhope moors and changing his clothes in a ruined house. He had been captured in Shiretown, where he had aroused suspicion when pursued from a gentlemen's toilet by a group of astonished farmers who, having recently imbibed freely of the local ale at the Magpie and Stump, showed no hesitation in giving chase. It was reported that they took exception to his frock and the fact that he was wearing lipstick, despite its being the latest fetching shade of Blush Pink.

After that there was no holding the boys. They boasted incessantly of their cleverness in recognizing a spy and we were bombarded by talk of war, which in the daily routine of the farm formed only a distant dark background to our lives. They had moved the war to the forefront in various ways – first by their military march that sent the goat on the rampage, then by searching the moors for morbid souvenirs of the crashed enemy plane, and lastly by discovering the spy. And to cap all, in a rare rash moment, Aunt Dot told them of Mr Shoeman's suspicious activities, so from then on it was as if the whole valley abounded in spies. They spent the rest of the week spying for spies, and imagined they could see one behind every sheep.

In retrospect it seemed to me that they had somehow brought the war with them, and I hoped that they would take it away again when they left. For with scant regard for my feelings, isolated as I was in Sourhope because of the hated war, they talked of little else, telling the spy story over and over until I felt heartily sick of hearing it. And since a tale never loses in the telling, so it was that they convinced themselves that they had been instrumental in capturing the spy, whereas in truth all that they had captured amounted to five billy-cans of blackberries.

Chapter 11

For the Rain it Raineth Every Day

My family departed on the Sunday, leaving me bereft once more. This time I declined to go to Thorny Edge to see them off, not wishing to repeat that previous bitter experience of watching the red bus take away from me the person I loved most in the world. I had tried what seemed like a thousand times to persuade my mother to change her mind, asking my favourite question 'Why?' again and again, until my persistence drove the entire household to distraction, but I received no satisfactory answer.

'You're safer here,' was all she said, though safer from what or from whom was never properly explained.

'You might get bombed if you go home with us,' was David's helpful contribution, and Neal agreed with a pleasurable glint in his eyes that the Nazis would be sure as anything to drop a bomb on me.

'I don't know why they should,' I retorted. 'You two deserve to be bombed a lot more than I do.' But they just laughed at my annoyance and frustration.

What puzzled me was that I was supposed to be safe in Sourhope, yet I had never felt less safe than in those recent weeks of separation. Without my mother, my sense of security, my sense of belonging had been badly shaken. And now I began to worry on her account, for her safety, as it stood to reason that whatever danger kept me shut away in these remote hills must constantly threaten her. Of course I knew about the war, and vaguely envisaged an immense and powerful force, a sort of fierce army of Mr Shoemans, moustached and militant, terrorizing and killing indiscriminately, but in my child's mind there remained a mystery: why would such a mighty fighting force concentrate its efforts on attacking an inconsequential little person like me if I should go home, yet consistently ignore my brothers' permanent presence there? I resented being treated differently, being singled out and cruelly excluded from all that I

149

held dear, but by the time departure day dawned I had at least become numbly resigned.

In any case it was a morning when the weather took charge, and the sensible thing to do was to stay indoors. So fiercely unremitting were the wind and rain that I was not even allowed to follow my family to the car. Yet in a curious way the turbulent weather was a comfort to me, expressing my feelings far more eloquently than I could myself. At any rate I liked to think so, to imagine that the elements had gathered round on my behalf to express their sympathy and support. For it happened that overnight a storm blew up, lashing itself by degrees into such a fury that by morning it had gone completely berserk. The wind raged at the house, howling at doors, wailing at windows, moaning round the chimney pot and whistling angrily down the chimney, scattering trails of soot across the hearthrug. Outdoors it sent buckets rattling over the flagstones, rolling like drums and clashing like cymbals, and tore at the rowan tree till the branches groaned, bending fit to break. And the rain joined in, weeping for me, rapidly developing into a deluge that swirled round sinks and brimmed over the trough, to flow in floods across the yard.

My mother gave me a quick kiss, assured me that the war would soon be over, and promised faithfully to return at Christmas. Then, holding a borrowed coat over her head, she ran out into the storm. The boys followed, sharing an umbrella that kept blowing inside out, and I stood rigid in the doorway, determined to show no emotion, but conscious of a dull ache in my chest, and unconsciously clenching my fists until the nails dug deep indentations. Despite the wet weather, the perverse car started first time, and I caught a brief glimpse of blurred faces and frantically waving hands. I waved back slowly and sadly, struggling to control my tears.

Then for some reason the engine backfired with a loud report, startling Uncle Matt into lifting his foot and losing first gear. The hand-waving became more spasmodic, and feeling rather stupid, I stopped waving at all. Then a sound like a machine cutting through stone, followed by the noise of a knife-grinder at work, indicated that he was trying to regain the gear, and after a few attempts the car spluttered forward and was gone. And curiously the storm abated a little, but the deluge stayed with us, raining on and on remorselessly day after day, completely overdoing its gesture of sympathy. I had never seen such rain, and began to envisage a flood of biblical proportions.

'Will it *ever* stop raining, Uncle Matt?' I enquired of my oracle.

'Your guess is as good as mine, pet,' he answered lugubriously. 'My meanin' is, up here at this time of year it could keep on comin' down till we all grow gills and fins and turn into fish.'

'And will you have to build an ark like Noah and take the animals in two by two?'

'It's an idea, Emma. You never know. It might come to that.'

'Can we take Beauty as one of the chosen calves and Gertie as one of the two hens, Uncle Matt?'

'Oh, I'll leave that up to you, pet. You're good at choosin'.'

'Then I think we'll leave all the geese behind,' I decided, finding a bright side to adversity.

'And mebbe your aunt Dot an' all if things don't improve,' he said with a wink. 'Right now I wouldn't mind sailin' away from her tongue.'

I knew exactly what he meant. Aunt Dot had become steadily more and more depressed, and characteristically took out her displeasure on her nearest and dearest. Her small face was forever puckered in a frown, rather like October's pig before my improvements, and her shrill voice reached new ear-piercing heights as she railed against the weather and the extra work it caused. For no one suffered life's vicissitudes as keenly as Aunt Dot.

'I'm just so sick of the rain,' she complained one morning to the postman. 'Sick to death of it. It's really too bad to bear. The worst I can remember. I can't stand much more of it. Really and truly, I can't.'

He stood wavering on the outside mat, full of ambition to attain the second, inner mat. He kept leaning forward for shelter and optimistically raising one foot off the ground as the rain cascaded in tiers over his various waterproof layers, dripping off the brim of his sou'wester, dribbling from his yellow cape, and running down over his high-laced boots. But any aspirations he nurtured of being invited in were doomed to disappointment. Aunt Dot would never tolerate a human fountain in her spotless kitchen. In fact, she gradually edged forward, casting indignant glances at the pools he was forming on the outside mat, which was rapidly turning into a footbath. Without moving too close to the downpour, she insidiously eased him out, and he finally took the hint and stepped back, rummaging in the mail bag under his oilskin cape for her letters and handing them over as he spoke.

'Aye. It's gay hard. A reet clashy spell.'

Gobbledegook, I thought, but she seemed to grasp his meaning.

'Clashy? Oh, it's clashy all right. It's got me clashed to death, I can tell you. It makes so much extra work. Work, work, work! That's all I do. Nothing but work. I'll be so glad when it's spring. I just can't wait.'

But he soon put her right on that score, muttering lugubriously in his doom-laden way, 'Aye. Ne doot. But spring's a canny bit off. It's still only back-end remember. There's worse than this ter come. We hev the howl o' the year yet.'

'The – er – what was that?' she asked, wishing she had an interpreter.

'Why, winter, of course,' he said gloomily. 'An' onny-hou, up here we reckon on six months o' winter and then six months o' bad weather.'

So much for the Sourhope climate, I thought. It sounded a bleak prospect, leaving little to look forward to, and for the present we were always wet and often soaked to the skin. Another chore had been added to my aunt's unending workload, that of drying clothes, and it soon began to cause problems. She always claimed that she never looked for work because it found her soon enough, so when it came to the weekly wash she only laundered what was strictly necessary. But those items she did wash she treated harshly and without mercy, being very heavy-handed for a small person. As I watched her on washdays I formed the impression that once the clothes had offended her by allowing themselves to get dirty, she punished them by torturing them almost to death.

First she soaked them in Oxydol powder or dipped them in bleach, then she scrubbed and pummelled and rubbed them roughly over the corrugations of a washboard until the more delicate sufferers turned threadbare under the strain. Then some of her victims were boiled alive like lobsters, and the rest were pounded with a copper-bottomed poss stick, otherwise used for removing goats from the garden. She moved around the zinc tub as a witch might circle a cauldron, stabbing and stirring the clothes as she scurried through clouds of soda-smelling steam. Next she drowned them all in cold water, rinsing them until they surrendered, squeaky clean, when she wrung their necks by hand before winding them through the mangle, wrenching impatiently at the handle, often cracking their buttons, while they squealed in protest. Some turned pale from the effect of a whitener called Dolly Blue, deliberately added to the water, and some were starched till they stiffened, emerging rigid as boards. Then at last, weather permitting, there followed a good blow outside, where they hung propped high in the air, stretched and pegged on the line and soaring in the wind, flapping and leaping like so many demented spirits straining to fly away. I sympathized with their plight, for I too felt pegged on a line, straining to fly away home.

Nor did the torture end there. When the washing had been recaptured it was pressed with a flat iron, which she wielded as fearlessly as a blacksmith forging iron in a furnace. She dropped her iron into the fire, adroitly hooked it out with heavy tongs, and tested the heat by flicking water on the bottom so that beads of moisture danced on the hot surface and spat off it, propelled into the air. Then she clipped the hot iron into its metal case and wielded it like a weapon, pressing it down with a hiss on the damp defenceless captives like someone branding cattle, and flattening them as if attacking her worst enemy. But with the battle won and the washing defeated, she smoothed, patted and folded everything to crisp perfection.

Finally acceptable to her, the sufferers were forgiven and placed to be aired on a long wooden rack, suspended in front of the living-room range, and raised or lowered by means of a pulley. Normally this contraption was scarcely noticeable when the washing hung in neat rows covering the slats, but with the ceaseless bout of wet weather, the whole business had gone totally out of control, the pulley perpetually in operation and the rack overflowing with garments not yet washed or ironed, casual hangings festooned overhead as though it were Flag Day. A supplementary dryer had to be brought into service, a makeshift clothes horse that stood steaming in front of the fire, keeping the heat in and lending the habitually immaculate room the higgledy-piggledy chaotic air of a second-hand clothes shop.

Throughout the crisis Aunt Dot let her sufferings be loudly and widely known, and it never occurred to her that anyone else might also be inconvenienced. More than once when I hesitated on the threshold before venturing outside into a torrential downpour she pushed me out with the comforting words, 'Go on, girl. Off you go. You won't shrink and you won't drown,' and without another thought about my suffering, she returned to her self-absorbed pursuits. Fortunately, however, Joe always showed consideration for my welfare, and during this wet spell he made a special effort to arrive on time to collect the milk so that I could at least reach school fairly dry.

'Ah'll try an' get here sharp every mornin' fer a bit. Try me best, like. We hev ta keep ya dry, bonny lass. That skimpy coat's no good when it's dreepin' wet. Noo, if Ah can get here soon, Ah will.'

And he was as good as his word, which was just as well, because the school offered little provision for drying clothes, only a small stove which we in the infant class clustered round with steam rising in front of us like a valley mist. On wet days we were allowed to stay indoors all day, but it was the journey home that did the damage, and many a day I returned home looking like a drowned rat. If I took the short cut across the fields my feet sank in the mud, especially in the marshy pasture, which gradually grew soggier and soggier, deteriorating into a quagmire. The fields were awash like an enormous swamp, the Sourhope version of the Florida Everglades that I had read about, except that no alligators crawled out, though I would not have been surprised to see one, or a crocodile either, but I guessed that Sourhope would have been too cold for them. Instead I came across big pink worms wriggling with pleasure at the rain, and nasty black slugs and snails washed out of hibernation. Often I disturbed the cows huddled together in the meadow, their heads turned from the driving rain. They churned the mud as they stumbled away, and glowered at me as if they thought me responsible for their damp discomfort.

On the other hand, if I opted for the other route, which my aunt began to insist upon, the walk took much longer and in time turned just as wet, the road becoming almost a river, that swilled soil and mud and grass from the verges and gathered in depth and momentum as it ran downhill. I still wound up as drenched and bedraggled as a string of seaweed, and Aunt Dot's comments at the sight of me became increasingly caustic. One evening when the rain was driven almost horizontal, I burst into the living room, wringing wet and dripping on everything, and I saw her face fall even further than usual. I could never be sure of my welcome in that house, and when faced with a hostile reception I tried to be as little trouble as possible.

'It's just my coat that's wet, Aunt Dot,' I said, making light of the situation.

'Nonsense, girl! You're soaked to the skin,' she retorted angrily.

She stormed into the kitchen and returned dragging the tin bath.

'More work for me,' she moaned. 'You'd better take everything off and have a bath straight away. Dear heaven! Will my work *never* end?'

I complied quietly, though I would have preferred a hot drink first while I thawed in front of the fire. But as she began filling the tin bath I reflected that the same procedure would probably have applied at home, my real home, had I returned from school in such a state, the difference being that it would have been done with concern and loving kindness. Then Aunt Dot noticed my shoes, and I cringed. I had to admit that they looked dreadful – saturated and discoloured where the dye had run, marbling my socks with unsightly brown streaks. Both shoes and socks lay in a sodden heap oozing dirty liquid, like an unspecified but unpleasant creature that had been drowned and recently retrieved. The depressing spectacle of that sopping pile seemed to be the last straw, and while I shivered in the cold room, she stiffened in every limb.

'You've walked up the fields, haven't you?' she said grimly, more an accusation than a question.

'No, Aunt Dot. I came up the road,' I answered honestly, but looking guilty in my nervousness.

'Don't tell lies, girl. You're always telling lies. I can see by your face you're lying.'

'No, Aunt Dot, I'm not. Honestly. The road's almost as bad as the fields right now. Just as squelchy. Like a muddy river. And the rain came on really heavily halfway home.'

'You haven't been on the road, you wicked girl. Tell the truth for once.'

'It is the truth. Honestly it is. It *is!*' I protested, wide-eyed with fright.

She stared at me with icy grey eyes. Then suddenly something seemed to snap, and she bent down and began smacking my legs, hitting out in temper, blaming me for the weather, for the extra work, and for her own frailty and fatigue. Vulnerably naked and trembling with cold and fear, I recoiled in shock. Not that she greatly hurt me physically – my legs were too numb with cold to retain much sensation – but my feelings were a different matter, the depth of that hurt in my insecure circumstances being immeasurable.

'No, Aunt Dot. No, don't! I haven't done anything wrong,' I cried, my voice shaking, but she just went on hitting and hitting.

'Wicked girl! Wicked, wicked! Thoughtless, selfish, naughty girl!'

The blows kept time with the words, and I tried to protect my legs, to fend off the blows, only to have my arms smacked as well.

'I'll tell my mother. I will!' I shouted in panic, an idle threat with my mother so far away, yet it seemed to make her all the more incensed, and she retorted in a piercing shriek, 'Don't worry. I'll tell her myself!

I'll tell her what a wicked, wicked girl you are. Dear heaven! Just look at all the work you've made me. Look! Look!'

Furiously she grabbed the shoes and socks and held them up, thrusting them in my face until I smelled the stench of mud and soaking wet leather. Then she threw them angrily across the floor, and the blows came again, thick and fast. My mother had never hit me, nor needed to, and the sheer injustice of being cruelly punished for something that was no fault of mine filled me with indignation and despair. Again the suffering was more mental than physical, and in the dim recesses of my young mind I half-understood. I vaguely realized that she was not so much hitting me as hitting out at the deal that life had dealt her, at the harsh climate and hard work, the constant struggle and futility of trying. I could see the exhaustion on her face and knew that she was fragile in everything except will power. But sadly this insight lessened neither the pain nor the humiliation.

In abject misery I took a silent bath and ate a silent meal. As usual my tea consisted of a boiled egg with bread and butter, every bite of which turned to ashes in my mouth. I could not even be bothered to cut the bread into the customary soldiers to dunk in the egg yoke, or finish with a slice of fruit cake, though like most children I had a sweet tooth. After tea I sat white and trembling by the fireside, ostensibly reading a library book, but reading the same page over and over again and taking none of it in. I felt utterly lost and unloved and very much alone.

Aunt Dot, on the other hand, recovered quickly. She had a mercurial temperament, which I put down to the mysterious qualities of her red hair, and her moods changed quickly and totally. By the time Uncle Matt came in she had calmed down and begun to behave as if nothing had happened. She bustled about attending to things, betraying no sign of her explosive temper except for two bright scarlet spots like dabs of rouge on her cheeks. My smarting red legs were hidden under a clean white nightdress, long enough to cover their punishment, and now, freshly laundered like the clothes on washday, I had become acceptable again. Nevertheless, Uncle Matt seemed to sense something wrong, perhaps alerted by my prolonged silence, because I usually waited eagerly for him and prattled away fifty to the dozen. He scrutinized me keenly and stroked my hair in passing.

'You're very quiet, Emma. Are you all right, pet?'

I could feel Aunt Dot's grey eyes boring into me, watchful as a cat, and I answered without looking up.

'Yes, thank you.'

'Sure now, Emma? Haven't heard a peep out of you so far tonight.'

'I'm all right, Uncle Matt.'

He set off towards the kitchen, tripped over my soggy shoes, and returned, carrying them and looking puzzled.

'What on earth are these doin' here? That's not like you, Emma. You're generally tidy as anythin'. And they're soakin' wet! Now, Emma, why didn't you have your wellies on today?'

'One of them has a hole in the sole, Uncle Matt,' I said, still with my head bent.

'Oh heck, Emma! That's awful. Why didn't you say? We'll have to put that right. You'll catch your death wearin' femmer shoes like those in this clarty weather. I'll buy you some new wellies on Tuesday. I will, pet. That's a promise. Now you can count that as definite,' he said, with a touch of defiance, as if threatening anyone who might try to stop him.

'Thank you, Uncle Matt.'

'And mebbe a pair of ridin' breeches as well. They'd keep your legs nice and warm. But you must have had terrible wet feet. No wonder you look chilled to the bone. You're not sickenin' for somethin', now are you, Emma?'

'I don't think so,' I answered tonelessly, still bent over the book.

He patted my head fondly and turned to my aunt.

'She's not herself, Dot. Definitely not. She's probably got a chill. We'll all catch pneumonia if this blasted weather keeps up. I reckon she should have an early night. Tell you what – I'll nip up and put a hot water bottle in her bed.'

I struggled to smile at him, grateful for his concern, needing at that moment the warmth of affection even more than a warm bed, though I thought a warm bed would be nice. I glanced nervously at Aunt Dot, but unpredictable as ever, she had become benevolent again. Like turning on a light switch, the dark mood had lifted and she now radiated kindness.

'That's all right, Matt. You have your tea. Kettle's boiled. I'll fill a bottle for Emma's bed. A stone one I think. It'll warm the sheets through thoroughly.'

She took the piping hot water bottle upstairs, and then busied herself over the range. In a little while she advanced upon me, and not knowing what to expect I shrank back in apprehension. With a cold smile she handed me a steaming mug, which I accepted with caution in case it should be scalding or poisoned, and placed it on the hearth, allowing it to cool. But as Aunt Dot constantly inspected me through narrowed eyes, I finally tasted it, and it turned out to be a delicious drink of boiled milk stirred with demerara sugar and ground ginger – warm, sweet and aromatic. I took some comfort from its rich sweetness, savouring every mouthful, and then collected my book and candle and well-hugged teddy bear, the only toy brought from home, and retired thankfully to bed, away from prying eyes. There I curled up with the stone bed-warmer, which I liked better than rubber bottles because it slid easily round the feather bed and kept its heat longer. But I lay awake long after I had snuffed the candle and long after the bottle had grown cold. I lay uneasily, feeling like an alien in a hostile house, wondering what had happened to my hitherto pleasant existence and whether I could be in any way to blame for the painful turn in my life.

And sadly I was to spend numerous nights in such unhappy speculation, because that beating was the first of many, featuring as a regular and demoralizing part of my new life. Once she had embarked on the pattern of punishment, Aunt Dot revealed herself to be a lively flyweight fighter, hitting out compulsively at whatever small misdemeanours on my part happened to annoy her. But worse than that, she usually waited until I had fallen asleep and then woke me, often brandishing the evidence in my face as she had with the muddy shoes, like 'Exhibit A' in a court of law. Then, having appointed herself judge, jury, and executioner, she proceeded to administer a painful reminder of my faults, all the more upsetting because I was still half-asleep.

After a while I began to sleep badly, tending to lie miserably awake for ages, listening to the musical spring below, now a torrent, a full orchestra of sounds, and adding my own contribution to the watery ensemble by crying myself to sleep. Eventually I confided in Uncle Matt, but he scratched his head in bewilderment as he contemplated the impossibility of taking either side. He did his best to protect me, but his task was similar to that of standing in the path of a typhoon and trying to hold it back. From then on, however, he started bringing me back small surprise presents whenever he went anywhere, spoiling me as much as he could. But as he had a fondness for rituals, there was always a teasing procedure to be gone through each time before the gift came into my possession.

'Guess which hand, Emma?' he would say, with both hands behind his back and a beaming smile on his face in anticipation of my pleasure.

And somehow I never chose the correct hand until he had tired of the game, but I bore the wait patiently, fully aware that the presents he brought, from liquorice laces to dolly mixtures, from ribbons to hair slides, and from puzzle books to magic tins of coloured bubbles that you blew through a metal ring, would be of little use to him or my aunt, and even less to Split. So the final ownership was never in doubt, and as well as these welcome offerings, he offered advice based on his own experience of dealing with the difficult and exacting Aunt Dot.

'Now, Emma, this is what you do. Don't ruffle her feelings, pet. My meanin' is, her feelings ruffle faster than anybody I know. Faster than Sandy gallops when he's on the run. So you be nice and butter her up a bit. She likes that. You'll definitely be on a winner there. Give her a bit of the old soft soap. Does no harm, even if you don't mean it. And it keeps her happy. Leastways as happy as she ever gets.'

'But I always try to be nice, Uncle Matt.'

'Yes, but you've got to try harder, pet. Lay it on with a trowel. That's what I do. You can't have too much of a good thing, Emma. And never, ever, argue with her. Even when you're sure you're right. Never contradict. She doesn't like to be put in the wrong. She really hates that. Oh Emma, I tell you, she does hate that!'

I took these wise words to heart and observed him carefully, noticing that he hardly suffered at all from the backlash of my aunt's Jekyll and Hyde personality. For a start she refrained from hitting him, as far as I knew, and rarely sharpened her tongue on him the way she regularly did on me. It soon became apparent that he had learnt to handle her with finesse, better than he handled the horse, the goat, or the dog. Perhaps it was because the animals were not susceptible to flattery, and he usually persuaded them of his point of view with a sharp kick in the shins – a convincing argument, but one that would never have done for Aunt Dot. With her he trod warily, always letting her think she was boss, and always covering his tracks, never accepting blame for anything. I knew that I had to become more like him, more devious and less spontaneous. My aunt, the perfectionist, sought to turn me into a mirror image of herself, but instead she made me defensive and diffident, secretive and deceitful.

So I vented my pent-up emotions on November's pig. Though the

159

month was well advanced, I had hesitated putting finishing touches to this particular portrait because of her dark skin, appropriate for dreary November but difficult to colour over. The pig of the month was described as a Berkshire Gilt, a gilt being – according to Uncle Matt – a pig that had never had piglets, and would have no experience of family life. And there was something about this pig that reminded me of Aunt Dot. Perhaps it was the peevish expression, the slightly sharp snout, the determined thrust of the jaw, or the cold bright eyes that followed me round the kitchen as if warning me not to start anything. Even her build suggested the comparison, because though nothing could be further from my aunt's dainty figure than the ample proportions of a pig, this breed looked smaller, leaner and younger than the rest. So as soon as I was alone in the house I took the stool and set to work. I needed only my thick black pencil to achieve the desired effect, that of a demon pig, and with a few deft strokes I sketched in horns and a forked tail, enlarged the cloven hoofs, and then climbed down to consider the likeness. 'Devilishly good,' was my verdict, despite being my own severest critic, yet I knew that there was an essential something missing, and pondered for days on whether I dare add the distinctive absent feature.

At last, however, I threw caution to the winds and climbed up with a bright orange pencil, colouring in a mane of fiery hair that fell down the demon pig's back in a pageboy style, thereby completing the likeness to Aunt Dot. While up there I added a few other orange touches, then replaced the stool and waited nervously for the consequences, which I was convinced would be dire. Curiously, however, nothing happened, and it appeared that my fleeting rebellion had gone unnoticed. Obvious as the resemblance between aunt and demonic pig seemed to my eyes, it had never occurred to me that it might not register immediately with her. But remarkably I escaped punishment and silently cheered every time I passed the calendar and caught the pig's blood-shot eye.

I wrote to my mother every week, but told her nothing of the distressing turn of events, because I could not be sure that my letters, though sealed by my own hand, would leave the farm without being censored. I had witnessed Aunt Dot's Secret Service methods with regard to other people's correspondence, in particular the Shoemans' mail, those mysterious missives, often unfathomably foreign, which she tampered with whenever the postman conveniently left them in her safe keeping. In her determination to pin down Mr Shoeman as a Nazi once and for all, she steamed open his envelopes, eagerly perusing the contents, and doing so without a qualm of conscience, always able to justify in herself conduct she would deplore in others.

'I could never bring myself to do such a thing normally,' she said, wearing her virtuous expression while building up a good head of steam on the kettle. 'But after all, everyone says he's a spy and it's up to us to find out for sure. It's our bounden duty. It's obviously our job because we live the nearest. We have the opportunity. We owe it to ourselves and to the war effort. We owe it to our brave troops fighting abroad. We owe it to Winston Churchill!'

Uncle Matt agreed wholeheartedly. Regardless of the rights and wrongs of their investigations, he simply disliked the Shoemans, and the prospect of exposing them as Nazis had become something of an obsession with him, so he aided and abetted her efforts. Patriotic fervour filled the house as he helped her to steam the envelopes and carefully tease them open, getting down excitedly to the inside stuff. Closely united in a common purpose, and heads together as they worked, they pored over papers, speculating as to the meaning of unfamiliar words, and quick to condemn anything remotely suspicious, though they seldom understood the significance of their findings.

'Look at this, Dot. To me it looks kind of incriminatin'. I mean, it's not English, is it? Oh, they're a bad lot and no mistake. They're spies all right. Them and their fancy ways and high and mighty manner! And turnin' their noses up at my produce, which is far and away too good for them. And dressin' their sheep in woolly clothes, goin' against nature. Why it's like takin' coals to Newcastle, that is. No, he's definitely no farmer. Hasn't a clue. So why does he pretend? It's odds on he's a spy, the greasy toad.'

'Yes, and what do you reckon to that, Matt?' she asked, thrusting an envelope bearing a harmless southern Irish stamp into his hand.

'Yes, by heck yes, that's a foreigner for a start,' he said, and they soon had the letter opened and scrutinized for incriminating evidence.

For a time, however, they found nothing conclusive. For one reason or another, perhaps because of the language barrier, they were none the wiser for reading Mr Shoeman's mail. But the finger of suspicion pointed strongly at him, so they went on investigating, thereby satisfying their curiosity and at the same time salving their uneasy consciences by telling themselves that they were doing their bit to

help win the war. Meanwhile I dared not risk writing anything controversial in case my letters came under the same kettle treatment.
Discretion being the better part of valour, I decided to wait until
Christmas and tell my mother my tale of woe in person. That way I
would avoid at least one beating.

And as it happened, Uncle Matt had been prophetic in suggesting
that I might be sickening for something. Coughs and colds were rife
in school, and I soon succumbed to an influenza epidemic – two new
words to me, long in syllables and presaging an illness longer than
I had hitherto experienced. For more than a week I lay feverishly in
bed, and then by degrees was permitted downstairs beside the fire
for a few hours each day during my slow recovery. In Sourhope folks
rarely 'bothered the doctor' as they put it, as he was based several
miles away in Aidensmead. So Aunt Dot undertook to nurse me back
to health herself, fitting in my welfare between her multitudinous
tasks. She nursed me well enough in that I did get better, but any
resemblance between her and Florence Nightingale relied only on the
lamp she often carried. Otherwise she totally lacked a bedside manner,
and her medicine came straight from the chamber of horrors. She
began my treatment with castor oil, holding my nose till I stopped
retching. Then she graduated to large doses of cod liver oil, bearing
down on me twice a day with unmistakable menace and a dose of
her cure-all, having a belief that its efficiency equalled its odiousness.
The more my health showed signs of improvement, the larger the
doses became, until I began to imagine that I must smell as fishy as
a cod on a slab and feared I would come to resemble one. Vehemently
I protested, but all to no avail.

'Drink it down!' she ordered. 'You'll feel better in no time. Trust
me. You'll soon see I'm right. You know I'm always right.'

'Ooergh!' I cried, reeling from the nauseating smell. 'It's horrible.
Really horrible! I hate it! Even the smell makes me sick!'

'Nonsense!' she said. 'Hurry up and get it down, you big softy.
What an almighty fuss about nothing! Drink it down before I lose
patience. I can't stand around here all day. I've work to do and no
time to waste. Now drink it all. It's the best medicine in the world.'

And indeed it might have been good medicine, left to itself and
taken quickly, from a spoon perhaps, with something sweet to follow,
but she stirred the oil into a glass of milk, where it floated in thick
globules of grease, and became difficult to keep down on an empty
stomach. I ate little; my diet consisting mainly of soup thickened with

barley, and highly peppered Bovril with dry cream crackers. No other tasty morsels were offered to tempt my invalid's appetite, and Aunt Dot stood over me while I took my medicine – swallowing, regurgitating, and swallowing again till at last it stayed down.

One day, after drinking half the mixture, I was left alone for a while and ran quickly into the kitchen looking for somewhere to jettison the other half. Noticing Split skulking by the back door, avoiding work, I offered the milk to him, and my hopes ran high as I held out the glass. I knew he was completely undiscriminating in his tastes. I had seen him tuck in heartily to rancid raw meat and sink his teeth into a rotting rabbit's foot. He would try to make a quick snack from a passing hedgehog's head, regardless of the sharp spines piercing his mouth, and happily quench his thirst at any muddy ditch or dirty puddle or watery rut in a cart track. With evident satisfaction he even licked the soapy suds from the discarded washing-up water round the outside sink.

So all in all, Split was not the least bit fussy in his diet, and looking at this greedy rascal with his tail thumping the ground in greeting and his tongue lolling out expectantly, I saw my saviour. But after taking the merest sniff of the oily milk he twitched his nose in disgust, baring his teeth and rearing as if he suspected me of poisoning him. With a hurt look he slunk off, tail between his legs, and it was some time before he put his trust in me again. Not for the first time, it occurred to me that he was by no means as stupid as Uncle Matt claimed. But sadly I could not escape the medicine so easily, and after what seemed like months of torture, even thoughts of school became attractive by comparison, and I was driven by an excess of oil in my diet to suggest I resume my education.

'I'm really a lot better, Aunt Dot,' I said, 'and it's not raining any more. And anyway, I've new wellies. So I think it's time I went back to school.'

She wrinkled her forehead and considered me critically for a moment.

'You still look pasty, and scrawny, and all googly-eyed,' she said at length, boosting my morale as usual.

'But I feel a lot better, Aunt Dot. Honestly, I'm fine.'

'Well, you're over the worst, certainly, but to be safe I'd say you need a few more days. After all, I'm responsible for you.'

'It's really boring, Aunt Dot, sitting around all day, especially when I'm by myself.'

'Oh, if you're bored I'll find you some nice little jobs. I wish *I* had time to be bored.'

'But I should get back to school,' I persisted, dangerously flouting Uncle Matt's advice never to argue. 'You see, I help the teacher and she needs me.'

She smiled her sarcastic little smile.

'My, oh my, Emma, but you do give yourself airs and graces. I'm sure Miss Speedwell can manage without you. She's a trained and experienced teacher. Somehow I think she'll cope.'

Somewhat abashed, I tried another tack.

'And then there's my library books. They need changing, and I've nothing to read.'

'I'll find you something to read,' she said in a tone of finality, and true to her word, she found me a *Shiretown Journal*, a *People's Friend*, and a *Farmers' Weekly*, none of which were of the slightest interest to me, being strong on boring substance and light on pictures.

Then, in a fleeting moment of generosity, she presented me with a brand new book, an advance Christmas present, which she had hidden away, and I accepted it with alacrity, eager to delve into its pristine pages. Alas, it turned out to be worse than the *Farmers' Weekly*, with less plot than the pig calendar. It was an improving book about a saintly girl who went about doing good deeds and after several selfless acts ended up dying young. I was of the opinion that it served her right, since she certainly bored her readers to death, and hard as I tried I could not relate to this heroine. I suspected Aunt Dot had given me the book to convey an underlying message, a sort of warning to mend my wicked ways. And as for the heroine's untimely death, the reason was merely hinted at, but I was convinced that she died of an overdose of cod liver oil.

So my convalescence slowly passed, and such was the depth of my loneliness that I missed not only Miss Speedwell and my class-mates, but also the little old lady hens and my two pet calves, Tiny and Beauty. But during my enforced confinement to the house I did learn something of the overall routine governing Windlestraw, and had the opportunity to meet our neighbours from the three nearest households. And also, and quite unforgettably, I experienced my first encounter with a mysterious stranger.

Chapter 12
Neighbours and Nazis

High Windlestraw stood at the end of the road, which then widened into a T-shaped turning point, and afterwards narrowed into a rough track, suitable only for horses and farm machinery. In the regular course of events a variety of vehicles came to the road end. Lorries collected milk and eggs, wagons transported cattle to and from Shiretown mart, horses pulling carts brought animal feed or coal, and every week a horse-drawn dray delivered orders from the local Co-op, some eight miles away in Aidensmead. Small vans brought the meat ration and occasionally fish, but the only vehicle to travel past the road end was the simplest one – the postman's bicycle.

For most residents of the valley shopping was mainly done at the door, but those who lived beyond the road end had to make their way to Windlestraw in order to meet the various tradesmen. These unfortunates, from farthest to nearest, comprised the Phillips of Nettle Head, Miss Titchmarsh of Moss House, and the Shoemans of Dyke Head. They came to the road end on the appropriate day at the appropriate time and waited for the particular service they required. Sometimes they had a long wait, but however long the wait and whatever the weather, it never occurred to my aunt to invite them into her home. Indeed, she would have hated the queue to form inside her house because it would mean an invasion of boots and shoes, all undoubtedly dirty and bearing smelly and unpleasant traces of messy farmyards. She regarded strangers' feet, even when wiped on her three mats, with the utmost suspicion, preferring to keep them firmly on the outside. Other than that, she laid down only one rule, an unwritten but strictly enforced one, that in the business of shopping she was always served first. After all, she insisted, it was her road end.

I was very surprised, therefore – though I knew my aunt could be kindness itself if the mood took her, especially to animals – when I heard her comment in concerned tones about Miss Titchmarsh standing outside in a storm one day.

165

'Poor woman!' she cried, speaking from the kitchen. 'Poor Miss Titchmarsh. The wind's almost blowing her over. I can't leave her out there. It's really too bad.'

'What's wrong, Aunt Dot?' I enquired, rising from the little rocking chair.

I had been sitting in the living room feeling sorry for myself, sniffing and sneezing, and hugging the warmth of the fireside. But when she spoke I left the fire, instantly feeling the loss of it, and stood in the doorway where the uncurtained kitchen window afforded a clear view of the road above the bank outside. Rain ceaselessly battered the window pane like a host of tapping fingers, and through the downpour I could see a figure swaying and struggling at the mercy of the elements, as if on the deck of a storm-tossed ship. In fact, to my childish imagination she might have been part of a ship herself, so tall was she, straight as a mast, her long gabardine mackintosh flapping round her, billowing and swelling like a wet sail, and her head rounded off like a masthead by two scarves, a woollen one for warmth and over it a waterproof one tied tightly under the chin.

Miss Titchmarsh always came with a big bag and a fat grey umbrella, and at first she tried to shelter under this umbrella, but the gale kept blowing it inside out, dropping it to half-mast, then wrenching at the spokes and tugging at her arm until I quite thought she would sail away. As yet no one else had turned up to collect their Co-op deliveries, and Aunt Dot kept a watchful eye on the situation while she pulled on her wellingtons and collected her coat, scarf and purse. Then she too tied on a headsquare, leaned out of the door and shouted through the wind in a voice that was shrill but as far-reaching as a foghorn.

'Miss Titchmarsh! Can I have a word? Miss Titchmarsh! Down here!'

I watched as Miss Titchmarsh shivered with anticipation before she got under way, and then, buffeted by the wind, struggled to the steps, navigated them successfully, and hove to at the welcome mat. I waited, peeping round the door, half pleased and half apprehensive, thinking I would soon have company by the fire and feeling a little shy about it. As she hovered in the doorway I peered at her with interest, this being the first time I had studied her at close range, and I had to admit that in describing her as plain my discerning uncle had not exaggerated. He had once remarked that even without her moustache and the large mole on her nose she would have been a rank outsider in a beauty contest, but in likening her face to that of a horse, I felt he went too far. True, she had been blessed with more than generous-sized teeth, but to my mind she had a nice face, shining with goodness and kindness, qualities that I had recently come to appreciate. And at that moment her face was lit by a pleasant smile as she stood there, fully expecting to be invited in.

'Good morning, Mrs Wheatley. I'm saying "good" morning and it's anything but. It's a truly terrible morning.'

'Yes, it certainly is,' agreed Aunt Dot, still barring the entrance. 'In fact, I was just thinking that as it's such a dreadful day to be out I should offer you refuge inside. It occurs to me that you could shelter in the wash-house. You're more than welcome to wait in there.'

I cringed, feeling embarrassed for Miss Titchmarsh, as I saw her face fall, looking more than a little deflated.

'Oh – oh, I see. Oh yes, of course. The wash-house. How generous. I'll do that, Mrs Wheatley. And thank you for the kind thought.'

'Not at all,' said my aunt, magnanimously. 'You can wait in there any time you want. In future you don't need an invitation.'

'Well, thank you again, Mrs Wheatley. That really is very good of you. You're too kind,' said Miss Titchmarsh, recovering her composure, and no doubt grateful for any port in a storm, she moved off to the wash-house and dropped anchor inside.

I returned to my seat by the fire, but could not help worrying about Miss Titchmarsh, wondering if she would be all right in the wash-house, cast away among the odds and ends of household effects with only spiders and beetles for company. For some reason that I could not have explained I felt guilty monopolizing the cheerful fire, but Aunt Dot suffered no such qualms of conscience. She wore the complacent expression of one who has dispensed charity and been a good Samaritan. So it was some time before I plucked up the courage to question her notion of hospitality.

'Couldn't you invite Miss Titchmarsh in here to get warm, Aunt Dot?' I suggested tentatively, and she stared at me for what seemed like a fortnight, as if I had taken leave of my senses.

'In here, girl? Inside my house? My spotlessly clean house? Whatever are you thinking of? If I invited one I'd have to invite all, and then where would we be? We'd have water everywhere, we'd have mud everywhere, and feet everywhere. Dirty, dirty feet! More work for me. And I've nothing but work already. Where would it all end? What a pity you don't think before you speak, girl. Why don't

167

you use your common sense and keep your silly questions to your-self? Just be thankful that *you're* not sitting in the wash-house.' And so from that day on, in inclement weather the wash-house was where Miss Titchmarsh always waited.

On these delivery days, Uncle Matt found employment close to home so that he would be on hand to help carry in the provisions, thereby setting in motion one of the little ceremonies of which he was so fond, one that he and my aunt enacted every week. Having collected the groceries, they sorted and inspected them, approved and gloated over them, and finally arranged them in storage, some in the warm living-room cupboard and others in the icy larder. They behaved like a couple of contented squirrels chattering over their hoard of nuts, and more so at this time of year when they stocked up against the onset of winter. They pounced on any tinned food available to add to Aunt Dot's 'rainy day' collection, and though she had her favourites, preferring salmon and peaches, she usually had to make do with more mundane products, such as Spam and golden syrup. But she always hung around and kept a sharp lookout that no one else fared better, especially the beautiful Mrs Phillip.

It was brighter weather on the day the Shoemans paid their unso-ciable call. They were the second visitors to disturb my convales-cence, banging imperiously on the front door, fit to break it down. Both aunt and uncle scurried from the kitchen where they had been sorting and boxing eggs, putting aside the cracked ones for cakes and selective distribution. Like Miss Titchmarsh, the Shoemans were kept outside, where they stood submerged under layers of clothing, swathed in scarves wrapped round and round like bandages on an Egyptian mummy. Mrs Shoeman wore .a long beaver coat, her husband a military-style jerkin with deeper pockets than a kangaroo, and both sported felt hats sprouting feathers, giving them the look of startled pheasants.

'Just out for a walk,' Mr Shoeman boomed, and I noticed that unlike Mr Clout's moustache that rippled like the wind through wheat when he spoke, Mr Shoeman's stubbly black moustache barely moved, but stayed squarely and stiffly defined under his bulbous nose like a dirty smudge waiting to be wiped off. 'I thought it good to call and collect the milk, straight from the cow – you know, while it is fresh.' His tone and the significant lift of his eyebrows cast doubt on the freshness of the delivered milk.

'Our milk's always fresh,' asserted Uncle Matt. 'Ask anybody. They'll all tell you,' and he waved his hand in an expansive gesture that took in the geese and cows grazing the front meadow, a few sheep exploring the stack yard at Todd Tindale's, and the goats mountaineering on the slopes of the dene.

Mrs Shoeman twittered nervously.

'Oh yes, I'm sure it is. Hans didn't mean – he wasn't implying – though it can be a bit blue at times – but I expect there's – a reason?'

'Shut up, Betty. Who asks you?' growled Mr Shoeman, handing Uncle Matt a covered container. 'I vill take it anyway, as we are now here.'

'Any particular cow you'd like?' asked Uncle Matt disarmingly.

'Just you get the milk,' said Mr Shoeman austerely, 'and I vill take the eggs as well. Also most fresh. And vith no cracks.'

'Brown please,' interjected Mrs Shoeman, simpering at Uncle Matt.

'Shut up, you stupid woman!' advised her husband. 'Nobody vants your opinion. Keep your trap shut.'

Nervous of Mr Shoeman and his nasty habit of producing a gun, I followed Uncle Matt into the kitchen, where I noticed that in collecting the eggs he gave them a swift surreptitious shuffle, deftly as a card trickster, so that he included some of the cracked ones, recently sorted and suitably camouflaged with a little dirt. Then eggs, milk, and money changed hands, and business having been successfully transacted, Uncle Matt turned away. But the Shoemans seemed to have taken root on the doorstep.

'Just von moment, Mr Wheatley,' said Mr Shoeman with an air of superiority.

He handed the dairy products to his wife and reached into one of his capacious pockets, causing Uncle Matt to start back nervously, but he only took out a pair of steel-rimmed spectacles, which he put on, temporarily dislodging his feathered hat. Having adjusted both, he fixed my uncle with a penetrating stare, like a Gestapo officer interrogating a suspect. When he spoke it was with a hint of menace, and he weighed his words carefully.

'I vish to ask you the questions, Mr Wheatley.'

'Fire away,' said Uncle Matt airily, 'though I can't guarantee to know the answers. If it's about your milk again . . .'

'No, no,' interrupted Shoeman with a touch of asperity. 'It is about the letters.'

When disposed to be awkward, Uncle Matt had a habit, irritating to some, of gaining time by being deliberately obtuse.

'Lettuce? You're too late for lettuce. We haven't had any for weeks. Wrong time of year, an' that. At a pinch I could let you have a couple of leeks, but they're scarce, 'cos the goat's had a few. So they'll cost you.'

A frown darkened Mr Shoeman's bulbous face, and he raised his hand, waving the leeks aside.

'Lett-*ers*, Mr Wheatley. My post. It is now and then left here, and the letters they look as if they have been opened. What have you to say?'

Aunt Dot, who had been hovering in the background in a supervisory capacity, now stepped forward, joining the discussion and giving Uncle Matt no time to answer.

'I know what you mean, Mr Shoeman. Not about your letters, of course. I haven't time to go examining your letters. But I've noticed repeatedly that ours look as if they've been opened. I blame the weather. All that rain. They're often damp and wrinkled. I expect yours are the same, are they?'

Mr Shoeman turned his interrogating stare on her instead, and his asperity became more marked. He shook his head dismissively.

'The weather? That nonsense is. Surely the letters are in the mailbag?'

'That's right, Hans. Quite right,' interposed Mrs Shoeman, her nose twitching involuntarily like a ruminating rabbit.

'Shut up, Betty,' he replied irritably. 'Just shut your stupid mouth.'

Then Uncle Matt took up the debate.

'You might think that if you hadn't thought it through. Stan Sparke, now, the postie, he calls at a lot of places before he gets here. You might say we're out on a limb here. And at every place he rummages in his mailbag with wet hands and the bag wide open. Stands to reason with all that rummagin' that the letters get wet.'

'Well, that's a thought, Hans,' said Mrs Shoeman, half convinced.

'Oh, it's more than a thought,' declared my uncle. 'It's a fact. Here, I'll show you a letter of mine that came only yesterday.'

He dived into the living room and returned with a bill for cattle feed that he had spilt his tea over in shock and agitation at the final total. He thrust it under Mr Shoeman's nose and grimaced as if his theory had been proved beyond dispute.

'Just look at the state of that!' he said, and Mrs Shoeman gasped.

'Good gracious! That is dreadful. Worse than ours.'

'Vill you shut the mouth, woman!' shouted her loving husband. 'That is beside the point.'

170

'Well, what *is* the point?' asked Uncle Matt brusquely. 'I have things to do, you know. Can't stand here all day chewin' the fat with you.'

'The point is that my letters they look as if they have been tampered vith and that is the criminal offence. I vould like to know who such a vicked thing does.'

'A lot of letters are opened nowadays,' pointed out Aunt Dot. 'Some are censored for security reasons. Are your letters from foreign parts, by any chance?'

Mr Shoeman's spectacles flashed coldly and his head jerked in annoyance, causing the hat feathers to quiver.

'I vill ask the questions, not you!' he shouted. 'The censored letters, they are officially opened. Mine are opened by the steam, I think. And I vould like to know who such a liberty takes.'

Aunt Dot drew herself up to her full height, an indignant four foot eleven inches.

'And why ask us? You've got a nerve. It has nothing to do with us. If you're so concerned about your precious letters, then complain to the post office or even the police. They'll soon sort you out.'

He looked a little startled and an uneasy silence followed, during which he replaced his spectacles in his pocket. It occurred to me that such a capacious pocket could easily contain a gun, and I shrank away from the straight line of fire he would have from the door, but after directing a threatening look at both aunt and uncle, he took a step backwards.

'Perhaps I vill – take some sort of action. Perhaps I vill do something,' he muttered darkly. 'I think, however, that we now understand each other.'

He pivoted on his heel and began to walk away, and I thought Uncle Matt would have been glad to see him go. But my intrepid uncle, indefatigable as ever in his pursuit of business, was reluctant to let any customer get away without a further contribution to the farm's annual turnover. He stepped outside and followed, gaining ground on Shoeman's sullen back.

'I just thought – since you're here anyway – I don't suppose you've changed your mind about that side of bacon?' he enquired optimistically.

Mr Shoeman rotated furiously.

'No! Certainly not!'

'It's a bargain, but my meanin' is, I could reduce the price at a pinch.'

'No! I vant no bacon now! You hear? And I bid you good day!'

He glared at Uncle Matt, then turned and strode through the stack yard, face reddening with anger and hat feathers fluttering like a flustered pheasant as he marched on to the road, leaving his wife to simper half-apologetic goodbyes and to follow behind carrying the eggs and milk. They left Aunt Dot unrepentant and undeterred from her covert operations, while Uncle Matt gazed after them, swivelling his cap thoughtfully.

'I'll sell him that bacon if it's the last thing I do,' he said.

'Careful, Matt. It might be. He's a nasty bit of work.'

'And you know he really wants it at the bottom of him. Did you notice he said "no bacon now," an' that? That means he'll likely take it next time. We had him wrong-footed today, but he'll buy it. You know, I think he suffers from high blood pressure. He's on a short fuse just now. Maybe you should lay off tamperin' with his letters for a bit. You're right – he's gettin' nasty.'

'Nonsense, Matt!' exclaimed my aunt, who would have none of any such spineless capitulation. 'If we stop now he'll know for sure it was us. No. I'll just have to be more careful, take more time over the steaming. I'm blessed if I'll be intimidated by him. Do you realize – he was threatening us? The very idea! What a nerve! Complaining and insinuating and threatening us! And him a foreigner. A Nazi, most likely. And in our country! Our precious England!'

So it was that the investigations on behalf of the war effort continued unabated and it appeared that I alone felt any alarm. It seemed to me that Mr Shoeman was capable of anything, even murder, and if he did turn out to be a Nazi, then my aunt and uncle were playing a dangerous game, and by association, implicating me. Fortunately for my peace of mind, the postman did not always leave the Shoemans' letters at Windlestraw. It depended upon how late he was, whether he had other deliveries beyond the road end, and, of course, what the weather was like. But whenever my aunt did get her inquisitive little fingers on his correspondence, and despite Shoeman's unmistakable warning, she continued to take a keen interest in its contents.

Meanwhile, towards the end of the second week of my illness, another visitor arrived, one I had heard of but not yet seen – the famous Mrs Phillip. Uncle Matt happened to answer the door, and she was the first caller allowed to step inside, walking straight into the living room with the easy confidence of one accustomed to being welcome everywhere. Nor did he try to deter her, but gave a tweak of his cap and a sort of courteous bow, quite out of character for him, as he ushered her to a seat by the fire. I had the feeling that if he had owned a red carpet he would have rolled it out for her. Yet once again he was living dangerously. He knew the house rules full well. He knew that uninvited guests were not admitted, but, overcome by the glamour of his beautiful blonde neighbour, he cast aside caution and treated her as a special guest. He noticed that she appeared distraught, so distraught that he felt obliged to plump up her chair cushion and pat her shoulder comfortingly, showing an excess of solicitude that Aunt Dot would have wondered at. Then he hovered over her, wearing a rather fatuous expression, I thought.

Young as I was, I readily understood why he liked and admired her and Aunt Dot did not, the reason in both cases being obvious. The two women had little in common, apart from their mutual role of farmer's wife and sharing a youthful attractiveness. My aunt had a pertly pretty face, spoilt only by her habitual expression, which was generally careworn and as sour as if she had just bitten deeply into a lemon. On the other hand, Mrs Phillip was a beauty, blessed with the sort of looks that turn heads. She was the epitome of perfection in her trim figure, her peaches-and-cream complexion, and her blonde curls. In particular she had remarkable eyes – large, limpid, and violet blue, which, despite their colour, Uncle Matt once romantically compared to a young cow's eyes, gazing contentedly across a field of clover. Nor did she dress like a typical farmer's wife. Not for her were the pinafores and knitted clutter of the tweeds-and-brogues brigade. She dressed with style, and even discounting the silk pyjamas worn in the hayfield – not that Uncle Matt could ever discount that often-remembered vision – her everyday attire seldom fell short of the chic. On this occasion she wore a royal blue coat with a grey astrakhan collar, a matching pillbox hat from which her hair curled attractively, smart court shoes and silk stockings. She looked simply stunning.

'Er – would you care for a cup of tea?' asked Uncle Matt, who laboured under the delusion that tea was all that any woman wanted.

'No thank you, Mr Wheatley,' she answered in her soft, harmonious voice, as different from Aunt Dot's grating tones as a nightingale from a corncrake. 'I just wondered if I might ask for some advice.'

At once he became effusive.

'Advice? Certainly, certainly. I mean to say, definitely. Anythin'. Anythin' at all. You name it. How can I help? What can I do?'

'Well, actually,' she said, after a moment's hesitation, 'it's your wife I really need to see. Do you think I could have a quick word with her?'

'Wife?' he queried vaguely, having temporarily forgotten he had one. 'Oh – er – wife. Yes of course, wife. Just a minute now. She's – er – she'll be – er – of course, she's in the byre,' he said, making it sound as if she was part of his livestock. 'I'll just get her.'

Looking rather disappointed that it was not his advice that was in demand, he reluctantly departed, leaving me alone with Mrs Phillip. She smiled, and I had not experienced such a warm smile since my mother left.

'And how long have you been living up here?' she asked pleasantly, her big blue eyes studying me with interest.

'About four pigs,' I said, and paused, blushing to the roots of my hair.

'Four . . . ?'

'Months. I should have said months, not pigs. I'm sorry.'

I knew what I meant, but felt very foolish. I had begun to measure time in terms of calendar pigs, and so far I had survived the Tamworth Sow, the Lincolnshire Curly Coat, the Middle White, and the Berkshire Gilt. Now I cringed with embarrassment, convinced she would think me stupid, a dunce, maybe even the village idiot. But she pretended not to notice my slip of the tongue, and smiled again in a kindly fashion.

'And don't you have to attend school at all?'

She did consider me a dunce, I thought, mortified.

'Oh yes, yes. I go to school. I go there all the time. Honestly. I'm in the – er – second class,' I said, thinking it would sound better than the infant class. 'But I've had the flu. I'm still getting over it.'

'Oh, you've been ill? What a shame. You poor thing,' she murmured sympathetically. 'I do hope you're soon recovered – er – what's your name, dear?'

'Emma,' I answered shyly.

'Ah, Emma. A pretty name. A pretty name for a pretty girl.'

There and then I decided that with regard to Mrs Phillip I was once again on Uncle Matt's side. Already I liked her a lot.

'I think *you're* ever so pretty,' I replied spontaneously. 'Really beautiful, like a princess.' But I instantly wished I had kept the thought to myself, because just then Aunt Dot breezed in like a human tornado and flashed me a disapproving look.

She had paused at the entrance to remove the protective pinny that she wore for work, a back-and-front affair from which her rolled-up cardigan sleeves protruded in an unattractive lump, looking like she meant business. She had also slipped out of her wellingtons and into shoes with a higher heel, because she could never face visitors without a little extra height, being as sensitive about her lack of inches as Uncle Matt was about his lack of hair. Now ready to compete, she entered, her face registering surprise and her tone some slight annoyance.

'You wanted to see me?'

'Yes please, Mrs Wheatley. I'm sorry to disturb you, but I desperately need advice. I heard you were a hairdresser before you married.'

'Yes, that's right. But I don't do hair now, I'm afraid. I haven't time. My life's all farm work now. Nothing but work. Anyway, what's the problem? Your hair looks all right.'

'All right?' echoed Uncle Matt, who had followed her in and remained hovering over Mrs Phillip like a bee over a flower. 'All right? It's lovely. Just lovely.'

'Oh, it's not *my* hair that's the problem,' explained Mrs Phillip. 'It's poor John's. It's gone purple.'

'Gone purple!' exclaimed Aunt Dot. 'I've never heard of such a thing. I've heard of people going grey overnight, or even white. But never purple.'

'Well, you see,' she said, blushing prettily, 'he dyed it, for my sake.'

'Understandable,' said Uncle Matt gallantly. 'Quite understandable.'

Aunt Dot directed a frosty glance at him and then turned back, bemused.

'I don't understand. Why would he want to go dyeing his hair purple at his age?'

'Oh, he didn't intend to dye it purple. Naturally not. Just to darken it a little. John went grey very early, you know, in his twenties. He wanted to look younger – well, for me really.'

'You can't blame him for that,' said my uncle, grinning inanely. 'Definitely not. I mean – well – I wouldn't blame him, like.'

Aunt Dot rounded on him, hitting out where it hurt most.

'Well, that's one problem you don't have. You haven't enough hair to dye purple, or any other colour. We could dye your bald head, of course. We could tie it up with coloured cloths and onion skins and pattern it like we do Easter eggs.'

He winced and stepped back a pace, looking disconcerted, but the tactful Mrs Phillip showed no sign of having heard. She proceeded to plead with my aunt, her big blue eyes turning rather watery.

'Oh please, Mrs Wheatley, can you help? I'd be so grateful if you could suggest something. My poor John. He can't go to Shiretown. He can't go near the mart. He simply daren't go out.'

'Sounds as if you should knit him a balaclava,' said Aunt Dot unfeelingly, smiling her sarcastic little smile. 'I'm afraid he's paying the price of vanity. There's not a lot you can do. You could try peroxide to bleach the colour out, but I should warn you, he'll go mauve first. He'll just have to keep his cap on – like Matt.'

'Peroxide. Oh yes. We have some peroxide,' cried Mrs Phillip, clapping her dainty hands.

'Yes, I thought you might have,' said my aunt, with a significant glance at the blonde curls. 'Well, I'm afraid it's a gradual process, and he'd be well advised to condition it each time, because too much bleaching rots the hair. What a pity men are so vain!' she added, patting her own thick mane of hair.

'Rots the hair, does it, Mrs Wheatley? Dear, dear. Condition it, you say? We'll certainly do that. Thank you so much for your advice. I feel better now, thanks.'

She rose and turned her intensely blue eyes on Uncle Matt as she elegantly pulled on her gloves.

'And thank you too, Mr Wheatley, so much. You've been so kind and helpful.'

She gave him the benefit of her dazzling smile and he reeled slightly, clutching at a ladder-backed chair for support.

'My pleasure,' he said fervently, 'and I mean that. Definitely. You're very welcome. You know – any time.' He tweaked his cap and, simpering nervously, added, 'And I hope your husband is soon better. I mean – less purple. I mean – back to himself again. I mean . . .'

'I think we all know what you mean, Matt,' interrupted Aunt Dot, with a withering look.

'Yes, well, perhaps I can see you out, Mrs Phillip,' he said courteously.

'No, I'll do that,' insisted Aunt Dot and, having opened the door and closed it without ceremony on Mrs Phillip, she returned to her slightly apprehensive husband, who was busily trying to deflect trouble by making tea, banking on the fact that though other women might be more demanding, that magic beverage usually won the day with his little woman.

'Just thought you might like a cuppa, Dot,' he said, with as much suaveness as he could muster.

'I would,' she said shortly.

'That was a turn-up for the book, wasn't it, Dot? Mrs Phillip was in here and sat down before I knew what was happenin'. Isn't that right, Emma?'

I nodded, helping him out, but Aunt Dot smiled dubiously.

'Oh yes? So what did you think of your blonde bombshell? Your bottle blonde?'

'Well, I think the same as everybody else. She's known as an absolute knockout.'

'Is she now?'

'Well, she is a bit of a cracker. She kinda suits her name – Phillip. She's a fillip all right. A rare treat for the eyes, it has to be said.'

'Does it?' she enquired sourly.

'Almost as bonny as you, Dot,' he added hastily, recognizing her tone.

'Fancy the poor man being driven to dye his hair!' she exclaimed. 'There's no limit to the depths of idiocy that a man will sink to for a bit of skirt. What a dance she must lead him.'

'Yes, what a dance,' said Uncle Matt dreamily.

He winked at me behind my aunt's back, and drifted into a few steps of a slinky tango, swaying with an imaginary partner. Aunt Dot poured three cups of tea and took a thoughtful sip of hers before returning to the subject.

'She certainly wears plenty of makeup. And mascara and lipstick. You'd think she was on the stage.'

'Like a film star,' murmured Uncle Matt.

'And those clothes! Quite unsuitable for a farmer's wife. Does she do any work?'

'Dinky hat though but,' he remarked. 'A little hat like that would suit you, Dot.'

'Hat! Call that a hat? It's absolutely useless for round here. She'll be lucky if she manages to keep it on. It has a good chance of blowing away down the dene. Yes, everything about that woman is frivolous. Absolutely everything.'

Uncle Matt slowly sipped his tea, apparently pondering in depth on the frivolous image of Mrs Phillip. And he would have done well to keep his ponderings to himself, but he allowed himself one more observation, softly, almost inaudibly.

'Silk stockings, eh? By heck! Such luxury. It sure makes you think.'

Aunt Dot turned on him, snatching away his almost full cup of tea.

'Does it?' she snapped. 'Well here's another thought to conjure with. After you've mucked the byre out thoroughly, the cooler-house floor needs attention. Save me a job. That should cool your ardour for a bit.'

Uncle Matt sighed noisily and with a despondent gesture headed for the door and stood with his hand on the handle. He looked like a man who has glimpsed the promised land and been diverted elsewhere, and we heard him mutter bitterly, 'From the sublime to the ridiculous. Who says romance isn't dead?' Then he stepped outside and closed the door before Aunt Dot could make a retort.

I felt sorry for him, and conscious of the fact that Mrs Philip had had an effect on all of us, though a different one in each case. She had reminded me of the softer, warmer, happier life that I had lost, and I hoped that I would soon see her and talk with her again. I also hoped to meet her husband of the purple hair, a new phenomenon for me. After that visit I thought of her a great deal at first, as I imagine did Uncle Matt, but I little knew that she would one day feature importantly in my life, coming to my aid when I was in dire straits and in need of a friend.

Meanwhile, the sweet impression she had left behind, together with the sense of menace left by the Shoemans and the ignominy of Miss Titchmarsh's banishment to the wash-house, were all driven dramatically from my mind, eclipsed by the last visitor to call at Windlestraw during my convalescence. Like Mrs Phillip, that final caller also enjoyed the privilege of entering the house, but she did so uninvited and unannounced, like a ghost in the night.

Chapter 13

Mad Mary

It was early evening and I sat alone in the house. Aunt Dot had lit the hanging lamp before leaving for the byre, and as sometimes happened, it began to burn low with a shimmering blue flame, filling me with dread in case it went out altogether. Gradually the lamp grew dimmer and dimmer, the circle of light smaller. Dark shadows encroached on my space, closing me in, and I became increasingly nervous. But what to do? I knew that full power could be restored by fiddling with the little brass knob below the lamp wick, and was sorely tempted to climb up and attempt to adjust it, but hesitated. Aunt Dot had forbidden me ever to touch the lamps and I disobeyed her at my peril. Besides, what if I twiddled the knob the wrong way, plunging myself into total darkness? It was a discouraging thought, and I dithered, weighing up the pros and cons of doing something, anything, and in the end did nothing. Yet I sat uneasily, frequently glancing over my shoulder, starting at the slightest sound, and though not over-fond of my aunt's company, constantly hoping against hope that she would soon come back.

She had set me to finish one of her 'nice little jobs', the simple but monotonous task of making butter. At this stage the only ingredient was cream, though she would add salt later on, and she had placed the glass churn on a tea towel spread on the table next to one of the tall chairs. All I had to do was sit there turning the handle that activated the wooden paddle inside, turning it continuously round and round until, as if by magic, the liquid changed into a solid pat of butter. I soon found that I could turn the handle and read at the same time, but as the flickering light cast moving shadows over the page, it became more and more difficult to read or even see the print.

Suddenly, already tense and nervous, I heard the back door open quietly and someone making stealthy but circuitous progress through the kitchen. I stiffened with fear, straining to hear the curious sounds – not exactly footsteps, but rather an erratic shuffle, a sliding, swishing

179

sound, like large feet shunting over the flagstone floor. I was reminded of the slipslop sound of my own feet when I tried to walk in my mother's shoes, scraping the soles forward and dragging the heels after them, except that this sound was somehow sinister. Whoever or whatever was making the harrowing noise seemed to be deliberately prolonging my suspense by approaching and retreating as if moving in circles. I doubted that it could be human, and I wondered if an animal had found its way into the kitchen by mistake. But the farm animals were already in their stalls for the night. A wild animal then? To the best of my knowledge, even wild animals seldom lifted latches and opened doors. An eerie visitor? Supernatural even? But did ghosts need to lift latches? Surely they simply materialized, after drifting through walls like wisps of smoke?

Then came the chanting, an unintelligible chant that rose and fell along with the shuffle, stopping when the shuffling stopped, and breaking into a demented chuckle. I sat glued to my chair, afraid to get down and investigate, afraid to move, no longer turning the churn handle, though my hand still gripped it tightly, frozen in position. I tried to speak, hoping for a reassuring answer, but my voice when it came sounded faint and tremulous, unrecognizable even to me.

'U – Uncle M – Matt?' I ventured, since the sound suggested big feet.

No answer, except for renewed chanting.

'A – Aunt D – D – Dot?'

Still no answer.

'Who – whooo – who's there?' I managed to utter, sounding like a startled owl.

Silence. I listened intently, but the chanting had ceased, as had the shuffling and chuckling. I waited, still and terrified, afraid to breathe, my frightened eyes riveted on the kitchen door. And suddenly an apparition filled the doorway, a swarthy, dirty, ragged apparition, with wild black hair and dark staring eyes. It stood suspended there, unmoving but menacing, as darkly brooding as the picture of the black vulture that hung in the school hall. I gaped at it, transfixed, trembling with fear at the frightful spectre, more terrible than anything I had ever seen or even imagined.

Then the thing smiled horribly, advancing slowly towards me, and by a miracle I found my feet. I had no desire to meet this hideous manifestation at close quarters, and with a strangled cry I was off the chair and out of the door in a flash. Fresh from an early bath and clad only in nightdress and slippers, I fled through the manure-spattered byre, giving no regard to my aunt's wrath or to the rats' eyes that watched me from the darkened cake bins as I passed. I ran straight to the main byre where milking was in progress, and stood white-faced, wide-eyed, and shaking like a leaf. Uncle Matt stopped milking and gaped in astonishment, while Aunt Dot turned sharply, instantly scowling at the sight of my slippers.

'Emma? You wicked girl! What on earth are you doing out here? In your nightclothes and everything! After all the precious time I've spent nursing you through the flu.'

I opened my mouth to answer but no words came.

'A – er – a – a' I stuttered.

I had lost my voice but my hands said it all, as eloquently as a mime artist. The danger, the fear, the panic were all expressed as my fingers pointed and gestured, clenched and spread, waved frantically, and finally clung most uncharacteristically to Aunt Dot's skirts. Nevertheless, Uncle Matt needed a translation.

'Emma, pet! Whatever's the matter?'

'G – g – ghost' was all I could say.

Aunt Dot bent down and gave me a quick shake.

'Calm yourself!' she said firmly. 'Now what is it? What's the matter? Take a deep breath and spit it out.'

I regained speech but not articulation.

'B – b – black – thing. In there – kitchen – hair – all hair – and eyes – oooooh, awful. Awful eyes.'

My aunt rose and sighed resignedly.

'I'd better go and see what it is, Matt. You carry on milking. It's probably just a mouse or a stray dog that's frightened her. What a pity she has such a vivid imagination.'

'No, no!' I protested, shaking my head vigorously. 'Big – black thing!'

'I'd better come too, just in case,' insisted my uncle. 'It's likely you're right, Dot, but my meanin' is, you never know.'

We returned to the house in a procession, all of us anxious except for Aunt Dot, who fearlessly led the way, ready to take on any number of big black things. Split, reluctant to take on any but too cowardly to stay on his own, brought up the rear as usual. I hid behind Uncle Matt, peering past his elbow, fearful of the apparition, yet in an odd way hoping it had not, as ghosts tend to do, disappeared, and with it my fragile credibility. In my haste to escape, however, I had left the door open, and with a curious sort of relief I could see the dark shape of the hideous caller now occupying an armchair. It was the same armchair in which the lovely Mrs Phillip had recently reclined so elegantly, but the present occupant provided a striking contrast, and I wondered if the same thought had occurred to Uncle Matt.

I had fully expected to see in the other members (including Split) of the procession of which I was a part, something of the shock that I had experienced, and in my uncle to some extent I did. As for my aunt, however, she never hesitated for a second. I might have guessed that she would take the apparition in her stride. No mere apparition, no matter how frightful, would intimidate her. Uncle Matt, on the other hand, after one glance inside the room, looked distinctly uneasy and disinclined to enter. He snorted disgustedly, rather like Sandy when turning down the opportunity to work, and I had the impression that he would have preferred to deal with the anticipated mouse or stray dog, or indeed anything other than this ragged horror, making herself at home in his living room.

Split plainly felt the same. His nose twitched and he snarled his disapproval, but, true to form, could not decide on an appropriate course of action – whether to attack or retreat. Instinctively he favoured retreat, but after much aimless darting about, he ended up doing both. He repeatedly ran forward, barking furiously, then backed away nervously, cringing on the ground, then came forward again and went back again, achieving nothing positive, but getting entangled in Uncle Matt's feet. So all in all it was left to Aunt Dot to act as the welcoming host, and she did so to perfection, stepping straight over the threshold and giving a smile of recognition.

'Oh, it's you, Mary! Well I never! I wondered who it could be,' she said in a matter-of-fact tone, and strode confidently up to the armchair. 'We haven't seen you for quite a while. Where've you been keeping yourself? How've you been, Mary?'

The sinister creature addressed as Mary, who I now realized must be the Mad Mary of whom I had heard rumours, gave no answer as such. At our approach she grasped the chair arms, digging long black fingernails into the upholstery and leaning forward as if gathering momentum for flight. But having ascertained from my aunt's tone that there was no immediate danger, she relaxed. Some sixth sense seemed to tell her that, though not exactly welcome, she would at least be tolerated, and she shook her tangled mane and sat back at her ease, though her eyes flitted restlessly to and fro. Aunt Dot attended to the failing lamp, pumping the knob briskly in a manner that brooked no nonsense, and thereby lit up Mary's sombre aspect in all its frightful detail. Then she put the kettle on, talking all the while, and I was driven by the cold night air to creep cautiously inside, but chose a chair near the door, ready to flee again if necessary.

'I'm just making some tea, Mary. There's nothing like a nice cup of tea to keep the cold out,' said my aunt pleasantly, 'and I expect you'd like a sandwich? I'm sure you would. By the way, Mary, I haven't introduced you to Emma. That's Emma over there. She'll talk to you while I'm busy. She loves to talk, don't you, Emma? That's after she's given her feet a good wipe of course. The naughty girl's been in the byre in her slippers.'

She pointed to the corner where I sat huddled and uncomfortable, doing my best to pass unnoticed, as I suspected she realized. But for once I had nothing to say, absolutely nothing. Only Aunt Dot felt able to talk, holding forth in an effortless flow of chit-chat, an inconsequential monologue, like a mother trying to soothe a child, expecting no answer, receiving none. Nor did Uncle Matt help her out. Repulsed by his first glimpse of the gloomy figure, he allowed his natural aversion to take control of his limbs, and with unseemly haste, legged it back to the byre.

Split must have followed, leaving me without friends and with an acute sense of desertion, especially after Aunt Dot had banged the door shut, cutting off escape. I curled my legs up on the corner chair, as far away from Mary as possible, and though it was a cold and draughty seat, I felt nothing of that, but only fear. I clung to the sturdy wooden arms as if my life depended on it and, forgetting my manners, stared at Mary as she had first stared at me, with my eyes on stalks. She looked at me still, but now with covert glances, and I hardly dared move lest I incurred the full frightening glare once more. Her dark, menacing presence at our fireside disturbed me. She had settled there like a big black thundercloud threatening at any moment to burst into a violent storm. I had seen nothing like her, and I could smell the foul stench of her clothes right across the room.

She wore a motley collection of garments, one layer overlapping another, culminating in a threadbare skirt that hung in shreds to her feet. All were torn and tattered, all stained and soiled, all little more than filthy rags. Her once substantial shoes now gaped open at the front like a mouth fed with fragments of newspaper – an explanation, I thought, for the strange slipslop sounds that I had heard earlier.

As for her luggage, it consisted of a coarse, crudely sewn cushion, buttoned down one side, which plainly contained all her worldly goods and served as both pillow and seat on her travels. It was her face, however, that fascinated and repelled me, and after a while I realized that what I had taken for a swarthy complexion was partly ingrained grime. Every wrinkle and crevice was filled with permanent dirt, like caked mud forming a brown crust. By contrast, the whites of her eyes stood out starkly, giving the impression of a fierce glare, the frightening look that had originally startled me. Her tousled mass of hair, long and black as jet beads, bushed round her head in tangles of grease, and straggled untidily over her forehead.

Not for the first time, Aunt Dot amazed me. Cool as a cucumber, she served her unwelcome intruder with tea and Spam sandwiches, a slice of her precious fruit cake, and two ginger biscuits. She might have been entertaining a duchess, so attentive was she, generously spooning out the sugar, stirring in the milk, and as if Mary would care about such niceties, cutting the crusts off the sandwiches. Only in one respect did she hold back from full hospitality. Mary was not invited to sit at the table, but was restricted to her chair, utilizing as an occasional table the all-purpose kitchen stool.

Surprisingly, I noticed that Aunt Dot seemed to have some kind of empathy for Mary, treating her with the compassion tempered with caution that she would have used in dealing with a wounded wild animal. And Mary responded like a wild animal, acting purely on instinct. She had no need of table manners, or social graces, or even speech, simply grabbing what she wanted and eating it greedily. She tore ravenously at the food, ramming it into her mouth with both hands, and gulped her tea quickly, hot as it was, while her watchful eyes darted round the room as if afraid the refreshments might be removed before she had had her fill.

For the most part she remained silent, except for the occasional grunt of satisfaction interrupting the steady sounds of chewing and slurping. But from time to time she muttered in incoherent ramblings not intended for our ears. She talked only to herself, and – to my horror – looked only at me. She watched me intently, glancing through her wild fuzz of hair like a wary animal, eager to be friendly but afraid of rebuttal. I felt terrified of this intense scrutiny, in mortal dread in case she snatched me up on her way out and took me with her. For some reason I had little confidence that Aunt Dot would stop her, and my grip on the chair steadily tightened till all the veins in my hands stood out like main roads marked in blue on a road map.

Then I had an idea born of desperation. I curled up as small as I could and pulled my nightdress so it would cover me, up over my ears, down over my hands, tucked under my feet. Since it was a white nightie, I hoped by that disguise to become invisible. I thought that Mary, being mad, might forget I was there and mistake me for a pillow or a pile of white linen. But as I glanced at her I detected a glimmer of amusement on her face, a fleeting smile, no sooner there than gone.

Meanwhile, Aunt Dot continued to chatter incessantly and Mary, once she had finished eating, soon grew restless. After a while she rose and picked up her cushion, ready to depart, and it occurred to me that maybe she was as tired of listening to my aunt's shrill incessant voice as I was, and maybe she was not so mad after all. But now I concentrated all my energies on holding on to my friendly chair arms, clinging so tenaciously to the limited security they offered that I would have had to be forcibly prised apart from them. And Aunt Dot bustled about in her inimitable manner, speeding her guest's departure, though trying to disguise her relief.

'Oh, are you off then, Mary? Well I suppose the time is getting on, and you'll want to be on your way. So we mustn't keep you. Look, Mary you might as well take a couple of biscuits with you for later. I'll put them in a bag. There you are now.'

She dashed to the door, but Mary reached it first. Thankfully, she had passed me – gone right by me with only a momentary pause – and I breathed a sigh of relief, slackening my hold on the chair arms. But having opened the door, she stood indecisively on the threshold, then turned and looked directly at me. Revealing teeth that had been small and straight but that were now as dirty and distressed as the rest of her, she smiled again, a strange smile, the sort that one shy child gives another. I tried to smile back. Good manners demanded no less. But somehow my face seemed stiffened in a fixed expression of fear, and anyway the nightdress presently hid my mouth. Still she hesitated and, misinterpreting her motives, Aunt Dot suddenly offered her accommodation for the night.

'Would you care to sleep in the barn, Mary?' she asked, with her usual flair for hospitality.

Mary shook her head and pointed towards the village, indicating that she had other plans, and once again I detected relief on Aunt

Dot's face as she shivered in the draughty doorway, pulling her heavy cardigan tightly round her, and sniffing the cold night air.

'Well, if you're sure. But it's very cold out. I know I wouldn't want to sleep rough tonight.'

Then for the first time Mary tried to speak, making a supreme effort to answer. Her face contorted in intense concentration and her lips moved as if struggling to find words. Finally her face softened, and in a hoarse and hardly audible whisper, like the wind rustling dead leaves, she breathed the words, 'Annie. Come out to play.'

After a second's thought Aunt Dot nodded as if she understood, and gazed at her sympathetically.

'But Mary, don't you know? Have you forgotten? Annie's . . . ' she began, then changed her mind, and on an impulse took hold of Mary's tattered sleeve.

'Just a minute. Wait a minute. This might help.'

She reached behind her to the coat rack, lifted off an old coat belonging to Uncle Matt, and slipped it over Mary's shoulders. I gasped in shock. The coat had undoubtedly seen better days, but I knew that my uncle had a particular regard for that coat, a quite irrational affection bordering on obsession, perhaps even superstition. His coat was as old as his marriage and he looked upon it not only as a useful garment, a veritable topcoat that fitted comfortably over other coats in stormy weather, but also as an essential companion – loyal, faithful, and long serving, a coat of many winters, never to be discarded. He did not, as in grand opera, go so far as to sing arias in its praise, but only because the idea had not occurred to him. The sentiments were there in full, so much so that he truly believed that if he lost the coat something terrible would happen to him.

For some reason, however, my aunt had always loathed the coat, perhaps because he loved it so much. She claimed that it made him look scruffy, like a disreputable old tramp, and more than once I heard her suggest that he donate it to a worthy scarecrow. Of course Mary knew nothing of the coat as a bone of contention, but accepted it merely as an extra layer of warmth, barely glancing at it, having no notion of its worth, real or imagined. She simply pulled it on and, like the ghost that I had first thought her, vanished wordlessly into the night.

I had hardly moved during her visit, every minute of which had gripped me with terror. I now discovered that my legs were frozen, numb to the knee, and when the door finally closed on her repulsive figure I crept thankfully to the fire, sat by it as close as could be, and silently recovered in my rocking chair, watching Aunt Dot. She now proceeded to attack the well-creased cover on the armchair that Mary had vacated, first with a stiff brush, then with a clean towel wrung out in warm soapy water. She sponged every inch of it over and over, rubbing vigorously, with the persistence of Lady Macbeth obsessively washing her hands, punishing herself as well as the chair until all possible traces of Mary had been wiped away, and both chair and aunt looked exhausted. Then she pushed the offending chair near the fire to dry.

I sat rocking to and fro, my thoughts occupied with the paradox of my aunt's personality. She treated me very strictly, and confined others to the doorstep or the wash-house. Even Uncle Matt, her nearest and dearest, often complained that she kept him around like a whet-stone for sharpening her tongue. Yet in dealing with a demented waif and stray, and despite her evident abhorrence of such a filthy, smelly guest, she had shown kindness, gentleness and hospitality. I could only guess at the reason – that Mary, having lost her wits, had become helpless, like a pet lamb, or a day-old chick, or a sickly calf, and help-lessness seemed to bring out the best in my contrary aunt, revealing a sort of repressed motherly instinct. She had even liked me better when I was ill. Admittedly, it was my uncle's coat she had given away, not her own, but there was a limit to her compassion and also to her coats. All the same, I found her relationship with Mary puzzling, and when she had finally finished cleaning the chair and its envi-rons I foolishly determined to probe the matter to its depths.

'Won't Uncle Matt be upset about his coat?' I began tentatively.

'Probably. And mind, Emma, you say nothing! You hear me now? Nothing! Now you've been warned. Well and truly warned.'

'Poor Uncle Matt. He loves that coat,' I answered incautiously, and noticed that her face registered annoyance that as usual I had taken his side, so I changed the subject slightly. 'Aunt Dot, where does she live, that Mary?'

'Oh, nowhere and everywhere. She's homeless. Homeless and harm-less. She sleeps anywhere. In barns and outhouses. In the fields and on the fells.'

'No wonder she smells so terrible. Where was she going, Aunt Dot?'

'Oh, I'm guessing she's headed for Lot House. She used to play there with Annie Pearson as a girl. The poor, sad, confused soul –

she still thinks she *is* a girl. Annie and she were great friends, but if she's expecting to play with Annie now she's in for a disappointment. She'd have more chance of playing with you.'

'Why?' I enquired, shuddering at the thought, and then worked out the answer. 'Because Annie's too old to play?'

Aunt Dot nodded grimly.

'Not only that, but she died five years ago, at the age of thirty-nine.'

'Why didn't you tell her?' I asked, now surprising myself by feeling sorry for Mary. Aunt Dot looked quizzically at me.

'She wouldn't have understood, and she'd have been upset. She might have stayed, and I didn't think you'd want that.'

'No,' I admitted frankly. 'She gave me a fright. An awful fright.'

Aunt Dot smiled mischievously.

'Well, all I can say is that it's a good job it isn't snowing. We couldn't have turned her out in the snow, now could we? I'd have had to put her up for the night. I'd have had to put her in with you.'

My green eyes widened in terror. I found her words sinister and ominous.

'My bed's much too small for two,' I pointed out quickly.

'Yes,' she said with a hint of malice, 'you'd have had to snuggle up close.'

I stared at her, horror-stricken. Could she possibly be serious?

'You don't mean it, Aunt Dot. You couldn't! You wouldn't!'

She smiled again, her shrewd grey eyes watching me.

'Where else could she sleep? We've only the two beds.'

'You offered her the barn before,' I pointed out, thinking I had her there, but once again she smiled maliciously.

'Yes, but it isn't snowing at present, is it? And besides, she took a real fancy to you. Didn't you notice? You must have noticed. She couldn't take her eyes off you. She gazed fondly at you the whole time she was here. I've never seen her take to anyone like that. She could hardly bear to leave you. Had to drag herself away. Yes, Emma, if she comes back here it'll certainly be to see you.'

I felt choked with fear. Was she only joking? Desperately I hoped against hope that she was joking, but I couldn't be sure. And now I had something else to keep me awake at night – not just the cruel absence of my mother, not just the terror of Mr Clout and his sinister cat, not just the constant threat of half-expected beatings from Aunt Dot, but now the most frightful prospect of all: the ghastly possibility of Mary – dirty, smelly and mad – climbing into bed beside me.

Night after night that image haunted me, dominating my thoughts, and the Mary of my imagination grew even worse than the reality, though that was bad enough. In my child's mind she gradually became bigger and blacker, dirtier and smellier, wilder and altogether more oppressive, like a clinging black blanket smothering the breath out of me. My aunt had described her as a poor lonely soul in search of a playmate, and it occurred to me that when she discovered the loss of Annie she might remember me and return. As Aunt Dot had said, there was no doubt that Mary had shown a disturbing interest in my every move. Those dark eyes under that black hair had watched me all the time, and before she left she had given me that awful, almost possessive smile.

So every night I prayed fervently that she would never come back, and – attempting to guard against all eventualities – that there would be no snow, none at all, that winter. A futile prayer. For the worst of it was that from then on the weather grew steadily colder, making the advent of snow not only inevitable but imminent. Meanwhile, only one day passed before Uncle Matt discovered that his beloved coat was missing, and he instantly instituted a thorough search, dragooning our help and devoting all his energies to finding it.

'Help me hunt for my overcoat, Dot,' he pleaded, and my aunt pretended to look for it, urging me to do the same. She had resolved not to tell him the truth, and I dared not disobey. So we searched in all the likely places, then in the unlikely places, then in those that were downright impossible. After that he started again, becoming totally obsessive about it, searching frantically every spare second, beset by feelings of guilt as if he had lost the coat through his own carelessness or neglect. I understood those feelings, having experienced a similar sense of guilt at the loss of my mother. In my eyes she was so perfect that I felt her rejection of me must be my fault. So I sympathized with him by keeping him company on his searches, ashamed of my duplicity, but doing my best to comfort him. Then one day, quite out of the blue, he dashed into the house, looking as if he had seen a ghost, frantic with worry, his face flushed and his eyes troubled.

'Dot! Are you there, Dot?' he cried. 'I've been thinkin'. About that coat. My coat. It just came to me – I haven't seen it since that scrounging Mary was here. Is it possible that she could have taken it?'

'Mary? Oh yes, Mary,' answered my aunt innocently. 'I'd quite forgotten about her. Well, I just wonder. Now you come to mention it, she did leave by the front door, didn't she, Emma? I suppose she could have snatched it on her way out. After all, it was dark.'

He stared at her, aghast.

'But didn't you see her? Didn't you watch her? Couldn't you stop her?'

'Oh, you know what Mary's like. She's a will-o'-the-wisp. She'd be off and away with it before I was aware she'd gone.'

He sank into a chair and groaned. I had never seen him so crestfallen, so stricken, his face gaunt, and his eyes dull with hopeless agony.

'Oh no! Not that!' he cried in anguish. 'Oh no, no, no, no! Not Mad Mary with my lovely old coat!'

'She must have needed it desperately, poor thing,' argued my aunt. 'Her clothes were hanging in shreds. It's an act of charity you've done. You'll get your reward in heaven.'

A low moan escaped him, and I realized the full extent of his suffering when he removed his cap and, revealing his bare head to the world, clasped the bald dome distractedly.

'I don't want a reward – in heaven or otherwise. My meanin' is I'd *give* a reward to get it back. I want my coat and I want it now! I hate the thought of it being close to that horrible filthy smelly creature.'

I looked curiously at Aunt Dot. Her face was an impassive mask, but anyone who knew her well would have detected an uncharacteristic nervousness in her manner. She did her best to placate him, showing such uncustomary patience and sympathy that I wondered why he was not suspicious. But even when she offered to buy him a new coat as soon as they could afford it, he still showed not a vestige of suspicion, apparently unable to consider her capable of such a dastardly act. He would not, however, be placated by a substitute coat, but raged unreasonably like a spoilt child, quite unlike his normal behaviour.

'Don't want a new one. Want my old one. Want it back. Want it here, with me. Now! My own lovely coat.'

And finally, despite her guilty conscience, she lost patience, clicking her tongue and giving him a piece of her mind, in the hope of settling the issue once and for all.

'For heaven's sake, Matt! You really are too bad. What a paddy you're in! The way you're carrying on! It's ludicrous! I tell you, I can't take much more of this. Surely you don't want the coat back after Mary's worn it all this time? Show some common sense, man. Goodness knows where it's been!'

That thought struck home, but only served to depress him further, and all he could do on the conversation front was to moan about his coat, expressing the same sad sentiments over and over again. For some two or three weeks he was a broken man, seething with feelings too deep for words, no longer whistling around the farm, no longer serenading the cows, not in any sense his usual buoyant and resilient self. He still brought me carefully selected gifts on market days, but now he handed them over straight away, as if he had no heart for the teasing ritual that had hitherto so entertained him.

'You know – it's only an old coat, Uncle Matt, not like – a person,' I said gently one day, thinking of my own truly sad loss, but he stared at me reproachfully.

'Well you see that's where you're wrong, Emma,' he said. 'To me, now, it *is* like a person.'

It was evident that he had regarded that coat as a medieval knight might view his armour, as a shield that had long protected him from the perils of the outside world, from storms and the treachery of fells and bogs. The sense of mourning went deep, and he grieved for the coat as if for someone close who had died, or gone away for good, only revealing their true worth too late. I grieved with him, and worried for both our sakes lest Mary paid us a return visit. I worried too in case something terrible happened, as he had ominously predicted, simultaneously indulging himself in almost masochistic pleasure as he conjured up visions of impending disasters.

Nothing did happen just then – nothing out of the ordinary, that is – though for some time afterwards he blamed every little mishap or misfortune on the absence of the coat. Gradually, however, he recovered his spirits, crawling slowly out of his Slough of Despond, and after a decent period of mourning, he became his old self again. But he never entirely got over his loss, and never missed an opportunity to give the coat an honourable mention, to my aunt's evident annoyance. Only she appeared to survive Mary's visit unscathed, and though we were all to face that disturbing apparition again, she never revealed the secret of the coat's change of ownership, and nor did I.

As the weather grew intensely cold and the longed-for month of December finally dawned, the calendar displayed the last pig portrait of the year, and for once I knew at a glance what I had to do. I felt well disposed towards this particular pig, because it represented Christmas and all the joys that season heralded, most especially the arrival of my mother. I needed a festive pig, and instantly recognized the potential of the jovial-faced Wessex Saddleback. A black pig, like Miss November, she differed in her accessories – hairy white cuffs and collar to match. Leaving these cuffs and collar pristine white, I merely reddened the dark body with a crimson crayon, added a red hood, and outlined a long white beard, and there it was – my Santa Claus pig.

I was reminded of happier days of carol singing with friends, tramping round neighbouring streets, singing a festive selection outside each door, but always finishing with a specific seasonal ditty. It began 'Christmas is coming, the geese are getting fat', and ended 'If you haven't got a ha'penny, God bless you'. The geese at Windlestraw were indeed getting fat, but I had no one to sing with, no one to sing to. The song, however, was short and soon remembered, so I secretly polished up my performance of it for the benefit of the calendar pig, a silent but uncritical audience.

Few children are immune from the special excitement of Christmas, even those without great expectations, and as it approached, my spirits rose. I hoped that this December pig, the last of the year, would also be the last to require the use of my coloured pencils and crayons, marking the end of my stay in Sourhope. And to add to my excitement, an advance Christmas present arrived from my mother, a parcel containing new winter clothes that delighted me. She had sewn or knitted everything herself, and I unpacked two skirts with matching jumpers, several pairs of long socks, and two woollen hats with pompoms. Every pretty thing in the parcel pleased me, and when alone in the house, I modelled the red outfit for the benefit of the calendar pig, and sang the song to a silent reception, putting heart and soul into the rendition. Then I smiled at the Christmas pig, and I could have sworn the pig smiled back.

Chapter 14

Golden Eggs

On the Saturday before I went back to school I tested the extent of my recovered health and strength by keeping Uncle Matt company on his various rounds, a busy schedule, to which he had added an additional task. The weather being so alarming – what with the mercury in the thermometer seemingly jammed at zero, the barometer, by which he set great store, now registering its worst, and the forecasts, both official and of folklore, all predicting a long, hard winter – he took it into his head to bring the sheep closer to home. Normally they lived on the fell above and beyond Brackenfield, but it was a good distance from the farmhouse should it be necessary to deliver feed.

'Don't want to make them soft,' he explained. 'Heaven forbid! And maybe they'll be all right up-by all winter, but I read in the paper that it's to be a bad one, and all the indications point to that. We've got red skies in the morning, and the moon's on its back, and it's a right frosty one at that, and I've noticed a few ravens about. Yes, definitely, there's all the signs and portents an' that. So the sooner I move them sheep the better. If there's heavy snow it'll be a deal easier if they're near at hand.'

So I helped him to bring the sheep down from the fell, along the track, and into the top lot behind the farmhouse. He kept a flock of Swaledales, and they travelled under protest, all looking as sheepish as their name and reputation suggested. Drifting ahead of us in a shambling mass of wool, they moved like rugs on spindly legs, surging forward one minute and faltering in disarray the next, swerving or bumping into each other, and tripping over their feet like an ungainly girl in her first long frock. All the way to their new winter home they bleated pitifully, their appearance matching their distress as their shaggy winter coats flapped round their ankles, snagging on heather, tearing on barbed wire, trailing through mud.

Progress was slow, made slower by Split's well-meant but clumsy efforts. By rights, at such times he should have come into his own, rounding up strays and stragglers, but as usual he proved more bother than the sheep. Refusing to keep his distance, he trailed their skirts, made sudden darts and gave sudden yelps, sending the scatty sheep off at a tangent in a frantic trot. Whatever the instructions he was given, Split did the opposite, and Uncle Matt shouted at him to no avail and whistled till he was blue in the face, but Split happily pleased himself.

As Uncle Matt remarked later when the gate finally closed on the sheep, if Split were entered in local sheepdog trials he could only win a prize in the novelty class. He was more of a circus performer than a trained sheepdog, and could do all kinds of clever tricks not normally required of him. He could dart and dodge, disappear when called upon to work, and miraculously reappear at mealtimes. When he wanted to ingratiate himself with Uncle Matt he could take a flying leap at him, turn over in the air, and land in his arms all curled up in a ball. But as a sheepdog he left much to be desired, and the hills resounded with harsh language as Uncle Matt cursed and swore and threatened a hundred times to cut the dog's legs off, while Split gazed back at him devotedly and wagged his tail as if he were being praised.

Nor was Split the only one to be confused that day. I had heard Uncle Matt mention that he had something called 'stints' on the fell, and in my innocence I thought we would be bringing them home along with the sheep, assuming that stints were rare animals, hitherto unheard of by me. I was excited about seeing them and had formed a clear picture in my mind as to how they would look, based on what little I knew of them. They must be heather coloured because they blended in, and similar to sheep because they lived on the fell. But the word 'stints' sounded more like a sneeze than a name, so I imagined them to be small and slight, with delicately pointed faces rather like whippets. Ever since Uncle Matt had mentioned them I had been intrigued, and as we approached the fell to collect the sheep I was determined to satisfy my curiosity.

'Where are the stints, Uncle Matt?' I asked eagerly.

'The stints, Emma? Right in front of you. Over there,' he said, gesturing vaguely at the heather, where I could only see sheep, as still as stone boulders and difficult to distinguish from them.

'But I can't see them,' I said, and he smiled teasingly.

'Can't you, pet? That's because they're invisible.'

Invisible animals. This was exciting.

'Then how do you know they're there?'

'I just know. And I know exactly how many.'

'But how do you count them, Uncle Matt?'

'I don't. They're already counted.'

'But how do you know you haven't lost any?'

'Why, 'cos they can't run away.'

'Then how are we going to bring them home?'

'We aren't. They're stuck out here. They can't move,' he said, grinning broadly.

Strange animals indeed, I thought, if they had to be glued to the spot, and he amused himself with his teasing answers for quite some time, plainly enjoying himself, and pushing the peak of his cap up high on his forehead the better to see my reactions. The more bemused I became, the more he laughed, until at last he explained.

'Stints aren't live animals, you see, Emma.'

'What are they? Birds?'

'No, nothin' live, Emma.'

'They're not dead animals, are they?'

'No, no. They're not animals at all. They're not real. They're nothin' you can put your finger on. Stints are – well, stints are – just a sort of entitlement on paper to graze so many sheep. That's about the size of it. Understand, Emma?'

I did. I understood that stints were simply a legal right to graze a flock of a certain size on the fell, and I understood that once again I was being teased for an adult's amusement. But it was gentle teasing, and though I felt rather foolish, I laughed with him. Anyway, the whole episode was driven from my mind by the trouble I found myself in that evening through no fault of my own, just because I followed my uncle and aunt round to the byre at milking time. I paused in the small byre to have a word with Tiny and Beauty, and two new baby calves cosseted there since birth. But I soon became aware of the rats skulking in the darkness behind me, their bright, malevolent eyes watching my every move, and I hurried into the big byre in search of more congenial company.

The cows were being fed before milking with a little of the cowcake they shared with the rats, and I kept well back out of their way. Before my illness I had helped to feed the calves, but only once did I try to feed the cows, because of the difficulty of squeezing past them. They either shuffled sideways, feet all over the place, clumsily thrusting me aside with their fat stomachs, or if they happened to be lying down, they reared up suddenly, lurching with scrambling legs and careless of where they tossed their horns. Aunt Dot, being thin, could dart in and out swift as a shadow, and Uncle Matt had his own method. He patted their rumps in passing and made soothing noises of 'Cush-cush, cush-cush' – cow language, he said it was, but I noticed that if he swore at them they leapt aside even faster.

They were now confined indoors every day with nothing to do but contemplate the whitewashed walls and chew their cud. In the close confines of the byre they had little room for manoeuvre, but rattled their tethering chains like restless convicts as they stirred in the gloom, turning large, soulful eyes on intruders like me. I preferred to stay at a respectful distance, because to me they seemed as enormous as prehistoric monsters with their massive bodies and lumbering gait, their sharp horns and steamy nostrils. They made a monstrous noise too, their deafening moos seeming to come from the very depths of their fat stomachs, echoing in the byre as if they were moaning in sorrow. And an unexpected moo was even worse, rumbling along the wide tunnel of a neck and emerging with the sudden blare of a foghorn, catching me unawares so that I leapt nearly out of my skin.

I had only been in the large byre a few minutes that evening when I noticed Aunt Dot frowning at me as if I were a trial to her. She stood with an empty milk pail at her feet, scrutinizing me with cold grey eyes, an appraising look that I had come to recognize when there was trouble ahead, when she had in mind some unpleasant purpose. Instantly I regretted that I had not stayed in the house, away from that calculating stare. Her head moved slowly and almost imperceptibly from side to side, like a snake's head before it strikes, and as she stared she smiled thinly. Finally she spoke.

'I wonder – I just wonder,' she began, gazing at me speculatively, and then with a curt nod she made her decision. 'I've just had a good idea,' she proceeded. 'What a pity I didn't think of it sooner.'

I glanced at Uncle Matt, my heart sinking – his too, I could tell. I was always apprehensive when she had an idea of some significance, as was he. It usually boded ill for one of us, or both of us, and he gave me a sympathetic wink and a wry smile.

'What's that then, Dot?' he enquired guardedly, not yet knowing which of us was to be the target of her latest brainwave.

'Well, I was just thinking that Emma could learn to milk a cow. You know – make herself useful for a change.'

The suggestion came as a bombshell, and I stared at her in disbe-lief, while Uncle Matt stopped milking and did the same.

'What in heck's the point of that, Dot?'

'Well, it's another pair of hands, and you never know when we might need one.'

'But the child's only eight!'

'She's nine next birthday, and anyway, that makes no difference. She could still learn. Lots of farmers' children learn to milk when they're young, and she's a fast learner and good with her hands. You're always telling me how quick she is.'

'Yes, but she's just a little girl. Look at her. She's only knee high to a butterfly. In fact she's not much bigger than the milk pail.'

'Nonsense! She's twice as big.'

'Well, Dot – twice as big as a milk pail isn't very big.'

'She's big enough. She'll be fine. She can learn on Dolly – a quiet enough beast. Very docile.'

'And who's goin' to do the teachin'?'

'Well, you are of course.'

'Somehow I had the feelin' it would be me.'

'Well I have enough to do. Heaven knows I have! I'm trying to *save* myself a job. Emma sits for hours in the house. She must be bored to death, and she might as well be doing something useful. I'm sure she'd like to learn. Wouldn't you, Emma?'

'No, thank you, Aunt Dot, I'd much rather not,' I said, with a slight shiver of distaste, but as carefully polite as if refusing a second helping of one her glutinous semolina puddings.

'Why ever not?' she asked, pretending surprise, as if everyone's ambition must be to milk a cow, and I took a deep breath before blurting out my answer.

'Because I'm frightened of the cows. Because I'm terrified, if you want to know. They're so big! They're huge! And they scare me half to death.'

'Rubbish!' she retorted. 'They're more frightened of you than you are of them. Anyway, you'll soon get over that. You'll enjoy milking once you know how. You spend too much time moping over books.'

'I *like* books, Aunt Dot. I love to read, and Miss Speedwell says you can never spend too much time reading. She says a good book is the best of friends.'

'Does she now? Well, what a pity Miss Speedwell isn't here to keep us right. You see, it's what *I* think that matters round here, and I think you need a change. You can make friends with a cow instead. Learn something new. It'll help to while away the long winter evenings, and what's more to the point, it'll help me. I usually have the job of milking Dolly. And as I say, she's docile.'

She moved along the byre with the milk pail as if considering the matter settled, and Uncle Matt muttered quietly to me from behind his hand.

'She's got to be docile when your aunt milks her. She has no other choice.'

He grinned wryly at me, but I could hardly raise even the vestige of a smile in return. Bitterly did I regret showing my face in the byre, prompting such terrible consequences. I had only taken my teddy bear for a walk and was looking for friendly company. Yet child though I was, somehow I knew that it was the sight of me standing there cuddling the bear, young and apparently carefree, that had sparked her discontent, causing her to unload onto me one of her own many responsibilities. She felt tired and had been suffering from a headache all day, and if she suffered, she made sure we all suffered. She now turned, advancing determinedly upon me, and, consumed with horror, I backed into the manure-spattered wall. She placed her pail beside Dolly's back legs and I braced myself, trembling in craven fear. My first impulse was to run – a pointless exercise. My second was to plead for mercy – equally pointless. But fear gripped me and reason fled. So with tears running down my cheeks, I pleaded.

'Aunt Dot, no! Please no! Not that. Let me do something else to help you. I'll do anything you say, but not that. Please Aunt Dot! Please!'

But the more I pleaded the more adamant she became, pushing me brusquely towards the big barrel of the cow's belly.

'What an almighty fuss!' she declared. 'Such a fuss about nothing. Now stop wasting time and get on with it. Now's as good a time as any to start.'

Uncle Matt looked at me in a resigned sort of way, and I too knew the futility, and indeed danger, of protesting further. But over the steady champing of cows I could hear my heart pounding nervously as he brought another three-legged stool. He sat my teddy bear on a window ledge out of harm's way, and there being no sign of a last-minute reprieve, I tearfully allowed myself to be led to face my ordeal and Dolly's ample hindquarters. I crouched between the cows, dwarfed by their massive bulk and thoroughly terrified, not knowing where or how to start. Fortunately Uncle Matt totally understood my fear, and cradled me with his arms and legs, effectively fencing me off from proximity to the cow until I had, to some extent at least, gained confidence. Then he taught me how to curl my fingers round the cow's teat and run them down it as I squeezed – a baffling and initially unproductive process.

'It's kinda like movin' your fingers along a violin string to get the different notes,' he explained fancifully, as time wore on and he struggled to keep his temper.

There followed numerous demonstrations on his part, and feeble attempts on mine, proving so clumsy that Dolly made her objections felt in many ways – by tossing her head, rattling her chains, flicking her tail like a dirty feather duster in my face, and shuffling her feet in the restricted box of a stall – forward, sideways, backwards, sideways, as if practising steps for a rumba. Docile she was, but it seemed that she could detect an unfamiliar pair of hands, and resented the incompetent fumbling of an apprentice with no notion of the art of milking, or even, as it happened, of playing the violin. But after many abject failures and bitter tears from me, and snide remarks from my aunt, and barely suppressed outbursts of impatience from my uncle, who clearly regarded the whole sorry business as a complete waste of time, I did finally manage to squirt milk. First I squirted it accidentally into Split's eye as he sat close by, taking a keen interest and no doubt in his own way cheering me on. Then at last I succeeded in shooting it straight and true into the milk pail.

Eventually I did master the peculiar skill, and could milk Dolly all by myself. I was occasionally called upon to do so, but not often. It seemed that Aunt Dot, having out of some strange perversity forced me to learn to milk the monster, soon lost interest once I had acquired the skill, and on the face of it had overcome my fear. But I never really did conquer my nervousness of the cows, especially when housed indoors. Nor did I ever understand Uncle Matt's violin theory, finding no similarity at all between the two pursuits, the one cultural and the other patently not. A diverse assortment of noises came from the cows as I sat there milking, but none by any stretch of the imagination could be described as musical, or in any way entertaining. And to add insult to injury, on the day after my traumatic initiation into milking, I encountered yet more trouble when the geese re-entered my life. I realized that my convalescence was well and truly at an end when Uncle Matt blithely suggested that I resume feeding those ferocious birds.

'I've been lookin' after your poultry while you've been poorly, Emma,' he said virtuously, 'but I guess they'll have missed you like mad. They'll sure be glad to see your little face again.'

'Oh, I'll be happy to see the hens again, Uncle Matt, but do I *have* to feed the geese? I do hate them. Really hate them.'

'Why, they'll be no bother to you now, Emma. There's just a handful of the beggars left,' he said, cheerfully waving aside my concerns. 'The older blighters went to market for the Christmas trade, so you'll hardly notice the rest. Take my word for it. And it'll be one job less for me, an' that.'

I racked my brains for a way out of these daily confrontations with the hated geese who now spent most of their time in the old hen-house. And though indeed fewer in number, the remaining youthful warriors formed the more energetic and forceful element, fiercely determined by casual pecking at my arms and legs to find out whether I was or was not edible and being offered as part of their diet. That evening, however, quite by chance, I happened to re-read an old library book, and was struck by the story of the goose that laid a golden egg. Instantly I became alert to the wonderful possibility of finding such an egg and could hardly wait to question Uncle Matt on this exciting prospect. I began to see the geese in a new light, a twenty-four-carat light, and if there were golden eggs going, I had no intention of missing out. Next feeding time, I plucked up all my courage to face the junior gaggle, and once the big beaks were busily occupied attacking their food instead of my legs I cautiously searched their premises, risking my skin for a very special reason.

I knew, strictly speaking, I had no right to the eggs, golden or otherwise, but rather hoped that the rule of 'finders keepers' that decided ownership at my new school might equally apply in this case. Nevertheless, I wanted to be honest and above board in my dealings with Uncle Matt, and suspected that I might be more knowledgeable about golden eggs than he was, supposing myself, from what I knew of him, to be more widely read. I had never seen him read books or stories of any kind, though he often furiously described his various invoices and household bills as pure fiction, reading them again and again with heartfelt grunts of dismay and resentment, as if he needed to be convinced that they could possibly be true. But he confined his serious reading to newspapers and free agricultural leaflets, and his light reading to Mr Shoeman's correspondence. So, having no wish to take advantage of his possible ignorance, I approached him openly before I continued searching.

'Uncle Matt, have you heard that some geese lay golden eggs?'

He pursed his lips and shook his head.

'No, Emma. Can't say as how I have, like.'

'Well, they do. I read about it.'

'Oh, do they now? Is that a fact? Well, you do surprise me. I can honestly say I've never come across one. And never's a long, long time.'

'Uncle Matt,' I continued, getting down to brass tacks, 'could I keep a golden egg if I find one?'

'You can that, Emma. You certainly can, pet. Definitely,' he said, with surprisingly lavish extravagance.

'Uncle Matt,' I persisted, 'I couldn't possibly have two, could I? I really need two.'

'You want two? That's fine. No bother. Help yourself,' he said agreeably.

I felt pleasantly surprised, and concluded that I must have caught him in a particularly good mood, so uncharacteristically generous had he been. He had a reputation stretching way beyond the valley for being canny with money, and even I noticed that it was a struggle for him to part with it, and that he rarely did so without bidding it a long and reluctant farewell, almost with a tear in his eye. On such sad occasions I thought he looked like a jailer watching a prisoner escape, yet here he was, donating golden eggs to me, right, left and centre, and actually smiling about it. I was astonished and slightly taken aback, and to add to my bewilderment, he waved his hand expansively and went on with even greater munificence.

'Two, did you say, Emma? My meanin' is, if you need two, you have two. Now are you quite sure you wouldn't like three?'

Plainly, I thought, he must be on a spendthrift spree.

'You mean it, Uncle Matt?'

'I do. Definitely.'

'I can really have three? Really?'

He smiled kindly at me and nodded his head.

'Emma, my pet, you can have as many as you find,' he said with astonishing largesse. 'You can have every golden egg there is. You can have all of them. Just as long as you throw a bit of feed around while you're at it.'

My heart leapt with excitement, and I skipped for pure joy as I set off to feed the dreaded geese.

'Oh, thank you, Uncle Matt! Thank you, thank you! I'll never forget you for this. I really hope I find some.'

'I hope you do, Emma,' he said, suddenly rather serious. 'I hope you find all of life's golden eggs.' He swivelled his cap, gazing at me meditatively, then added, 'Though I have to say, pet, they're thin on the ground. They've always stayed hidden from me.'

I searched diligently every day, my small fingers sorting anxiously through the straw and feathers in eager anticipation of wealth to come, though my keenness was not entirely motivated by material gain. I wanted two golden eggs for two good reasons. The first would make a wonderful Christmas present for my mother. I had in the past always bought her some pretty trifle out of my pocket money, but in the absence of both shops and pocket money I had nothing to give her this year, and I could imagine her pleasure on unwrapping such a glittering prize.

The second egg, should I be lucky enough to find two, would serve a more subtle purpose. I had a shadowy notion that rich people did what they wanted and got what they demanded. So the possession of a golden egg would give me that authority, that power. I could, for instance, live where I liked and with whom I liked. If I were rich enough I could go home to my mother, and no one could stop me. A golden egg represented freedom, my escape from Sourhope. So I pursued my quest every day without fail, but sadly found nothing – no glint of golden eggs – and oddly enough, no ordinary eggs either. Indeed, that latter shortage began to trouble me, niggling away at the back of my mind, until one night I spent some time thinking about the mystery, the unaccountable absence of goose eggs of any description.

It so happened that on that particular night I had been wakened in the small hours by a nightmare in which Mad Mary was climbing into bed beside me. Her dark clothes hung over me like a blackout curtain, and though I knew for sure it was Mary, I could see nothing of her face except for the whites of her bulging eyes as she closed in. I woke with a start, petrified, and lay in a cold sweat, motionless in the pitch-black bedroom. The dream had been so real that when I plucked up courage to move I cautiously stretched out exploratory legs and arms to the icy far reaches of the sheets, nervously seeking assurance that Mary was not in the bed. Thankfully she was not. And hearing no sounds other than those that were normal, I gradually grew confident that she was not anywhere else in the room either. With immense relief I realized that it had only been a nightmare, but a frightful one at that, upsetting me so much that it was some time before I could get back to sleep. I lay tossing and turning, thinking of this and that, determinedly trying not to think of Mad Mary. Finally I tried counting the Swaledale sheep as I remembered them coming down from the fell, and when that failed to work I tried counting the geese instead. And suddenly it struck me quite forcibly that the lack of goose eggs of any sort was suspicious, so suspicious that it warranted investigation, and before eventually falling asleep I made the decision to tackle Uncle Matt on the subject first thing the following morning.

'I've decided to give up searching for eggs, Uncle Matt,' I said. 'I've been thinking about it, and it seems to me you have the wrong kind of geese.'

He looked disappointed, probably in case I rebelled against feeding them, once the incentive had gone.

'Give up? Why, that's not like you, Emma. You're never defeatist. What do you want to give up for? You should never give up on some-thin' you've set your mind to. I dare bet Miss Speedwell tells you that all the time. Now doesn't she? Ten to one she does. No, you've got to keep on tryin'. Try, try, and try again, as they say. You get nothin' if you don't try.'

'But I don't think your geese are the kind that lay golden eggs. In fact, they don't lay eggs at all, and that's a funny thing, Uncle Matt.'

He looked thoughtful, scratching the stubble on his chin reflec-tively, and pursing his lips as he did when taxing his brain for a telling phrase to clinch a deal at the mart. Then he turned to me with wide, innocent blue eyes.

'I think I know what the trouble is. They must be upset about somethin'. They don't lay if they're upset, you know. You haven't upset them, have you? You haven't been saying, "boo" to them or anything like that?'

'I don't think so,' I said doubtfully, for who could remember what was said in extreme circumstances?

'Ah, but you're not sure. So you might have. Well, there you are then. You've heard the expression "daren't say boo to a goose" haven't you?'

'Yes, but . . .'

'They don't like it. They get upset. No wonder they're not layin'. Of course, it's up to you, pet, if you want to give up, but if I were you I'd keep on lookin'. There's always an outside chance that you might be lucky. And that *would* be somethin', now wouldn't it? But my meanin' is, just watch what you say in front of them.'

Fool that I was, I took him at his word and went on looking for golden eggs, braving the danger zone, and risking pecked legs. I endured daily disappointment, but it never occurred to my rogue of an uncle to tell me that the geese only started laying in the spring. I had been so careful not to take advantage of his possible ignorance, but he showed no such scruples in taking advantage of mine, using my gullibility to get his geese fed for him.

One day I recalled Droopy, a goose in some ways different from the rest, a goose singularly marked, and I wondered if she was the one that laid golden eggs and he had foolishly sold her. Perhaps the agreeable young man he had duped into buying the troublesome goose had reaped the reward for his soft-hearted acceptance of her. I hoped so because, fond as I was of my uncle, I felt he did not deserve a gold mine of a goose. Meanwhile I remained my gullible trusting self, waiting for my mother to take me away.

Chapter 15

The Teacher

My return to school was an unexpected triumph, even though I was late again. It appeared that without the need to be early on my account, Joe had slipped back into his old hitty-missy ways of unreliable time-keeping, and on that particular Monday morning he was running late, very late. So my pleasure at seeing his handsome face again was spoilt, as was my enjoyment of the elevated ride in the lorry cab, by the additional worry of making a conspicuously late entrance. This anxiety increased the sense of unease already troubling my mind at the prospect of returning to school after such a long absence, and my heart thumped loudly all the way there, echoing the throbbing engine. Joe did his best to hurry things along, springing about like a veritable jack-in-the-box, hurtling cans on and off the lorry with reckless haste, and vigorously revving the noisy engine till I could hardly hear myself think, let alone speak. But he made up little of the lost time, and as he dropped me off at the school gates he grimaced ruefully.

'Sorry, bonny lass,' he shouted. 'Ah canna help things as the day answers, but Ah'll see tha forst thing the moorn. My word on't.'

'That's all right,' I shouted into the cold wind, smiling wanly at his pleasant face, knowing that indeed he had done all he could for me and I had no real cause for complaint. He was under no obligation to transport small girls to school, and under even less to race against time trying to beat the school bell. 'Bye, Joe. See you tomorrow then,' I called out, prolonging the parting.

'Chin up, bonny lass,' he yelled back over his shoulder as he started to turn the lorry and, reluctant to let him go, I stood watching as he clanked and rattled up the road to Blackcleugh Farm.

Then I walked through the iron gates feeling as timid as on my very first day, once more overawed by the deep silence of the deserted yard. This time, however, I faced the ordeal alone, without my dapper uncle tagging along, weakly hanging on to my hand. Nor could I take Joe's advice and keep my chin up, because the yard's surface had turned very hazardous, thickly covered in a crisp white frost, which numerous busy boots had criss-crossed with slippery slides, now frozen hard. Cautiously I picked my way between the icy tracks and crept into the classroom, nervous as a new girl, and after placing my absence note on Miss Speedwell's desk, stood timidly waiting. The note was a tightly folded missive, painstakingly shaped to fit my small pocket, and in its creation Uncle Matt had burnt the midnight oil, straining every brain cell to the utmost, and sustaining an ink-stained mouth in the agonies of composition. Unable to use the regular excuse, designed for a short absence and subtly suggesting that Aunt Dot's cooking was to blame for any indisposition, he had had to start from scratch. But he wrote plainly and simply, much as he spoke and straight from the heart, waxing eloquent only in his determination to convince any doubters of the absolute legitimacy of my absence. The final version, which I had timidly presented, was written in his best copperplate hand, and read as follows:

Dear Miss,
Emma's been laid up with an uncommon bad cold, through a hole in her shoe brought on by the teeming weather of late. My meaning is, it was more like the flu she had. Definitely. In fact she's still a bit femmer, but now has new wellies.
    Yours truly,
    Matthew Wheatley

Splendidly informative as the letter was, Miss Speedwell simply laid it aside to digest at her leisure and hurried round the desk. And a moment later I might never have been away. I was welcomed with open arms, literally, because she gave me a big hug, and all my class-mates followed her example and gathered round excitedly.

'Oh, Emma, Emma, how lovely to see you!' she cried. 'How are you, dear? I've missed my little helper. We've all missed you, haven't we, everyone? Even the twins. They don't remember much, as you know, but they do remember you. We're delighted you're with us again. Welcome, welcome!'

I blushed with pleasure, and could scarcely resist skipping as I made my way to my old familiar desk. I had almost forgotten the joy of being missed and wanted, and was gratified to be greeted by everyone in turn, each boasting some new possession or accomplishment, from a dead woodlouse secreted in a matchbox to an impressive paragraph of joined-up writing. Of course the girls were more interested in showing off new clothes, and Betty Heslop, the baby of the class, paraded in a complete new outfit, which hung loosely, fitting where it touched, so that she did not so much wear it as move about inside it, emerging here and there as required.

'Me mam says I'll soon grow into it,' she explained earnestly, and we all wished her every success with her best endeavours to do so.

Then Tommy Noble triumphantly announced that three times tuppence ha'penny made sixpence, and not to be outdone, Jimmy Nixon attempted to empty a celebratory ink pot over Jack Reed's head. I reflected happily that nothing much had changed in my absence except that Miss Speedwell seemed to get nicer and nicer. I sat swinging my legs contentedly, glad to be with friends, and she brought me two books, a slim volume and a big fat tome, and smiled warmly as she handed them over.

'I've saved these specially for you,' she said. 'I know you'll appreciate them more than anyone else. This one's about Dr Dolittle, who talks to animals, and you can take that home to enjoy. The other may be difficult for you in parts, but I'm sure you'll love the illustrations. I thought of you the minute I saw them – I thought you might like to draw some copies of them and colour them in your own special way.'

I accepted both books with immense pleasure. I had missed the joy of choosing library books and soon found that ready access to *Farmers' Weekly* and the *Pig Keepers' Gazette*, though they constituted recommended reading by Uncle Matt, was no substitute at all. Having a tendency to talk to animals myself, I looked forward to reading *Dr Dolittle*, and as for the second book, a compendium of *Arabian Nights* tales, it filled me with awe and wonder. It was so large that when open, it entirely covered the desk, and I knew I would love it even before I opened it because it was bound in cerulean blue leather cloth embossed in patterns of gold. Nor did the contents disappoint, for as I rapturously flicked the pages I found them rich in exquisite illustrations, each one more brilliant than the last.

I became bewitched, absorbed by the book of wonders, which transported me from my bleak, drab life to a charmed world of immense beauty. The stark grey houses of Sourhope were transformed into exotic minarets and lacy-walled palaces; the dour and soberly clad farming community became sultans, viziers and princesses, flamboyant in turbans, curly-toed slippers and diaphanous silks. My aunt's clippy mats became flying carpets; the hurricane lamps, magic lamps; the farm scythes, scimitars; and the hateful geese, fabulous giant birds. I could hardly wait to reach school and return to the book's entrancing pages. I treated it with reverence, guarding it jealously from other small fingers. Indeed, on occasion I had to tear myself away from it, forcing myself to concentrate on less exciting subjects, until such time as I could return to my magic book and re-enter its enchanted world. I was glad to be back with Miss Speedwell again, glad to be learning again, and I soon settled into my old routine, resuming my role as her assistant and passing pleasant days in her company.

One morning I told her the tale of Mad Mary and confessed my fear of a return visit. She listened with rapt attention and then persuaded me to write an essay on the subject and to paint my impression of Mary. She praised both my efforts, giving them high marks, though the portrait turned out so ghoulish, so darkly sinister, that it frightened the twins at first. Nevertheless, the wise Miss Speedwell mounted the work on pale cream card and pinned it on the display board, where it was exhibited all the time and therefore gradually went unnoticed. Mary's frightful image became commonplace, a non-event that frightened no one. And though in the night it still came to my mind, to some extent it haunted me less.

Sadly, as I passed those pleasant days of learning in an easy and sympathetic environment that suited me well, I little knew that they were numbered and about to come to an end. To my dismay, Miss Speedwell soon grew pale and feverish, showing all the symptoms of becoming the next flu victim. As she struggled more and more each day I worried about her, and also about the infant class. What would we do without her? What would become of us? To lose our lovely teacher would be bad enough, but the alternative of being taught by Mr Clout did not bear thinking about. Then one day disaster finally struck. We arrived to find our teacher missing, and we clung together in teeth-chattering trepidation, waiting for inevitable doom in the terrifying shape of Mr Clout.

At five minutes to nine we heard the scuffle and shuffle of feet as some twenty-five to thirty seniors, give or take absentees and truants, lined up for assembly in the large classroom, which also served as a school hall. A hush fell on all of us except for Betty Heslop, who began to whinge and then to weep softly. Miss Speedwell had always shepherded us in and out of assembly, and huddled beside her at the entrance, we hardly noticed we were entering alien territory, but now we were on our own and very insecure. Yet so ingrained were we in the habits she had instilled in us that we automatically formed a smart single file at the door, standing wide-eyed and woeful, waiting to see what would happen. I took Betty's hand to comfort her, and at nine precisely we heard the rustle of tweeds, and a grizzled head appeared round the door.

'Assembly!' barked Mr Clout. 'Come along now. Chop-chop!' And we were marched into the main room and shunted sideways to form a front row, a small, anxious band of latecomers.

Assembly began and, except for the lack of our teacher's reassuring presence, it proceeded much as usual. The service conducted by Mr Clout combined Christian principles with his own apparently pagan philosophy of striking first and reasoning later – if at all. He threw in a little of one, then a little of the other, all mixed up like potpourri. The religious parts, consisting of prayers, a short reading from the Bible, and a hymn, were periodically interrupted by his unpredictable prowling, especially during prayers, when eyes were closed, increasing his advantage and the surprise element when he pounced. Casually and indiscriminately he meted out sharp reminders of his presence, like a big bear freed from captivity and amusing himself at random. Though not built for speed, he moved purposefully, and even in the act of pouncing, there lurked a threat of worse to come. His loud growl of 'There! That's for nothing. Now do something!' resounded through the room, affecting even the most innocent of us with a sense of impending misery. A prod here, a smack there, a salutary cuff round the ear, or an instructive push back into line – these were all part of the service, and prayers were punctuated by strangled cries as he trod on vulnerable toes.

It seemed to me that, as on a battlefield, those of us in the front line were most at risk. His affliction of deafness made him sensitive to the slightest movement, the merest twitch, and he reacted irrationally, venting his frustration by selecting culprits at random – often the usual suspects who in his opinion were bound to be guilty of something or other – and inviting them to join him at his study door during break. I fully expected to be included sooner or later in that ominous invitation, because my position at the end of the front row was perilous. So I stood uneasily, stiff as a steel poker, frightened to make the slightest move yet feeling oddly conspicuous, as if my head had grown so big that it would be bound to catch Mr Clout's roving eye. Petrified as I was, I wondered how Uncle Matt had had the temerity to bargain with this growling bear, boldly offering him half a crown for his sentimental watercolour, and once again I saw my uncle in a new light.

Then came the hymn, and in the absence of Miss Speedwell, our pianist, it soon degenerated into a tuneless cacophony, which even Mr Clout, deaf as he was, could hardly fail to notice. Miss Speedwell always managed to keep the singing moving along smoothly, drowning out the discordant voices, but Mr Clout had no musical accomplishments, being more at home with a trowel or a dibber than a piano. He was deaf like Beethoven, but there the resemblance ended, and once he had played the starting note he had reached the end of his repertoire. As the singing began to falter, he tried to revive the flagging sound by waving his arms about, acting as a choirmaster.

'Right, everyone! Watch me!' he shouted, bristling importantly, and struck the air with a hairy hand and a jerky action, like an automaton winding down, as the hymn collapsed in confusion. 'Pay attention! Watch the beat!' he bellowed, and wiggled his formidable eyebrows encouragingly.

But remarkable as those eyebrows were – the sort that would prompt a barber to reach for hedge clippers rather than scissors – their effect was not sufficient to rein in runaway singers. The hymn turned into a pell-mell race to the finish, with the senior pupils taking the lead and the infants lagging well behind, and the pace grew faster and faster, more and more chaotic, until a furious Mr Clout held up a flat hand like a traffic policeman and thundered 'Stop!', whereupon the singing floundered altogether and gradually petered out. No further hymn was attempted for the duration of Miss Speedwell's absence.

Mr Clout now glared round the room, hoping to spot other offenders to punish, since he had not yet reached his daily target. But a wary silence had fallen, a silence so profound that anyone could have heard a pin drop – anyone except him, that is, unless it had been a rolling pin. So, in some disappointment, he moved on to the announcements, beginning with a reminder to all pupils of the areas that were out of bounds.

'Two boys have been caught climbing the bell tower,' he thundered, 'and will be severely punished. You all know very well that the bell tower is out of bounds. As is the newly erected tool shed. Stay away from that. Don't go near it. Don't even think of it! The shed is absolutely and categorically out of bounds. Yes, indeed!'

For the first time that morning a ripple of interest spread through the seniors, girls as well as boys. Whereas the custom of climbing the bell tower was a time-honoured tradition, regarded by some as rather old hat, the tool shed was new, bang up to the minute, offering intriguing and unmissable possibilities. But Mr Clout heard nothing of this excited buzz, being too busy offering alternative amusement.

'Those of you who are bored with the playground should come and see me. Satan finds mischief for idle hands and I can usefully employ those hands. There is much to be done in the vegetable garden before winter.'

A subdued groan spread through the room but he heard nothing.

'There is soil to be dug, mulching to finish, manure to spread. There is no need to be bored when you can commune with nature among the onions and leeks, or keep yourselves busy in the Brussels sprout bed.'

A louder groan followed this suggestion, but if he heard it he ignored it, finally coming to the anxiously awaited announcement concerning Miss Speedwell, confirming our fears that she would be absent for at least a week. He tweaked irritably at his moustache while he considered what to do about this difficult situation, glaring balefully at the infant faces at the front as if he had never seen such a depressing sight, as if holding us directly responsible for his present inconvenience.

'Oh dear me! Dearie, dearie me!' he muttered, striding restlessly back and forth. 'As if I haven't enough to put up with, enough idiots to teach! Upon my soul! Another class to look after! Infants indeed! Babies no less! Gracious me! What to do? Yes, indeed, what to do?'

He shook his shock of grey hair and his beady eyes swept along the front row as if seeking inspiration, while we stood rigid with fear, hardly daring to breathe. At length he threw his hands in the air with a dramatic gesture, suggesting that it was all too much to bear, and suddenly bellowed at us, enunciating every word painfully slowly as if we infants generally spoke a foreign language.

'Right! All – right! Go – back – to – your – classroom. Sit – down – at your – desks – and – don't – make – a – sound. Not – a – sound, I – say, until – I – have – time – to – attend – to – you.' He added ominously, 'I'll – be – coming – for – you – shortly.'

It was a sobering thought. And in a subdued line we filed out as instructed, glad to be away, albeit temporarily, from the scrutiny of those sharp eyes: though heavily camouflaged by hair, they seemed

211

to bore holes right into the brain, reading thoughts that were better concealed. Having fully expected to be pounced upon like so many other unfortunates, I led the way out with alacrity and feeling light as air, with something of the relief experienced by someone sentenced to sit under the sword of Damocles, who hears the suspending hair snap but the sword miraculously miss.

Again as instructed, we sat at our desks and remained quiet – at first. Then Betty burst into uncontrollable sobs, the twins followed suit, others joined in, and the hubbub grew in volume. It was a disturbingly miserable sound, and for a few moments I sat with my hands over my ears, trying to think. I was very conscious that the classroom had turned into a sort of Wailing Wall, and I could imagine Mr Clout's reaction should he come in at that point. I knew I had to do something. But what? Then, after a moment's hesitation, I did the first thing that came to mind – I gave out the textbooks. And taken by surprise, my charges stopped wailing to watch me. So I continued passing out the necessary equipment – pencils, paper, rulers and rubbers. I chose pencils because of Jimmy Nixon's nasty habits with ink, and paper because Miss Speedwell was so particular about her exercise books, and rubbers because in the infant class they saw more action than any other piece of classroom equipment.

Unwittingly, I took over the class. I knew the particular stage that each pupil had reached – from young Betty struggling with the simplest words and the easiest sums to the three six-year-olds who worked in all subjects from Book Four. And thinking that Tommy Noble would be a problem, having as he did a natural resistance to learning, I suggested that he copied the alphabet in large straight letters from the wall chart, a ponderous and painstaking task involving such considerable heavy breathing and pencil-point licking that he was still occupied with the letter 'K' when Miss Speedwell returned. I copied her methods in everything I did, and was busy writing page numbers on the blackboard when I became aware that all eyes were on me, or rather were staring goggle-eyed at something directly behind me, and I turned to confront Mr Clout, hovering silently and menacingly at my heels. He must have sneaked in soundlessly because I heard nothing of his approach, so intent was I on the task at hand. One minute the room was totally devoid of hairy monsters, and the next we had one too many. It was almost as if he had simply materialized in his hairy grey form, like a short and substantial Dracula.

'Aaaaah – hah!' he exclaimed, as if he had caught me red-handed in the act of stealing his leeks.

Naturally I leapt in fright and hurried back to my desk, and we all began to work feverishly, silent except for the frantic scratching of pencils working overtime. The small room seemed filled with Mr Clout's hairy presence, dominating our every thought. He moved round our little desks with a clumsy shuffling gait, his shrewd eyes flitting to and fro, like an inquisitive bear taking a close interest in new surroundings – too close for comfort. He crouched over each of us in turn, placing a hairy paw on each desk as he did so, snorting at our humble efforts, and giving an occasional grunt, as bears are prone to do. At last he reached my desk and stopped, his beady eyes boring into my blushing face as he took a thoughtful pull at his beard and growled softly. Convinced that he was about to pounce, I shuffled uneasily along the seat, but instead he stepped back from me, the better to see me.

'And what's your name again, young lady?' he enquired, not unkindly.

'Sir, it's Emma Emmerson, sir,' I replied, loudly but deferentially.

'No, it's not. It's – er – on the tip of my tongue – yes – I know it – it's er – Weakling. That's it. It's Weakling, isn't it?'

'No, sir. It's Emma Emmerson.'

'Are you sure?'

'Yes, sir. Quite sure.'

'I think you're wrong there.'

'No, sir.'

'I'm certain your father told me Weakling.'

'No, sir. And he's not my father, sir.'

'Not your father? Not your father! Oh, indeed! So that's the way it is. Well, I can't say I'm surprised, having met him. Dear me! Dear, dear! Whatever are things coming to? The careless way some people live! No wonder their children don't know who they are. I can assure you, young lady, that I've never forgotten *my* name. I've always known I was a Clout, but you don't seem to know that you're a Weakling.'

'Really, sir! My name's Emma Emmerson. Honestly, sir.'

'Well, we won't argue, young lady. I have it written down somewhere, and of course it'll be right there on the register,' he said triumphantly, as if he could easily prove my ignorance of my own name. Then he added, 'You're a forward little thing, aren't you?'

I kept quiet on the grounds that to answer might incriminate me.

To admit being forward, putting myself in the wrong, or to deny it, contradicting him again – both might equally well annoy him, and I had more sense than to bait a bear. Besides, he seemed to be verging on being in a good mood, showing a faint, but for him unprecedented, glimmer of a smile through the fuzz that was his face.

'There, there. Never mind,' he said benignly, seeing the growing distress on my face. 'For goodness' sake don't upset yourself, Emma – er – whatever you're called. You've done very well. Got the little perishers all working. And all by yourself. That's quite remarkable. Yes indeed, remarkable! It's first rate in fact. Splendid! Now carry on, everyone. I'll see you later.'

He bestowed a final searching glance on me, no doubt remembering our earlier chat about onions and cats, and I shifted uncomfortably in my seat, experiencing a twinge of concern for the unwelcome attention I had brought upon myself. Then he moved ponderously to the doorway, filling the width of it, and stumped out, slamming the door behind him, and we all breathed a sigh of relief, though it was too soon, because the door suddenly opened a crack again, and round it came his grizzled head.

'I'll leave this door ajar just in case,' he growled. 'And remember – I'm only next door. Just a seed fling away. If I hear so much as a peep out of any of you I'll be back before you can say – cat.'

The head vanished and heavy footsteps clumped away, this time leaving us in shock. There it was at last – *The Cat*. Out in the open. A direct mention, a direct threat. We all began to whisper simultaneously, asking each other if anyone had seen the cat, and what it was like – where kept, when used, and how fed. The others followed my lead, and because I assumed the cat to be a live animal, so did they, except for two objectors with older brothers and sisters, who expressed doubts. They insisted that the cat was used for hitting people so it must be a dead cat. But that theory seemed altogether too far-fetched and they were outnumbered and outvoted. And after we had all twittered for a time in nervous speculation I began to worry in case Mr Clout should hear us and settle the argument by producing the disputed cat, so I brought everyone to order and we settled down to work, trying to put the feline mystery to the back of our minds.

Gradually the class began to accept me as its teacher, and after a few days I occasionally found myself addressed as 'Miss', and even Mr Clout sarcastically called me 'Miss Weakling'. Of course, without

Miss Speedwell being present, I lost the privilege of staying in at breaks, but fortunately I discovered that I had my choice of peaceful sheltered corners near the school building, because most pupils now congregated at the tool shed, the popular and fashionable place to be. I heard rumours that the shed was full of bright and shiny brand new tools, spied through the window, but so far Mr Clout's security system of locks and more locks, as well as padlocks and chains, had defied entry to even the most enterprising of amateur burglars.

On the whole Mr Clout left the infants to themselves. I knew more about the class than he did, and he knew a good thing when he saw one. But he frequently checked up on us, forever haunting the room with his hairy presence. Constantly I heard the door creak as he tried to push it open without our knowledge, and constantly I saw his apparently disembodied head peering through the opening, observing us like some grizzly spectre. He called in often, sniffing round in the manner of a school inspector looking for faults, but I followed Miss Speedwell's timetable and her excellent example, storing completed work in neat piles of separate subjects. He examined them, poring over my work in particular, especially in Nature Study, while I tried to keep out of his way as far as possible, and avoided speaking to him. One day, however, he caught me off guard. He had been studying my newly completed cross section of a cowslip, and he sighed with pleasure.

'Aaah, the wonderful wild cowslip, Primula veris. A beautiful drawing. Yes, indeed!' he murmured. 'That's the stuff to give the troops.' And for once my natural curiosity overcame caution.

'Please, sir, what exactly would the troops do with it?' I enquired, interested, but he gave me a wooden stare and departed, leaving me none the wiser.

I never for a moment flattered myself that my humble efforts as a teacher constituted anything more than a holding operation. In fact, if any of my class fell asleep, as some were inclined to do, I left them alone and tried not to wake them, especially if the snoozers happened to be Tommy Noble or Jimmy Nixon, who were considerably less trouble that way. At the beginning of Miss Speedwell's absence I had locked away the beautiful blue book, and conscientiously followed the normal timetable with no privileges. Like the others, I missed our teacher tremendously and danced with delight when she returned, just a few days before the Christmas holiday, but in time to give us end-of-term tests, and to put up paper streamers and set us to work making Christmas cards. Nevertheless, she praised my initiative and hard work in her absence and presented me with a leather pencil case, bright blue like the Arabian book, and filled with gleaming new pencils. I loved the present – the look of it, the rich leathery smell of it, and most of all the fact that it came from Miss Speedwell. I spent a blissfully happy day, and that evening treated the calendar pig to six choruses of the special Christmas carol. But so often in life pride comes before a fall, and my downfall came next day at school with a visit from Mr Clout.

'What's the name of that little thing?' he asked Miss Speedwell, waving a hairy paw at me.

'It's Emma Emmerson, Mr Clout.'

'Are you sure? She told me it was, but the chap who brought her said it was Weakling. I distinctly remember that. I have it written down somewhere.'

'That gentleman was her guardian, Mr Clout. Her uncle. And his name's Wheatley. Emma's an evacuee.'

'An evacuee, eh? Well I don't care what she is. She's a clever little thing. I've had my eyes opened about her while you've been away. She's even good at Nature Study. Her – er – guardian told me she was well ahead of her years but I didn't believe him. He was such an odd bod. No hair. And he kept trying to buy my picture, right off my wall. I've never experienced an interview like it. I expected him to make an offer for my desk and chair next. Anyway, he was right about her after all. She's good.'

Miss Speedwell glanced anxiously at me.

'Yes, Emma's a clever girl,' she answered quietly, 'and she's beginning to settle down nicely.'

Mr Clout frowned accusingly at her, his shaggy eyebrows like two hairy caterpillars meeting in the middle of his forehead.

'So, Miss Speedwell – you've noticed! Yet you failed to draw the matter to my attention. That was most reprehensible. Yes, indeed! I'm surprised at you. But never mind. No harm done. Now that I'm aware of her outstanding ability we'll move her up straight after Christmas.'

'With all due respect, Mr Clout, I'm not sure that's wise,' said Miss Speedwell bravely. 'She's a very sensitive child and she's just settled down. And after all, she's had enough to put up with, being uprooted from home, separated from her mother.'

He frowned darkly, exercising the caterpillar eyebrows. Academic decisions were always open for discussion with Miss Speedwell, but only as long as she agreed with him. He wagged a playful finger at her, but his eyes smouldered angrily.

'Now, now, Miss Speedwell, this won't do. It won't do at all. You mustn't hold her back.'

'Oh, I assure you I'm not,' she replied heatedly. 'As a matter of fact she's been working at the level of your ten-year-olds.'

'Exactly!' he cried triumphantly. 'She's in the wrong class. She's well beyond this one. She's as bright as a button. I can see her *easily* passing the eleven plus. She's nearly there already. And I could certainly do with someone of her intelligence next door. Half the time I'd swear I was talking to myself. They're a lot of philistines. Even when it comes to Nature Study. Heaven knows they live their lives with nature in the raw, but they have absolutely no appreciation of its finer points. Ask them about sheep dipping or peat digging and you're on their wavelength. Catch them on wild orchids or the haunts of the ring ouzel, and you catch them wanting.'

I silently seethed with indignation. I was well aware that this assessment of his pupils was a far cry from the line he had taken with Uncle Matt, when he had suggested that their brains were in direct ratio to the size of their clodhopping boots, and I, being small, had been dismissed with contempt. He talked whichever way the wind blew, I decided, adopting one of Uncle Matt's expressions. But again he waved a hairy paw in my direction.

'That child is different. Yes, indeed! You're right in saying she's sensitive, and she's also perceptive. She has a natural appreciation of beauty. That child can draw a butterfly so precisely that you can count the scales on its wings and wouldn't be surprised if it fluttered away. She can capture the detail of a wild flower minutely, so that you find yourself sniffing it, half expecting to catch hay fever. And as for essays, she can describe a kestrel so that it soars off the page. The top and bottom of it is, Miss Speedwell, that child's in the wrong class.'

Despite the praise I stared at Miss Speedwell in horror and misery, my big eyes imploring her to save me. Was this to be my reward for looking after her class? Surely she could intervene. But she too looked agitated, fearful on my behalf but helpless to prevent the inevitable. Yet she made a final protest, tactful but insistent.

'Yes, she's doing well, Mr Clout, but perhaps it's not wise to move her just now. She's been away for weeks with a bad dose of flu and needs to settle in again. As I said, she could easily be knocked back, and anyway I think she's possibly too sensitive for the senior class. After all, she's only eight.'

He waved a dismissive hand and shook his head.

'Nonsense!' he said firmly. 'Next door is where she belongs, and next door is where she goes. It's all settled.'

He puffed his chest out and gave his beard a self-satisfied tug, taking credit for discovering talent plainly under his nose all the time. Then he turned to me with a triumphant and possessive look, like a racehorse owner who has just acquired a likely winner of the Grand National.

'By the way, young lady,' he said imperiously, 'just for the record – your name *is* Emma Emmerson.'

'Yes, sir, I know,' I answered with lip trembling, tearfully wondering why he was telling me what was not news.

'Just as long as you *do* know,' he said with a self-important air. 'You seemed somewhat confused earlier. You certainly had me confused.'

Then he departed, returning to torment his class next door, and leaving me to wallow in self-pity. Tears started in my eyes, and I lowered my head onto the desk and sobbed into the scribbles and ink blots, just like little Betty on a bad day.

'I won't go into his class!' I cried. 'I won't! I just won't! Please don't make me.'

Miss Speedwell stroked my hair soothingly, upset but out of her depth. She too was annoyed at the turn of events, but helpless to alter them.

'I'm sorry, Emma. I'm so sorry. But there's nothing more I can do. Mr Clout's the headmaster and what he says goes. But you'll be all right. You can hold your own anywhere. I'll keep an eye on you. And you can still come and see me at breaks, and I'll still save you the best library books.'

That helped, but not enough, and for a while I was inconsolable. Then I remembered – how could I have forgotten? My mother was coming for me. Surely this time she would take me away. Of course – I would never reach Mr Clout's class! I was safe. Everything would be all right when my mother came. And so it was that with the often-misplaced optimism of youth I stopped crying, pulled myself together and cheered up, returning to the *Arabian Nights* tales to absorb every last detail while I had the chance. The term ended with good wishes all round. I said fond – and I hoped final – goodbyes, and the Christmas holiday began. But sadly I ran into trouble straight away. As soon as Aunt Dot spotted the pencil case she took me to task.

'That looks expensive,' she said in accusing tones. 'Your Uncle Matt didn't buy you that. Where did you get it? You haven't taken it from school, have you? Have you, Emma? Tell the truth now! Tell the truth and shame the Devil.'

'No, of course not, Aunt Dot.'

'From one of the other children then? Tell me! Have you stolen it?'

'No, no, Aunt Dot. I'd never do such a thing!' I exclaimed, affronted.

'Then where did you get it? Explain that if you can.'

'It was a present. Given to me by Miss Speedwell.'

'What on earth for?' she demanded suspiciously.

'Well – for – sort of helping her.'

'There you go again, giving yourself airs and graces,' she said disbelievingly. 'Now where did you get it? The truth now. Out with it!'

I began to cringe, feeling like a heretic under interrogation by the Spanish Inquisition. Nothing I said was believed. Then Uncle Matt came to my rescue.

'Was it for doin' good work, Emma?' he enquired kindly.

'Yes, that's it, Uncle Matt.'

'Kinda like a prize, an' that?'

'Yes, I suppose it was.'

'Admit it now, Emma. Was it for bein' top of the class? Go on, tell me. *Was* it?'

I gazed into his eager blue eyes, now twinkling with excitement, and I knew I could not disappoint him. Besides, in a way it was the truth.

'Well – yes, Uncle Matt,' I said, taking the easy way out.

He smiled radiantly, finally able to forgive himself completely for putting his aspirations of owning his dream picture before my best interests. Not that I imagined he had been greatly troubled by remorse, knowing him as I did. I guessed that he would have justified his conduct to himself ages ago. Nevertheless, he began to crow, exuding complacency and self-satisfaction.

'There you are, Emma. There you are, girl!' he cried triumphantly. 'Didn't I say you'd be top of the class? Didn't I now? My meanin' is, I told you so. Didn't I tell you? And I was right. By heck, Emma! I was one hundred per cent right. There now! How about that!'

I smiled at his pleasure in my supposed success. But there was no top of the class among Miss Speedwell's charges, no class to be top of – just ten little individuals, developing at different rates, struggling to make sense of it all. Little did my uncle know that I had been left in charge of that composite class, which he had abandoned me to, and that for several days I had in my own small way replaced the teacher. But I said nothing. I guessed that such a revelation would at the very least be received with scepticism and, as far as Aunt Dot was concerned, would come into the category of telling lies, an offence meriting serious punishment – in her eyes, possibly even hanging. So I told no one except the calendar pig, who I knew from experience to be the soul of discretion.

In any case, while I counted the minutes until my mother's arrival, the routine at Windlestraw was suddenly disrupted. There was little time to spare for me, even less than usual, because both aunt and uncle had become obsessed by food, leading to a long-fought battle of wills in which one of the casualties was a pig.

Chapter 16
Cheesed Off

For some time now, especially since the onset of winter, Uncle Matt had grown discontented with the monotony of his diet, and on this vital issue, as on so many others, I totally agreed with him. I too found the boring predictability of Aunt Dot's food disappointing, neither tempting in content nor sufficient in quantity to satisfy the appetite of a growing girl. Often of an evening he and I would engage in critical analysis of the meals served that day, commiserating over the burnt offerings, or the frugal portions (though sometimes a small portion could be a blessing in disguise), and the subsequent indigestion or stomach upsets or lingering hunger. Of course we conferred in private, out of earshot of Aunt Dot, so that we could reminisce freely about favourite foods, drooling over thoughts of steak and onions or Yorkshire puddings or chocolate éclairs, the memories of past feasts being all we had to sustain us in the current famine.

'By heck, Emma! When you cast your mind back,' he would remark ruefully, 'to the way things were before the war an' that, it sure makes you think.'

'It does, Uncle Matt,' I agreed companionably, although in truth I retained only dim memories of those halcyon days.

'Aye, things are always changin'. And like as not it's for the worse.'

'That's so true, Uncle Matt,' said I, with feeling.

'Mind you,' he pointed out during one of our clandestine discussions, looking rather guilty, 'make no mistake about it, I think the world of your aunt Dot. I do, Emma. Definitely.'

'Do you really, Uncle Matt?' I asked, finding the concept difficult to accept and unable to conceal my surprise.

'Oh yes. Though I don't think so much of her cookin', you understand.'

'I know, Uncle Matt. Me too.'

And so it was that, having little else to sustain us, we wallowed in nostalgia, and for a while that unhappy situation prevailed, the question occupying both our minds being what, if anything, could be done about it. As he gravely pointed out, the thorny issue of my aunt's cooking could not be tackled lightly for fear of repercussions. In the case of open mutiny she held all the weapons to quash it. The daily fare, such as it was, whether burnt, small, or otherwise found wanting, could be reduced still further, or withdrawn altogether, or even, as had been known, hurled in temper at the mutineer's head or into the all-consuming fire.

'No, Emma. You just can't rush into these things. A sensitive matter like this requires careful handlin'. A man needs a deal of tact and diplomacy,' he said sagely, and as I rarely thought of him as Uncle Matt the diplomat, I naturally watched subsequent events with great interest.

His rebellion, when it finally came, was in itself unusual, because he rarely interfered in household affairs in case he found himself roped in to help with them. Outdoors was his province, indoors hers, and as she was in charge of all things domestic he criticized her methods at his peril. But suddenly events took a downward turn, plunging us both into despair and driving him to take defensive action, whatever the consequences.

'By heck, Emma! It's hard to believe that our meals could get any poorer, but they have. They're actually goin' from bad to worse, as they say.'

'You're right, Uncle Matt. They are. But what can we do about it?'

'Do? I dunno yet. But I'll definitely think of somethin'. That I will!' he vowed, pulling his cap down squarely in fierce determination.

The farm's store of bacon and hams had been running very low, even the dubious ones tinged with green that he tried to palm off on the unsuspecting. Nor did the butcher's van come to his rescue as it used to before the war, tantalizing his taste buds with succulent cuts from the chopping board. Indeed, by the time the van reached Windlestraw there was not much left from which to choose, the choice cuts having been distributed on a first-come-first-served basis.

There again, as I could hardly help noticing, Aunt Dot lacked my mother's flair and imagination to stretch the rations by making tasty meals from very little meat. I well remembered the savoury meals I used to come home to every day, the pies and suet puddings, the soups and stews and hotpots that my resourceful mother made from our rations. Aunt Dot, however, spent too much time scrubbing and cleaning to have much energy left for cooking, and the less successful her efforts, the less interested she became, and consequently the less she tried. But what made matters worse, bringing everything in this period of deprivation to a head, was that she embarked on a health-food diet, or, as my uncle described it, 'a daft food fad', and as far as he was concerned this was the last straw.

The *Shiretown Post* could claim initial responsibility for the decline in the already low standard of culinary creations produced in the Windlestraw household. It published an article on allegedly healthy eating, and the minute Aunt Dot read it on a sheet of newspaper wrapped by the butcher round a neck end of lamb, she was lost to real food. She adopted its recommendations lock, stock and barrel, embracing its stringent principles like a religion, with all the fervour of the newly converted.

'We'll all benefit from healthier eating,' she insisted self-righteously. 'It says in the article that we should just eat to live, whereas most people live to eat.'

'Not in this house they don't,' muttered Uncle Matt woefully, his whole aspect registering despair.

'We'll be all the better for eating the right things, better both phys-ically and spiritually,' she reiterated emphatically, but we two strongly suspected that the diet appealed to her simply because it involved hardly any cooking.

She showed no regard for the fact that neither of us shared her faith, nor for the lack of availability of all the ingredients necessary to promote good health. She adopted the principles of the diet but ignored its finer details, and the result was hunger and misery for us all. In the cold weather we longed for a hot meal, but day after day we faced a near-starvation diet consisting mainly of carrot juice, stewed raisins, raw cabbage and oatcakes. I gradually acquired a taste for the oatcakes, they being the nearest thing to food, but I loathed the cloying taste of the carrot juice, and was constantly on the lookout for places to rid myself of the nauseating liquid, the discriminating Split having turned it down at the first sniff. As Uncle Matt commented when we were alone, a little of that foul sickly stuff went a long way.

Aunt Dot kept herself going on constant cups of tea and ginger biscuits, and seemed determined to see the thing through to the bitter end. But once her food fad was in full swing I began to notice in Uncle Matt the signs of burgeoning rebellion, though at first he adopted a softly, softly approach. Making no mention of the controversial diet, he harped on incessantly on the subject of food – what he liked, what he disliked, and what his particular preferences were, until I wanted to scream with hunger. Sausages featured highly in his list of preferred foods, and he took to muttering to the world at large about them at every opportunity.

'I want sausages. Give me sausages. I like to know what I'm eatin'.'

I tried to put him right there, but to no avail.

'Nobody knows what's in a sausage, Uncle Matt. There's all kinds of funny things in them. My mum says it's hard to fathom sausages, especially nowadays when there's so much sawdust mixed in.'

'I love 'em,' he declared, unrepentant, and defiantly kept on muttering about sausages, often bursting into the refrain 'When we are married we'll have sausage for tea, sausage for tea, sausage for tea . . .', tantalizingly repeating those three words until finally ending with a triumphant bellow, 'Oh how happy we will be!'

The songs he sang round the house now tended to feature food rather than romance, and we were regularly regaled with snatches of 'Boiled beef and carrots' and 'Pork chops and gravy', and his favourite chorus, ending in a defiant shout of 'You get no bread with one meatball'. He even extended his repertoire in the byre, when serenading the cows, to include 'Hey little hen, when, when, when will you lay me an egg for my tea?' and, using poetic license for the old lyric 'I'm in the mood for love', changed the words to 'I'm in the mood for stew'.

But if he thought he would wear down my aunt's resistance so easily he was greatly mistaken. She steadfastly ignored the message in the songs, and though he sang as loudly and emotionally as a plaintive street singer in an effort to ram home his dissatisfaction, she showed not a flicker of interest, passing him with a cold, impassive expression as if studiously biding her time. I could therefore barely conceal my trepidation when he ventured a step further, launching into a modified version of the popular but provocative song which went something like 'Ma, I miss your apple pie, Ma, I miss your stew, Ma, she's treating me all right, but she can't cook like you', putting so much elongated emphasis on the 'Mas' that Aunt Dot was heard to remark to no one in particular that he sounded like a constipated sheep.

I realized that he was at last working himself up to taking a stand; that these tactics were not just a cry from the heart but a broad hint. But no one took the hint, neither the inflexible butcher nor my equally inflexible aunt, though Uncle Matt and I were both convinced that it had registered with her. Soon we all began to look under-nourished and to lose weight though none of us could afford to, and when hunger pushed Uncle Matt to the limit, he became a force to be reckoned with. First he tried another tack, more direct yet still pursuing his tactful approach. While I sat open-mouthed in astonishment, he simply and politely requested a variation in the menu.

'You see, Dot, I could just fancy somethin' a bit different,' he explained guilelessly. 'What I'm gettin' at is that raisins and carrot juice are all very well once in a while, but a man likes a change. Call it a quirk if you like, but a man likes a bit of variety. Some sausages would be nice, very nice, but failin' that, some bacon and eggs would go down a treat.'

'So!' she said, managing to put a lot of venom into that short word. 'So you're tired of a healthy diet already. You'd like something a bit different. Is that right?'

'That's it, Dot. They do say that variety's the spice of life, and a man likes to be surprised.'

'And that's what you'd like, is it? Something completely different, and you'd like to be surprised?'

'That's it, Dot. That's exactly it. Definitely.'

She turned to me, a sly little smile playing about her lips, and gave me a penetrating stare.

'And what about you, Missy? Would you like to be surprised?'

I hesitated. Clearly she regarded us as co-conspirators, and I thought hard but fast, weighing up the subtle menace of that malicious smile I knew so well against the ever-present threat of carrot juice. I asked myself: which was the greater of the two evils? And carrot juice won by a short head, as Uncle Matt would have put it.

'Yes please, Aunt Dot,' I said, living dangerously, especially since Uncle Matt instantly deserted me, wiping the perspiration from his neck and quitting while he was ahead.

'Things to do in the byre,' he muttered, beating a hasty retreat to that safe haven, craftily removing himself from an atmosphere charged with tension.

But the following day Aunt Dot did indeed surprise us. Out of the blue she produced what was for her a surprisingly innovative dish, to be served with the unsurprising oatcakes. It was an experimental attempt at goats' cheese, which my uncle later graphically described as 'the final sickener', and as soon as I came in for tea he intercepted my progress to the table, discreetly pressing a strong brown envelope into my hand.

'Here, Emma, cop hold of this, pet, and hide it up your jumper,' he advised in a hoarse whisper. 'You'll be glad of it when you taste what's for tea. Believe me, I know. I've sampled it.' And he grimaced as he wiped his sticky forefinger on his handkerchief.

'What's wrong?' I whispered back, and he jerked his thumb at the table. With an expression of acute distaste, he indicated three plates, two of them unusually full, containing some sort of white mess, like paste scrambled to a sticky, lumpy consistency, which, together with the oatcakes, comprised our evening meal.

'Your aunt's made it,' he muttered warningly. 'It's supposed to be cheese.'

I took the optimistic view.

'Oh, we haven't had that before. It might be tasty.'

'Pigs might fly,' he said shortly.

'Well, it's a change at any rate. That's good, isn't it?' I whispered, but he shook his head firmly.

'No, Emma, it's not good. It's anythin' but good. It's plain awful in fact. The taste is sickenin' and disgustin'. I don't know how your aunt does it. Ruinin' good food like that. Must be a knack, a natural gift. No, the word for that cheese, Emma, the first word that springs to mind, is diabolical. Yes definitely, diabolical. Take my advice, pet, and pop what you can't eat into the envelope. Pass it to me when you're finished, but on the sly, like, under the table. Be very, very, careful though. It'll easily give you the slip, and she's sensitive about her abominable cheese. She's real huffy about it.'

I took his advice. I hid the envelope, and as he had predicted, was glad of it. For as I tentatively tasted the surprise cheese there was no doubt in my mind that it was strongly redolent of goat – the smell of goat and the taste of goat, so powerful that my imagination conjured up the very aura of goat hanging over the table and I could have sworn I could see its horned and shaggy shape. Then I noticed the texture of the cheese, which slopped around the plate in glutinous globules, and when I put it in my mouth it stuck to my teeth, refusing to be swallowed. I glanced at Uncle Matt and for an instant thought that he was foaming at the mouth, and wondered if I appeared similarly afflicted. Certainly I could hardly prise my jaws apart, and though to my knowledge I had never eaten wallpaper paste, I felt sure the taste and consistency must be similar.

'This cheese would stick paper to the wall for ever, Uncle Matt,' I murmured thickly. 'It would even hold the wall up.'

He grunted in agreement, his spoon hovering over his plate, his puckered face poised, sniffing like a fastidious cat suspicious of an unfamiliar cat food. While Aunt Dot was out of the room he raised his plate to his nose, took a deep sniff, and recoiled.

'Anybody who takes two sniffs of that's a glutton,' he whispered with a wink at me, and hastily put the plate down.

He had his own thick brown envelope at the ready, and whenever opportunity presented itself he spooned his cheese into it and then balanced it on his knee, hidden under the hang of the tablecloth. I cautiously followed suit, but we were obliged to eat some of the acrid curds when Aunt Dot was in the room. She watched us like a hawk, and when I tried to eat oatcake without cheese she gave me a warning look, a look that promised a beating if I failed to treat her cheese with proper respect.

'You asked for a surprise,' she said austerely. 'You asked for something different. You both wanted it. Well, you've got it. And by heaven, you're going to eat it.'

With a show of enjoyment I scooped a spoonful of the sickening stuff onto an oatcake and chewed stoically, but it was all I could do to swallow it and keep it down. Fortunately Aunt Dot rarely sat still during mealtimes, but kept topping up the teapot at the stove or dashing into the kitchen on undisclosed errands. In fact, later that evening when my fellow sufferer and I exchanged views on the so-called meal, we agreed that she had left the table considerably more often than usual. Uncle Matt said it was odds on that she was also trying to avoid eating the cheese, because she had served herself with the smallest portion by far, and he added that he considered such selfish behaviour a bit sneaky, not to mention underhand. But be that as it may, during those brief respites we carried out our cloak-and-dagger enterprise, busily transferring the odorous cheese to the receptive envelopes, filling them to capacity.

It was a dangerous game, requiring strong nerves and split-second timing. First the disgusting goats' cheese had to be transferred without spillage. Otherwise the game was up. Then, when it was me carrying out the manoeuvre, the soggy envelope had to be balanced on my knee before finally being passed under the table to Uncle Matt's waiting hand as he reached blindly underneath the tablecloth. The entire procedure was fraught with heart-stopping moments, for to be caught in the act meant a beating for me for sure and no doubt some unpleasantness for my accomplice. Nor was that the end of the matter, because the sticky cheese was served up again the next day, and the next, and though it was hard to credit, each time it surfaced, the nauseating dollops seemed even stickier and smellier. I had been reading about a witch's brew and now I had the feeling I was tasting it.

'It's the killer cheese again,' Uncle Matt whispered on the second day. 'It sure smells high. I'd sooner smell the manure heap – it's a healthier pong.'

'What did you do with yesterday's envelopes?' I enquired discreetly.

'Emptied them into the pig swill,' he muttered, hardly moving his lips.

'Hard luck on the pigs, Uncle Matt.'

'Well, pigs'll eat any old swill dumped in front of them. Even your aunt's cookin'. Even her diabolical cheese. They never turn their snouts up at anythin', and you see, they'll never even notice the smell.'

I felt better knowing that, and happily on the fourth day he finally put his foot down – not before time, I thought. We were running out of envelopes, and when the pungent smell of goat met him at the front door, invading his nostrils, his forbearance suddenly came to an end.

'Hellish dark, and smells of cheese!' he muttered, remembering a line from one of the few books he had read, his face grimacing in disgust as he finally confronted my aunt. 'The whole house smells of cheese. I bet they're sniffin' it down at Thorny Edge. Maybe even in Shiretown. No, that's it. Definitely. No more goats' cheese, Dot. Not an ounce. Not a teaspoonful. Not even a minuscule amount. No more ever, ever again,' he announced, reeling from the smell. Then, seeing her face darken like storm clouds over Lornhope, he added, 'Not that it's not good. In fact I've never tasted anythin' like it. It's in a class of its own. But the sad fact is, most regrettably, Dot, goats' cheese disagrees with me.'

Aunt Dot's eyes narrowed.

'I knew you didn't like my cheese. Why didn't you say so? I just knew it. Right from the start.'

'It's not your cheese, Dot. It's any goats' cheese. It's always upset me. Even when I was a nipper. That's why I've never suggested you make it. And there again, I thought I might've grown out of the trouble, but I haven't. I'm still allergic to it. I think Emma is too. She's lookin' a bit peaky. Thinner than a fourpenny rabbit.'

I directed a grateful glance at him. I had been wondering what my fate would be if he managed to wriggle out of eating the cheese, and whether I would have to dispose of twice as much – perish the thought. I waited hungrily as he brought eggs from the kitchen, cracked them into a pan and fried them, two each, sunny side up for him, once over lightly for me.

'Save you havin' to cook something else, Dot,' he said diplomatically. 'My meanin' is, you can enjoy your cheese in peace.'

That brave gesture, which to my mind merited a medal, signalled the beginning of the end of the health-food diet, and secretly I thought that Aunt Dot had seen it coming. But she never gave in lightly, never went down without a fight, and for a while she tried to make us suffer while she acted the martyr.

'What a pity I bothered to make the cheese. Such a waste of time and effort, not to mention good milk. As if I didn't have enough to do. But you did say you wanted something different.'

'Yes, and it certainly was different,' he conceded.

'I'm a fool to myself. All that work and all for nothing,' she complained bitterly, and in a voice suggestive of an angry corncrake, embarked upon a catalogue of all the tasks undertaken that day, and the day before, and the day before that, until, fearing that she might keep going back to the day they were married, Uncle Matt looked up from forking his eggs and stopped her in full flow.

I was lost in admiration. Before me, with egg yoke running down his square chin, sat my hero. 'Now, Dot, that's enough. We all know how hard you work,' he said placatingly, leaving me wondering who 'we all' were, and whether he included the dog. 'But I just can't work on goats' cheese and carrot juice. This cold weather I need somethin' hot and nourishin'. So does Emma. She's a delicate little thing and she's gettin' awful skinny. There's no need to go to a lot of trouble. A boiled onion'll do at a pinch, with some nice brown bread, or a couple of eggs, an' that. You know. Anythin' does me.'

'And *what*,' demanded Aunt Dot angrily, 'what do you suggest I do with all that cheese? I made some more today.'

I could see temptation written all over Uncle Matt's face as a pithy and heart-felt answer sprang to his lips, but instead he played the peacemaker.

'Yes, it would be a shame to waste it. Must be good for somethin'. Tell you what – we'll sell the fresh stuff to the Shoemans. Serve them right. I mean, it'll serve them well. It'll go nicely with their sauer-kraut or whatever.'

For the first and only time I felt sorry for the Shoemans, but after all, I thought, this was war, and Aunt Dot's cheese a powerful weapon. So Uncle Matt had his way at last, and to a certain extent the menu changed, but not the monotony. Aunt Dot was down but not yet out. Raisins and carrot juice were relegated to the status of an option, but Uncle Matt's victory was by no means complete. Having rashly asserted that he would be happy with eggs, he soon found that eggs became the dish of the day every day – once, twice, and occasionally three times a day. He went out after eating eggs and came back to face more eggs, cooked in different ways, but eggs all the same. Whenever Aunt Dot went into the kitchen he winked at me and made clucking noises, now recklessly careless of whether or not she heard him.

'If I eat one more egg I'll start layin' them,' he declared, cackling like one of my hens on the nest. But he had a final card up his sleeve, and one day when he came in frozen stiff from repairing dry stone walls and caught sight of his overcooked omelette sitting in a pan, he played it.

'We have a pig needs killin',' he said, quite out of the blue.

'What do you mean, *needs* killing?' Aunt Dot demanded suspi-ciously, emptying the pan of its rubbery brown contents onto his plate.

'One of them pigs is too fat for her own good. She can hardly stagger to the trough. In fact, I'm practically hand-feedin' her, 'cos she's so weighed down.'

'Pigs are supposed to be fat,' my aunt pointed out crossly.

'Not so fat that they can't move,' he asserted. 'That's no life, even for a pig. And my first thought was, instead of feedin' her, like, she might as well be feedin' us.'

'I can't be bothered with pig killing, just before Christmas,' Dot cried. 'It's a lot of work and we've got visitors coming.'

'That was my second thought,' Uncle Matt said agreeably. 'Plenty of grub to feed the visitors.'

'The meat won't be cured for at least three weeks,' she argued, 'and it's just a few days to Christmas.'

'Ah, but we needn't cure all of it. In about a week we could have a roast or some chops, and meantime we'll have kidneys and liver and black puddin' and white puddin' and big juicy *sausages*. Think of that!'

'It sounds like a whole load of work to me. It seems no time since we killed the last pig and I was shattered afterwards for weeks. Just plain tired out.'

'Yes, it's too much work for you, Dot, far too much. So I thought I'd ask Bill and Elsie to help us out. They can have a share of the produce if they share the work, and Elsie's a dab hand at sausages and black puddin'. She's a right tasty cook.'

'Is she indeed? That's nice for you,' Dot said dryly.

'Just like you, Dot,' he said, winking at me behind her back. 'But Elsie'll be willin' to give you a hand, though you'll be in charge, like.'

She held out as long as she could, but he kept playing up the poor health of the pig.

'It has to be done, Dot, before she dies. She's in a bad way. Could hardly stir today. Didn't even poke her snout out of the sty. The big, fat, lazy lump of lard.'

In the end she agreed, and in a rush to beat the Christmas visitors, final arrangements were hastily made. The local pig killer, Sam Cullen, was discreetly sent for, not on the usual grapevine but by more cloak-and-dagger means, strictly hush-hush, there being wartime regulations governing the private slaughter of pigs. And that very Saturday, Bill and Elsie arrived after breakfast to keep us company for the day, a social event which in itself went against the grain as far as Aunt Dot was concerned. She could not help glancing at their feet, and had to force herself to refrain from dwelling on where those offending appendages had been before they tramped around her pristine kitchen. But I always enjoyed company and was drawn to Elsie at once. She brought me lemon sherbet, and both she and Bill fussed over me, providing a pleasant change in my solitary existence. As soon as Bill came in he looked around, seeking me out, and then nodded, and with the air of one disposed to conversation, took a seat, beaming through the pipe smoke that preceded him.

'So *there* ya are, little Emma,' he said kindly, his blue eye winking as if we were old friends. 'I see the elves haven't got ya yet.'

My answer surprised even me, and Aunt Dot shot a sharp glance in my direction.

'There's worse things than elves,' I said solemnly. 'They're well down my list of things to worry about.' He laughed heartily.

'Aye, Emma. Reckon yer right at that,' he said. 'But those elves are a bit slow, like. You're that bonny that fer two pins Ah'd steal ya meself.'

Then Elsie advanced to greet me, bending over to shake my hand, making me feel very grown-up and important.

'Well now, so you're Emma. Bill said you were a bonny bairn and for once he's right. We'd have loved a little lass like you, but God in his wisdom sent us five lads. Never mind, Emma, you'll make a lovely wife for our youngest some day. He's turned nine. Just the right age.'

I smiled pleasantly, but privately I thought what a terrible fate that would be, to be marooned forever in this bleak valley, enduring the harsh drudgery of life as a farmer's wife. Such a future by no means fitted my romantic dreams. I expected my life to be more like one of the *Arabian Nights* tales, full of beauty and excitement, accompanied, of course, by a handsome prince, even now waiting in the wings somewhere for me to grow up. But I hated to disappoint people, and she seemed very set on the idea, and she *had* brought me lemon sherbet, so I decided not to mention that I was already spoken for, and went on smiling. After her next remark, however, the smile faded.

'You're a bit skinny though,' she said kindly. 'Thank goodness we've a pig to kill and we can get you fattened up.'

Until that moment I had never really thought about the origins of meat and its progress to the dining table. I vaguely realized that meat came from dead animals, but exactly how the living creatures ended up cooked on my plate had never entered my mind. Naïve as I was, I must have imagined that they conveniently died 'peacefully in their sleep', a phrase found frequently in columns of deaths listed in the local newspaper, and which I understood at that time to mean that they knew the best way to die and took advantage of it.

So it was that Elsie's remark came as a terrible shock. To me the pigs were like people and I knew them personally. There were five pigs living at Todd Tingate's and I often fed them, hanging over the fence to have a civil word with them and scratch their bristly backs, and they grunted back in a friendly way until we gradually built up a meaningful relationship. In order to tell them apart I had christened them according to their outstanding characteristics – Snooty, Snorter, Snuffle, Blacky and Grunt. And now it appeared that one of these friends was threatened with extinction. Like the rabbits before her, this pig would die purely in order to put food on the table. That sad situation was suddenly brought home to me in all its frightful poignancy, filling me with abhorrence. Yet I had not the slightest inkling of the extent of the suffering in store – not only for the unsuspecting pig, but for me as well.

Chapter 17
Pigs Might Fly

The pig destined to add trimmings to the Christmas table – for we were to have goose on Christmas Day – turned out to be Snooty, so called because of her superior expression arising from the possession of a snub snout. She was an elderly Middle White, a calendar portrait of whose younger relative I remembered improving by adding spectacles and a bow tie. In pig terms she had reached the age of retirement, and though Uncle Matt had exaggerated the extent of her infirmity, she did lead a sedentary life, keeping exercise to a minimum, and spending her days snoring in the sty. It was as much as she could do to stagger to the trough and consume her fair share of pigswill and potatoes, which formed the huge calorie intake that made her what she was – a very fat pig.

Like the victims of the French Revolution, she was brought in an open cart to her execution, transported from Todd Tingate's to

Windlestraw to meet her doom. And directly contradicting Uncle Matt, who had insisted that she could hardly walk, she miraculously recovered the use of her legs to make several waddling runs for freedom, but in vain. On her arrival, the men took her into the small byre and tied her up, and at that point she began to squeal, squealing and squealing in sheer terror, just as if she knew her fate. She squealed so loudly and so piercingly and so persistently that the sound filled the house, and whatever I did I could not shut out the harrowing cries. I clasped my hands over my ears and stuffed cotton wool into them, but still the sound penetrated. I crouched face downwards in an armchair, pulling a cushion tightly over my head, but the shrill sound filtered through. Nothing could give me the silence I craved from the terrible sound of those plaintive squeals. Indeed, I seemed to hear the sound for weeks afterwards, long after the pig was dead. Yet Uncle Matt had assured me that the pig would feel no pain.

'Are you absolutely sure, Uncle Matt?' I asked him repeatedly before she was killed. 'Cross your heart and hope to die?'

'Sure I'm sure,' he said, crossing his fingers instead. 'Definitely, I'm sure. She'll be gone in a flash and off to pigs' heaven.'

'Will she really? Honestly, Uncle Matt? Is there really a pigs' heaven?'

'No doubt about it,' he said, doffing his cap and lowering his eyes piously. 'And you see, Emma, she's always been a good pig. All her life she's never put a trotter wrong, so to speak. Yes, she's a good virtuous pig all right, and I reckon she deserves to go to heaven. It'll be a blessin', and the sooner the better, I'd say, from her point of view, like.'

What a fool I was to believe such a story. To some extent his words had consoled me at the time, believing that the pig would be happy. I imagined pigs' heaven as an everlasting lawn, crossed by an endless trough forever filled with pigswill and potatoes, and edged with woods crammed to infinity with truffles. She would be all right there, I thought, safe and warm before the worst of winter. But now, like the pig, I felt betrayed. By my reckoning she should have been in heaven long ago and yet she was still squealing. The sound was torture to me, and in an attempt to make the ordeal bearable, I forced myself to dismiss from my mind the horror of what I suspected was happening and seek more acceptable explanations for the prolonged and pitiful ear-splitting squeals. Remembering Uncle Matt's expression 'Pigs might fly', I deluded myself into thinking that she had done just that – raised her hefty bulk from the ground and literally taken flight. I tried to imagine that the squeals were not of fear or pain but were rather of delight, as she flew freely round and round in the air, cleverly escaping her executioners.

Alas the truth, which I learnt later from the men, could not have been more different. The problem was that, try as they might, they could not stun this particular pig, not even with a sledgehammer. Like all Middle Whites she had an inbred tendency to a wrinkled forehead, but advancing years had magnified this inherent characteristic and dug deep furrows behind her short, sharp snout. Between these furrows had formed several thick layers of gristle against which the sledgehammer, intended to knock her out instantly, simply bounced off. Blow after blow was struck, thudding down onto the heavily reinforced forehead, but without result, until the men began to lose control and bedlam broke out. A terrible struggle ensued, with the pig staggering and reeling from side to side and squealing with all her might, the men slipping and sliding on the damp byre floor, and everyone shouting at once.

'Giss-giss, giss-giss,' called Uncle Matt urgently but ineffectively, in an attempt to calm the pig down, but sounding so frantic that he had the opposite effect; meanwhile, Bill tried to restore order by shouting directions, but nobody could follow them.

'Ho'd on a bit. That's it. Pull your end. No, t'other way, man! Whoa!'

Sam, being the professional and therefore, in his opinion, in charge, shouted the loudest, bellowing unintelligibly throughout the prolonged hustle and scuffle.

'How-way! Pull harder. Yank it roond, man. By, but she's heavy. Man alive! Had on! Noo then – pull your end. Mind there! Look oot! Mind, she'll dunch tha!'

Only the pig appeared to understand the confusing directions, because she stayed one step ahead of the game, one move ahead of her attackers, constantly confounding them. Later Uncle Matt admitted that she deserved to live because she fought so hard; but the men fought harder, holding on to the ropes as if they were waterskiers whose lives depended on it. They slid under the pig, and rolled over her, and rode her, and slithered past her, and got kicked by her, and accidentally thumped by her, and still the poor persecuted pig stood her ground and squealed. In the normally peaceful byre the terrified calves shied away from the noisy hustle and tussle, huddling together for comfort; the disturbed rats buried their bright eyes deep in the protective darkness of the cake bins; and Split discreetly retreated from the scene to hide in the reeds behind the wash-house. The fierce tug-of-war degenerated into a battle of wills, lacking any real skill or finesse, so that in the end, Bill suddenly pulled the rope with a jerk, unsynchronized with the actions of the other two combatants, and overbalanced, arms frantically flailing the air and legs sliding along the slippery floor, bringing the startled pig down with him.

'Divn't let her get up, lads!' he yelled, whereupon Sam Cullen grabbed his knife and pounced, hastily slitting her throat.

Seconds later peace descended. I lifted the corner of my cushion and peeped out at a blissfully still and silent house. But the peace lasted for only a moment. Then everyone came rushing through the room from front to back, and the mayhem transferred itself to the house, as all five adults charged past me carrying buckets of blood and the gory remains of the pig. Then, as I soon discovered to my horror, they began to turn homely Windlestraw into a slaughterhouse, and to incarnadine with blood the previously spotless white kitchen. Now I used the cushion to cover my eyes. I wanted to see nothing of this dreadful carnage, to detach myself completely from it. But all at once I remembered the Santa Claus pig, hanging on the kitchen wall facing the grisly carve-up, and I steeled myself to dash in and save her feelings by draping a duster over the calendar. I tried not to look to right or left on this errand of mercy, but could not avoid seeing the women making blood into black puddings. I saw enough – too much in fact, for as I scuttled back to the protective cushion I knew that I would never eat black pudding again as long as I lived. Or white pudding. Or liver and kidneys. And I had my doubts about bacon.

Uncle Matt suffered no such compunction, however, but was tucking in to sausage sandwiches by lunchtime, laughing and joking as he shamelessly talked through an overfull mouth, and strutting proudly in front of his guests like a genial host overseeing a lavish feast for which he claimed sole responsibility. Furthermore, he ended the day, as did all the rest of the company except me, by sampling each of the newly produced savouries in one monumental fry-up that covered every inch of a large plate. He revelled in the tasty fare, and for once could not bring himself to sell any of it, especially to the Shoemans, firmly declaring that it was much too good for them.

His lack of conscience at such over-indulgence was justified in his mind by recollection of his recent dietary deprivation, and after the famine he wallowed in the feasting. I alone mourned poor Snooty and the manner of her passing. I puzzled my uncle and annoyed my aunt by refusing to eat any produce from the pig, because to me, eating Snooty would be tantamount to cannibalism. Much unpleasantness ensued, but I stood firm, wasting whatever was forced onto my plate, until finally, after a lengthy peroration from Aunt Dot in which she cast blame on my self-centred obduracy for the plight of all the starving people in the world, Uncle Matt undertook to straighten me out.

'Now I want you to know, Emma, that I respect your principles, pet,' he began. 'I do, Emma, I really do. When it comes to sausages and puddings and liver and the like, I don't share your feelin's but I understand them. Definitely. You fed the pig, you knew the pig, and you liked the pig. And that's all fair enough. But you see, girl, you could still have a bit of bacon because it's not from that pig.'

'Surely, Uncle Matt, it must be!' I protested, unconvinced. 'I saw the carcass carried in.'

'Ah yes, Emma, and you'll see it still if you care to look, quartered and lying in a box of salt in the larder, all intact,' he said triumphantly. 'You see, you don't know everythin', even if you are a good scholar and top of the class. And what you don't know is that pork – leastways ham and bacon and stuff – has to be cured. Salted an' that. Takes time, pet. Takes a few weeks. So the bacon we're eatin' at present comes from no pig that you know. No pig you've ever met. It's just like bacon from the bacon counter at the shop, and you've always eaten that.'

'Are you quite sure, Uncle Matt? Cross your heart and hope to die?'

'Certain sure, Emma. Definitely sure. Now trust me,' he said, returning my gaze candidly, as well as performing the reassuring crossing of the heart, though in the light of previous experience I never knew why I still believed in the sincerity of that ritual.

And somehow, according to his reckoning, we never did get around to eating Snooty, the hams having been hung and mixed up with the others. Whether he told the truth or had his fingers crossed behind his back whilst spinning me a yarn I never knew, but I believed him, and conceded to eat bacon, but only bacon, no other parts of a pig. I believed him because I wanted to, because I was hungry and sick to death of nothing but eggs and raisins, not to mention goats' cheese, and because the singularly appetizing smell of frying bacon betrayed me, melting my resolve.

Then, sadly, I had just begun to forget the pathos of the pig's death when it was swiftly followed by another death, that of the docile cow Dolly, who died as she had lived, peacefully in her stall.

'She's died of old age,' said Uncle Matt mournfully, once again a prey to gloom. 'It's a sad loss, but she's likely had enough of this pesky hard life and rotten climate, so she's handed in her dinner pail, so to speak. Yes, she's kicked the bucket for the last time. And who can blame her?' he enquired rhetorically, removing his cap to scratch his head thoughtfully as he considered his next course of action.

In the end he acted quite quickly. He put in motion the ever-efficient bush telegraph system and sent urgently for the dead cart – or at least that was what I called the filthy truck that arrived to dispose of Dolly. Afterwards I sincerely wished I had stayed in the house that day, because disturbing memories of the dead cart haunted me for some time. Natural curiosity drew me out to make the acquaintance of the driver and his grim-faced assistant, both liberally spattered with grease and blood, and some sort of horrible fascination caused me to glance in the back of the truck. The grisly assistant was slithering over a surface oozing with slime, hauling various carcasses about with undignified and disrespectful zeal to make room for Dolly, and I noticed with horror that several of them were already crawling and wriggling with maggots. The putrid stench was overpowering, and not wishing to see poor Dolly join the stinking inmates of the gruesome truck, I rapidly made myself scarce. At least, I thought, we were not about to eat Dolly. That was my only comfort.

Meanwhile, as Christmas week arrived, the weather suddenly grew even colder. The pointer on the barometer slipped back to 'Change' and then to 'Stormy', conjuring up expectations of snow, and with the first white flurry, black portents of Mad Mary. Every morning the paths round the farm sparkled with icy patches, crazed and glittering like broken glass; the rough track to Brackenfield froze hard and spiky in its ridges; and the peaks of Lornhope Fell were powdered with snow like sieved icing sugar on chocolate buns. Even my bedroom windows were patterned with frost, inside as well as out, like a double layer of lace curtains. I dreaded the weather worsening, and waited impatiently for my mother to come. Once she was with us nothing else would matter, even if the worst happened and snow followed.

My aunt and uncle now made preparations against the onset of snowstorms. Aunt Dot filled every available container with fresh water, made two batches of brown bread, and hung heavy curtains behind both the front and the back door. Uncle Matt took delivery of extra bales of straw, tightened the knots on the tarpaulin over the haystack, transported peat and logs from Todd Tingate's to supplement the coal store, and secured all animals, including the geese and hens. The four surviving pigs curled up cosily in their sty and, ignorant of Snooty's fate from overeating, guzzled their way through the winter. I warned them and warned them against this reckless gluttony, but they would *not* listen. Nor did they appear to miss their fellow lodger, probably taking the selfish view that her sudden disappearance meant more pigswill for the rest of them. They had been joined in Todd Tingate's outbuildings, though in separate quarters, by the goats, but Sandy, who had cleverly grown a special winter coat, stayed outside until Uncle Matt considered it imperative to house him, that being the only time the horse ever came quietly.

We were now ready, as ready as we could be, for Christmas and for winter, though in truth nothing could have fully prepared me for the trauma of winter in Sourhope. My mother and brothers were due to arrive the day before Christmas Eve, and that very day, just as we were about to set off to meet them, a telegram arrived, such a rare event in Sourhope that a chill of apprehension turned my blood to ice, even before Aunt Dot opened and read it. It said: 'Can't come. Snowed in. Love, Ellie' – only six little words, but it seemed like a long sentence to me, longer every time I read it, and I read it over and over again, incredulously and tearfully. To me it was like a jail sentence, a death sentence to all my hopes. For the best part of an hour I cried bitterly, unable to stop until Aunt Dot rounded on me with scant patience.

'And you can turn the waterworks off right now, Missy,' she said brusquely. 'They're not coming and that's that. So stop whingeing or I'll give you something to cry about.'

I took myself to my room and cried into my pillow. That night I slept fitfully, and the next morning, still in the depths of despair, I looked out on another gloomy day, the sort of day that grows steadily darker instead of lighter. A single raven sat still and black in front of the house, perched like an omen of doom on the gatepost. It had not moved when I went downstairs for breakfast to find Uncle Matt gazing at it through the window.

'Folks are superstitious about a raven bringin' bad luck,' he said, 'but it's more likely a sign of bad weather. He winters on the crags, and he'll have come down in case there's a storm.'

'Yes, somehow I'm sure it'll snow today,' I said woefully. 'Not that it matters now, one way or the other.' He turned to look at me.

'Cheer up, Emma,' he said kindly. 'It's not like you to be so down. My meaning is, Christmas isn't Christmas without a bit of snow. And as for your mother, well to be honest I've been expecting just such a telegram. I read in the paper that the whole country's been hit by snowstorms, and they're steadily movin' north.'

'She could still have come,' I complained illogically. 'She promised. And it's Christmas.'

'Now, Emma, you wouldn't really want that, would you?' he reasoned, taking my hand, which I snatched away in pique. 'It would be madness to travel in such weather. She could be stranded anywhere or lost in a drift. Then you'd *never* see her again.'

'But she promised,' I repeated, not to be diverted.

'Yes, and I'm sure she'll keep her promise. Soon as she can. Soon as the weather improves. Why, if it's not as bad as folks forecast, she might get here for New Year.'

'New Year? Honestly?'

'Yes, next week. That's if things get better. And meantime, Emma, it's Christmas, and my meanin' is, we'll have a grand time. Plenty to eat for a change, and presents an' that, and – oh – everythin'. You'll enjoy it. See if you don't. I dare bet we'll all have a whale of a time.'

I listened in misery and dejection, accepting none of it, refusing to be comforted. Despite his promises of the fabled jollity of Christmas at Windlestraw, I felt nothing but despair, my brain numb, my heart heavy, and my spirits weary. It was not only the fact that my mother had cancelled her visit that upset me. Indeed, so much more in my life than Uncle Matt realized had hinged on her coming to take me away, and once again I had been let down. Besides, it *was* Christmas, and Christmas without my mother was unthinkable, unbearable. But he persisted in looking on the bright side, determined to cheer me up.

'Tell you what, Emma, as it's Christmas we'll have a party tonight. We'll get the gramophone out and have a singalong, maybe even a dance, eh? Now that's somethin' to look forward to, isn't it? You've been stayin' here all this time and you've never even heard our gramophone. That'll be a treat for us both just as soon as I've finished the milkin'.'

True to his word, as soon as he came in from the byre he unearthed the gramophone, packed away at the bottom of the cupboard under the stairs. It was a rectangular black box with blued-steel corners and clasp, and a handle that folded away inside. Aunt Dot glowered in disapproval as she saw him staggering out with it, and in a trice she whipped off the clean white tablecloth, replacing it with folded newspaper. He blew a little dust off the gramophone lid, the box having lain unused in the cupboard for years, then placed the device on the newspaper and slowly and carefully wound the handle.

As he lifted the lid I noticed on the inside a small picture of a white terrier listening intently to a large horn, shaped rather like an ear-trumpet. The same musical dog featured on the centre of some of the records he produced from a compartment in the lid, and he chose one at random and set it away, judging the positioning of the needle with great care and precision. A maudlin tenor, whose voice was muffled by the crackling sound of the scratched record, sang mournfully about an old rugged cross that he seemed inordinately fond of, but Uncle Matt soon wearied of the song, pulling a critical face as he took it off before the finish.

'Heck no,' he said. 'That's no good. Load of misery, that is. It's a canny tune right enough, but more suited to a funeral. What we need is somethin' cheerful. Ah now, here's one – "Blaze away" – that should fit the bill,' and he stood swinging his hands like an expressive conductor, swaying his head from side to side, and tapping his foot to the marching rhythm. 'That's put me in the mood for a dance,' he added. 'Let's have a dance, Emma. I'll just see what I can find.'

This time it was a young lady's voice singing 'He flies through the air with the greatest of ease, the daring young man on the flying trapeze,' and Uncle Matt bowed politely, and smiling down at me asked, 'May I have this dance?' Then, suiting his action to the words, he put his arm round my waist, gripped my hand tightly, and proceeded to fly through the air, whirling me with him in a sort of frenzied crouching polka, round and round the table. We were both breathless when the record ended, and for my part a little flustered as my feet had hardly touched the floor, so he looked for something slower and more sedate, finally settling for what he called a modern waltz, a romantic song, 'Who's taking you home tonight?', universally popular as the last waltz of the evening.

I had always imagined that dancing would come naturally to me and that when I found my Prince Charming I would take to the floor with instinctive grace. But I had no experience of dancing the waltz, and my head only came up to Uncle Matt's waist. Besides, the coconut matting that covered the stone floor, though worn to a shine, was not an ideal surface for dancing, and the scattered clippy mats tended to get in the way, so I kept tripping over his feet and several times he swept me off mine. Then the gramophone began to run down, the singer's voice growing steadily slower and slower, deeper and deeper, more miserable than romantic, and he had to leap to it to give the vocalist a much-needed boost with a quick wind of the handle. What finally put us both off, however, bringing the dance to a sudden close, was the untimely arrival of Aunt Dot, who stomped into the room, stopped dead in her tracks and stared at us with the intensely sour expression of someone who has just bitten a large lump out of her tongue and dislikes the taste of it.

'Nothing better to do than prance about like an idiot at full moon?' she enquired acidly. 'There's been a few flurries of snow, and I'd strongly advise you to get finished outside and locked up for the night.'

Silently and sheepishly Uncle Matt folded away the handle, replaced the records into a flap that fastened with a press stud under the box lid, and cleared the table, returning the box to the cupboard, and I assumed that the Christmas jollifications were over. But he winked at me before leaving, and spoke in ringing tones across the room, a touch of defiance entering his voice.

'We'll have some more of that tomorrow, Emma,' he said. 'And you never know – maybe your aunt Dot'll join in. She's a dab hand at dancin', as light on her feet as a wagtail. Now, while I'm out, you find me your longest stockin' and we'll get it hung ready for bein' filled. Tonight's the night for hangin' it up. Tonight's the night, girl.'

Then, obedient to Aunt Dot's impatient scowl, he scuttled away like a fieldmouse caught in the beam of a hurricane lamp. By the time he returned I was ready for bed, just waiting to say goodnight, and he had regained his determinedly festive mood.

'Christmas Eve, eh, Emma?' he said, grinning inanely at me. 'Well, well, Christmas Eve. How about that? Just the job, eh? Well, it's time to get that stockin' hung. That all-important stockin'.'

He then proceeded to hang my stocking with great ceremony and a piece of rough string, tying it to the brass mantel rail with as many different knots as a seaman might use on a sailing ship, and proudly applauding his own efforts.

'That's a good sturdy job,' he said, looking to me for approval. 'I just thought that we'd better get your stockin' hung up in good time. As it happens, I swept the chimney a fortnight ago, and it's a grand wide one. Plenty of room for a fat Santa to get down. Though he's in for a shock when he lands, 'cos we never let the fire go out.'

'You'll have to move that stocking. It's in the way,' said Aunt Dot predictably, just as he stood back to admire his handiwork. 'For heaven's sake, Matt, hang it round the corner. We don't want to burn in our beds, do we? Starting a fire with a stocking! You never think ahead, do you?'

'Well, I dunno about that. They hang stockin's at the front of the mantelpiece on them Christmas cards,' he demurred.

He jerked his thumb at one of three cards on the sideboard, the others depicting a snow scene and a Christmas tree, sadly the only Christmas tree in evidence in the house. And oh, how I remembered our big Christmas tree at home, with its exquisitely fragile glass baubles and trails of tinsel, silver and gold.

But Aunt Dot shook her head disparagingly.

'Yes, Matt, and if you look more closely at the card you'll notice they're all smiling,' she retorted. 'You see, it's not true to life.'

Obligingly, he moved the stocking round the side of the rail and performed the hanging ceremony again, while I watched the ritual without much expectation. It seemed to me that such a lot of string was involved that it would be difficult to get anything in the stocking, and I was not anticipating any other presents. My only hope was that Santa Claus would manage to squeeze himself down the permanently sooty chimney and, despite all the hazards of his journey, would arrive in a generous mood. As for Christmas, my heart was not in it. I had to swallow a hard lump in my throat whenever I compared my dream of Christmas with its harsh reality, and I could no longer bring myself to sing to the Calendar pig.

Nevertheless, the niceties had to be observed. I had persuaded Uncle Matt to buy me two pretty handkerchiefs to give Aunt Dot, and used my precious sweet coupons on a bar of chocolate for Uncle Matt. I had wrapped them in coloured tissue paper that I had begged from Miss Speedwell, and after writing and decorating fancy labels, arranged the presents artistically on the sideboard before going to bed. I appreciated Uncle Matt's attempts to brighten my Christmas, to infuse some vestige of festive spirit into the cheerless atmosphere of Windlestraw, and I thanked him profusely for his painstaking efforts in hanging my stocking so securely. As I pointed out, to his amusement, whatever the value of the contents might turn out to be, no one could steal it, that was for sure.

Privately, however, I climbed the stairs to bed with a very heavy heart, feeling that I had never missed my mother as much as on that Christmas Eve, the first without her. Then, as I went to draw my bedroom curtains and looked out of the window, suddenly it began to snow – softly and slowly at first and then harder and faster in huge blinding flakes. And as I was soon to discover, once started, it almost forgot to stop.

Chapter 18

Comfort and Joy

When it snowed in Sourhope it snowed abundantly, as if the Clerk of the Weather had been called away and forgotten to switch off the snowfall button. The wind that whistled through the hills all winter now whirled the snow in blinding blizzards, obliterating the familiar landscape. Everyday objects in the farmyard, from buckets to troughs and from hay-rakes to reapers, lost their old identity and, covered in steadily accumulating snow, took on fantastic new forms, white, weird and wonderful. The whole valley merged into one bewildering white mist, and the steep road to Windlestraw narrowed to nothing and then vanished, like a conjurer's trick – now you see it, now you don't.

I could scarcely believe my eyes as the wilderness that was Sourhope became magically transformed into a thing of beauty, but the magic soon palled on the hard-pressed farmers, and despite his keen eye for natural beauty in all its forms, Uncle Matt was no exception. Snow fell remorselessly day and night, and life for both aunt and uncle degenerated into a war against the elements, a fight for survival. Muffled up like Eskimos, with fierce winds battering their bodies and driving snow cutting their faces, they struggled to reach the various outbuildings to tend their animals or bring in fuel. Every day, Uncle Matt battled against blizzards in a daunting trek to Todd Tingate's and Brackenfield; every day in the top lot he dug his sheep out of deep snowdrifts; and true to character, every day on returning home he wasted no opportunity to bemoan the loss of his beloved missing coat.

'I'm just remarkin', Dot, that if I had that old coat of mine it would add that extra layer I need this bad weather,' he said again and again, for what seemed like a thousand times a day, and she listened with ill-disguised exasperation.

'With all our problems in this terrible weather, with all that's happening to us right now, you're still grumbling on and on about that wretched ragged old coat! Get a sense of proportion, can't you, Matt?'

'Yes, but you see, Dot,' he persisted, looking as pathetic as a newly shorn lamb on a cold spring day, 'you see, I should have it, like, and I don't half miss it.'

'Lest we forget,' she muttered grimly, clenching her teeth, but he showed no mercy.

'Well, Dot, I was mighty attached to that partic'lar coat. I miss it in all sorts of ways, and it has to be said that at times like this I miss it more. I really do. I miss it somethin' terrible.' And with the bereaved air of one who has sustained an irreplaceable loss, he sighed fitfully.

So it was that in an odd way, when beset on all sides by other troubles, lowering his resistance in general, he began grieving all over again for his lost coat, thereby testing my aunt's limited patience and once more pricking her uneasy conscience, a strategy not conducive to harmony in the home. Meanwhile the snow stormed on and on relentlessly, and for a while nothing and no one got through to Windlestraw – no deliveries or collections, no neighbours or postman. We led a hermit-like existence, marooned in our square igloo, and I felt doubly marooned, for in addition I was often waiting alone for hours on end, thriving only on neglect, and missing my mother more than ever.

On Christmas morning I experienced my first intimation of the severity of wintering in Sourhope. As if out of respect for the occasion, there came a brief lull in the storm, and I looked out of the window through peepholes in the patterned frost onto a totally strange world. With a pang I remembered that it was Christmas, a day when I would normally be up at the crack of dawn, excitedly opening presents with my brothers. This house was silent, and the air freezing, even colder than usual, and I washed in a bowl of icy water, dressed as quickly and warmly as I could, and rushed downstairs. There I found everything deserted, with no Aunt Dot, frosty as the weather, stoking the fire or boiling the kettle or clattering the overworked egg pan, and no Uncle Matt to wish me a merry Christmas. So – no breakfast either. And for once the ever-burning fire looked grey and almost lifeless. Clearly it was dying, but both the coal scuttle and the log box stood empty, and I crouched over the warm embers, appreciating what paltry heat they gave.

I noticed that my stocking, hung so elaborately from the mantel rail, had mysteriously been filled, and that a present addressed to me in Uncle Matt's distinctive hand – bold and lavish in curlicues – occupied the centre of the mantelpiece between the Christmas decorations, such as they were. Aunt Dot's notion of house decoration was as minimal as her notion of house furnishing, her only concession to the festive season consisting of four sprigs of berried holly, acquired by Uncle Matt from a secret source at Thorny Edge, and placed so precisely at either side of the mantelpiece that I suspected her of measuring the leaves with a ruler.

I saw that my presents to aunt and uncle lay undisturbed on the sideboard, as did the breakfast plates on the table, and I deduced that the missing adults had drunk a quick cup of tea and departed, leaving me to my own devices. *And a merry Christmas to you too*, I thought, feeling sorry for myself, and reflecting on the splendid Christmas my brothers would be enjoying, undoubtedly warm and snug and happy. Even so, I could not help being a little bit curious as to the contents of the festive stocking and parcel, but I estimated them to be situated just out of my reach, and I dared not scale the dizzy heights of the mantelpiece without permission. It seemed to me that Uncle Matt had made such a thorough job of attaching the string – a job intended to last, and involving the same convoluted methods that he used in mending barbed-wire fences – that if I pulled the string I might well bring the brass rail down on my head, if not the entire mantelpiece.

I could not stop shivering, so I put my coat on and, in search of help and company, attempted to open the front door, but it resisted my efforts. I tugged hard with both hands and all my strength until the door yielded so suddenly towards me that I staggered back, losing my balance. Yet it only opened a few inches, revealing another door, a solid white screen of icy snow that had stopped it from opening any further. The snow had drifted all night along the exposed front of the house and frozen hard, cutting off that exit. I put on wellingtons and tried the back door, which opened easily, and saw that paths had been cleared in all directions – to the coalhouse, to the washhouse, up the steps to the road, and down to the front of the house. I followed this latter path and found that the snow on either side of me gradually grew higher, forming a deep trench and then a deeper narrow passageway, the snow rearing above my head and feeling icy cold. Ahead I could see two figures labouring in the snow, clearing a space in front of the byre door, and I could hear the grating sound of shovels scraping in unison. Uncle Matt wielded a long-handled

shovel, cutting huge swathes of snow and hurling them aside. Aunt
Dot followed with a smaller shovel, tidying up the track, and in relief
I shouted at her, 'Aunt Dot!' and again, 'Aunt Dot!'

They stopped working, straightened up and turned towards me,
looking from covered heads to wellington boots like Mr and Mrs Jack
Frost. Once again Aunt Dot had made free with Uncle Matt's clothing,
borrowing his old gabardine, which hung loosely and long, reaching
to her feet, and though her red hair was hidden by a tightly bound
scarf, her face was ruddy enough from frost and exertion to compen-
sate. Uncle Matt had tied a ragged old cardigan over his jacket, knot-
ting it in front by the sleeves. His cap was secured with a long scarf
so that only the peak remained visible, and under it jutted his sharp
nose, which constantly formed a drop on the end, that he constantly
wiped off on the back of his glove. Flakes of snow had settled on
both of them, clinging to their shoulders and defining their eyebrows
like distinguishing chalk marks. Uncle Matt was the first to shout.

'Emma! Be careful, pet. It's very slippy!'

It was indeed slippery and intensely cold in that trench. I could
see my breath hanging in the air and freezing in front of me.

'Aren't you coming in for breakfast?' I shouted hopefully, and Aunt
Dot leant briefly on her shovel, half-turned away from me, anxious
to make progress.

'Won't be long Emma. Have some bread and milk till we're finished.'

'Can't I get the coal shovel and help?'

'No!' she shouted abruptly. 'You'd just be in the way.'

I was always in the way, I reflected ruefully, and I looked to Uncle
Matt for support, but he echoed her sentiments.

'No, Emma, it's best if you go inside and keep warm.'

'But it isn't warm,' I argued. 'The fire's nearly out and there's no
coal or logs.'

At that an anguished cry came from Aunt Dot.

'Oh no! Not the fire! Oh, that's dreadful. The thought of a nice cup
of tea is all that's keeping me going. Put a couple of logs on it, Emma.
Fetch them from the wash-house. But be careful.'

I felt heartened by her unusual concern for me. It must be the
Christmas spirit, I thought, but she shouted again, dispelling my illu-
sions, and making her priorities clear.

'Now be very careful, Emma, or you'll put the fire out.'

Then Uncle Matt joined in with different priorities.

'Watch it, Emma. Watch your fingers near the hot fire, and be careful of the hot kettle and that hot pan. My meanin' is, pet, they'll be hot.'

I brought logs and fed the fire, which spat back at me ungratefully, but in time took hold. So I brought more logs and a few lumps of coal, which I placed with due care to encourage flames. I steadily filled the coal scuttle and log box, and then, snuggling close to the fire, drank a cup of cold milk and ate a chunk of bread, the sort of stale crust that you would throw out for the birds. I had a long wait before Aunt Dot came in because she finished off the milking so that Uncle Matt could feed the sheep. He was gone for ages and Aunt Dot kept looking at the clock and clicking her tongue and brewing cups of tea for him, which she drank herself. Then she began to make the Christmas dinner. We were to have had a goose for the occasion, one of our own, but Uncle Matt, not being by nature a warrior, kept putting off the evil hour of catching and killing the creature. And once my family had cancelled their planned visit, Aunt Dot considered the effort that would be involved in preparation too much for just the three of us, as I had overheard her explaining to Uncle Matt.

'All that work of plucking and singeing feathers, and the chances are that Missy won't eat it anyway,' she pointed out, her shrewd grey eyes darting disapprovingly at me. 'She's something of a goose herself, and if she thinks she has even a nodding acquaintance with the goose you kill she'll not touch a bite. Besides, we're worked off our feet already without looking for more work. I think we'll just forget it, Matt.'

So now she stoked the fire till it blazed like a furnace, placing a joint of pork, which she tactfully referred to as 'meat' for my benefit, into the oven to roast, and a Christmas pudding into the black pan to boil. I helped her prepare vegetables and waited patiently for Christmas to begin. But when Uncle Matt finally arrived he looked exhausted and sadder than I had seen him since he lost his coat. He removed his outdoor clothes, shook the snow off them at the door, and then stood in font of the fire to thaw out, stamping his feet and flapping his arms across his chest like a penguin flapping its flippers. Aunt Dot handed him a steaming mug of tea and he sipped it slowly, gazing with doleful eyes into the fire.

'Are you all right, Uncle Matt?' I enquired sympathetically.

'I've been better, Emma,' he said, sounding troubled.

'Have you lost something, Uncle Matt?' I asked, hazarding a guess.

'I have, Emma. I've lost a couple of sheep.'

'Can I help? Can I help you find them?'

'No. 'Fraid not, Emma. You see I know where they are. They're dead. I've just set them against the wall for buryin' later.'

Aunt Dot stopped basting the meat and eyed him sourly.

'What's that? What did you say? Dead sheep?'

'Yes, just a couple so far, thank goodness. Thought it might've been more. They were nearly all under the snow, but most of them had sheltered behind the dyke where there's a current of air. I only found two that were dead.'

'What a pity you let them die!' she cried. 'What a pity you didn't go up there first. You might have saved them. Or one of them anyway.'

'But you wanted the paths cleared and the milkin' done first,' he pointed out irritably. 'I can't be everywhere at once, much as you'd like me to be.'

'No, I suppose not,' she acknowledged reluctantly, as if she considered he was showing a deplorable lack of effort. 'But it's a pity. Two sheep – a big loss.'

'Yes, I hate to see healthy animals die like that. Especially at Christmas. Should be a time to celebrate birth, not face death. Still, I guess things could be worse. At least it's stopped snowin'.'

I took his hand and squeezed it comfortingly, and with a visible effort he pulled himself together and smiled down at me.

'Well, this won't do, pet. I seem to remember promisin' you a lovely Christmas. So we'll have to do better than this. Definitely. This isn't much of a Christmas Day for you, is it? For a start I expect you'd like to see what presents you've got an' that.'

He proceeded to undo the stocking, unravelling the coarse string with fingers still half numb from the cold. He tackled the task with intense concentration, brow furrowed and nose wrinkled, and while he worked he whistled tunelessly through his teeth, oblivious of the suffering he was inflicting on Aunt Dot. Some time later, with a proud grin and a dramatic flourish, he laid my stocking on the rocking chair and I relaxed. The mantelpiece and its brass rail had survived intact.

'You'd better open your aunt Dot's present first,' he said, giving me a sly wink. 'It'll likely be the best.'

'And don't you dare eat anything,' chimed in Aunt Dot on a high note. 'I'm not doing all this work for nothing, so don't go spoiling your appetite.'

Having only eaten a morsel of bread that morning, I had plenty of appetite to spoil, and could have been tempted by the juicy pear

I found in the stocking, or the bright red apple on top. It looked as rosy as the apple the wicked queen gave Snow White, and it crossed my mind to wonder if it could be poisoned like hers, but it was so long since I had seen such a delicious treat that I intended eating it anyway. Further investigation revealed some assorted nuts caught in a little net, and a modest bag of mixed sweets, all of a tiny variety like hundreds and thousands and Dolly mixtures, sweets that gave quantity to the four-ounce measure and that, if eaten slowly and individually, would last well into the New Year. Next came a lacy red scarf, which I had seen before but was now shorter and neatly darned at one end. It had been cut from a scarf given to Aunt Dot, which she seldom wore because it clashed with her red hair and was so long that it tripped her up. And finally, the bulging foot of the stocking had been stuffed with a pair of khaki socks, specially knitted, so Aunt Dot said, to wear over other socks in wellingtons. A kind thought at least, I reflected, but later Uncle Matt confided the truth.

'Them socks you've got were knitted for the army, like,' he explained apologetically. 'Women are supposed to knit for the army – you know – scarves, and balaclavas, and socks an' that. But your aunt Dot's efforts turned out all wrong, one bigger than the other, but both far too small for a man. So, like it or not, you've benefited. You've reaped the reward of her endeavours for the war effort.'

'Khaki's not really – my – favourite colour, Uncle Matt,' I said hesitantly, not wishing to sound ungrateful.

'No, I don't suppose it is. And I expect they're far too big for you an' all, one in partic'lar. But never mind, eh? They might come in handy to fill out your wellies. I tell you, Emma, I'm a great believer in that extra layer against the cold, and them thick socks should keep your chilblains at bay. Besides, you never know your luck, and they just might shrink. Most things do when your aunt has a go at them.'

'It'll be a blessing if the long one shrinks more than the short,' I observed sagaciously, but Uncle Matt pulled a dubious face.

'I reckon that's too much to ask of life, Emma. But we'll keep our hopes high and our fingers crossed.'

So it was that on that Christmas morning I surveyed the contents of my Christmas stocking with emotions as mixed as my bag of sweets – on the one hand grateful for anything, but on the other, despite low expectations, somewhat disappointed. Once I had eaten the edibles, which would take no time at all, I was left with a darned scarf and a pair of odd socks. And I strongly suspected that it was

Uncle Matt who had provided the edible goodies, having obtained them by hook or by crook in Shiretown. Fruit was a very scarce commodity in wartime winter, and he must have scoured the town to find apples and nuts. That pleased me, but otherwise I could not help feeling slightly aggrieved at the 'waste not, want not' gifts from my aunt.

I was reminded of Mr Clout's words of wisdom, repeatedly delivered with a certain sadistic relish in assembly: 'He who expecteth much receiveth little' – from which I naturally drew the opposite inference that he who expecteth little receiveth much. Therefore to expect little and receive little seemed somehow unfair, and in a nebulous way I felt cheated. I had, however, learned to be thankful for small mercies, and I now advanced upon Aunt Dot intending to kiss her, much as I would my mother. But somehow she always presented me with an invisible barrier, holding me back from showing affection, and just then she had her back turned to me as she manipulated the heavy kettle, so I edged forward slowly, uncertain of correct procedure.

'Thanks very much, Aunt Dot. Everything's lovely,' I said shyly.

'Oh, that's all right, Emma,' she answered, not bothering to turn round but busily topping up the water in the pudding pan. 'It's the very least I could do' – and I silently agreed that the very least she could do was what she had done. 'After all,' she went on, 'Christmas comes but once a year, as they say. But what I say is, thank goodness. Gracious me, it's a lot of work! Quite unnecessary extra work.'

I backed away and kissed Uncle Matt instead, because he seemed to expect it, and because I liked his presents. He had bought me a sketch pad, a set of drawing pens, and six small bottles of coloured inks, which, when held to the light, reflected vibrant colours like a stained-glass window. I praised them to the skies, but he seemed strangely troubled once he had handed them over. He waited until Aunt Dot went into the kitchen and then engaged me in a conversation conducted in urgent whispers.

'For heaven's sake, Emma, be careful of them inks. Don't suck your fingers after you've used them 'cos they must be poisonous. I've just this minute noticed that they're inedible.'

I stared from him to the bottles and back again, uncomprehendingly.

'But, Uncle Matt, who would swallow ink?' I whispered. 'Even Jimmy Nixon only pours it on other people. He's not daft enough to drink it, and neither am I.'

'Well, I dunno, but it must be dangerous when they've put a warning on the bottle. See? See that, Emma?'

My bewildered eyes followed his pointing finger and read the label. All was instantly clear.

'No, Uncle Matt, that's not inedible. It's indelible. That means it won't rub out.'

'Won't rub out? Won't rub out! By heck, Emma! That's nearly as bad! What if you spill them on the tablecloth, or the coconut matting, or that beige clippy mat, or even your clothes?'

'I won't. I'll be very careful. They're too good to waste.'

'If you spill any of it, just the teeniest drop, we'll both be in the soup. Your aunt'll be after me with the carving knife. She's always wantin' to cut me down to size.'

'Don't worry, Uncle Matt. I'll be very, very careful. I promise.'

'Good girl,' he whispered hoarsely. 'My meanin' is – good girl.' And he wandered off to collect the wherewithal for a shave and general spruce-up as a concession to Christmas Day.

Dinner was served rather late, but could be called an unqualified success, in both senses of the expression. It was the only appetizing meal I ever knew my aunt to cook, and though acutely aware that this was my first Christmas away from my mother, even I managed to enjoy the food. The appetite we brought to the table undoubtedly helped, but with the exception of the gravy, which as usual turned out grey with mysterious black floaters drowning in its murky depths, everything tasted better than usual, and Uncle Matt revelled in an abundance of roast pork. I ate charily of that, lest I should be eating an old friend, though Aunt Dot said not. Sometimes, however, she told me what she called 'little white lies', claiming that they were not real lies but harmless fibs told for my own good. In my view, confused as to what to believe, they were still lies whatever their size and colour, so I concentrated on eating the vegetables, especially the roast potatoes, and begged a second helping of the surprisingly delectable Christmas pudding, which simply melted in the mouth.

The pudding was the star of the meal and would have caused the best cordon bleu cook to nod in approval. Not even the lumpy custard could spoil its light and fruity taste, and though I had half-forgotten the sweet taste of puddings, suddenly nostalgic memories of others I had had before flooded my mind – fresh fruit, and ginger, and chocolate – and I wondered if we might indulge in such delicacies more often. Every mouthful of that pudding surprised me.

Undoubtedly, I thought, Aunt Dot had been hiding her light under a bushel, and all I had to do was follow Uncle Matt's advice and compliment her on her cooking, flattering with fulsome praise, and for as long as I remained at Windlestraw I would face a rosy future, enriched with mouth-watering puddings. For once I could be sincere and convincing in my appreciation.

'This pudding is absolutely delicious, Aunt Dot,' I enthused, savouring every mouthful. 'My mum would love this recipe. It's just wonderful. The best I've ever tasted. It's really scrumptious. I know you've a lot to do, but I do wish you'd make puddings more often.'

I thought I was doing rather well, and glanced at Uncle Matt, anticipating his approval and support, since we were usually as one in the matter of food, but to my amazement he began to grimace and make frantic signs, like a ticktack man at the races, and when I embarked on further flattering comments he shook his head so vigorously that I stopped in mid-sentence. Meanwhile Aunt Dot fidgeted about a bit, straightening her pinafore and patting her hair in place. Then she stared at me with an odd expression, as if deliberating between telling the truth and substituting one of her little white lies, but after a short struggle the truth won, and she spoke forcibly.

'Well, Emma, you may as well know what's what. I suppose I should tell you something. I should tell you that your mother made that pudding and sent it on ahead, just in case anything stopped her from coming. Which it did, of course. That terrible storm. So there it is. Now you know. It's your mother's Christmas pudding.'

After this confession she gave me a searching speculative look as if wondering whether I intended making something of it, but what could I say? I played safe and said nothing, but kept my eyes on my plate, toying with the remaining portion of pudding as if expecting it to comment for me and account for itself. A tense moment passed, and then she went on.

'Oh, and by the way, I nearly forgot – I've had it hidden, that's why. She sent you a little parcel at the same time. You can open it when you've finished eating.'

Suddenly the pudding tasted even sweeter. A present from my mother was guaranteed to be exciting, and the fact that she had tried, albeit from a distance, to make my Christmas special filled me with pleasure. Perhaps she did still care about me after all. Perhaps she would come for me at New Year. Uncle Matt had certainly held out that hope. Moreover, it *had* stopped snowing. I settled down at last to enjoy Christmas, and the parcel exceeded my expectations. Opening it eagerly, I unpacked a pair of slippers, cute and cosy, then a cardigan matching my red jumper, providing that extra layer that Uncle Matt always advocated, and underneath that, two small but interesting-looking boxes. The first contained a shiny pink mirror complete with brush and comb, so I could now see myself at any time and do my hair without having to beg for the shaving mirror from the wall. I loved the brush set, but the best was yet to come. When I lifted the lid of the second box, joy of joys, five little porcelain faces looked up at me, five little dolls each five inches long, each slightly different and dressed in different colours. Although so small, they lacked no detail, even to the jointed limbs and wisps of hair. And behind each head, slotted in the cardboard casing, were five little cups, saucers and plates, patterned with minute flowers. That present was exactly what I needed, a family of my own to care for. No present I ever received thereafter, no matter how expensive or sophisticated, meant as much to me as those five little dolls that day. I lavished them with love, served them imaginary tea, talked to them incessantly, and taught them all I knew.

Ever since arriving at Windlestraw I had been plunged prema-turely into an adult world of worries and responsibilities, a world in which my childhood concerns were largely pushed aside. Now for a while it was wonderful just to be a child, to play with dolls and be eight again. But I played alone, the dolls my only companions. Almost before we had finished Christmas dinner the sky turned dark and threatening, and Uncle Matt left the table and set off post-haste to Todd Tingate's and Brackenfield. Another storm undid most of the morning's work, filling in the recently cleared paths, which had to be dug out again and salted in case they froze overnight.

I seldom even glimpsed my aunt and uncle for the rest of Christmas Day, not until mid-evening, when they returned exhausted, and, regaining her customary skills, Aunt Dot managed to burn the fried leftover vegetables accompanying the cold meat for supper. None of the traditional fare was on offer – no Christmas cake and no mince pie to provide a wish of any sort. And soon both aunt and uncle were off again, leaving me alone, and I kept the fire going with logs and peat and tried not to think what my mother would say if she could see my small hands so close to the flames.

That was Christmas Day, a memorable day, but on the whole best forgotten, and there were to be many such solitary days that long winter, causing me to become increasingly nervous and intro-spective. Most evenings I sat with my dolls ranged round me, talking to them out loud to counteract the interminable silence. Yet the silence troubled me less than the strange noises. At night the house seemed alive with startling sounds – sudden and inexplicable. Ever since Aunt Dot had threatened to lodge Mad Mary in my bed should she pay us a return call during a snowstorm, I constantly expected a visit from that sinister creature. I had come to equate snow with the imminent appearance of her black presence, so that any unex-plained noise filled me with dread. At times I sat rigid with suspense, knowing that the back door had been left unlocked, listening for the chilling click of the door latch, or the slithering shuffle of shabby shoes, or the eerie croak of Mary's voice. In the lamplight, when shadows danced on the walls, trivial sounds that in daylight would have passed unnoticed were amplified, their momentary threat magnified out of all proportion. Harmless sounds, insignificant in themselves, suddenly occurring in the dim light and deep stillness gave me such a start that I tensed, petrified, trying to trace their source.

Sometimes the culprit was the grandfather clock, which ticked deaf-eningly when I was alone, delivering an extra loud click as it approached the hour, and vibrating like Big Ben when it struck. Sometimes the upstairs floorboards groaned with age, and the down-stairs furniture creaked in sympathy. Then the fire would join in, catching me unawares. It crackled for no good reason, made a star-tling racket when logs shifted, and shattered my nerves with a loud crack when foreign bodies in the coal exploded, spitting out fiery fragments. At times the weather made its contribution, rattling doors and windows. The wind howled hauntingly down the chimney or hooted like the short-eared owl in the pasture, and sleet constantly pelted the window panes, sounding to my childish fancy like little lost souls trying to find their way inside. Imagination took over, distorting everything around me, filling me with apprehension. And, imprisoned as I was in that lonely house, I shivered in fear.

New Year came and went, but my mother did not. Only the snow kept on coming. I suffered silently but my resentment grew, and I took revenge on the calendar pig. January's pig, the first of the new calendar, was labelled as a Danish Landrace. She was very large, plump and pink, with a self-satisfied expression and a litter of piglets gathered round her trotters. I took a dislike to this pig, a dislike aggravated by the happy family scene she flaunted in the face of my intense loneliness.

So it was that I began the New Year by killing the paper pig. Imitating my elders and betters, and making copious use of my red pencils, I dissected her, ruthlessly carving her up into ham shanks and chops, rashers and sausages, heart, liver and kidneys, trotters and knuckles. Then I drew a sharp line round her neck, cutting her head off, and sketched an apple in her mouth, colouring it acid green. I left the piglets alone to fend for themselves – just like me. Sadly I had come a long way in a short time; from protecting the feelings of December's portrait to butchering January's.

The following morning, after the execution of my masterpiece, I noticed that on her brief visits to the house Aunt Dot gave me curious and uneasy glances and kept shaking her head in an angry and bemused way. But she said nothing, and that afternoon was kept very busy because the snow renewed its relentless attack. As for Uncle Matt, he was too occupied wielding his shovel and saving sheep to notice me, let alone the calendar. I wondered – had I got away with it? This time I thought not. But at that depressingly low point in my life, I no longer cared.

Chapter 19

Wee, sleekit, cowrin', tim'rous beastie

Nothing in my brief life had prepared me for the daunting prospect of that winter in Sourhope. The short dark days, unremittingly dreary, were spent in constant drudgery by both aunt and uncle, and in constant loneliness by me. Most days it snowed, seldom relenting for more than a few hours. Other days it froze, hanging long icicles like glassy stalactites down the house walls and turning the garden spring into clustering grapes of ice. The ground hardened to marble, less suited to farming than to winter sports: the paths became slippery slides, the yard a skating rink, and the track to the netty a dangerous ski slope down which I hurtled slithering till I cannoned into the door. The two sheep that died on Christmas Day turned out to be the first of a succession that would be found suffocated or frozen under the snow, and sometimes Uncle Matt buried several together in one grave. Every morning at dawn, in fair weather or foul, he began his day by wading through snowdrifts in an urgent search to save trapped sheep.

'You see, Emma,' he explained one day while setting off for the umpteenth time with his shovel, 'you see, I have to keep lookin' every chance I get. You see, them sheep can live up to three weeks if they've settled in an open drain or near a wall where there's a whiff of air.'

'Why don't they all do that then, Uncle Matt?' I asked, puzzled, as if the sheep knew very well how to save themselves, and died out of sheer perversity.

'Oh, 'cos they haven't the sense. They're short of common sense are sheep. Daft as that brush yonder. And they will huddle together, like. Well, you've seen them huddle, haven't you? They're always at it. So if they happen to fall down they get trampled on by the rest, and then the snow covers them and that's the end of them.'

'But they won't *all* die, will they, Uncle Matt?'

'I hope not, Emma. By heck, I do hope not! Or we'll be finished an' all. But it's a bad lookout, 'cos even the survivors can die if they've

258

been under the snow for more than a week. They lose strength an' that. They go as weak as water, too weak to live.'

Not for a second could he rest for worrying about his sheep, and gradually a deep depression settled over him. To lose sheep was a manifold disaster, bringing grief for the dead and resentment at being defeated, as well as a financial loss that he could ill afford. Time and time again during daylight and again at night by torchlight he went out searching, taking a long crook to prod down into snowdrifts and a reluctant dog to nose up the sheep. Sometimes he was bent double, blown back by the wind blasting his face and straining to balance the sacks of hay he carried to try and save his sheep. But as the weather worsened the sheep went on dying.

The road to Windlestraw was regularly opened by the council snow-plough and then closed by drifts driven by the wind. It could be cleared and closed again within an hour, thereby causing Uncle Matt's second biggest problem – how to dispose of the milk. Several days might pass without a sign of the milk lorry, leaving gallons of milk to freeze in their churns, and in time he was left with no alternative but to pour precious milk over the snow, white on white, in a useless, wasteful stream. Of course Aunt Dot skimmed off the cream, increasing our butter ration, but as food supplies dwindled and fresh orders failed to arrive we often found ourselves short of something to spread it on. Aunt Dot, always thin as a lathe, now shrank to a feather-weight, and Uncle Matt grew gaunt, his face beginning to droop and sag like a mournful bloodhound. He no longer serenaded the cows, having, as he said, nothing to sing about. And needless to say, in the midst of all this gloom and doom no one had time to spare for me. Whenever Uncle Matt passed through the house he always spoke to me in passing, but now he did so with a hurried and preoccupied air.

'Hello there, Emma, pet. You all right?' he asked, kindly enough, but I noticed that he rarely waited for an answer.

And Aunt Dot's attitude was even more impersonal. She seemed largely oblivious of my existence except when leaving the house on her outside rounds, and only then did she give me her full attention. Only then did her pinched little face peer intently at me from a veri-table turban of scarves as she issued her last-minute instructions.

'Now listen, Emma. Listen to me. I want you to make the beds and take a duster to the furniture. It'll give you something to do. Oh, and polish the sideboard thoroughly. It needs a proper do. But first wash those dishes. I've left a bowl of warm soapy water. And peel a few potatoes for later. Put them in the black pan in cold water. And whatever you do, keep that fire going. Bring some logs in a few at a time till the box is full, and keep on feeding the fire. Now don't let me down, Emma, or else you'll be for it, well and truly for it. I can promise you that.'

I hated to think what lay behind that threat, so I tried as hard as I could to fulfil my new role of housekeeper, but felt that neither aunt nor uncle saw me any longer as a child or even as a person. I had somehow lost my identity and become nothing more than a fire stoker, a scullery maid, a beck-and-call skivvy – a Cinderella. For the most part I was restricted to the house, which was little warmer than the temperature outside. Freezing draughts kept me company, creeping out of all the corners to circulate through the rooms, and as if drawn to warmth, clinging to me with over-friendly fingers of ice, refusing to be shaken off. A chill seemed to settle on everything, even curtains and clothes. My fingers constantly felt numb and my feet perpetually frozen. Snow forced its way through the old sash windows to freeze hard on the inside sills, and so bitterly cold did my bedroom become that one night I woke in the early hours, horribly aware that something – I had no idea what – but *something* had taken refuge in my bed. Something small and furry was crawling inside my nightdress, creeping up my leg, and I froze rigid, and sat up in bed, electrified. Then, with no thought for the consequences, I screamed and screamed as if I had seen a hideous ghost.

My reaction surprised even me. The thought of Mad Mary sharing my bed filled me with stark but unutterable terror, yet the realization that some other unknown creature had taken this liberty sent me into hysteria, and I screamed until I woke the entire household. Still screaming, I leapt out of bed, fumbling blindly and frantically for matches, dropping and scattering them over the floor, my hand shaking as I finally managed to light the candle. When I turned round and looked fearfully at the bed it was to see a mouse emerging from my sheets, its shadow on the wall behind grotesquely exaggerated in the flickering candlelight, larger than a rat. At least it was *not* a rat, I thought, slightly relieved but still shaking, while my desperate bedfellow crawled to the foot of the bed and paused, just looking at me. I never forgot that look, at once both sad and reproachful. Not at all threatening, and yet I shivered with fear.

A moment later Aunt Dot rushed in, closely followed by Uncle

Matt, who, in addition to red, white and blue striped pyjamas, was wearing an agitated expression, and looking somehow naked without his cap. I had always assumed that he wore the indispensable cap in bed, or substituted one of those old-fashioned nightcaps, but there he was, bare at both extremities, having wasted no time in putting on slippers. I had never seen either relative in nightclothes before and they looked strangely vulnerable. Aunt Dot reminded me of a rag doll as she stood clutching her voluminous nightdress close to her neck, her hair wound in pipe cleaners in lieu of curlers and her face glistening from the cold cream and glycerine that she spread on it every night. Like me they were both shivering, but only from the cold in my room after their warm bed, and Uncle Matt was busily massaging the arms of his patriotic pyjamas and dancing from foot to foot on the icy floor. My bedroom offered none of the luxury of soft carpeting that I took for granted at home, the floor comprising a sheet of glacial linoleum with just one small rug for comfort, and it was to this rug that he headed, lifting his feet gingerly as he minced towards it. But he minced speedily, and having reached the haven of the rug, he began his interrogation.

'Crikey, Emma! What's up? What is it, girl? Why on earth were you screamin'? What the heck's goin' on?'

'There! That creepy thing. Right there!' I exclaimed, pointing with a shaky hand at the offending rodent. 'That thing's been in my bed. Crawling up my leg. Under my nightie and everything!'

'It's a mouse,' he said, always a shrewd observer.

'It's *only* a mouse,' said Aunt Dot, annoyingly changing the emphasis.

'Yes, it's a mouse all right. Definitely,' concluded Uncle Matt.

'But – it's a *mouse*!' I cried indignantly, resenting their casual attitude. 'How would you like a mouse in your bed?'

Aunt Dot glanced sideways at Uncle Matt as if tempted to point out that she already had one, but she resisted, and bestowed on the mouse a glance even colder than the temperature. I marvelled that the timid creature never flinched. I expected it to shrivel like a spring flower in a late frost, but it held its ground on the counterpane, keeping a reproachful gaze riveted on me.

'Is that all?' demanded my furious aunt. 'That harmless, insignificant little mouse? What a fuss about a triviality! I can hardly see the thing. After all that screaming I expected something the size of an elephant and savage with it. But that! Tchah! I need a microscope just to focus on it. And to think I'm losing a night's precious sleep for that! What a pity you had to wake us up for nothing!'

She glared at the unwitting animal and then at me with a Medusa-like stare that should have turned us both to stone on the spot, and while Uncle Matt persisted in reminding everyone that the intruder was indeed most definitely a mouse, she set off back to their room, patting her pipe cleaners into position. They had gone slightly askew, spiking from her head like spines on a nervous hedgehog, and she smoothed them into place ready for sleep. I thought she had abandoned us, leaving the urgent matter of the mouse unresolved, but two seconds later she reappeared carrying Uncle Matt's slippers, which she dropped carelessly on his recoiling toes.

'Deal with it, Matt,' she said peremptorily. 'I'm absolutely perished. I'm going back to bed and I don't expect to be disturbed again. I hope that's quite clear.' And turning on her heel, she departed.

To my relief the mouse finally withdrew its gaze from my face, and now showing signs of being injured, clawed its way clumsily to the floor and began to follow her. At first I thought and fervently hoped that as she apparently shared none of my aversion to sleeping with mice, the poor disabled thing was off to spend the night in her bed. But to my disappointment the creature changed course, and proceeded to crawl in a dazed fashion back and forth, making a weird clicking noise as it went. This alerted Uncle Matt, who ever since identifying my visitor as a mouse had been gazing round the bare room, looking for a weapon with which to hit it on the head. To my horror, he had just cast a covetous eye on my new and pristine pink hairbrush when he heard the peculiar click and leapt to attention, cupping his hands round his ears.

'Listen to that! He's been damaged,' he cried, automatically assuming the intruder to be male. 'A hundred to one he's been in a trap. That'll be his trouble for sure. He's hurt, so catchin' him'll be a doddle. Now you keep an eye on him for me.'

He disappeared and I watched the mouse scrattling across the floor, making a clearly audible click-click, his long tail trailing over the linoleum. He moved stiffly and mechanically, for all the world like a clockwork mouse, and when Uncle Matt returned carrying a shovel and a sturdy hammer (concealed behind his back), the mouse offered no resistance. There was not a squeak out of him.

'This should do the trick. This'll see him right. Put him out of his misery,' he said compassionately, and brought the hammer down on the mouse's head, adding, as he picked him up by the tail, 'I'll leave him on the shovel till mornin', like.'

'Is he dead, Uncle Matt?' I asked, unaccountably upset.

'Oh he's dead all right. Definitely dead, Emma. Dead as a dodo, you might say. I can honestly state that I've never seen a deader mouse.'

'But I didn't know you meant to kill him. I thought you'd just give him his freedom. Put him outside.'

'Oh he's better off dead than out in that blizzard.'

'You're quite sure he's dead?'

'Sure as eggs is eggs. *You'd* be dead if I hit you with this partic'lar hammer, and you're a lot bigger than he is. Don't you worry, pet. He was damaged anyway, and sufferin'. But now he's off to mouse heaven.'

'Is that the same place as pigs' heaven?'

'Well – on and off. My meanin' is – near enough,' he said non-committally, adding after a moment's thought, 'But maybe they serve more cheese. Anyway, I dare bet he'll be a darn sight warmer up there than down here. Which reminds me, Emma, how do you stand the cold in here? This floor's nitherin'. That's the only word for it – *nitherin'*.'

'I just have to, Uncle Matt,' I pointed out resignedly.

'Yes, I suppose you do at that, pet. We must fix our minds on improvin' things when the bad weather lifts a bit. I had no idea it was that cold in here. Now, jump into bed and put the candle out and curl your feet up and get some shut-eye. I'm off to do the same, though it won't be long before that pesky alarm goes off and I'll have to rise and shine. So I'll say goodnight, Emma. What's left of it.'

Bearing the small furry body on the shovel ceremoniously before him, like a butler bearing a glass of port on a silver salver, he left the room, closing the door quietly. And I did as bidden, curling my feet up inside my winceyette nightie, but I lay awake for a long time listening to Uncle Matt's snores. I also heard his alarm go off, a sudden shrill ring, loud and persistent, as he tried to sleep through it until jabbed in the ribs by Aunt Dot, when he gave a cry that caused me to sit up in bed, stiff with shock. Nor could I settle down again. I felt frozen and tormented by guilt, because not only had I been respon-sible for the untimely death of a helpless fellow creature, but I had deprived my aunt and uncle of much-needed rest and, unlike me, they had to rise very early. Besides, my feet refused to be warmed, so finally, with Uncle Matt's constant advice in mind, I lifted the rug from the floor onto the bed, thus benefiting from that much-extolled extra layer.

I slept late the following morning. There being no school to attend, I could sleep as long as I liked, and Aunt Dot actively encouraged me to sleep late rather than 'get under her feet', as she put it. School was closed, and as the weeks passed and the roads continued to be blocked it remained closed. I might have worried about this gap in my education had it not been for my lively apprehension about the threatened transfer to Mr Clout's classroom and the spectres therein that haunted me – Mr Clout himself, his terrifying cat, and his class of giants. In the light of those three frightening prospects, I was glad to stay away as long as possible, preferably for ever, and endeavoured to spend my days peacefully, doing innumerable little jobs around the house, reading and drawing when I had time, and most importantly, keeping the piles of fuel high and the fire warm and bright.

I tried to stay out of Aunt Dot's way as much as possible, because relations between us were increasingly strained. She became ever more obsessed with the unfairness of the weather, and just as she had previously repeatedly praised a fine day in a superstitious way in case it changed, so she now continually railed against the snow as if her disapproval would put a stop to it, make it think twice about persisting. And her temper soon grew as short as her small person. It was perhaps understandable that she should become so fractious and irascible, but she lost her temper faster than Uncle Matt could hide a furtive cigarette, and he could do that like greased lightning. Any supposed misdemeanour on my part, however insignificant, was followed either instantly or belatedly by retribution on hers, until I came to expect punishment as an inescapable fact of life. And once again it was my imagination that often led me into trouble. During the fierce storms that confined me to the house, only my mind was free to roam, and my imaginings irritated my aunt more than anything, causing her to regard me as a liar, or as slightly mad, or – worse still in her eyes – as totally wilful.

I loved talking to people, and in the absence of real people I invented them, populating the valley with figments of my fertile mind. Unwitting of the harm it would do, I invented colourful strangers coming to call, crossing the yard or approaching the house from the front meadow. One afternoon as I sat daydreaming on the window seat I described a whole family passing through the fields, walking quickly in a hail of sleet. Aunt Dot was working close behind me, busily preparing a corned beef hash to be heated up at suppertime. I could not help thinking that 'hash' was an appropriate name for most of her concoctions, but in this case the smell of simmering onions for once gave the promise of something tasty. I played my game in happy anticipation of a hot meal to come, and as I talked she seemed unusually interested, giving the impression that she was joining in the game, just as my mother used to do.

'A family, did you say? My word! Out in this weather! Who on earth can they be? I must say, I haven't seen a soul for days and days.'

'I don't know, Aunt Dot, but I see a man, a woman and two children.'

'Gracious me! What a day to be out with children!' she exclaimed, lifting her pinafore to dab her eyes, wiping away what I took to be tears of sympathy, then realized they were caused by the onions.

'Oh, don't worry, Aunt Dot,' I said. 'They've got the right clothes on. The man's wearing a long coat patterned with stars and high boots and a tall pointed hat. And the woman's wearing a crinoline and carrying a fur muff. The boy has gold pantaloons on, and the girl's wearing a blue poncho with a silver fringe.'

It was an absurd description, patently not to be taken seriously, but it was all too much for Aunt Dot, and she rushed to the window, rubbing a clear circle in the condensation and peering through.

'Where? Where? I can't see anyone. Not a living soul.'

'Just there,' I pointed, still lost in my daydream. 'Hurrying through the meadow. The wind's blowing their clothes. They're halfway through the field. See them?'

I had conjured up a childish fantasy but I brought down a furore on my head. Aunt Dot flew at me, flapping wildly at any part she could reach, squawking and screeching with the fury of a threatened bird defending its nest.

'You've made it all up, haven't you? Made the whole thing up just to provoke me! You wicked, tiresome girl! Wicked! Wicked! Wicked!' she shrieked, each accusation emphasized by an angry blow. 'It's all just lies. Lies! Lies! Lies! I hate lies. I'll knock the lies out of you if it's the last thing I do.'

At that moment I rather hoped it would be, so that the beating would stop. I made no sound, so as to let her know that the lies had indeed been knocked out of me, knocked for six in fact, but she went on flapping and screeching with tireless perseverance and all her tiny might. She thought I intended to trick her, to make a fool of her, whereas no such intention entered my mind, nor did malice of any sort, but only childish play. Eventually, she calmed down and got on with her work, but for the rest of the time that she remained in the house I hid behind the curtain, crouched and stiff with cold on the chilly window sill, afraid to move a muscle. I kept as quiet as a mouse, in fact much quieter than the mouse of recent acquaintance, while she made enough noise for both of us as she stormed about her business, clashing and banging utensils, and muttering furiously to herself.

'Pointed hats, indeed! Crinolines, for mercy's sake! And, of all things, pantaloons! Gracious heavens, the child's crazy! I shouldn't have to tolerate such lunatic behaviour. I don't deserve such aggravation.'

She left me in no doubt that I was firmly in her black books, and I sat worrying lest I had jeopardized my chance of supper. Food was scarce and most of the time I felt starving. Besides, though she was inclined to be heavy-handed with the pepper in all savoury creations, the simple corned beef hash was one of the few dishes that even she found difficult to spoil. My worry was that Uncle Matt was not there to defend me. He had spent the early hours rescuing sheep, then called at the house for a change of clothes and a bite to eat and left for Thorny Edge, travelling by horse and sledge and taking Mr Phillip with him. He had met John Phillip the day before at Brackenfield, and after discussing their desperate need for various provisions, they arranged the trip together for mutual safety. Then at the last moment Mr Shoeman joined them, determined to collect his undelivered mail. Uncle Matt was intrigued by the value Shoeman put on his mail when there were so many more pressing problems, as I had overheard him telling Aunt Dot the previous evening.

'I must try to get to the village for supplies, Dot,' he said anxiously. 'John Phillip walked as far as Low Nether the other day and heard a rumour that they're droppin' food by parachute, to be shared among the farmsteads, so we must go down and get our share. Definitely. I know we're badly in need of flour and yeast, but they're droppin' bread to tide us over. And we're right short of paraffin, so I'll try for that and anything else I can lay my hands on.'

'You'll never make it, Matt. Not all the way to Thorny Edge,' Aunt Dot protested, torn between needing supplies and risking Uncle Matt, not to mention the horse.

'Maybe not, but we have to try. It means leavin' you to feed the hens and pigs, but things are very scarce around here, and it's not just food and paraffin. That last blizzard did a power of harm – sheep dyin' like flies, and hay wastin' in the snow. We're beginnin' to run out of hay and straw. So I need to cast about and see if there's any to be bought, else if the weather doesn't kill the poor beggars then hunger will.'

He returned at dusk, soaked through but glowing with the exhilaration of a successful expedition, and as I listened to him from my subdued corner I had the impression that he could have been home much earlier had he not been tempted to hob-nob with the neighbours congregating at Thorny Edge. He described the village, usually quiet as the grave, as a hive of activity, buzzing with the noise of neighing horses and boisterous men, all lively with purpose. Some, like him, were simply seeking provisions, some were helping to keep the main road clear, and others were cutting big swathes with business-like shovels through the snowdrifts to free stranded vehicles.

Word had gone round the lower valley that supplies had arrived from two directions – brought from Aidensmead by snow cutters, and dropped from an aeroplane like manna from heaven. Hopeful residents gathered at the church hall, forming an orderly queue, and Olive Featherstone and other helpful ladies busily distributed the goods, and as a welcome sideline provided hot cocoa, sticky buns and the latest gossip. The men circulated, stamping feet and flapping arms, slapping backs and lighting pipes, their breath and smoke and cocoa steam combining in vaporous clouds to rise and freeze in the icy air. Reluctant to disperse and face the lonely and hazardous journey home they lingered, greeting friends and exchanging winter tales and experiences, each more harrowing than the one before. They told of loss and damage to livestock and livelihoods, of bravery and bereavement, of brides carried piggyback to the church, and of coffins pulled by sledge and borne on mourners' shoulders through knee-deep snow to the graveyard.

As soon as Uncle Matt had filled his bags and boxes with provisions, wheedling as much as possible on account of living so far out, he joined the various groups. He partook eagerly of the local gossip and in full measure of the available cocoa and sticky buns, rejoining the queue several times when he thought no one was looking. He even took a turn at wielding a shovel, talking non-stop as he hurled the snow high and wide. He was a gregarious soul, and weeks spent

267

in the company of dying sheep had made him crave human companionship. Fortunately John Phillip felt the same, but the reclusive Mr Shoeman, for reasons better known to himself, was in a hurry to leave. The moment his business was transacted, his shopping done, and his correspondence stored in a leather shoulder bag, he set off on his return trip alone.

John Phillip tried to dissuade him, but in vain.

'He's taking a big risk, all by himself and on foot,' he said, gazing after Shoeman's stubbornly retreating back.

'Yes, the blighter might end up in a fifteen-foot drift,' said Uncle Matt rather wistfully. 'With a bit of luck, that is. He was mad keen to get hold of them letters and be off. Did you notice that? I'd love to know what was in them. I reckon he's a spy all right. Odds on he is. Anyway, they say the Devil takes care of his own.'

And the Devil did, because Mr Shoeman not only survived unscathed, but beat the others home by over an hour, which feat naturally led to suspicion on Aunt Dot's part that Uncle Matt was out enjoying himself. She happened to notice Shoeman's fur hat passing her kitchen window, and the long wait that followed did nothing to improve her temper. She was ready for her wanderer's return, and if he expected the fatted-calf treatment he was doomed to disappointment. He staggered in like a tired but conquering hero, threw off his wet clothes and flopped into a chair in front of the fire, stretching his feet towards the heat as happily as a pampered cat, and was soon steaming gently.

'Thank goodness I'm back, Dot. Absolutely jiggered but safe and sound,' he said proudly. 'What a day I've had. Terrible. Drifts ten to fifteen feet high. And I'll tell you what – you nearly lost me. Once or twice I thought we were goners. Still, never mind, eh? We made it, though by the skin of our teeth at times. And it sure is good to be home. That's a grand smell coming from the range. A grand smell. My meanin' is, Dot, whatever you've been cookin' sure smells good, and I can't wait to sample it.'

Compliments on Aunt Dot's cooking were as rare as golden eggs from geese, but instead of accepting this one gracefully she dismissed it, just as she dispensed with the hero's welcome. She made him a cup of tea, handed him a slice of bread and butter, and then proceeded to give him what he called 'the third degree'. She questioned him closely as to where he had been till this hour, and why he was so late, and how come Shoeman's hat had sailed past the kitchen window over an hour ago, and how was Olive Featherstone looking these days, and was she still as fat and frumpy as ever, to all of which questions he gave guarded replies. She listened intently to the answers, and just as he began to relax again, she held out a dry coat and hustled him into it and straight out to the byre.

'But what about my hot dinner?' he protested, looking pitifully over his shoulder as she propelled him to the door.

'Cows first,' she answered stubbornly. 'They still have to be fed and milked. I'll be out in a minute to help you, so that you can check on the sheep afterwards while I heat up the meal. Then I dare say you'll be good and ready for it.'

Almost two hours passed before we ate and he had the chance to dwell at length on his adventures, but though the first flush of excitement had faded from his delivery, he still gave a detailed account, lingering on his own bravery and the many times he had saved the day despite the efforts of his wayward horse to lead him astray.

'Awful dangerous conditions, Dot. You have no idea. A man needs the heart of a lion for a journey like that. Ask anybody,' he said, waving his hand vaguely from grandfather clock to empty chairs as if Windlestraw were full of witnesses willing to corroborate his story. 'Yes, you're very lucky to have me back in one piece, I can tell you,' he added, puffing his chest out with patriotic pride. 'We're heroes, we are, me and John. Yes, that's it, heroes. Just like the lads from Dunkirk.'

'Oh, yes?' said Aunt Dot, sceptically. 'Well, we'll have to see if we can get you a medal. A medal as big as a frying pan. That should do.'

She smiled her tight sarcastic smile, and turned her attention to the containers he had brought back, but having briefly ascertained that they were all full, she relaxed somewhat, and listened to his tale with surprising patience while we ate our supper. Though it had dried out a little, it still tasted appetizing, and as Uncle Matt remarked in fulsome praise, it filled an empty corner. She showed less interest in learning of the trials and tribulations of his journey than in hearing the local gossip, and could hardly wait to investigate fully the contents of the bags and boxes.

Eagerly but critically she appraised them, item by item, remarking as she stacked them on the table that she wished he had brought more tins of this rather than that, or more packets of the other, while he kept reminding her that she was lucky to have anything, and that he had not only risked his life for that small quota, but twice had to slip Olive Featherstone a threepenny bit to persuade her to part with certain extras.

'Oh, I know you've done your best,' she conceded, 'but I'd have liked just a bit more. Heaven knows when you'll be back to Thorny Edge.'

'Well, as to that, Dot, I'll have to go back next week, come what may. I could only get one can of paraffin. It's very scarce and everybody's shoutin' for it. And there's no hay to be bought. But I bumped into Bill down there and he was tellin' me that there'll be hay at the crossroads on Tuesday and each farm can take ten bundles. They say it's damp black rubbish, but better than nothin', and I must have my share.'

On the whole he seemed in sunnier spirits after his trip, and chatted pleasantly to me as he warmed his hands before supper. He smiled a lot and winked across the table, greatly to my relief, because Aunt Dot stolidly ignored me. I might have been invisible the way she looked straight through me with her cold, stony stare. Even when she slammed a third dinner plate onto the table, bouncing it fit to break it as if it too had wronged her, even then she did not summon me to the table. It was Uncle Matt who patted my chair invitingly and winked, so that I hastily climbed up and tucked in hungrily. I had been tormented by that tantalizing smell for hours and would have eaten my portion even if it had been served in Split's dog bowl.

Throughout the meal I remained quiet, knowing that Aunt Dot was still nursing her grudge and might fly off the handle before I finished eating. Fortunately Uncle Matt monopolized the conversation at table, but afterwards I overheard a discussion taking place in the kitchen, a heated discussion about me during which Aunt Dot entered into a lengthy catalogue of all my faults, particularly those of recent origin, and all the extra work that in her view I deliberately caused her, while Uncle Matt did his best to defend me. Time and time again I heard him make the same patient comment, as he tried to calm her down.

'She's only little, Dot. Give her a chance. You forget that she's just a little girl.' But time and again she gave him the same sharp answer.

'She's big enough to tell lies. Big enough to be deceitful.'

'Well now, Dot,' he sighed, 'I wouldn't say they're lies exactly. Not really lies, like. It's just make-believe. She has a powerful imagination, I'll grant you, but it's natural that she plays like that, and dreams people up that don't exist. She's stuck out here on her own with nobody to talk to, and she's not used to this isolation. She must be real lonely at times. In fact, I met Amy Leadbetter in the post office and she was saying that her niece often visits at weekends when the weather's decent. She needs a playmate too, so we kinda settled it that the next time Ida – that's her niece – comes for the weekend our Emma can go down and visit.'

'Oh yes, that's right, you'll take her side as usual,' declared Aunt Dot bitterly. 'You spoil her. You always take her part against me. You think more of her than you do of your own wife.'

'Not at all, Dot. Course I don't. I understand your viewpoint. You work too hard and Emma tries your patience. As a matter of fact, I was thinkin' that if the weather's fair tomorrow I'll take her with me. Out from under your feet. There now.'

He emerged from the kitchen to my gratified gaze, his face the impassive mask he always wore when he wanted to look inscrutable, concealing any indication that I had recently been the subject of Aunt Dot's bitter criticism.

'Oh, there you are, Emma girl,' he began in surprised tones, as if there were somewhere else I might be. 'I've just been confabbin' with your aunt, and we're agreed that if it's fine tomorrow I'll take you with me. It's time you had a breath of fresh air, and you can help me feed the hens and goats an' that. But mind you, you'll need to wrap up very warm – scarf, hat, gloves, the lot. And put them riding breeches on that I bought you. They'll fit nicely inside your wellies. Now as to the breeches, Emma, I won't take no for an answer. They cost good money and they're just the ticket, so put them on. And by the way, it nearly slipped my mind that I've a present here for somebody. Some comics. I managed to scrounge a *Beano* and a *Dandy* at the post office, and they're yours if you can guess which hand they're in.'

So it was that the following morning, which dawned bright and sunny with a bracing wind, I was taken out of my cold prison for the first time for weeks and led into an arctic world of dazzling white, almost blinding to my unaccustomed eyes. The price for this pleasure was acceptance of the riding breeches, which I had hitherto shrunk from wearing. Whatever the practicalities of this alien leg wear, I felt it would make me look quite ridiculous. But after some thought I decided that it would seem ungrateful to refuse, and anyway, scarcely anyone would see me, so I would wear the riding breeches if it would

271

please him. It did, and as an added bonus I found them exception-ally warm and comfortable. I forgot all about my earlier prejudices, even about the lack of a pony to complete the picture, and from then on the breeches and I became inseparable.

'Didn't I tell you, Emma, that they'd be warm as toast?' cried Uncle Matt triumphantly. 'Didn't I now?'

'Yes, you did, Uncle Matt, and so they are, but they're really just for riding and I think they make me look like a boy.'

'Boy? Stuff and nonsense! They're girls' breeches, and anyways, I've never seen a boy as pretty as you. No, Emma, you look like a proper little toff. You'd pass for a gentleman farmer's daughter. One of the county set.' And though I knew that the breeches weren't really appropriate, I accepted his compliments as sincere.

Most of the track leading to Todd Tingate's had frozen hard, and we proceeded cautiously but without incident, Uncle Matt carrying a few provisions for Miss Titchmarsh, and I clinging to his other arm. The animals gave us an ecstatic welcome, and Split growled and barked them into submission, but only because they were securely locked up and he could be as menacing as he liked. It was when we left for Moss House that we ran into trouble because the lane had filled to the brim with snow, now turning soft, so that we soon began to sink down into ten-foot drifts. Uncle Matt had acquired the knack of tightrope walking along the tops of walls, but I tended to slip off, or lose a wellington, leaving it embedded in the snow. I constantly had to be rescued until I found a way of half-crawling along, holding on to the top stones as best I could, and glad of the thick breeches and khaki socks.

Eventually we reached Moss House, where Miss Titchmarsh was crouched mournfully over a low fire. She brightened instantly, espe-cially when she saw the contents of Uncle Matt's bag, in which he had included a few treats, for though he often made fun of her behind her back, he felt sorry for her and always tried to help. Besides, her obvious adulation flattered him, giving a welcome boost to his ego. She offered us a late breakfast, spreading toast with condensed milk, which I loved. Then Uncle Matt carried in coal and cleared paths, while I thawed out and dried my socks.

'I'm so pleased to see you both,' she kept saying. 'I haven't spoken to anyone for days. And you, Mr Wheatley, you're a gentleman. An absolute gentleman.' At this he shrugged his shoulders modestly, but tweaked his cap as if to prove her right.

She was most reluctant to let us go, but my hens were waiting to be fed at Brackenfield. I had been so looking forward to seeing them again, but despite their lady-like pretensions, I soon realized that they were by no means house-proud. An oppressive smell met us at the hen-house door, and Uncle Matt attempted to give the premises a quick clean out, but the hens squawked in protest, fluttering in his way, all fury and flapping feathers, only interested in food. At length, locking them back in their warmth and darkness, we retraced our steps to Windlestraw, and from then on whenever the weather allowed, I accompanied Uncle Matt on his errands, though my short legs were frequently buried in snowdrifts and I had to be hauled out igno-miniously by the scruff of the neck, as helpless as a floundering puppy.

On stormy days when forced to stay home, I turned to the calendar pig for company. Like everything else that month, February's pig turned out to be a snowy colour, a White Ulster, of pale complexion and fine hair, almost bald in fact. So with only a light dusting of white chalk I transformed her into a snowman pig, adding the tradi-tional accoutrements. I blackened the eyes to look like nuggets of coal and coloured in a checked muffler, but I left out the carrot nose as she was already endowed with a more than substantial snout. Finally, to remind myself of Uncle Matt, I substituted a cap for the traditional top hat and a cigarette for the pipe. I found it comforting to see this familiar face in the kitchen during the long hours that Uncle Matt spent outside, stoically braving the elements like a snowman come to life.

Chapter 20

Eye-catching Breeches

The coming of March should have heralded spring, but apart from the timely activity of local birds beginning to build nests, there was little evidence of that longed-for season. Briefly the winter storms abated, and in that brief respite March came in like a lamb rather than a lion, but not a lively lamb full of the joys of spring – more like the cold wet lambs struggling for life that began to be born on the farm. Nor had winter loosened its grip entirely, for, as Uncle Matt pointed out, thick slabs of snow lay hard as icebergs along the dyke bottoms – a sign of more to come, he said. Definitely. And sure enough, sudden snowfalls that he called lambing storms persisted for weeks, catching us unawares and killing yet more sheep as well as weakly lambs.

For the moment, however, a fresh wind brought fresh problems; it caused a quick thaw, so that we walked ankle deep in thick slush that moved like a slow river over the land. It was weather just fit for ducks, and I often thought it a pity that we kept none at Windlestraw, considering that duck ponds had formed all over the place, really big ponds, enough and to spare. Everywhere we went we paddled, or 'plodged', as Uncle Matt would have it. Acres of melting snow now swashed and splashed underfoot, sometimes hiding dangerous ice.

So it was small wonder that in those hazardous conditions no one had time to consider me, or the two major events in my life – my birthday, and my return most unwillingly to school. Somehow these two events became inextricably linked in my mind, perhaps because they occurred simultaneously, and perhaps because I was made to feel that the one was to blame for the other. Every protest, every excuse, every plea that I put forward in the hope of a reprieve from school, or at the very least of a postponement, all met with the same unsympathetic response from Aunt Dot.

'That's enough, Emma! Quite enough! Now stop whingeing this

minute. You're always whingeing about something. Gracious heavens! You're a big girl now. You're nine! Goodness' sakes! You shouldn't be making a fuss about school at your age. Especially when you've had such a nice long rest from lessons. What a pity you've nothing better to worry about. If you had my worries you'd know what hit you. You'd know when you were well off. Anyway, it's high time you went back to school. I'm sick and tired of having you under my feet all the time.'

And even Uncle Matt, on whom I could usually rely to take my part, inexplicably let me down, for once siding with my aunt and adding to my confusion and despair. Like the changing weather, his priorities had also changed, as the arrival of spring brought new worries, needing extra vigilance and effort of a different kind. He was now busy lambing ewes at all hours of the day and night, causing him to be constantly tired and fractious, and therefore inclined to give short shrift to my juvenile problems.

'This isn't like you, Emma,' he said gravely. 'Not like you at all. I mean to say, you're mostly brave as a little lion. And after all, you're nine now. A big girl now.'

'Am I really a big girl?' I asked in some bewilderment. 'Aunt Dot keeps saying so, but I don't feel any bigger. I feel just the same, and you know – all my clothes still fit.'

'Big? Course you are. Crikey Moses! Nine years old! Why it's practically grown up. By heck I wish I was nine! I'd have a whale of a time. I'd be glad to get back to school. Best years of your life, your schooldays. I'd be off like a shot, I would.'

I took that assertion with a large pinch of salt since I already knew the truth of it. He had often boasted to me of his schooldays, and of the painstaking efforts he made in deliberately shirking those so-called best years of his life, showing an aptitude bordering on genius at persistent truanting. He had described how brilliantly he bamboozled the school-board man, gaining high scores only in the number of absence noughts against his name on the register, and achieving success solely in his studious avoidance of school. Yet now he sought to pull the wool over my eyes, as he sat on his three-legged stool, his cap pushed well back on his head, the peak forming a halo, and looking as angelic as a cherub decorating a harp, radiating self-righteousness.

It occurred to me, however, that it was not in my best interests to highlight his hypocrisy, so I said nothing just then about his earlier confessions, but instead tried to elicit his sympathy by reminding him of Mr Clout's formidable personality. As I remembered it, their September encounter had resembled a clash of Titans, and my uncle had lost the conflict hands down. It was my impression that Mr Clout had treated him more like a doormat than an Uncle Matt, metaphorically wiping his feet all over him.

I recalled that my determined uncle had begun the interview with a modicum of confidence, which grew out of all proportion as he launched into negotiation to buy a painting never up for sale, and he had achieved nothing but raised tempers all round. The coveted painting still hung undisturbed in the headmaster's study. Uncle Matt had been shown the door, I had been placed in the wrong class, and Mr Clout had been driven to kick petulantly at the antique patina of his rather splendid desk. At least, that was how *I* remembered events, but I soon discovered that Uncle Matt remembered things quite differently. One evening I stood patiently behind the cows while he hurriedly milked them, as he intended checking his sheep again before dark, and at length, with some difficulty, I engaged his attention.

'I just daren't go back, Uncle Matt,' I pleaded miserably. 'If I do I'll be put in the big class, in Mr Clout's class. You know – you remember – the dreaded Mr Clout.'

'Well of course you will, girl. That's what you get for comin' out top of the class,' he said, sticking his chest out with pride. 'Nothin' wrong with that as I can see.'

'But you know how scary he is. Like a big wild grizzly bear.'

'Oh now don't exaggerate, Emma. I wouldn't say he's scary, once you get to know him. I did find him a bit high and mighty at first, but we were soon right as rain. We had a real friendly chat, as I recall. Got on fine. Yes, definitely. Talked about art, an' that. Shook hands and everythin'. I was surprised really, 'cos he has quite a superior air about him that would put some people off, them that's easily discouraged, like. He's quite the gentleman I grant you, with his fancy whiskers and waistcoats.'

It was evident that my negotiations, like his with Mr Clout, were not going well, and in acute disappointment I plucked up the courage to contradict.

'No, Uncle Matt. I'm afraid you've got him all wrong. He's not what he seems, not what you think. He's no gentleman. He's just a big bully. He's frightening and cruel. He yells and growls and pounces and hits, and I hate him.'

'Hmm. Well, if you say so, Emma. I don't deny that he can be strict. He's noted for it. But likely he *has* to be strict. Likely he has some big louts to contend with. They'll not all be as keen to learn as you. And you've got to hand it to the man; he does know his stuff, especially when he's spoutin' off on nature. And he certainly can talk. Talk the hind leg off a donkey. And there again, he's got great taste in art, same taste as me as it happens. Which reminds me, Emma, maybe when you get settled in, like, you could jog his memory about that watercolour I fancied. You know the one, don't you, pet? Well, I've been thinkin' it over, and what with the nice gold frame it had and everythin', I'd definitely go to three shillings and ninepence.'

I stared at him in horror, scarcely able to believe my ears. Would he never learn? Did he really understand so little about me? Not in a million years would I dare approach Mr Clout voluntarily about anything, least of all about an incident which had driven him to complete exasperation, clearly convinced that he was dealing with a couple of crazy people. It had taken weeks to live that disgrace down and I had no intention of stirring it up again. I fastened imploring green eyes on Uncle Matt's newly animated face, as he basked in recollection of the painting that had temporarily got away but that still tantalized.

'But, Uncle Matt, don't you understand? I couldn't possibly do that! I'm terrified of Mr Clout – of the big class – of the school! Terrified to go back at all!' To which outburst he shrugged his shoulders and swivelled his cap, looking somewhat at a loss.

'Ah but, Emma, pet, you have to, girl. Everybody has to go to school.'

'*You* didn't,' I finally could not resist pointing out, and for a moment he seemed taken aback, but quickly recovered.

'But times have changed, Emma. Things have moved on since them days,' he said vaguely. 'Now it's the law an' that. Just as long as the school's open you have to go. And it's open again now. Anyways, I was just a daft lad, but you're a clever girl. You don't want to grow up higorant, do you? A bright girl like you? Top of the class an' all. Surely you can see the sense of that? After all, as your aunt's fond of remarkin', you're a big girl now. You're nine.'

I seemed to be going round in circles, and it was frustrating to say the least. So in desperation I attempted a last throw of the dice, my last chance to convince him of what to me was a very real danger.

'But Uncle Matt, what about the cat? What about that, then? You know – the vicious cat that nobody talks about. *The Cat!'*

In a rare expression of disapproval he frowned deeply at me and turned away, then moved off to the cooler-house, plainly losing patience, and looking disappointed.

'Now, Emma, don't start all that again. Don't go on about that dratted cat! You saw how Mr Clout disliked all that silliness. That's how you got on his wrong side in the first place, by harpin' on about cats. Just when I had him eatin' out of my hand, so to speak. Anyway, a big girl like you shouldn't be frightened of cats.' And then, inspired by an afterthought, he paused at the door, adding a final pithy comment. 'I'll tell you one thing,' he said emphatically, as if this riposte would clinch the argument once and for all, 'one thing to be said in Clout's favour. Very much so, in fact. Credit where credit's due – he's kept a magnificent head of hair. Magnificent! Yes, I just wish I had a tenth of it. There now!' And with that he vanished with his milk pail, victorious.

I left it at that, bowing to the inevitable, but felt constantly bemused by the suggestion, now frequently hinted at, that since reaching the mature age of nine I had undergone an overnight transformation reminiscent of Alice in Wonderland. Apparently I had aged and grown out of all proportion to the unremarkable event of being one day older. Without a full-length mirror I could neither dispute nor verify this phenomenon, but I held my little hand mirror at maybe a dozen different angles and could not detect even a smidgen of change. Perhaps I had grown an inch or so taller in the seven months since coming to Windlestraw, but nothing to justify the sudden appellation of a 'big girl'. And curiously, this inconsistency, which both aunt and uncle insisted upon, was never satisfactorily explained, and I puzzled over it many a day but never solved the mystery.

As for my birthday, it passed almost unnoticed. Whatever slight excitement I felt at the start soon fizzled out like a damp squib when I received neither cards nor presents, and it was completely extinguished at the sight of my birthday tea. This celebration meal featured the habitual boiled egg with bread and butter, but as a concession to the occasion, Aunt Dot had baked a sponge cake, slightly burnt round the edges and soggy in the middle. She had unearthed a single birthday candle, which she stuck into a little tin candleholder shaped like a rose. This she speared into the centre of the cake, lighting the candle with a spill from the fireside, but she instantly hovered over it, like a moth attracted to the flame. She seemed curiously eager to snuff it out, so, just like my birthday hopes, no sooner had it flickered into life than it was gone.

'Hurry, Emma. Hurry up now,' she cried, her thin little hands gesticulating in agitation. 'Make your wish and blow the candle out. It would be a shame to spoil the cake with drips of candle grease, and a sin to waste the candle. Living way out here, you never know when you might need an extra candle.'

I doubted if any wish would come true when made in such haste and over one candle instead of nine, but I whispered my wish swiftly, rushing to complete it before the candle was removed, and so earnestly that it came out half wish and half prayer.

'I wish – I wish I had the power of red hair – and could go home and live with my mother – foreverandeveramen.'

And no sooner had I blown the candle out than Aunt Dot snatched it away, replacing it in the cupboard; then, with a cursory cry of 'Happy birthday' called over her shoulder, she vanished into the kitchen. Meanwhile, Uncle Matt gazed mournfully at the unappetizing candleless cake.

'We're not exactly pushin' the boat out here, are we, Emma? Not makin' much of a splash,' he sighed. 'My meanin' is, pet, this is a poor show for a birthday tea, and it has to be said, a poor birthday cake. In fact, to be brutally frank – but don't quote me to your aunt Dot – it looks more like a cowpat than a cake.

'It's fine, Uncle Matt, *really*,' I whispered quickly, glancing nervously at the kitchen door, anxious to avoid trouble on my birthday. 'I think it's very kind of Aunt Dot to make me a cake when she's so busy, and I'm sure that with a spoonful of treacle on it, it'll taste lovely.'

'I wouldn't put money on it, Emma,' he murmured gloomily. 'As cakes go it's a definite disaster. It looks sad – in fact, proper sorry for itself, and sinkin' fast in the middle. But anyway, pet, many happy returns of the day, and I'm sorry there's no cards or presents, but as you know, I've been nowhere near the shops lately.' Then, brightening a little, he added, 'I'll make it up to you, Emma. See if I don't. And in the meantime, here's two threepenny bits for you. Put them away nice and safe, and don't spend them all at once.'

That frugal celebration more or less constituted my birthday party – short and not particularly sweet. It should have been enlivened by a parcel from my mother, but sadly that was delayed, arriving some three days later. It was, however, well worth the wait, enclosing as it did a pretty card and a loving letter, as well as sweets, a small iced fruit cake, and a warm coat, which Aunt Dot declared too good for school, so it was put away for best and seldom worn. Two things occurred to me regarding that coat my mother had made for me, the first being that it was clever of her to guess the right size, considering my rumoured overnight growth, and the second, that it seemed a shame after she had used up part of her precious ration of clothing coupons that the coat should hang upstairs, largely neglected. But only one week back at school convinced me that Aunt Dot might be right at that. By then both my new ruler and protractor had mysteriously disappeared, and I guessed that my new coat might well have suffered the same fate.

I soon learnt that accommodation of senior pupils' coats was governed by the weather. Normally they hung in the porch like dead hares on iron hooks, and the end of the school day signalled a joyous stampede through the porch to the outer door, so that the fleetest of foot could, if unscrupulous, claim the best coat. But on wet days coats were draped on the fireguard round the stove, where steam rose thickly like sudden fog to the lofty ceiling, filling the air with earthy vapours and releasing strong smells redolent of byres and barns, stables and sheepfolds. Nevertheless, the same rule applied – first come, first served – and after the final bell the frantic tussle round the stove resembled a free-for-all with no holds barred. Fortunately my coat was too small and worn to be in demand, so I waited patiently for the despised left-over to be released, and often found it lying trampled to dusty shapelessness on the rough and splintery floorboards.

To combat my fear of returning to school, I had formed a cunning plan to help me cope. It seemed to my naïve mind that after such a long absence the teachers might well have forgotten about my transfer to the senior class, and that I in turn could be forgiven for a similar lapse of memory. At any rate, the strategy was worth a try, I thought, and, arriving later than usual, having been persuaded to wait for the milk lorry, I brazenly presented myself in Miss Speedwell's class, intending to sneak into my old desk. But here I encountered my first obstacle, finding the seat already occupied by a very small boy.

He was engrossed in chewing a pencil and spitting the splinters onto the floor, gnawing at the wood like a hungry rodent, and so concentrated was he in this absorbing enterprise that he never even noticed me. He had clearly reached that stage in life which most children go through and some grow out of faster than others, of regarding anything in front of him, from a lump of coal to a garden worm, as something specifically designed to put in his mouth. And though intent on demolishing the pencil, he was even now eyeing with interest other potential snacks lined up for later consumption. He had found a jelly baby covered in fluff in his pocket, someone's lost mitten in the desk, a half-eaten biscuit on the floor, and one of Miss Speedwell's rubbers, which he was saving for dessert. I could envisage no immediate prospect of prising this insatiable infant from my seat, and having never met the usurper before, I stood nonplussed, at a loss how to proceed. Then Miss Speedwell saw me, smiled warmly, and gave me a hug.

'Oh, Emma. How lovely to see you!' she cried. 'I wondered if you'd be in today, but I thought not, since you live so far away. Well, you're a brave girl, and Mr Clout will be pleased. He asked about you yesterday, so I'd better take you straight through to his class. But don't worry about a thing. You'll be just fine. Really, you will. And remember, Emma, you're always welcome to pop in here and talk to me.'

And with that she led me into the senior classroom, and with my heart sinking and all hope gone I followed, though once inside and trembling like an aspen leaf, I hesitated and drew back, seriously considering making a run for it. But she turned and squeezed my shoulders and whispered comfortingly, 'Chin up, Emma. You'll be all right. I promise.' We stood waiting nervously for Mr Clout's attention.

Only about half the class had bothered to come in, the rest having taken advantage of bad weather to stay home, and those present looked cold and dispirited, frozen to their seats and bored by Mr Clout's dull voice reading in flat tones from a history book. They brightened slightly at our interruption, relieving the monotony as it did, and a few hands went up to attract Mr Clout's attention to our welcome appearance. I glanced timidly at him, and he looked even hairier than I remembered, as if, like Rip Van Winkle, he had slept for twenty years and his hair and whiskers had gone on growing. No wonder Uncle Matt was jealous of such a mop head, I thought, feeling at once intimidated by the headmaster's shaggy presence and overwhelmed by the large room. I had never been in the spotlight before, the cynosure of all eyes.

Then, to make matters worse, Miss Speedwell suddenly removed my coat, folding it with others that had been flung in a forlorn heap over the fireguard to dry. And instantly the sound of tittering began, faintly at first, but spreading quickly through the room. Then I remembered! Oh, how *could* I have forgotten? The riding breeches! They had completely slipped my mind. Familiarity having blunted awareness, I had thoughtlessly put them on as usual, foolishly laying myself open to mass ridicule. I blushed with embarrassment, wishing for a hole in the floor to open and swallow me, and the titters intensified, causing Mr Clout to stop reading and glower round the room until his beady eye rested on me.

'Ah, it's the Weakling girl,' he growled. 'And about time too!'

Then the sniggers began, and I could hear amused whispers of 'Weakling' from all quarters of the room until Miss Speedwell frowned at the class and spoke up indignantly.

'This is Emma Emmerson, Mr Clout. You remember? Emma *Emmerson*,' she repeated, loud and clear. 'I'm afraid it's my fault that Emma's a little late. She's been helping me with something next door. But I'm sure you'll agree she's done well to come at all, living so far out. I notice that some older and much nearer pupils haven't made the effort.'

'What did you say?' demanded Mr Clout querulously. 'Em-er-em-er? That's not a name. More like a stammer. Anyway, I'm sure her name's Weakling. Told me so herself. I have it written down somewhere.' With that, he patted his pockets absently and looked vaguely about his desk.

'No, no, Mr Clout. She's Emma *Emmerson*.'

'Emm – er – Emm – er – son?' he droned, dragging the name out until it sounded an interminable and mortifying length, half a mile long it seemed to me, and whether intentionally or not, he now appeared to be playing to the gallery, to the easily amused big boys in the back row, who, whenever he spoke, pointed at me and laughed uproariously.

'That's right, Mr Clout. *Emm – a*. Her name's Emma.'

'Are you sure? It's hard to tell where her Christian name ends and her surname begins.'

'Quite sure, Mr Clout. And now if you'll excuse me, I must get back to my class.' After giving me a last reassuring smile she departed, while Mr Clout bestowed a critical look and sighed audibly.

'You're even smaller than I remembered,' he said disparagingly.

'Still, in this life we must hope for the best, expect the worst, and take what God sends. Anyway, I'm expecting great things of you, Emma – er – Whatever, and you'd better not let me down. Now sit yourself there where I can see you, next to Irene – er – Whatsername.'

He waved a hairy paw, directing me to a spare seat in the front row, fortunately fairly close to the stove, but unfortunately also close to his desk, and I sat down quickly, glad to do so, glad to face away from the back row and hide my eye-catching breeches out of sight. The desks were constructed like those in the infants' room, but larger of course, and joined in groups of four, mine being an end seat. Otherwise, the two rooms differed greatly in ambience, for whereas the infants' room was light and cosy, brightened by cheerful wall charts and row upon row of colourful books, the senior room struck me as oppressively gloomy and cold. The high windows let in little sunshine, and though the central stove tended to be stoked to its maximum capacity, so hot that part of its chimney glowed danger-ously red, beyond a radius of a few feet of its circle of warmth the air met an atmosphere so icy that at times pupils sitting on the periphery found difficulty holding a pen, let alone writing with it.

Nor did the decor lift the spirits. The walls had once been painted cream, but over the years had dirtied down to a dull khaki, appro-priate in wartime but depressingly dark. And their only decoration, apart from a large map of the world dominated by red areas denoting the British Empire, was a sinister pair of tall pictures in black frames, one of an eagle and the other of a vulture, which eyed us from above with piercing and predatory stares.

As I glanced nervously around, another singular feature puzzled me at first. The high window sills and every available surface held all manner of jars and bottles, of all shapes and sizes, crammed as in a chemist's shop. Most of them stood empty and washed ready for use, but some contained specimens of rotting vegetation – shriv-elled and decayed plants giving off a dank and putrid smell. In time I came to realize that these specimens related to Mr Clout's Nature Study lessons, and that in due season all the receptacles in the room would be filled with wild flowers, their fresh perfume overriding the stench of stale water. But for the moment the forgotten containers were of neither use nor ornament, and the only living plants – a tray of dry, withered cacti – shivered neglected, like dusty outcasts in the corner of the draughty room.

Initially my reception from Irene Whatsername, who turned out to be Irene Milburn, was as frosty as the atmosphere of the class-room, and I sensed that she considered the ignominy of sitting beside a refugee from the infant class quite beneath her dignity. She appeared to be some two years older than me, and darkly pretty in a gypsy-like way, with swarthy skin, warm brown spaniel eyes, and nut-brown curly hair with a fringe from under which she glanced at me disdainfully. As the morning wore on, however, and she discovered that I worked at her own standard and was more than willing to share my coloured pencils, her attitude relaxed and she softened towards me. But it was at lunchtime, when I found myself in trouble and she came to my aid, that the hand of friendship was truly extended. I had intended to knock on Miss Speedwell's door and beg permission to eat my sandwiches in her room as usual, but in the event I was not even allowed to rise to my feet before being hemmed in by hostile youths.

I must have presented an easy target for those of a bullying disposition – small, vulnerable, uniquely dressed in riding breeches, and already bestowed with the nickname of 'Weakling'. So as soon as Mr Clout left the room for a peaceful lunch in his study, away from the milling throng, the senior boys wasted no time. They swooped on me like the vulture on the wall, hindering my exit from the seat, which meant that, because she was sitting next to me, Irene couldn't escape either. They shouted, they jeered and jostled, pushing at my desk till it rattled, and towering over me like grinning gargoyles till I felt flustered and suffocated. I recog-nized the ringleader as Gormley, the flamboyantly dressed boy who had acted as guide to me and Uncle Matt on my first day, and now chief bully. I could feel his rough hand on my shoulder, his big feet kicking mine, and his foul breath fanning my cheeks as he leant over me, firing scornful questions, one after the other, into my cringing face.

'Where's yer horse?' he yelled, again and again, laughing raucously, while the rest joined in, applauding his wit.

I shrank away in fear and embarrassment, unable to answer. I had the impression that my throat had closed, so constricted did it feel, and that no sound would come even if I found the courage to speak. He thrust his face still closer, his freckled head with its popping eyes and protruding tongue reminding me of a large lizard – repulsive, intimidating. Then he became more personal in his attack.

'Why are ya wearing breeches, eh? Are ya a lad, like, or a lass?

Why don't ya tell us, Weakling? Why don't ya prove it, one way or t'other? Come on, Weakling, prove yerself. Show us yer knickers.'

Even in my acute misery, suffocated as I was by hot breath and harsh noises round my head, harassing and intimidating me, by hands prodding everywhere and elbows jostling and feet kicking – even then I felt a flash of indignation that a gaudy rag-bag such as Gormley should see fit to criticize my dress sense. But in the circumstances I hesitated to point out that he was no fashion plate himself. Fear gripped me till I trembled, yet I tried not to show it, though my heart pounded so loudly that to me it was deafening and I imagined everyone could hear it beating. I found myself praying for Mr Clout's return – the lesser of the two evils – because Gormley's face was now pressed up threateningly close to mine.

I bent back as far as I could, leaning away from his sour breath, but his eyes still held me helpless, mesmerized like a rabbit trapped in headlights. I could think of nothing to do or say to save myself, and despite my resolve to show no weakness, tears began to fill my eyes. The leering faces swam before me until I thought I might faint, and in a curious way I rather hoped I would as it might teach the bullies a lesson. Then suddenly I noticed Gormley's teeth, bared and grinning at me, a menacing blur of yellow that jolted me back into consciousness, and at last I spoke, blurting out the first thought that entered my head.

'Your teeth are yellow,' I said with quiet dignity, taking him by surprise.

'What's that? *What* did you say, Weakling?' he snarled, and for a second recoiled as if I had struck him.

'You have horrible yellow teeth,' I said, following up my advantage. 'You should clean them. They're disgusting.'

The unguarded words had emerged without thought for the consequences, but momentarily they stopped him in his tracks, perhaps because of the surprise element, or perhaps because the others were now laughing at him, turning the ridicule back onto the bully. Doubtless he would have recovered soon enough, but in that split second of hesitation Irene sprang into action. Flinging back the desk lids without regard to anyone or anything in the way, or to damage done to fingers and elbows, or to squeals of protest or yelps of pain, she grabbed my sandwich box, ducked under the desk and quickly crawled away, shouting to me to follow.

'Come on, Emma! Come on! Down you go!' she cried as she kicked her way deftly through the throng of legs and then jumped up and ran out, with only one backward glance.

I followed only too gladly, but on rising from the floor felt someone tall and strong take hold of me, so that I fought like a tiger to free myself, only to realize that this was an unknown benefactor, who had lifted me clear of my tormentors and set me down safely with two coats round my shoulders, near the door. I soon found myself in the fresh air, where Irene waited to take her coat, help me with mine, and hand me my lunch box.

'Phew! That was something!' she said calmly. 'You handled yourself very well there, Emma. Now hurry up. You can eat your sandwiches at our place. It's just over there, on the roadside. See it? If we take the short cut it's about a seven-minute walk.'

'Won't your mother mind?' I asked shyly, remembering Aunt Dot's dislike of guests and envying this easy sociability. 'After all, she's never even met me.'

'Oh no. She'll be pleased. Everybody's welcome at our house. Mam likes meeting new people, and I'm sure she'll take a shine to you.'

I paused to take a few deep breaths, having been shaken to the core by that threatening encounter with Gormley's gang. A great relief stole over me as I realized that for the time being I was safe, that I had eluded the bullies and was on my way to eat my lunch in a friendly home.

'Thank heaven,' I murmured, 'and thank you, Irene. I'm so glad to get away in one piece. But – oh, Irene – oh, my goodness! I've just thought – I'll have to go back after lunch and then they'll get me. They'll be waiting for me.'

'No they won't,' she answered airily. 'They won't touch or bother you again. As long as you're a friend of mine they'll leave you alone.'

'Really? Why is that?' I asked, marvelling at such power, nothing short of miraculous, and without even the potent influence of red hair.

'Simple. You see, the big lad that lifted you, that's my brother. He's by far the biggest in the school, and the best fighter,' she said proudly. 'And the best-looking one too, of course. Goes without saying. So, anyway, he rules the school. No contest.'

'Oh! Will he be coming home for his sandwiches?' I asked in some trepidation, remembering how hard I had struggled to fight him off.

'No, he prefers to stay at school and play football. But come on, Emma. We'll have to hurry or we'll be late back. Then we'll be for it from Clouty.'

The Milburn house, known as Wagtail Cottage, instantly intrigued me, appearing to my eyes quite magical in its construction. From the back it looked tall and multi-windowed, but from the front, which we approached via a steep flight of steps, it looked like a low bungalow, with a slab stone roof sloping sharply down and overhanging the facade, reaching towards the road as if trying to touch its toes. I had never seen a split-level house before, a topsy-turvy house in which the stairs led down to the bedrooms instead of up, and the house looked high and yet the ceilings hung low, apparently held up by dark beams. We entered through a long passage that cut the top floor in two and opened on the right to a large, hospitable kitchen with a blazing fire, where Mrs Milburn was busy ladling out three steaming bowls of vegetable soup. She was instantly recognizable as an older version of Irene, just as slim, just as dark, and even more gypsy-like since she wore hooped earrings and a bright red headband holding back her cloud of curly hair.

'I saw you coming across the field,' she said with a welcoming smile, 'and I said to myself, now there's a canny little body with a bonny little face and I bet she's coming to visit me. I dare say, I said to myself, that my young visitor would enjoy a few hot broth, so I've poured a few out to be ready and cooling.

'Yes, I would, thank you,' I said appreciatively.

'You can have them with your sandwiches,' she said, speaking about the broth in the plural, as was the habit in those parts, as if all the chopped onions and diced carrots had each been accounted for individually and were being served that way too. 'And there's plenty more if you can eat them. Let's just see what sort of sandwiches you've got. See if they'll go with the broth.' She peered into my lunch box, and with an expression of acute distaste opened up all four sandwiches.

'Oh dear!' she exclaimed. 'There's nothing in them. Nothing at all. Only something that looks like glue holding the bread together.'

'Oh, they'll be treacle sandwiches,' I guessed, knowing that whenever Aunt Dot was in a particular hurry she resorted to a treacle filling. 'The treacle sinks in and sort of disappears. They're not very nice really.' She shook her head in dismay and put the sandwiches aside.

'I think we'll give those a miss, don't you? We'll give them to the birds. It'll do the birds the world of good, that treacle. They're starving this weather. Or they can use it to stick their nests together. But you have some of this instead.' She broke some warm crusty rolls into a small wicker basket which she placed on the table. 'Now, take your coat off and sit up here by the fire. Help yourself while Irene introduces us.'

Irene duly obliged, explaining my unexpected presence, and with pardonable exaggeration outlining her brave part in the proceedings, while Mrs Milburn sympathized and praised in all the right places, making me feel important and protected. Tea and a delicious angel cake rounded off the meal, and as I ate I studied the comfortable kitchen. It seemed to me that everything about the room reflected Mrs Milburn's warm and welcoming disposition – the sunny glow of pale yellow walls, the inviting chairs with their soft feather cushions, the cheerful chintz curtains looped back to let in extra light, the colourful plates twinkling on the dresser, and the capacious cups standing at the ready, waiting to be filled. Meanwhile, conversation flowed, time flew, and in the end Irene and I had to run all the way back to school.

'See you tomorrow, Emma,' Mrs Milburn called after us as she waved us off. 'I'll cook you a baked apple with pink blancmange.'

So it was that for a time I felt a new sense of contentment. I had made friends at last in Sourhope valley, good friends at that. And from then on, most days I ate lunch in the upside-down house, always taking my own sandwiches, but always sampling other delights instead, an indulgence that I was careful to keep from Aunt Dot, especially since the neighbourhood birds were regularly fed from my lunch box.

The Milburn home smelled in equal proportions of furniture polish, lavender and apples, the latter having been picked from Mrs Milburn's own three trees and stored in every room in the house. From these fruits she made delicious desserts, rare treats in wartime. I loved my visits to that friendly household, and was sometimes allowed to go at weekends too, but not as often as I would have wished, it being a five-mile walk there and back from Windlestraw. But on those special occasions when I did visit Irene, we played in her 'boody-house', an old outhouse converted into a playroom, with a primus stove on which we cooked real food, happily frying potatoes and scrambling eggs made from dried egg powder, a wartime substitute, which to my mind tasted much better than hens' eggs. Like Uncle Matt, the Milburns were incomers. Mr Milburn had worked in the local lead mine, but like my own father, had joined the army and been reported missing in action. Mrs Milburn supplemented the family income by working as a cleaner at both the church and the school. At the time I thought her one of the kindest people I had ever met, and to this day I still do.

I made my visits last as long as I dared, putting off departure until the eleventh hour, reluctant to leave such a happy home. Now and then I took my leave too late for safety and peace of mind, and found myself glancing back nervously and running to outstrip the oncoming darkness. Of course, once past Fern Cottage and climbing the fields I had a dim view of my destination up ahead. I could see the glow of lamplight turned low in our living room, and often the intermittent flashes of a hurricane lamp flitting like a firefly to and fro from house to byre. These lights beckoned, but did so without reassurance, because I could never be certain of the warmth of my welcome, particularly if I was late. Most times I walked back at dusk, fearful and breathless, just as the birds sang a muted goodnight, and wary little animal eyes watched me from the reeds; the moonlit tails of rabbits were their only giveaway. .

As for the obnoxious Eddie Gormley, he never bullied me quite so openly again, but he did shamelessly torment me, using sly and insidious wiles. I have a lively remembrance of threats and indignities constantly inflicted, and he remained the bane of my school life, rivalling the cat-o'-nine-tails and even Mad Mary for occupying the prime spot in my nightmares. Indeed, he was so much in my thoughts that he seemed the obvious choice for the calendar pig of the month, and it happily transpired that the March pig was practically a double for Eddie already, being endowed with similar qualities to his worst aspects.

The Gloucester Old Spot turned out to be a scrounger, a pig of unrefined tastes and habits, who liked nothing better than to wallow indiscriminately in common pig swill, and, by coincidence, as the name suggested, it was a spotted pig. Perfect, I thought, and having noted the character resemblance as well as the physical likeness, I set to with my pencils. It was the first spotted pig to come my way, and I only had to give my orange pencil free rein, filling in extra spots until the pig looked like a victim of a virulent form of German measles, to achieve a representation of my freckled tormentor that satisfied my loathing for him and served to brighten my days.

So the month of March progressed, and having perversely come in like a lamb, it went out just as contrary-wise like a lion. Gales blew us into April, and as I struggled home each day with the wind blasting in my face, forcing me back, I had to comfort myself with the thought that it only held me there because it liked my company, and that it would soon lose interest. Indeed, so persistent was the Sourhope wind that at times I wondered whether Uncle Matt had gradually lost his hair to its savage force, and whether Aunt Dot invested in strong bootlaces in order to keep hers on, to fasten her mysteriously powerful but unruly tresses firmly to her head. I began to feel concern about losing my own hair, and was glad when the fierce gale dropped for a while, even though the change ushered in a return to continual rain, now masquerading as April showers. Little did I know, however, that April would bring other changes, not the least of which was my first sighting of *The Cat*.

Chapter 21

Bear-baiting

G. Jack

April is the cruellest month, so the poet says, and so it seemed to my impressionable young eyes, as little by little the brutality of spring came to be revealed. One thing after another sprang into life, flourished briefly, and then died. First the wild flowers shot up: coltsfoots, primroses, and violets bravely carpeted the bleak bank sides, only to be cruelly blasted by the weather or trodden by foot or hoof back into the ground. Then the birds busily built nests, which suddenly appeared everywhere, like new houses in an economic boom, but despite careful camouflage the eggs or chicks within were often destroyed by predators. These heart-rending scenes of devastation were there, plain for me to see, but Uncle Matt simply pooh-poohed my childish concerns.

'Don't upset yourself, Emma, now. It's only nature, and nature's like that. Tooth-and-claw survival. You see, Emma, it's a dog-eat-dog world.'

'What have dogs to do with it, Uncle Matt?'

'Nothing. Nothing at all. Just an expression. Manner of speakin', like.'

'Then why must the poor little birds die, Uncle Matt? Why?' I asked, distressed, and he swivelled his cap as he did when thinking hard and gazed at me with the philosopher's expression that had become so familiar to me.

'Ah well, Emma, you see nature's a beggar. Nature can be very cruel. Yes, she can be a blighter all right. It's as they say, pet, death is always with us, and my meanin' is, that's life.'

'That's really sad, Uncle Matt. I think that's terrible. It's so savage.'

'Maybe, Emma, but don't forget that them birds you're so fond of'll eat any little thing that moves, even each other. Take them hoodies now,' he said, pointing at two inscrutable crows perched on a wall, awaiting their chance. 'They'll take all the grouse chicks they can get their claws on. And that fine-looking merlin we saw t'other day, why he'll pounce on a ring ouzel, bite its head off, and feed the rest to his mate for breakfast. It's nature, pet, just nature.'

So much for nature in the raw, I thought, but cruelty soon raised its ugly head on the domestic front too. A number of lambs were found shivering and abandoned, and despite reuniting some with mothers and fixing others up with foster mothers, Uncle Matt was left with a pitiful band of orphans to be bottle-fed and reared as pets.

'Pesky nuisances, the lot of them,' he grumbled. 'I've never had so many hungry mouths to feed. Waste of time. Waste of milk. I've a good mind to cut their pesky little legs off. I have, definitely.' And though he managed to restrain himself from reducing his motherless flock to lamb chops, I noticed that the task of feeding them fell to Aunt Dot and me.

One sheep family in particular caused him hours of aggravation as he tried to pair up the mother of a dead lamb with a frail orphan. I watched in horror as he carefully removed the skin from her dead lamb and fitted it like a second skin over the orphan, thrusting mother and child together in the hope of mutual acceptance. But sadly the mother would have none of the impostor, repeatedly rejecting my uncle's efforts, until finally he gave up, bringing the miserable lamb into the byre to be fed. Holding her between his knees, he was about to offer her the bottle, when suddenly the reluctant surrogate mother came skidding to the doorway, looking as overwrought as a deadpan sheep can look, and bleating in a perfect frenzy. She had returned to where her lamb was born, picked up the scent, followed it to the byre, and was now in her own fashion accusing us of abduction. Using a front hoof as a door knocker, she rapped peremptorily on the byre door, and this time when Uncle Matt thrust the lamb at her, she nudged it affectionately, and to my delight the two went off together, firmly united at last.

Later another batch of orphans arrived in the shape of day-old chicks, and took up residence in a covered basket on a shelf of the kitchen range, the basket acting as a sort of mother hen keeping the chicks warm. Now and then I could not resist lifting out these yellow balls of fluff to play with them on the hearthrug, where they blinked their minuscule eyes against the light and teetered on twig-like legs, even lighter than their later feathers.

'What about a mother for those chicks, Uncle Matt?' I suggested as I listened to their plaintive cheeping. 'I think everyone should have a mother. The chickens at Brackenfield all have mothers, and there are plenty of hens without families that could take these ones.'

But he shook his head firmly.

'No good, Emma. You see, I've got no clocker for this brood.'

'What's a clocker?' I asked, bewildered. 'Is it some sort of time-piece for chickens?'

'Don't be silly!' said Aunt Dot sharply. 'You *are* a silly girl, Emma. He means a clucker, a broody hen that wants to hatch eggs. Not a clock!'

'Well, won't any old hen do for that, Uncle Matt?'

'By no, Emma. Any old hen won't do. My meanin' is, she won't do at all. If your hen's not a clocker she's liable to peck your chicks to bits.'

Cruelty again, I thought, but I readily understood, knowing from personal experience, the problems arising from trying to use a substi-tute mother. Nevertheless, about a week later he did attempt an unusual adoption. He had never kept ducks before, but while wheeler-dealing in Shiretown he acquired a bargain of a dozen duck eggs, and having by then found what he called a clocker, he set her to hatch the eggs.

'That daft hen's in for a shock when her chickens hatch. She sure is,' he said, much amused. 'She's got what you might call cuckoos in the nest. A dozen little Donald Ducks.'

Whether shocked or not we never knew, but the Rhode Island Red accepted her family of ducklings and they their unusual mother, her frill of red feathers being the first thing they encountered when they saw the light of day. At the beginning of their relationship they followed her faithfully, and I could hardly tear myself away from the sight of that wonderful procession waddling in single file after the hen. Then one day disaster struck. The procession came to a small pond and the little ducks, being ducks, waded straight in, happily sailing out of her reach. The hen became distraught, fluttering round and round the water's edge and squawking helplessly at the blameless pond. But the ducklings enjoyed their swim and took their time about it, and that incident triggered the gradual estrangement between duck-lings and hen. They soon cast her off like a quilt in August, and took to following each other instead, huddling together at night, inde-pendent of the poor deserted hen. I had named her Broody Bertha when she volunteered to hatch the duck eggs, and watched sympa-thetically as she struggled with her web-footed family. As Head Poultry Keeper I naturally felt responsible for her welfare and eager to find a way to help.

'It's so tragic, Uncle Matt,' I cried. 'She's just so pitiful. We must do something. What can we do?'

'Can't do a thing, Emma,' he replied, smiling at my dismay. 'Them ducklings don't want her any more and that's that. You can't make a chicken out of a duck any more than you can make a duck out of a hen.'

'What about the story of the ugly duckling?' I said. 'That turned into a swan.'

'No, Emma, it always was a swan. You are what you are, pet, and there's no sense wantin' to be somethin' you're not.'

I said nothing more about it, though I found his attitude unduly pessimistic, as I secretly entertained hopes of turning into something of a swan myself. In the meantime, however, I determined to explain matters to the hen, so as to put her mind at rest. But all I got for my pains was a fierce peck on the foot, bringing me down to earth. It seemed that I was standing in the way of the trough, and that the hen was as faithless as her waterbird brood. And I wondered – if this mother had forgotten her chicks so quickly, how long would my mother remember me? It was a distressing thought.

By now I considered myself something of an expert on nature in all its idiosyncrasies, but I soon learnt that I had only scratched the surface, and at school I was about to dig deep, literally, as the growing season progressed and Mr Clout began to weld together his two obsessions – Nature Study and Gardening with a capital G. Gradually he seemed to be confusing the distinction between them, and also between theory and practice, until his Nature Study lessons ceased to be even remotely educational and turned into tedious jobs in the vegetable plot. For the moment, however, he concentrated on theory, and his declared interest in Nature Study soon revealed itself as a consuming passion, so that those lessons lasted twice as long as other subjects and even then they often overran.

'Ah good, good, Nature Study next. Excellent!' he would observe with satisfaction, glancing at the timetable on the notice board – though he knew it by heart – and rubbing his hairy hands till they crackled. 'A treat for us all. The marvels of living things. Speaking of which, are you clods in the back row still living? Or have you died, silently and unnoticed by an unfeeling world?'

Expecting no answer and receiving none, he turned his attention to other forms of life, jumping from one area of interest to another, like an intellectual grasshopper. And while he held forth monotonously, we gradually froze in our seats, stiffening, not entirely from boredom, but from the Siberian draughts that whistled round our backs, chilling us to the very marrow. Even the aspiring delinquents who squeezed together in the back row, overhanging their inadequate seats, often slumped by degrees into an apathetic stupor, too numb to find the energy to rebel.

Only Mr Clout appeared at ease with his surroundings, enveloped as he was in his thick hairy suit of Harris tweed, warm woollen waist-coat, and knee-high foot-coddling socks – three pairs to be safe – and ensconced as he was, except for periodic prowls, in an armchair next to the well-stoked stove. In this enviable position with his legs stretched towards the stove and with no thought for those less fortunate, he took full advantage of whatever heat it emitted. As April advanced and the slowly stirring season that passed for spring in Sourhope began to mani-fest itself, he became if anything even more obsessed with nature. And more and more his lessons took on a practical slant, as he shared with us his enthusiasm for gardening, constantly extolling the virtues of lady-birds on account of the number of greenfly larvae they can eat in an hour, and loudly deploring the subversive habits of the carrot fly.

'The sap is rising,' was his joyful cry each morning, as he gazed out of the window at a budding hawthorn tree, the only tree within a half-mile radius. 'Good, very good! I do assure you, boys and girls, the sap is rising. The time is at hand.' And though I knew little of what was to come, I instinctively felt that we senior pupils were among the saps soon to be rising, condemned to hard labour in the vegetable plot.

Indeed, for some of the class, that sentence had already started, because since early March, whenever weather permitted, the boys from the back row had been sent out to 'dig for victory', as he put it, a wartime slogan that strongly appealed to him. And when they returned with chapped hands and muddy boots, smelling strongly of manure, the gleam in his eyes intensified. At odd moments he could now be observed discreetly cleaning his collection of trowels, or polishing his favourite fork, tenderly stroking its well-worn handle and trying out a few practice moves with it, developing the wrist action and the follow-through. Increasingly his lesson content veered towards the horticultural, and with our lack of appreciation of both of his hobby horses, it was not unusual for one or more of us to fall asleep. At such moments he had a tendency to shout, his voice suddenly trumpeting so loudly that we all shot up in our seats like leaping salmon.

'Hoi there! You there! Yes, I'm talking to you, dimwit! Wake up and pay attention! You dozy clod! Tell me what I just said, eh? What? What?' he yelled, sending an electric thrill of guilt through all of us.

Sometimes his beady eyes rolled round the room, looking for movement, especially lip movement, and having found the slightest sign, however innocent, he drew his own conclusions, right or wrong.

'Are you chewing, girl? No? Well then you must be talking. How dare you talk in lessons? Especially important lessons. Come out here at once!' And he promptly administered punishment with manifest impatience and an old leather slipper.

Had his face been less whiskered I might have detected a twinkle in his eye or a trace of geniality round his mouth, but any reassuring signs of humanity were masked by his fierce bush of facial hair. Ignorant of any rights as a pupil, I regarded him as omnipotent, ruling with a rod of iron, and exhibiting a cruel streak ranging in severity from humiliating sarcasm to corporal punishment. He was like a powerful and ferocious bear, escaped from captivity and taking his revenge on everyone within range. As far as possible I stayed out of his way and kept a low profile. I had been branded 'the weakling' and shamelessly played that part, trying to shrink into invisibility.

In this ambition, however, I had less success with my classmates because, small as I was, I rarely escaped their notice, and with the exception of Irene, who remained a good friend, they resented me. They were all much bigger, and from one to five years older, than me, so I simply did not fit in. I dared not adopt the prevailing attitude of indifference to learning, but worked conscientiously, often knowing the answers when others could hardly be bothered to listen to the questions. And this effrontery on my part naturally made me unpopular, being particularly galling coming from one so young, and an incomer at that. They always referred to me as 'Weakling' or 'Swot' but never 'Emma'. I tried to make friends, but tentative approaches met with stony silence, and I often felt hostile eyes boring into my back, intensifying the chill of the room. Clearly my fellow sufferers in the class regarded me as a minor irritant in their lives, like a speck of grit in the eye, but by and large they left me alone, except for Eddie Gormley, who maintained his subtle but persistent reign of bullying terror.

It was some time before I realized that I was not alone in disliking Gormley, that those apparently close to him were only intimidated into friendship, and that Mr Clout of all people shared my aversion, my sense of unease in Gormley's presence: just as this freckled bully was the bane of my life, so too was he the bane of the headmaster's. Just as I felt threatened by his sneaky presence, so, curiously, did Mr Clout – not in the same way, but he felt threatened all the same, like a grouchy bear plagued by a mischievous monkey. Eddie was a free spirit, impervious to criticism, immune to discipline; and Mr Clout viewed him as a potential time bomb that might go off at any moment.

Eddie had a number of irritating habits, exhibited most frequently during poetry lessons. He had a deep suspicion of poetry, and soon became restless. One habit was to rise from his seat when the icy temperature became too much for him, and restore circulation by jumping on the spot while flapping his arms and barking like a distraught seal. Another favourite was to drop on the floor and slither over it, as silently as an underwater swimmer, emerging abruptly elsewhere in the room like a diver breaking surface. And there were times when he would suddenly regale the class with personal thoughts that he considered more interesting than the lesson.

Worst of all, he had an endless fund of awkward questions, aimed at causing maximum aggravation, sending Mr Clout into paroxysms of rage. He was what Uncle Matt would have called 'a wise guy', and yet you could have counted on the fingers of one hand the subjects in which he excelled and still had five left over. Most of the time he got away with his wisecracks, but now and then he went too far, and one April day, as a result, I learnt much more than anything that was taught in my lessons. I learnt all there was to know about *The Cat*. It happened that Mr Clout had been trying to inspire interest in the industrious worker ant when Gormley raised his hand and, supporting one arm with the other, waved it from side to side like a human metronome, indicating a desire to speak. Mr Clout reluctantly nodded permission, whereupon Gormley began asking his questions.

'Did you know that ants have a short life, sir? They work too hard.'

'It'll never happen to you then, boy. You should live for ever.'

'Sir, why don't you tell us about other insects, sir?' enquired Gormley with pleasing deference. 'Like a centipede, sir. Why does it need so many legs when it's only a little thing?'

'Never mind, Gormley. Be quiet, boy.'

'Or earwigs, sir. If they have wings, sir, why don't they fly?'

'I said *quiet*, Gormley! You're trying to take over my lesson and you haven't the brain of a bean. Now that's enough! Quite enough!'

'Why is it called an earwig, sir? Does it crawl into your ear? Is that what happened to you, sir? Have you got one in your ear?'

It was a question too far and Mr Clout leapt from his chair, and with surprising speed for a man of his bulk, flew with flapping tweeds to the back row, pouncing on Gormley like the merlin upon the ring ouzel and capturing him by the scruff of the neck, though he stopped short of biting his head off. He dragged the struggling boy to the front, dropped him beside the desk, and reached into the bottom drawer, a deeper drawer than the rest. Gasps of horror and anticipation circled the class as the word *Cat* passed excitedly from mouth to mouth, and I waited apprehensively for the animal to be unleashed. At last, I thought fearfully, all would be revealed. But what emerged from the drawer was no sharp-clawed snarling cat – indeed, no live animal at all – but a leather strap with five thongs trailing from it, which Mr Clout brandished sadistically, giving it a practice flick, so that it cracked the air with a loud report like a ringmaster's whip.

'Hold your hand out, boy!' he growled, advancing menacingly with all whiskers bristling, and Gormley, suddenly realizing that he had gone too far – beyond punishment by the slipper and into the more serious realm of castigation by *The Cat* – tried to save himself, beginning to whinge and snivel.

'But, sir, Ah was just askin' a few questions, sir. Just takin' an interest, like. An interest in insects, sir. And, sir, you can't hit me, 'cos Ah've got sore hands, sir. A cut and two sore keens. Deep keens, sir.'

'No problem, boy,' said Mr Clout agreeably, and in a trice Gormley found himself bent over the desk with his hands lying flat and his nose pressed into the rugged oak surface, his bottom in the air, reverberating from every stinging lash of the so-called cat-o'-nine-tails.

For such the strap turned out to be, and now I knew *The Cat* for what it was – not the terrifying beast that haunted my dreams – no actual cat at all, but a leather taws or strap with only five tails, not nine, and used for punishment in the north; it was an all-round impostor that had been given its exaggerated nickname by the senior boys. A faceless monster, it was still frightening in its effects, still viciously cruel. I was both relieved and at the same time horrified. In a vague way I half-admired Gormley for his bravery, which I felt I lacked, for he took his punishment like a man, with no further protests. And as the leather strap whipped through the air, and he writhed, convulsed with pain and expelling tortured gasps of air in noisy outbursts, rather like a sink plunger, I vowed that I would never let myself incur his public humiliation – I would never subject myself to punishment by *The Cat*.

'My brother's had *The Cat*,' said Irene proudly, as we walked to the Milburn house for lunch. 'He got it for a dare, when he climbed the tower and rang the bell.'

'Really? Well, I'd hate it, Irene. Just hate it! You and I must be very careful. Ever so careful never to be punished by *The Cat*. I'd die if I had to face that.'

'There's not much chance of you getting *The Cat*,' she said, grinning. 'You're always so well-behaved. You're like Goody Two-Shoes, you are. You always mind your Ps and Qs.'

I felt sure she was right – that though I had finally been introduced to *The Cat* at second hand, I would never encounter it myself at first hand. Situated as Irene and I were under Mr Clout's watchful eye, we were always mindful of where that eye was directed, so we were very careful and circumspect.

Then one afternoon something unexpected happened. Perfect harmony reigned in the classroom, the class being engaged in writing up notes on the metamorphosis of tadpole into frog, and Mr Clout being busy perusing an instructive book. He was reading Dibbler's *Growing Prize Vegetables*, a manual which served him as a Bible, never far from his reach, and to him totally absorbing.

All was silent but for the regular scratching of pen nibs, but that sound was soon stilled by the sight of a mouse darting across the floor, doubtless sharing the popular view that the room's extremities were too cold for man or beast. The class rarely enjoyed the diversion of visitors, two-legged or four, and elbow nudged elbow until all eyes were riveted on the mouse, which, while luxuriating in the warmth thrown off by the stove, still seemed restless and evidently hungry in that it crept boldly round the toasty environs, picking up crumbs and sampling a wizened apple core.

At length it noticed Mr Clout's shoes, stretched as ever towards the heat, in such close proximity to the stove that the soles steamed gently in filmy wisps, creating a rich aroma so appetizing to a hungry rodent that the mouse made directly for the gastronomic footwear. Perhaps the traces of manure and compost forever embedded under Mr Clout's heels had heated through, giving off an odour that reminded the fieldmouse of home. At any rate, the creature's nose worked overtime, twitching appreciatively at the steaming soles, as if it had discovered toasted cheese or some such irresistible delicacy. Then the mouth joined in, biting into a shoelace and nibbling speculatively. At this outrageous liberty, the class reacted with a mass intake of breath, and then, as with one voice, emitted a concerted 'Aaaaaaah', like a sympathetic sigh.

Despite this united and sustained sound, Mr Clout remained oblivious of the mouse fidgeting at his feet. Having warned the class to work silently and on no account disturb his serious study, he sat relaxed in a world of his own, engrossed in a book which, once opened, he found difficult to put down. As a result of merely glancing at the chapter on the secrets of growing bigger and better leeks, and even though he had consulted it many times before, he was at once absorbed by its captivating prose and helpful hints. It was only when the mouse moved in for the kill, nibbling the neat bow in the shoelace, and causing Irene to give an involuntary gasp and Gormley to hail the mouse with a loud 'Wey-hey!', that he returned abruptly to consciousness.

His hairy head shot up from the page, and he looked round angrily for a culprit,. As he did so, his gaze fell on my smiling face and on Irene's hand clasped over her mouth, belatedly stifling the gasp. Instantly he leapt to his feet, and while the real culprit scuttled back to its hole, he reached purposefully into the bottom drawer. What happened next was quite unreal to me. He glowered at the pair of us, his face flushed with fury, and flicking his supple strap to and fro like a sort of pointing device, he swished the thongs from where we sat cowering to where he wanted us to stand, shouting, 'Out! Out! Chop-chop! Out! Out!'

Gleeful whispers of '*The Cat*! Oooooh! They're getting *The Cat*!' again circulated around the astonished class, and I stood staring at him disbelievingly.

Surely, I thought, *he can't mean me? Not me! A model pupil! Everybody knew that. It must be a mistake.* And I looked behind me fully expecting someone else to step forward. No one did. No one except Irene, that is, who accepted her fate philosophically – holding out her left hand to save her writing hand, closing her eyes as the strap descended, and quietly returning to her seat. Alas, meek acceptance of injustice was not in my nature. My deep sense of fair play, which had often led me into trouble in the past, again compelled me to speak up. I had to defend myself, to present my case, fully expecting a last-minute reprieve.

'But, sir, I didn't do anything. It wasn't us, sir. It was a mouse.'

'A mouse, eh?' he repeated sarcastically. 'That's strange. The mice round here don't usually shout out. Must be a big one. Too big for its boots, I'd say.'

'It really was a mouse, sir. On your foot. Chewing your shoelaces.'

I turned to the class for confirmation, but no one spoke up to corroborate my story – partly, I suspected, because they were enjoying watching me taken down a peg or two, and partly because they were afraid of joining the punishment queue. Even I had to admit that the story sounded thin, and Mr Clout plainly thought so and acted accordingly.

'Hold your left hand out!' he ordered, and a second later the five thongs descended, bitingly thin, stinging my trembling fingers. 'Now, right hand!' and the thongs lashed and stung again. 'Anything more to say?' he enquired with an expression of exaggerated interest, whilst allowing the strap to swing like a pendulum between us.

'No, sir,' I mumbled, suddenly losing my desire for justice, for after all, I thought, I was not Joan of Arc.

'Off you go then and get on with your work. And mind it's done in your best handwriting. I'll accept no excuses. I must say, Emm-aah Emm-aah-son, I'm extremely disappointed in you.'

I moved away, fighting back tears but holding my head high, and caught a glimpse of Eddie Gormley's face, his expression half-admiring, half-gloating, his mouth as usual hanging open, giving the yellow teeth an airing. For years he had borne the brunt of *The Cat*'s punishing tails, but for once he was an amused and malicious spectator. I knew that we had come off lightly compared with the severe thrashings he suffered, when Mr Clout wielded the whip like a lion tamer. Nevertheless, angry weals striped my hands, and worse still, my pride was hurt. The punishment certainly did not fit the crime – and anyway, Irene and I were blameless. The unfairness of being publicly punished though totally innocent rankled with me – and went on rankling.

I kept my hands out of sight and told no one of my humiliation except Irene's mother, who was as comforting and supportive as ever. I had a vague notion that Uncle Matt might think less of me if he knew, and that Aunt Dot might punish me again. So I brooded silently, unable to forgive Mr Clout for his cruelty. From that moment on I never looked directly at him, never smiled at his praise or his jokes, and in assembly when we were asked to pray for others, I reminded God that Mr Clout was not included. I only began to feel a little better when I had buried the ghost of the cat-o'-nine-tails in its metamorphosis as a calendar pig. As it happened, April's pig, clearly identified as a Large Black, was just that – very large and very black – and I had little trouble transforming her into the demon cat of my imagination. Four extra tails, long lethal claws, and fiercely sharp teeth did the trick. Then I drew a dagger piercing the vicious cat-pig through the heart, thereby killing it in my mind and eliminating that threat from my life, and with it, hopefully, the real threat – Mr Clout's cruel leather persuader.

Moreover, a few days later something important occurred, something of such significance that it drove the whole undignified episode of *The Cat* to the back of my mind. I thought my luck had changed, and in the best way possible, because to my great joy a letter arrived from my mother, a brief note, but enough to send my spirits soaring. In it she proposed to visit us at the end of April and to come alone, my brothers having elected to stay behind with our grandmother. At once I felt sure she intended taking me home. Everything pointed to that happy ending, and I skipped on feet lighter than gossamer, to consult my oracle, Uncle Matt.

'Uncle Matt! Uncle Matt! What do you think's happened?' I cried excitedly as I approached, eyes shining and words tumbling out in a rush. 'My mother, Uncle Matt, she's coming, and I think she'll be taking me home.'

But without waiting for me to finish he chimed in, face grinning and manner conspiratorial.

'Emma, pet, you've just reminded me of somethin' I have to do tomorrow. There's a horse runnin' at Shiretown and I'm thinkin' of backin' it. If I can only manage to get a bet on. It's called "Green Eyes" and that name kinda reminded me of you. So when you came in just then it was the same as gettin' a tip. I reckon that horse is as good as past the post. Great odds as well. Definitely worth a couple of bob on the nose. Don't mention it to your Aunt Dot though, mind.'

'But, Uncle Matt . . .'

'I fancied it from the start, Emma. Strongly fancied it, but seein' your big green eyes just then reminded me of that horse.'

A dubious compliment, I thought, and tried again, determined to get a word in edgeways.

'Listen, Uncle Matt. Please listen for a moment. I want to ask you something,' I said, impatiently dismissing the subject of horses. 'Uncle Matt, my mother's coming. Is she taking me home with her or what?'

But to my disappointment, because to me the whole thing appeared done and dusted, he hesitated, slowly stroking the stubble on his unshaven chin.

'We – ll now, I dunno. She might be, and there again, she might not.'

'But it's to be a short visit, without the boys. That's different from usual. Surely that means something?'

'I really couldn't say, Emma. My meanin' is, there's still a war on. You see?'

I didn't see, but didn't say so, being intent on the main issue.

'Uncle Matt, please tell me. Why am I here?' I asked earnestly. And he gave his imaginary philosopher's cap a reflective turn and sighed.

'Ah, the big question, Emma. Why are we here? That's what we'd all like to know. The meanin' of life an' that.'

'No, I mean why am I *here*? Why am I up here in Sourhope when the boys are allowed to stay happily at home?'

'Why, to keep you safe from the war, pet. You're that little, you see.'

Once more I was struck by the duplicity of adults, who seemingly changed opinions on a whim, defining my size whichever way it suited them – now big, now little, as variable as my shadow on a sunny day. But before I could point out this inconsistency he aired a grievance of his own.

'Anyway, Emma, you seem mighty keen on the notion of leavin' me. I thought we were good friends an' all.'

'Oh we are, Uncle Matt. Very good friends. And I'd be sorry to leave you of course. But you'll manage without me, won't you? You did before I came.'

'Well now, I dare say I'd struggle along, but I sure would miss you, Emma. I've got used to your funny little ways.'

This was the first intimation that leaving Sourhope might not be as easy as I hoped, because other people had now become involved in my life. My heart sank. I had no wish to upset him.

'I'll miss you too, Uncle Matt, but I miss my mother all the time. So much! And I miss my home. And I hate this school. And I hate the cruel headmaster. And he whips people for no good reason.'

'Not you though, Emma? He hasn't belted you, has he? 'Cos if I thought he had I'd be down there in a flash, sortin' him out. That I would, Emma! Definitely! No question about it.'

Remembering his weak-kneed capitulation on the last occasion he had bandied words with Mr Clout, I felt unconvinced by this show of bravado. On the other hand, I knew he still coveted Mr Clout's painting and might visit school on the flimsiest of pretexts. And where would that leave me? Maybe hobnobbing again with *The Cat*. So I was quick and emphatic in my denial.

'*Me?* Oh no, not *me*, Uncle Matt. Why would he hit *me*? No, definitely not me! No, no! But we don't learn much you know. Only Nature Study all the time. I'm really fed up with it.'

'That'll be the war to blame,' he declared categorically. 'Shortage of everythin', you see. Teachers, books, everythin'. I reckon he's short of books on other subjects. You'd likely find the same if you went back to your old school.'

'No, it was a good school. And we didn't do non-stop Nature Study.'

'Well, I dunno, Emma. Let's wait and see. Let's hear what your mother has to say. No sense jumpin' the gun an' that.'

I was startled to notice that he looked hurt, suddenly saddened and careworn. The fine enthusiasm that had lit his face when I flew to his side after reading my mother's letter had died away, leaving it drawn, as if he had bet his shirt on the fancied horse and lost it. I too felt momentarily sad, and unaccountably guilty. To my surprise, and for the first time since being abandoned in Sourhope, I felt torn two ways. There was no doubt about it – I had allowed myself to become fond of Uncle Matt, and I would have walked alone to the summit of Lornhope rather than offend him.

Chapter 22

Digging for Victory

As things turned out, the worrying discussion as to whether I would stay or go was purely academic – a deep disappointment that I faced as soon as my mother unpacked. For once again she had brought me new clothes, pretty as can be, especially the cream bolero which she had made from a jacket of her own. Yet all I longed for, all I wanted to see, was an empty suitcase, because now I could read the familiar signs of rejection. Nor was I prepared for the emotional gulf between us, for after eight months apart we seemed to have as little in common as the ducklings and the hen. Nevertheless, she was my mother, and the realization that she intended leaving me behind a third time pierced through me like the pencilled dagger pierced the heart of April's pig.

I was left with only one ray of hope – my trump card, so I thought. I could tell tales of the many hidings given me by Aunt Dot, and surely that would force the issue. But as the days passed I found difficulty catching my mother alone. Then one day on my way downstairs I heard my name mentioned, so I stopped halfway and listened, sitting as quietly as the school mouse that had delivered me to *The Cat*. It is said that eavesdroppers hear no good of themselves, and so it was, because Aunt Dot embarked upon a lengthy catalogue of all my faults, surprisingly lengthy for such a small person as myself. Then finally she came to the point.

'Well, it's bad news, I'm afraid,' she said. 'Emma's a strange child, very strange, and I don't pretend to understand her. I've tried everything, even spanking her. Now don't look at me like that, Ellie. I don't hit her hard. Just a tap really. Anyway it does no good. Nothing works. In fact I can only see one solution. If you agree to it, that is. I think – I firmly believe, in fact – that Emma should see a psychiatrist. I really do.'

I cowered uneasily on the stair, the hairs on my neck prickling in fear. I had no idea what a psychiatrist was, any more than I had known what a cat-o'-nine-tails was, but experience had shown that in Sourhope the unknown often turned out to be even worse in reality than it was when simply feared. Judging by my aunt's tone, it sounded sinister, and if she was in favour of it, it was surely something to be avoided at all costs. Besides, my mother had greeted the suggestion with stunned silence, and when she did recover speech she sounded shocked.

'What? I don't believe it! A psychiatrist, Dot! Whatever has my little girl done?'

Aunt Dot then detailed my strange habits, deploring those occasions when I had drawn her attention to invisible people or imaginary events, and times when I had deliberately distracted her from her work by telling fictitious stories, and moments when I had been caught talking to myself – or to flowers, for heaven's sake – or even worse, to empty bottles! She spoke at length and my mother listened with a patience that became her well, but at the end of the recital she gave a deep sigh of relief.

'Oh, is that all, Dot? I thought it was something serious. That's just play. All children play like that. Trust me, they do. It's only make-believe. Perfectly harmless and normal.'

'Oh, you think so, do you?' retorted Aunt Dot furiously. 'Well, that's *not* all. I'll show you something that *will* convince you. And shock you too. Come with me.'

She led the way into the kitchen and paused just inside, and I guessed they were viewing my latest masterpiece, the recently created cat-pig. I held my breath, overcome with guilt.

'There now! What do you think of that? That's what little madam sees fit to do to our calendar,' she said grimly. 'Every month she defaces it with a different monstrosity. Hideously nasty productions of a warped mind. I've kept them all, and they're sickening. Come and see.'

The footsteps returned to the living room, and I heard the sound of the sideboard drawer being opened, evidently revealing the rest of the futuristic pig collection.

'What do you think of these then? You can't say they're normal. *Now* do you agree that she needs a psychiatrist?'

Silence followed and a twinge of alarm disturbed me. All those months I had thought my secret safe, assuming my improvements to the calendar had gone unnoticed, or been attributed to some other artist. And all that time Aunt Dot had been seething over them and storing them to use in evidence against me. A thought struck me and froze me to the stair. What if my mother disowned me, abandoning me to Sourhope and psychiatrists for ever? But suddenly my mother began to giggle and the sound rippled merrily on and on, as she laughed and laughed, so infectiously that I had to smile myself, while the happy peal drowned out my aunt's expostulations of anger.

'Oh, my goodness,' my mother gasped, finding difficulty controlling her voice. 'Oh my! That's the best laugh I've had for ages. Since this dreadful war started, I think. Look at that pig, Dot, with the spots, and that one with the red hair. And that! And that! Oh dear me, they are amusing. And talented too. I'll keep these, Dot, if I may. What a funny daughter I have, to be sure. But the answer's no, Dot. Categorically no! No psychiatrist! Absolutely not! And no more spankings either. This terrible war's done enough damage. Be kind to my little girl, Dot. I worry about her *so* much.'

For a time I remained on the stairs, mulling over events in my mind. Naturally I was pleased at my mother's response, but disappointed at losing my trump card. Sadly it seemed that for the time being I remained stuck at Windlestraw, and would have to find other means of escape from my prison camp. Not so easy. And I racked my brains for hours until finally I came up with a ruse that just might work. So on the evening before her departure I began to lay the groundwork.

'Mum, you know you said that the boys are taking piano lessons?'

'Yes, that's right, pet.'

'Well I don't think that's fair. I've always wanted to learn to play the piano. If I were at home I could have lessons too, but there's no piano or music teacher up here.'

She looked dismayed and for a while remained thoughtful. Then to my delight she agreed.

'You're quite right, Emma. It isn't fair. I'd no idea you were so keen to learn. I'll give that some thought. I must try to do something. Maybe on my next visit.'

Success at last, I decided. Next time I would be taken home. No doubt about it. Even Sourhope could be endured for another few weeks. I felt a rare surge of optimism as I climbed into the car taking my mother to the bus, and without the usual intense pain at parting, watched the red bus drive her out of sight. Next time I would be on the bus with her. It was, I thought, what Uncle Matt would call a 'dead cert'. Buoyant as my mood was, however, Uncle Matt's bettered it. I had noticed on the way down the valley that he kept grinning to himself, like the cat that got the cream. He whistled, he sang, and as soon as the bus had gone he led me into the post office and gestured airily.

'Pick what you want, Emma,' he said with unaccustomed largesse. 'Choose two things – or three – no, make it four. Whatever you want, pet. Help yourself.'

I stared at him, unable to comprehend this reckless spending. Was he, I wondered, quite well? Had a sudden rush of blood to the head affected his natural tendency to make prisoners of any coins that came his way? But he winked at me, smirking as he whispered, 'Green Eyes.'

'What about them?' I asked, bemused.

'I've been wantin' to tell you for two days,' he said gleefully. 'Our horse – you know – "Green Eyes" – came up at twenty to one. Great news, eh? But not a word to you know who.'

It should have been a pleasant journey back, what with the prevailing mood of optimism, and my recent acquisitions – ranging from liquorice laces and sherbet dabs to comics and puzzles – sitting securely on my lap, and the sun shining warmly for once, and Uncle Matt dangling a cigarette out of the open window and singing from the heart. He had remembered the words of the old song 'He played his ukulele as the ship went down', and was letting it rip, scattering nervous sheep from the verges. And indeed all went well until the car gave a loud cough and joined in, spluttering along in time to his jubilant warbling. Then in a fit of temperament it choked, shuddering to a halt as if going down in sympathy with the ship, and in an instant the prevailing mood changed. Uncle Matt swore like a trooper, frantically yanking at a mysterious lever situated on the steering wheel and marked 'Advance' and 'Retard'. But it was obvious that he had no idea what he was doing. Clearly, I thought, he had mastered 'Retard', but was a complete novice when it came to 'Advance'.

Nor in my opinion did he handle the situation well from then on. Only a few days earlier my very sanity had been called into question for talking to inanimate objects, yet here he was cursing the car soundly, swearing at it roundly, and thrashing its ageing bodywork with wild abandon, like a kick-boxer going in for the kill. The temperamental Morris was not impressed and remained unresponsive, sulkily silent. We had to push its heavy body for some yards, and beg assistance from a nearby farmer and his son and from a passing lorry driver to help us negotiate Slate Bank. I pushed and pushed, straining every muscle and sinew of my small person to the utmost, helping to persuade the reluctant Morris to crawl slowly and painfully up the hill so that the engine would start as it ran down the other side. Uncle Matt sat comfortably in the driving seat, steering the car and directing operations, shouting 'Onward and upward! Onward and upward!' encouragingly at intervals, and offering gratuitous advice which no one seemed to appreciate. Least of all me. Indeed, as I continued pushing and straining with the rest of them, I reflected that April had sustained its cruel streak right to the bitter end.

Happily, however, better times were in store, as April gave way to the merry month of May, and the emergence into my life of two neighbours together with the mysterious disappearance of two others. My new acquaintance was Amy Leadbetter, who lived in Fern Cottage in the lee of Low Windlestraw Farm. Her cottage stood at the point where I turned off the road to cross the fields on my way home, and was pleasantly situated, being sheltered by the farm at the back, and facing an ever-changing frontal view through willow trees of the burn winding by. I had often seen Amy's cheerful countenance in passing, but on the first Saturday in May, true to his winter promise, Uncle Matt escorted me to her door and formally introduced me, not only to Amy herself, but also to her visiting nine-year-old niece, Ida.

The smiling pair stood side by side, looking as fresh and crisp and round as two small cottage loaves, and very alike, the niece simply a younger version of the aunt. I warmed to them instantly, sensing kindred spirits, and for a time my loneliness seemed to be a thing of the past. I now looked forward to weekends, anticipating all kinds of pleasure in store, and feeling as contented as I could be in the absence of my mother. Besides, Amy was quite motherly herself, being of marriageable age though with no particular suitor in mind, or so Uncle Matt hinted as we walked down to visit her and he outlined her marriage prospects in his own inimitable way.

'You'll like Amy. She's a real nice lass, Emma. Not the bonniest I've ever seen, but all the same not bad lookin'. She's got fine features an' that. And she's a grand cook too,' he added wistfully. 'She'll make some lucky bloke a dashed good wife. She will, definitely.'

'Is she getting married then, Uncle Matt?'

'Well no, not right now, like. But I guess it's just a matter of time,' he said, adding with a wink. 'So far nobody's managed to hang his hat up.'

'Really? Is the hat stand too high for them?'

'No. I don't mean that, Emma. My meanin' is that no young man's managed to get his feet under her table.'

Low table or big feet? It was all very puzzling. And naturally his romantic turn of phrase fired my ready imagination. So it was perhaps unsurprising that I entered Fern Cottage labouring under a few misconceptions about both house and hostess. I fully anticipated furniture of an irregular height, specially designed so that Amy, like many a fictional heroine, could provide personal tests for potential suitors. I expected to see an unusual home, and so it was, though not in the way I had been led to believe. There was nothing unusual in the height of the furniture, but the astonishing variety of the furnishings was a different matter, for the simple cottage exterior belied its busy interior, and the small windows that frothed with white lace hid the profusion within. Once inside, however, I stared in amazement, confronting an Aladdin's cave of wonders, such an infinite treasure trove that I never did take all of it in.

Every room, though neat and tidy and scrupulously clean, was crammed to the ceiling with collections of one sort or another. Copper and brass lit up dark beams, stuffed birds gazed stolidly through glass domes at neighbouring clock faces, and pictures of all kinds lined the walls, leaving scarcely enough room for a space between the frames. Pottery and porcelain filled every accommodating surface, with jugs and teapots nudging bowls and plates, while figurines crowded into nooks and crannies. Flat-backed figures on horses rode the mantelpiece, and glass-eyed dogs shared the hearth with smug hand-painted cats. At first I was afraid to move in case I knocked something over, or worse still, broke it. But Amy seemed unconcerned about her wealth of possessions, giving their safety not a second's anxious thought.

'Tush, Emma, they're only things. It's people that's important, lass,' she said, handing me an exquisite porcelain shepherdess to hold. 'And anyway, I reckon I could spare quite a few ornaments and never miss them. Wouldn't you say so now?'

'But surely you'd be vexed if something like this got broken?' I suggested, thinking how angrily Aunt Dot would react in such circumstances, especially as she only possessed one ornament to break.

'No, not at all, honey. Don't disturb yourself on that account. It wouldn't matter. But in any case, I'm not worried on that score. You see, Emma, lasses are careful with things. I don't recall Ida ever breaking anything or spoiling anything in her life, bless her, and I dare say you're just the same.' I made no reply to this, remembering guiltily a certain pig calendar that I had evidently ruined.

'But, Amy,' I protested, changing the subject back to her, 'you've collected all these pieces. You must be fond of them.'

'Only for sentiment's sake,' she said. 'I haven't really collected them. Just inherited them. They were all handed down from my mother, and from her mother before that, and maybe from hers before. I keep the things in remembrance of the people, of my mother and Gran. You see, Emma?'

'What happened to your mother, Amy?'

'Oh well, she died, Emma. When I was little more than your age. Yes, about nine, I'd be, and it was scarlet fever carried her off. People died of it regular in those days. And Father followed five years ago. There was a terrible accident in the lead mine. A fair number died that day.'

'Oh Amy! But how awful! That's so much worse than my troubles. I'm just separated from my family, but you . . .'

'Now, now, Emma,' she said, patting my hand kindly. 'Time heals and life moves on. I still have family and friends, and company at weekends with Ida here, and now I have you, a new caller. I'm as happy as a lark I am. You must always look forward in life, Emma. You never know what good things are to come. Maybe something special around the corner. Or someone,' she added coquettishly. 'Someone special just around the corner.'

I then suspected that Uncle Matt had failed to assess the situation quite correctly. I guessed that Amy did have a young man in mind, perhaps the farmer's son next door. He was just around the corner. At any rate, she had set her mind on someone who would be welcome to put his feet under her table, and doubtless she had a peg at a convenient height reserved for his hat. I liked to think so, and, being something of a romantic myself, hoped for a happy ending. From that moment on I felt quite at home in Fern Cottage. Ida and I played with whatever took our fancy, often the grotesque character jugs and prancing horses that stimulated our imagination. But there were other delights too – toys, and a doll's pram, and a farm kitten, a cheeky black and white bundle of fur called Kitty, whom we dressed in dolls' clothes and pushed like a baby in the pram. But she seldom played the game for long, always managing to wriggle free and bound away with bonnet strings trailing through the farmyard muck.

For a while Ida and I spent most of the weekends together, much to my delight and Aunt Dot's grim disapproval, because when she wanted little jobs doing I was missing, wasting precious time in play. I stayed at Amy's for Saturday tea, when dainty sandwiches were served on gilt-edged plates smothered in printed flowers, or sometimes for Sunday lunch, when fat Yorkshire puddings rose like crisp castles in the oven. Amy introduced me to new culinary delights with wonderful names – to Maids of Honour, and Sly Cake, and Upside Down Cake, and Apple Turnover, made from dried apple rings. The war was forgotten in that comfortable home. All was bliss. Once again I had found warmth and kindness in austere Sourhope, and I knew that when my mother finally came to take me away, as I felt sure she must, I would miss my new-found friends more than I could say.

Looking back, I appreciate how fortuitous it was that Amy befriended me at that particular time, because apart from the enjoyment I derived from her company, she probably saved me from many a beating. Our acquaintance coincided with Mr Clout's decision to switch his syllabus from Nature Study to gardening, turning reluctant students of nature into rebellious garden slaves. So as it happened, without Amy's intervention I would have ended many a gardening day in trouble, with my clothes dirty and dishevelled, and no acceptable excuses to ward off the wrath of Aunt Dot. But Amy contrived to clean me up and brush me down, sending me on my way not only with a light heart but with a stomach refreshed by tea and cakes.

For some weeks past the senior boys had been sent outside in groups of six to prepare the ground and plant vegetables, but now it seemed that the whole class was needed to bring the growing beds up to scratch. An inspiring 'Dig for Victory' poster suddenly appeared pinned to the wall between the hooked beaks of eagle and vulture, its optimistic message somewhat at odds with the sombre stare of the birds of prey. Then the outdoor torture began in earnest one sunny but bitterly cold May morning, when Mr Clout started the day by making a dramatic announcement.

'Boys and girls, the sap has risen! The moment has come!' he boomed theatrically, whiskers bristling in happy anticipation of the joy of launching his prize vegetables into the world, and out we all went, I for one casting envious glances at the infants cosily reading as we trudged in a desultory crocodile past their inviting window.

After a quick conducted tour we were all allocated tasks. The boys continued the heavy work of digging and forking compost, and some, like the early Egyptian slaves, carried huge stones from a nearby

312

quarry to build various structures that Mr Clout had planned during the winter. Meanwhile, the girls were assigned the lighter but back-aching jobs of weeding, thinning, tidying and riddling soil. The garden plot was elevated and exposed to the elements, so I soon came to know why Mr Clout had once recommended the onion patch to me: it was because the wall shielding the onions helped to cut the bitter wind that so sorely nipped the ears. Naturally, however, there was much rivalry for this sheltered position, and, contrary to the old proverb that the weakest go to the wall, in this case they were pushed away from it, back into the wind.

At this stage Mr Clout's role was largely supervisory, keeping a sharp all-seeing eye on our labours. Only occasionally did he wield a trowel or fork, and then purely for demonstration purposes. I noticed, however, that he carried a long, pliable stick, which he had picked up from the path, taken a fancy to, and seemed reluctant to put down. He toyed with it the whole time, whipping it in the wind with a swishing noise similar to that of the cat-o'-nine-tails in the classroom. He had instantly recognized the stick's potential, and from then on, whenever he taught outside, it travelled with him like an extra elongated arm.

I kept away from him and his companion, the stick, continuing to avoid his gaze and proximity, but his menacing presence dominated the vegetable plot. Nor was he the only menace to thrive there, because the mere fact of being in the open air gave my arch enemy, Eddie Gormley, leeway to perpetrate mischief, tormenting me to his heart's content. He made his first approach as I came out alone from the garden shed, pinning me with outstretched arms against the door, his face close to mine, his cold eyes staring without emotion, his lizard-like tongue lolling through yellow teeth. I turned my face away disgustedly, heart racing and knees like jelly, but having glimpsed Irene coming to my rescue, I found the courage to slide down the door and escape, knocking his arm aside as I fled.

'Ah'll get ya fer that, gooseberry eyes,' he shouted after me, 'and Ah'll bury ya in the Elf Holes.' Then a few days later, when Mr Clout's attention was otherwise engaged in measuring a promising young leek's dimensions, the bully crept up behind me concealing a worm behind his back.

'Cuddle up to that, you little squirt,' he said, dangling in my face the longest, fattest, slimiest worm imaginable.

I shrank away in horror, my mouth open for a scream that never came. I was too scared to cry out, having been punished before merely on the suspicion of so doing. As always when threatened by Gormley I froze with fright, lapsing into my convincing imitation of a petrified rabbit, while Gormley cruelly pulled me towards him and began to push the worm down my neck. I struggled helplessly, glancing behind me in panic, and once again it was Irene who came to my rescue, deftly delivering a salutary kick to his shins and saving both me and the worm from further torment. In pained surprise Gormley uttered a loud yelp, like a puppy whose tail has been trodden on, and he dropped the worm, which made good its escape. Mr Clout swivelled round and, seeing the boy hopping on one leg and generally loafing about instead of working the soil, strode forward purposefully, waving his stick like a stern conductor intent on putting an orchestra through its paces. A frown darkened his hairy face and the stick quivered in his hand as if it were a divining rod discovering water. For a second he let it quiver, contemplating the sheer pleasure of employing it on Gormley, now bending and tenderly massaging the afflicted leg. Then he raised the stick and with a graceful swing administered a telling whack across the boy's trouser seat, stepping back with a gratified smile.

'I knew that stick would come in useful,' he declared. 'Knew it all along. Felt it in my bones.' And with that he resumed strutting round the various vegetable beds, containing everything from asparagus to turnips.

He strutted imperiously, the long flaps of his vented grey overcoat swaying gently in the wind, and issued all the while a sort of running commentary, a non-stop litany of instructions. He interrupted his recital only for frequent refreshment, in the form of the contents of a flask which he removed from his capacious pocket with gloved hands, and which was a wise precaution to keep out the cold, but sadly not one that the rest of us could adopt. And as if to give the proceedings a semblance of educational worth, he combined them with a lesson of sorts, constantly throwing to us as they occurred, like scraps from a table, spellings and snippets of information at random.

'Listen, everyone! This is important!' he yelled above the roaring of the wind. 'See that cloche there? Now leave that alone for the moment. It contains lettuce, spelled with a "c" not an "s", of course. Remember that. You there, cloth-ears. I told you to hoe carefully round the carrots. Carrot with a "c" not a "k". Carrots are said to be good for the eyes. Remember that. And you, bright spark, keep earthing up those potatoes. The potato takes an "e" in the plural, like tomato. Potatoes were introduced to this country by Sir Walter Raleigh, by the way. Remember that. Watch what you're doing there, bone-brain. They're my prize leeks you're trifling with. My leeks are *very, very* precious. The leek is, of course, the Welsh national emblem. That's leek with a double "e". Leak with an "a" is quite a different kettle of fish.'

So he rambled on, very much in his element, taking comfort from the thought that though he might not produce prize-winning pupils, he could certainly produce prize-winning vegetables. Yet seemingly he was unaware that the success of the one might well contribute to the failure of the other. In gardening circles at least he was a winner year after year after year. He was content with that.

Meanwhile, I kept a wary eye on Eddie Gormley and noted that he appeared to be lacking in motivation and concentration. He constantly took time out to massage his shins tenderly, and seemed to have lost all heart for any job that entailed turning his back and bending over. As for the memorable spellings enlightening the air, they passed over his head and blew away in the wind. He could never cope with spelling and that was that. In fact, he held the distinction of being the only pupil in the school able to write an essay without marring its consistency by a single recognizable word. So it was only a matter of time before Mr Clout noticed his lack of application on both fronts and, with a lordly wave of his versatile stick, summoned the boy to his side.

'Gormley, my boy, I have a special job for you,' he said with unexpected geniality. 'It's an important job, and one that I'm confident will stand you in good stead in later life, training you for your future career. Yes indeed, boy. Now this is what I want you to do. Take the wheelbarrow to that far corner where there's a wonderful heap of well-rotted manure. Beautiful stuff. Such stuff as dreams are made on. Keep filling the barrow with the manure and distributing it in the various beds. That'll be a job well worth doing and should keep you out of mischief.'

From my point of view, Eddie's banishment to the manure heap was a blessing, but with or without Gormley hovering near, I hated those lessons, if such they could be called. I hated the black fingernails and muddy shoes. I hated the scratches and keens I somehow acquired, and the ever-present threat of Mr Clout's stick. I hated the creepy-crawlies, especially the slugs and woodlice, and the suspicion that foreign bodies, both animal and vegetable, were finding their way into my hair. Most of all I hated the intense cold that numbed my ears and froze my feet. Besides, I was too small for the tools. I never managed to riddle soil without filling my shoes and socks with the overflow, or to weed without sinking my knees and elbows into the soggy earth. The soil was always heavy, retaining a gooey consistency that clung to clothes like glue, so that I was grateful to call at Amy's cottage and throw myself on her mercy.

'Sit by the fire, honey,' she would say, 'and have a cup of tea. Best to tackle the job of cleaning your clothes when they're thoroughly dry. The clarts brush off easier then. But I'll fetch you a bowl of warm water for your hands and knees, and a clean pair of Ida's socks. We'll soon get you smartened up. Now, Emma, do you fancy a jam tart or a rock cake? I made them both special like, but we mustn't spoil your appetite for your proper tea.'

'It's impossible to spoil Aunt Dot's tea,' I remarked ambiguously, but refrained from mentioning that there was seldom a proper tea to spoil, and what there was had usually been spoilt already.

I lingered at Fern Cottage as long as I dared, basking in the warmth of Amy's hearth and hospitality; then made my way home through the fields, enjoying the walk in the scented May evenings. For now I walked on wild flowers, serenaded by bird song. Marsh marigolds and celandines turned the pasture deep yellow, and millions of tiny pansies daubed the meadow purple, like pointillism on an Impressionist canvas. And from this carpet of flowers rose the constant cry of the peewit – a plaintive and repetitive cry of 'pee-r-wit, pee-r-wit', to which a curlew would reply with its flutey call of 'cour-li', forming a duet to sing me home. Both types of birds nested and cared for their young in the pasture, and were easily recognized, not only by the cries from which they derived their names, but from their distinctive features: the tufted crest of the peewit, spiking from the back of the head like a lady's tiara worn high in the hair; and the long curved bill of the curlew, shaped like a sickle.

The evenings were long and light then, longer than I could ever recall in my short life, and Uncle Matt explained that we were two hours ahead of ourselves because of something called double summer time, and that the clocks had been adjusted accordingly. It was a phenomenon of war, he said, and a good thing for farmers. But for me it could be confusing, and I often found myself behind the clock rather than ahead, mistaking the time and staying out too late for my own good. As long as Aunt Dot was busy in the byre or cooler-house, all was well, and I rapidly attended to various little jobs around the house, giving the impression that I had been home for some time. But if she happened to be in the kitchen, my heart sank when I confronted her basilisk stare as she stiffened at the sight of me, rigid and ready to strike, and I waited for the expected fulmination.

'Where've you been till this time?' was her shrill and hostile greeting, but without waiting for an answer she pounced, and in an instant I found myself dodging blows as best I could.

'You promised my mum you wouldn't hit me! You did! You promised!' I protested many and many a time as I fended off attack, but to no avail.

'I'm not hitting you! It's just a tap. Believe me, if I really hit you, you'd know all about it. By heaven you would! You'd know you'd been hit all right!'

'I do know, Aunt Dot. I really do!' I cried, as I tried to back away.

'Oh yes, I forgot – you think you know everything. You're a little clever-clogs. But believe me, you've got a long way to go before you've learnt sense. You're a stupid, wicked, wilful girl. That's what I think, and I know I'm right.'

So it was that she acted the harridan simply because I was late from school. The lashings from the sharp edge of her tongue kept time with the lashings from her well-practised hand – or whatever weapon she casually picked up, be it serving spoon, soup ladle, or tea towel flicked hard at my legs till they smarted. Sometimes it was the bread knife that came to hand. She referred to it as 'the gully', and used the long flat blade to tap the top of my head warningly, as if for two pins she would cut the whole thing off and have done with it. It was not surprising that I often reflected on my good fortune at surviving these tussles intact, and at escaping with the requisite number of eyes and ears, fingers and limbs, ready to face another day.

Chapter 23

Nazi Spies

One evening after I had greatly overstayed at Amy's, I ran frantically homewards, scattering songbirds and everything else in my path. I arrived breathless and apprehensive, fearful of my reception, expecting to be greeted by something in the nature of medieval torture. But even as I crossed the yard I could hear raised voices in the kitchen and stopped short, recognizing the Germanic tones of Mr Shoeman. Overcome by curiosity, I crept in quietly, perching myself beside the water buckets on the bench by the window, trying to look as if I had been there for some time. From that cramped seat I watched and listened, riveted to the scene being enacted before my amazed eyes. At first it resembled a pantomime, in that Shoeman kept bellowing, 'Oh yes you did!' with Aunt Dot retorting, 'Oh no I didn't!' Then everyone shouted at once, everyone except me, because astonishment held me dumb. Mr Shoeman, who had never previously been allowed to put a foot over the threshold, had now infiltrated the hallowed precincts of Aunt Dot's kitchen and had advanced as far as the third mat!

I soon realized, however, that he was not there by invitation. My intrepid uncle, presently occupying the second mat, kept dodging about like a cat on hot bricks, showing an aggression the like of which I had rarely seen in him, even when he was retrieving stolen geese. With clenched fists he repeatedly squared up to Mr Shoeman's substantial back as if sparring for a fight, superficially looking as brave as can be. But I could not help wondering what he would do if his opponent, with whom he was so skilfully shadow-boxing, suddenly turned round, and I was soon to find out, because suddenly Shoeman did just that.

Sensing movement behind him, he swivelled to face Uncle Matt, who instantly dropped all bravado, whipped off his cap, and pretended to be swatting a fly. Shoeman snorted contemptuously and turned back to Aunt Dot, whom he appeared to regard as his real opponent. His gaze remained riveted on her as she bounced angrily about the kitchen like a jumping firecracker, screaming hysterically at him. I could see that he too was seething with violent emotions and, having brought no wife with him on whom to vent his fury, he continually snorted like a bull gathering momentum for a charge.

By now it was evident that I was witnessing some sort of repeat of a previous argument, concerning suspicions of my aunt and uncle meddling with Shoeman's mail. So much was evident, but this time the signs pointed to a more serious situation. To me, Aunt Dot's denials had a ring of truth about them, and the package that Shoeman kept waving in such a frenzied manner did not suggest her handiwork. I had seen her in action and knew that with the aid of her ever-boiling kettle she could open and close any envelope, package or parcel immaculately, leaving scarcely a trace of interference, not even a wrinkle or smudge to show that she had tampered with it. She took pride in her work, and Shoeman had insulted her professionalism, an affront to her talents that she soon made plain.

'You're talking rubbish!' she shouted. 'Absolute tommyrot! I've never touched your stupid package. I've got better things to do. But anyone with half an eye can see it's been opened by somebody. It's been around for some time, that has. It's an old tear – soiled both sides. Yes, that parcel's had some wear and tear all right, and some of the contents are clearly visible. Plain as day. There'll be more than us had a chance to read that!'

Shoeman subsided a little and stopped shouting.

'You think so?' he asked, an expression of unease crossing his reddened face.

'You're darned right I think so. All the edges are dirty and frayed. People all over the country could have had a peek at what's inside. Nosey people could have had it translated. It's in German, isn't it? No wonder you're worried. I wouldn't be surprised if someone's alerted the police. Perhaps they're on their way already.'

'That's right, Dot. It's German,' interjected Uncle Matt. 'You tell him. Let him have it. Quite right.' His courage returning, he resumed his ducking and weaving.

Mr Shoeman stiffened and his head jerked militantly.

'So! You admit! My private papers you have read!'

'Who hasn't?' enquired Aunt Dot sarcastically.

Shoeman took a threatening step towards her and then hesitated for a second, and in that second Uncle Matt made a strategic blunder. For some reason better known to himself he suddenly leapt forward and hissed in Shoeman's ear.

'Nazi! You're a damned Nazi! A thoroughly nasty Nazi!'

He had issued an overt challenge and the effect was dynamite. Shoeman leapt nervously, reached into an inside pocket and pulled out a gun, which he pointed at each of us in turn, rotating on his heel and glaring malevolently, even at me. It was a moment for prompt action, and I wriggled off the bench – causing water to slosh about in the brimming buckets – and raised my hands in the air, surrendering as I had seen people do in gangster films at the cinema. Usually somebody said 'Stick 'em up!' and so far nobody had, but as the gun turned towards me I stuck 'em up anyway, hoping to live to fight another day. Uncle Matt stopped prancing about and stood gaping at the gun in horror and disbelief. Only Aunt Dot stayed calm, not at all fazed by confronting an armed Nazi in her clinical kitchen. A woman who has faced an angry bull without flinching is not intimidated by a mere gun. An inanimate gun pales by comparison, and in a voice as cold as the winter wind she dismissed the weapon and cut Shoeman down to size.

'And you can put that silly thing away for a start,' she said acidly. 'The colossal cheek of it! The very idea of barging into a person's home and having the unmitigated gall to wave a gun in people's faces and threaten them! Pshaw! Take yourself off, out of my house, out of my sight, and don't you dare come back. You hear me? Ever!'

'You vill shut up, woman!' shouted Shoeman wildly and, having selected her as his chief antagonist, he now ignored us and aimed the gun solely at her.

That being so, I lowered my hands and eased myself carefully back onto the bench. Meanwhile Aunt Dot tossed her head and answered without so much as a tremor in her voice.

'What? In my own kitchen? Don't you dare give me orders in my own kitchen! And you're hardly in a position to give orders anyway. I mean to say – *you're* the intruder. And *you're* the Nazi! Like as not you're a spy, in enemy territory, and if I may say so, out of your depth.'

'Definitely! That's tellin' him, Dot! He's a Nazi all right. We've proved it at last. A damned Nazi! A pesky Nazi!' interposed Uncle Matt, becoming his old confident self again.

'Quiet! You will both be quiet!' shouted Shoeman, in desperation rotating the gun again to frighten us, but Aunt Dot ignored him, resuming her remarks.

'And *you're* the one who's going to get caught. Then you'll be for it all right. And shooting us would only make things worse for you. A lot worse, as you well know. And surely you're not going to shoot a child? You coward! Oh, what a pity I'm not a man! I'd soon fix you and your bullying ways. Pointing a gun at a little child and a defence-less woman!'

I had never thought of Aunt Dot as defenceless, and it seemed to come as something of a surprise to Shoeman too. An uneasy silence followed during which he inspected each of us in turn, his eyes behind the steely spectacles flickering to and fro as he weighed up his next move. I raised my hands in the air again, respecting the gun, indi-cating my full co-operation, and at length he heaved a regretful sigh, as if disappointed that he was obliged to forego the pleasure of shooting us, and reluctantly replaced the gun in his pocket.

'There is some truth in what you say,' he admitted grudgingly, looking rather foolish. 'Perhaps we come to an understanding, yes? An arrangement for our mutual benefit?' With that, he suddenly reached in his pocket again, causing Uncle Matt to leap like a star-tled fawn for fear of what was coming out this time.

But it was an engagingly fat wallet that emerged into the light of day, and from it Shoeman began to peel off pristine five-pound notes. It was an uncommon sight, and Uncle Matt's eyes lit up. He seldom came across so much as a single fiver, but the rare vision of a bundle of them – large, white, crisp and crinkly – made him feel quite overcome, and his hand automatically reached out. Not so Aunt Dot, who in a state of angry amazement, pushed him aside, climbing on her dignity.

'How dare you insult us with money!' she exclaimed, outraged. 'Don't imagine for a moment that you can buy me off! I will not be bribed! Unlike you, Mr so-called Shoeman, I'm no traitor. So keep your filthy money and clear off.'

But as if in a dream, Uncle Matt glided forward, holding his hand up in arbitration.

'Hold on there, Dot. Let's not be too hasty,' he advised. 'I'm not so easily insulted.' And at that, he eagerly helped himself to a handful of notes from the over-stuffed wallet.

'But, Matt, we can't! We *can't* take money from a spy to keep quiet.'

'Of course we can't, Dot. Definitely not. That would be a terrible thing to do. Nothin' short of collaboration. But we *could* sell Mr Shoeman here some of that bacon he's always beggin' me for.'

'Bacon!' expostulated Shoeman contemptuously, spitting the word out as if the bacon had burnt his mouth.

'There you are!' said Uncle Matt triumphantly. 'There he goes again. Always shoutin' for bacon. And after all, Dot, we've been doin' business with him all the time we suspected he was a Nazi, so what's the difference? Even Nazis have to eat – until they're shot, of course.'

'But, Matt, it just doesn't seem right.'

'Course it is. Right as rain. Look at it this way – this Nazi's got too much money. Ill-gotten gains, no doubt. And we haven't enough. So deprivin' him of a bit slows him down and helps us forward. Think of it as part of the war effort. Now pop into the larder and get him a side of bacon. That special one at the back's just the ticket.'

He helped himself to another six fivers and would have added more to his collection, but Shoeman began to show resistance, forcing Uncle Matt to advance the economic argument.

'Off-ration food prices are goin' up all the time,' he explained. 'It's the war, you know. Damned Nazis! Oops sorry, I forgot. Ah, here's Dot, back with your bacon.' And with that, he extracted another note from the bulging wallet.

'I do not vant your rotten stinking putrid bacon,' protested Shoeman.

'What? Course you do! You've paid for it, haven't you? Through the nose, you might say. Besides, it's not stinkin'. Just a wee bit reasty. You know – a bit suspect, a bit tainted. Just like you, Shoeman. Anyway, beggars can't be choosers. And I'm sorry it's just wrapped in news-paper, but we've run out of greaseproof. There again, it's the war to blame. So here you are, and if I were you I wouldn't hang about.'

Shoeman scowled, turned on his heel, and with despair in his heart and a side of bacon under his arm, headed for the door and disap-peared. The following morning when the postman called, Uncle Matt set the bush telegraph system in motion to report the Shoemans to the police, and shortly afterwards, the day being a Saturday, he insisted that I accompany him on his morning rounds.

'We'll start with Dyke Head,' he said, fastening a tartan scarf round his neck in lieu of a tie, and adjusting his cap to a jaunty angle, the turn in his fortunes having boosted his morale.

I hung back, not wishing to repeat the experience of having a gun thrust in my face.

'I think I'll stay home today for a change, Uncle Matt.'

'What? That's not like you, Emma. I thought you enjoyed keepin' me company.'

'I do, Uncle Matt, but not to Dyke Head.'

'Nonsense. Dyke Head's all right. As it happens, I think you'll find it quite interestin' today. Now pop your coat on. The fresh air'll do you good, and you're not due at Amy's till this afternoon. So hurry up or the day'll be half over.'

'But what about Shoeman's gun, Uncle Matt?'

'Oh, we're not scared of Shoeman, are we?' he said, sticking his chest out, brave in Shoeman's absence. 'Anyway, I don't think he'll bother us today somehow. In fact, I dare bet one of his fivers on it. Come on now.'

'Aren't we taking eggs and milk, Uncle Matt?'

'No, not for the Shoemans. I've a feelin' they won't want any today. Or ever again in fact. No, we'll just walk up and snoop about a bit. Right! Let's get to it.'

Most unusually we found two gates open, and Uncle Matt nodded his head sagely.

'Yes, that's it. Just as I thought. Definitely. You'll see, Emma.'

And again unusually, as we approached the back door there was no sign of habitation. No one met us or accosted us, no smoke curled from the blackened chimney, and the house, always unwelcoming, now had a deserted air. All was eerily silent until the sheep noticed us. They stood huddled in the near corner of the field as if waiting for the morning roll-call, and they surged forward in a mass, bleating expectantly. They looked a bedraggled flock, some trailing tattered ribbons, some bedecked in woollen jackets and staring through tea-cosies dangling from their ears. Uncle Matt threw his hands in the air and swore under his breath.

'I've never got used to that sight, Emma – sheep wearin' woolly jumpers and hats! Mean to say, they've already got 'em, haven't they? Born with 'em, an' that. Nature provides. Talk about takin' coals to Newcastle! It beggars belief, Emma. The Shoemans must be barmy. Anyway, let's give their place the once-over.'

We found the door closed but unlocked and he stepped cautiously inside, calling loudly as he went, 'Hello! Hello there! Anybody in? Anyone at home?'

Silence greeted us and we proceeded into the living room, where even in the semi-darkness we detected signs of a hasty departure. The curtains were still closed, a stool lay on its side, chairs were strewn with discarded clothing, and the stale remains of a meal were being finished off by a big ugly bluebottle buzzing round the table, breaking the silence. Instinctively Uncle Matt attempted to restore peace by swatting the bluebottle with his upturned cap, but it eluded him and he persisted, cursing it soundly. I waited, peering through the gloom as he danced from side to side, wielding the cap like a phantom ping-pong player. Then suddenly I felt something circling my legs, brushing them gently back and front with the soft silkiness of a feather duster. It was an eerie sensation and I let out an involuntary scream, causing Uncle Matt to leap in the air, demonstrating a few steps of the Highland Fling, a nimble display that would have won acclaim at a gathering of the clans but was wasted on me.

'Whuh-at? What the devil?' he cried, and to throw light on proceedings, he dashed to the window and opened the heavy curtains.

Daylight revealed Split wagging his tail round my legs by way of testing his welcome. I realized that he must have followed us in, and I sighed with relief and stroked his head. Uncle Matt began cursing him instead of the bluebottle, advising him to buck his ideas up or else. He aimed a kick at the dog's behind, but with a Pavlovian reflex action Split swerved and, sighing, Uncle Matt abandoned both him and the bluebottle and turned his attention to the room.

'Just as I thought,' he said, replacing his cap on his head and smiling complacently. 'Exactly as I thought. You see, Emma, they've skedaddled. My meanin' is, they've done a moonlight flit.'

It sounded romantic, but there was little romance about the room that now met our gaze, a shabby, depressing room decorated in dismal browns, with a dirty threadbare carpet and dingy furniture covered in a thick layer of dust. Spiders had long since settled down there, making it their home and spinning countless webs that had trapped other insects, suspending them in various stages of decay. It seemed to me that the woman known as Mrs Shoeman must have hated living in that house and longed to escape. She had neither cleaned it nor cared for it, and it offered little more comfort than a prison cell. Uncle Matt, who was used to a dust-free environment, heatedly condemned the couple as filthy beggars, idle wasters, and an all-round bad lot. Then his roving eye fell on the fireplace, where cold ashes partly covered the remnants of burnt papers. He pounced eagerly on them, using nearby fire tongs to lift them carefully out, and perused their contents with exclamations of astonishment and disgust.

'Well, what do you know? The evil toad! Why, blow me! That'll flummox Dot. Who'd have thought it? By heck! Well, I'll go to the foot of our stairs! Fancy that!' Finally he looked up, putting the papers in his pocket and me in the picture. 'Well, Emma, it's a shame there's so much of this evidence burnt, but I can deduce that he's a Nazi all right. He deserves to be caught and dealt with, but I reckon he'll have gone to ground like the weasel he is. We'll just have to hope they pick him up when he surfaces. And as for her, I gather I was right. She's not married to the blighter. He's German, but she's British, and in my book that makes her worse than him. My meanin' is, she's a traitor, fraternizin' with the enemy. Betrayin' her own people, like. The brazen hussy. Well, at least we've put the skids under them.'

'What'll happen to her, Uncle Matt?'

'Goodness knows, Emma, but I hope she gets caught. She deserves to be locked up for the duration of the war at least. And to think she used to make sheep's eyes at me! She should be so lucky! Anyway, them papers might come in handy to the police when they arrive. Now, pet, let's see what else we can find before they get here.'

He gave the grate a spirited kick in passing, sending grey dust and particles of charred paper scattering in the air, and then led the way upstairs, where we found the main bedroom also darkened by drawn curtains, and this time he determined to open them first. There was nothing of hesitation about his entry into the room, but no sooner was he inside than he repeated his sprightly performance of the Highland Fling, adding the obligatory shriek and frightening the life out of me, not to mention Split, who bolted like lightning down the stairs. Ahead, a ghostly figure was advancing on my terrified uncle, coming straight towards him, rapidly closing in until they were almost face to face, at which point Uncle Matt suddenly leapt aside, colliding with the foot of the brass bed.

'Stay back, Emma!' he shouted bravely. 'It's horrible! Ooooh – a ghastly thing! Ooooh – awful!' As he did so, he limped to the window, frantically throwing the curtains wide.

Then, as light flooded the room, he sighed with relief, realizing that the mysterious menacing figure was none other than himself, reflected in a full-length mirror placed directly opposite the door. He sat on the bed trying to collect his wits, and gently massaged the foot that had come off worst against the bed's solid brass foot. I knew that he was feeling better when he began to curse the mirror, and the Shoemans for putting it there, and the bed for being brass. But he only regained his good humour completely when, in continuing our search, we came across a gentleman's overcoat hanging in the wardrobe. It was an imposing coat, double-breasted with big lapels and a belt, and he attempted to fold it neatly over his arm. But as if the owner were still wearing it, the bulky garment fought back, sleeves flailing in his face, and untameable lapels springing from his restraining grip, until finally he took a piece of strong cord from his pocket and subdued it into a tightly tied bundle.

'I'll have that for a start. It's a grand coat,' he declared, feeling the cloth approvingly. 'Pure wool and hardly worn. It's classy, that is. Though it'll never make up for the coat I lost. Crikey Moses! That *was* a coat. Still, this'll keep the snow out next winter. See how sharp the lapels are, pet? They could cut a swathe through grass they could. They're so big.'

'So's the coat, Uncle Matt,' I could not help but remark. 'Too big for you, surely?'

'Oh, I dare say it'll fit where it touches, though your aunt might shorten the sleeves. But it'll come in for somethin'. Even if it's just feedin' the pigs. That would be a fair tribute to Shoeman, Emma. Wearin' the Nazi swine's best coat to feed pigs.'

We continued our tour but found nothing more of interest until we reached the kitchen, where my uncle took a covetous fancy to an old red mangle, little used and accordingly in good condition.

'Now that's a canny little mangle,' he said. 'I dare bet your Aunt Dot would like that. My meanin' is, I could maybe do a swap and sell hers. I'll pick that up later with the horse and cart.'

'Who do these things belong to now?' I asked, always a stickler for honesty, and he swivelled his cap several times before answering.

'Hard to say, Emma. It's a rented house and it's between tenants. You see, it's as sure as eggs is eggs that we've seen the last of the Shoemans, or whoever they might be, so I reckon their things are up for grabs. A prize of war, you could say. And oh, look here, Emma. What do you know? They've left a side of bacon wrapped in newspaper. Might as well take that. No sense in wasting it. And here's a funny thing – there's an envelope underneath addressed to me.'

He took out a note and as he read it out loud I was struck by the thought that whatever the faults of the woman known as Mrs Shoeman, she was a shrewd judge of character. She had Uncle Matt summed up exactly. She had known he would search the house, known he would retrieve his bacon, known just where to hide the note. The message was short and simple, and in my opinion showed a kind and caring side to her nature. It said:

Dear Mr Wheatley,
    Please look after my darling lambkins, especially Curly and Fluffy, the sensitive little angels, and of course poor delicate Hobbles. You're a kind man and I know you'll treat them as your own. My best regards, dear friend,
    Betty

'Oooh. Look after the lambkins, eh?' said Uncle Matt happily. 'I'll do that all right. My meaning is – no problem there. Treat them as my own. See that, Emma? See that? That note's like a will. She's practically given me the sheep. You're a witness, pet, but I'll keep this signed paper just in case it's ever needed.' And he carefully pocketed the note and picked up the coat and bacon.

Then we closed the door on Dyke Head, leaving it to the bluebottle, though Uncle Matt, who never let the grass grow on his enterprises, returned that very afternoon to capture the sheep and the mangle. And now I saw another aspect of his many-faceted character. From some strange perversity, he treated the Shoeman sheep like prisoners of war, ceremonially stripping them of all ribbons and regalia, removing all privileges previously enjoyed, and for a time segregating them from his own flock, keeping them in a small separate pen. At odd moments he marched round the pen, checking that his prisoners were all present and correct, and inspecting them with a wary and critical eye, being particularly suspicious of one that he said reminded him of Mussolini. Sometimes on his last rounds at night he shone a torch on them, beaming it like a searchlight in a prison camp detecting would-be escapees. Night and day he counted his bonus flock, as if he could hardly believe his good fortune at having acquired spoils of war, tangible proof that Britain was on the winning side. Nor did he relax his strict regime for special cases. Ignoring Betty's touching note, he made no effort to identify Curly or Fluffy, and though Hobbles was easily recognized, he gave her no special treatment, despite the limp.

'Sheep's just sheep,' he said phlegmatically.

Though not a man to look a gift horse in the mouth, or a gift sheep for that matter, in his own way he always squared his actions with his conscience, and for a time he kept his distance from the Shoemans' sheep. Officials came and went, disturbing the dust and spiders at Dyke Head, but finding little more evidence than the charred papers that Uncle Matt had eagerly handed over. Only when he felt quite safe from enquiries did he brand the sheep, integrating them into his own flock. They became his, and somehow no one questioned his ownership, so he came to regard them as his by right – a sort of farming subsidy compensating for winter losses, and a reward for his unmasking of Shoeman, yet another of his contributions to the war effort.

It was left to me to round off the Shoeman story; my contribution in this respect was in the form of alterations to the pig calendar. I had resisted altering the calendar after it had been firmly established that Aunt Dot knew the identity of the artist. But the Essex Saddleback, representing May, stared invitingly at me day after day, and as the month drew to a close, living as dangerously as the times dictated, I finally succumbed to temptation. The Essex was a mainly black pig with a wide collar on which I drew row upon row of swastikas. I then topped the pig's head with a Shoeman-style Tyrolean hat, and perched steel-rimmed spectacles on the snout. Aunt Dot said nothing, but one day as she passed through the kitchen and glanced at the calendar I thought I detected the faint glimmer of a smile on her face. Perhaps she felt as I did – that we finally had Shoeman, the Nazi spy, properly exposed and pinned to the wall.

Surprisingly, however, the sudden departure of the Shoemans, though dramatic at the time, had remarkably little impact on our lives. In the valley nothing changed. The sun still shone on the June fields and the wind still blew cold from Lornhope. The birds still sang from dawn till dusk and wild flowers grew in ever greater profusion. Life soon returned to normal. Poultry and pigs were fed, sheep were sheared, calves were born, and cows and goats were put out to pasture. Uncle Matt found new outlets for his eggs – even the cracked ones, now fancifully marketed as 'cake eggs'. And for the first time in weeks, milk was plentiful in the house.

Throughout the winter, in one of my uncle's periodic bursts of enthusiasm for the war effort, he had sent away every last drop of milk, sometimes leaving us short of any for our own consumption. I often puzzled about this curious contradiction of living on a dairy farm and having to put up with black tea, like being adrift in the middle of an ocean without water to drink. Then I discovered that he had entered a competition run by the War Agricultural Committee for winter milk production, and all became clear. In June he was awarded a prize and a certificate, a palpable recognition of his farm management skills that made him swell with pride and show off the certificate to any casual callers at the door, whether they wanted to see it or not.

'Were you top then, Uncle Matt?' I asked, that being a question that he was wont to ask me in a regular way about school.

'Well no, Emma, not top exactly, but fifteenth in a field of a hundred and thirty. Now to my mind that's a good result in anybody's book. It is, definitely. And if you would care to read this here certificate, pet, you'll notice that I'm "complimented" – the very wordin' – for "high efficiency" – the very words. See there – "high efficiency". That's quite somethin', isn't it, Emma? It's a kind of honour an' that.'

'It certainly is, Uncle Matt. It's really very good,' I agreed, though I was secretly surprised that he had been proclaimed 'efficient' at all, let alone 'highly efficient'.

When it came to Uncle Matt's farming skills, I had always assumed that he sort of muddled through, succeeding now and then by the law of averages, more by good luck than good management. Now, however, in the face of this prized certificate, whenever I was called upon to make the sacrifice, I tried to drink my bitter tea with good grace, albeit without milk. He was immensely proud of the certificate, and I formed the impression that he would have liked it framed and hung in pride of place in the living room, it being his first of any kind. But Aunt Dot put her foot down firmly on that ambition, refusing point-blank to be swayed. She would tolerate no dust collectors on her walls, only the controversial calendar, and, curiously, a framed embroidered text which hung over my white wrought-iron bedhead and ominously warned 'Thou God See'st Me', a message that I never found conducive to peace of mind. Anyway, the valued certificate was relegated to the sideboard drawer where she had also stored my improved pig collection, that had been secreted away as evidence of my insanity. And Uncle Matt had to content himself with admiring this official tribute whenever he felt the need to have his efficiency confirmed, and whenever his hands were clean enough to delve into the drawer.

I had been sworn to secrecy by both aunt and uncle on the manifold facets of the Shoeman affair. I was forbidden to mention, on pain of dire penalties, the delicate matter of money changing hands; threatened with terrible consequences should I make the slightest reference outside the house to overcoats, mangles, bacon and, most especially, recently acquired sheep. I thought this reticence very strange considering Uncle Matt's assurance that Dyke Head was between tenants and its assets available to any opportunist, but, obedient as ever, I held my tongue and abided by that ruling.

Nevertheless, I had not been silenced altogether, and even the bare bones of the spy story went down well and kept my listeners spellbound. So with a certain amount of artistic license I related a gripping account of the terrifying moment when Shoeman, finally exposed as a Nazi, threatened to shoot us all, and had to be outwitted and persuaded to put his gun away. It was a riveting tale and I told it well, and was rewarded with rapt interest and admiration from all who heard it. They wanted to hear it again and again, and for once I basked in glory, the centre of attention.

'You poor little soul,' said Amy. 'And the size of you! Fancy threatening a wee mite like you with a gun! It's a wonder you weren't scared half to death, bless you. You brave, brave girl.' And Ida agreed, eyes shining in awe and wonder.

'I would've been,' she said. 'I'd have fainted clean away. You're so brave, Emma.'

The Milburns also heaped praise on my head, until, blanking out of my mind the memory of those weak moments when I had shamefully surrendered, I almost came to believe their good opinion.

'What a blessing you all stood up to him,' said Mrs Milburn. 'And in the right way too. Not batting an eyelid. You're lucky to be alive,

Emma. I've heard that the Nazis stop at nothing, not even at killing women and children. One false move, one wrong word, and it might have been curtains for you. You could all have been shot.'

And Irene, who made a habit of visiting Aidensmead cinema on Saturday nights to watch romantic films, also saw me as some kind of heroine.

'Ooooh! You're just like the girls in the French resistance, Emma. They stand up to the Nazis same as you. What happened to you could've turned your hair white. Their hair's always turning white. And you should have a medal like them.'

I accepted their congratulations and tributes with due modesty, and though honesty compelled me to admit that it was Aunt Dot, if anyone, who deserved the medal, my fame as a heroine spread. Even Mr Clout came to hear of it, condescending to pat my head and grunt his approval in passing, and more surprising still was Eddie Gormley's grudging glance of respect, which almost led me into reckless action.

'He'll think twice before taking you on again,' said Irene. 'Go on, Emma, have a go at him. Call him a rude name and see what happens. I bet he daren't do anything.'

I looked at the calculating slits that were Eddie's eyes, reminding me, but for the absence of albino flicker, of the furtive eyes of our former ferret. For an instant I was tempted to show off by taking the challenge, and then common sense prevailed. I decided that bravado has its place but also its limits, and rather than tackle the sly and pugnacious Gormley, I would sooner stir up a hornets' nest or even spill a pail of milk over Aunt Dot's newly washed kitchen floor.

'I've been brave enough for one week,' I answered nonchalantly.

Chapter 24

The Barrage Balloon

The beginning of June seemed to be a time when everyone caught up with things left undone, and while waiting for the grass to grow high and dry in the meadows, Uncle Matt caught up with odd jobs, some of them very odd the way he undertook them. I noticed that he did a great deal of digging for victory, digging peat for winter fuel, and digging endless ditches for no good reason that I could see. But his speciality was stone-walling, in both senses of the word, and whenever he wanted to escape from the house he found a section of wall urgently in need of repair. In fact, I suspected that he was not above pulling a few stones down, or at least helping them on their way, in order to strengthen his case, because the gap in a wall almost always coincided with some little job that Aunt Dot had lined up for him. Then he would sit for hours in the shelter of the crumbling wall, choosing stones and chipping away at them like a budding Michelangelo, carefully shaping his construction and whistling cheerfully as he reflected on what he might have been doing had he stayed at home.

Meanwhile Aunt Dot embarked upon an unnecessary splurge of spring cleaning, so his need to remove himself from the vicinity of the house increased, and in his absence she commandeered my help whenever I showed my face, as if she were extracting the last pennyworth of work from an overpaid employee. Unlike my uncle, I had no excuse, no wall to hide behind, so I worked long, tedious hours. But every spare minute I had I wrote to my mother, telling her of the recent danger I had found myself in, and remembering to stress how keen I was to begin piano lessons. I fancied myself as a subtle, not to say clever, correspondent, and awaited the results of my scheming with sweet anticipation.

At school Mr Clout also attempted to catch up, concentrating an entire academic term into a few gruelling weeks. Paradoxically, now that the weather had improved and the sun shone warmly, he decreed that we stop communing with nature and spend our lessons indoors. His vegetables were already expanding to prize-winning perfection, so he had time for the less important young things in his charge – his pupils. Certain aspects of our education had been sadly neglected, certain key subjects scarcely given an airing, and that deplorable fact suddenly struck home. He was like a man waking from a beautiful dream only to discover that he has fallen asleep at his job, done no work, and sighted his employer heading purposefully towards him. His educated whiskers bristled with urgency as he tried to pack the work of several months into one, force-feeding us facts that had to be digested and retained in time for the end-of-term examinations. One sunny morning when we expected to be out keeping the worms and beetles company, he settled us in the classroom instead, addressing us in accusing tones as if we were responsible for his negligence.

'There will be no Nature Study today, boys and girls. Whether you like it or not, our favourite subject must be put on hold. There is much work to be done in the core subjects – Maths and English. Really hard work. The importance of these subjects cannot be over-estimated, and I can't believe how far you've allowed yourselves to fall behind. Time is of the essence, and I want to see your shoulders to the wheel and your noses pressed firmly to the grindstone. It upsets me when no pupils from this school pass for Shiretown Grammar. But let past failures be a lesson to you – you dozy clods! The fault is yours and the answer is study. Study, study, study! For my part, I intend to crack the whip in more ways than one, and give you homework.'

This statement met with muffled groans and rebellious mutterings, which he heard only dimly, like the distant sound of waves breaking on rocks, and which, on account of his defective hearing and wishful thinking, he mistook for general approbation, and so he preened, taking a gratified pull at his moustache. There followed six gruelling weeks of fractions and decimals, of essays and comprehension, six weeks in which he attempted to catch up with the real syllabus instead of the dream syllabus he had drifted into, and to drag us along with him.

A sort of renaissance swept the school, a sudden burst of energetic learning, of which the occupants of the back row took a dim view, resenting being forced to think. And during this period of panic and stress, punishment was easily incurred. Mr Clout's slipper, which he used in at least ten different ways as a weapon, now resided permanently on his desk, and standing by for more serious offences lurked the dreaded cat-o'-nine-tails. Lessons, like life itself, became a dangerous lottery.

For me the new regime presented a few problems, but not of the academic sort. Although I worked at the same level as the older members of the class, I managed to do my homework quickly and easily, unless Uncle Matt insisted on helping me, when it could take much longer. But now that I had to carry more books back and forth, I needed a more substantial carrier bag, and after much pleading on my part, Aunt Dot unearthed a big old leather handbag which was anything but ideal. It was quite heavy in itself, and to my embarrassment looked every inch a handbag. So I suffered greatly from derisory remarks made by the boys, especially Eddie Gormley, who called me 'Old Mother Riley' or 'Charley's Aunt', until I was so fed up that one evening I blurted out my troubles to Uncle Matt.

'Oh, Emma, pet, why didn't you say so before?' he asked. 'The bag just needs a bit fettle, that's all. I'll soon fettle it. Don't you worry your little self about that.' And with that, he headed purposefully for the byre, tucking the handbag under his arm with all the style and nonchalance of a male model.

He returned some time later smirking in satisfaction at a problem solved, and I saw he had removed all the trimmings denoting handbag, replacing the handle with a long strap to sling over my shoulder. The fettled bag suited me much better, being less conspicuous and easier to carry, an important consideration just then, as I needed to move fast through the fields coming home from school. For while the grass grew long in the meadows I had to run the gauntlet of the cows confined to the pasture, as they favoured browsing in the middle of the field, selfishly obstructing the diagonal path. To my nervous eyes these massive beasts seemed to fill the pasture, leaving hardly any room for me, small as I was, to pass. Some lumbered towards me, grazing selectively, enormous as elephants. Some lay down, spreading themselves amply over their folded knees, fat and placid and apparently harmless, but inclined to scramble up unexpectedly, trampling everything underfoot. Others sprawled across the path itself, staring at me with large limpid eyes, and snorting warm steam from huge nostrils as I picked my way timidly past.

Unfortunately Beauty, now half grown and a fine, robust calf, always recognized me. In fact, I suspected that she waited for me, falling in behind and acting like an affectionate escort, licking me whenever she drew alongside. Tiny, my first pet calf, followed her, and then the rest of the herd, thinking it must be milking time, heaved to their feet and joined the curious procession. On the last stretch to the stile, as they surged forward gathering momentum I had to break into a sprint to keep ahead, and to a chorus of disappointed moos, I took the stile at a leap, landing breathlessly all in a heap in the front meadow.

As it happened, however, my problems travelling through the pasture were soon solved, but afterwards how I wished I had them back again, the solution being so much worse than the problem. Suddenly the war, which had recently made its mark on the valley with the presence of the Nazi spies, now for a time took over entirely, ruining lives, as well as my peace of mind, my valued friendships, and my childhood memories. One warm evening as I walked home as usual, pursued through the pasture as usual, dodging horns and tails and cowpats, I was so intent on finding my way safely through the maze of cows that I never once glanced at the sky. I felt no apprehension about impending disaster or any intimation of anything sinister approaching. Had I looked up I might have noticed an ominous speck against low clouds in the distance, but I kept my eyes fixed on the path, and once inside the kitchen, sat down happily beside Uncle Matt, who was busily sorting eggs. Blissfully unaware of the horror outside, we sorted the eggs into categories – first cracked or 'cake' eggs, then small, medium and large. We talked as we worked, listening to the clatter of teacups and smelling the familiar smell of burnt toast as Aunt Dot prepared our meal.

Then Uncle Matt pulled a disgruntled face and whispered, 'I bet it's boiled eggs again, Emma. Stone me! I thought I'd cured her of that habit, but no. She's in another boiled-egg rut. I keep tellin' her and tellin' her – a man needs somethin' to stick to his ribs after a hard day's work. He does, definitely. I'll tell you somethin', pet. I'm sick of the sight of pesky eggs.'

He made a sweeping gesture at the eggs cluttering the table and looked so put out that I squeezed his hand consolingly and whispered back, 'There's toast. That smells nice. I always think toast smells kind of comforting.'

'It smells *burnt*, Emma. She *will* let it burn. Everything she cooks is kizzened. She never learns,' he muttered. 'And anyway, a bit of fried bacon would smell nice, a fat spicy sausage would smell nice.

And my meanin' is, a juicy steak or a pork chop would smell even better.'

Despite his mutinous mood, he made no complaint as he sat at the table, and I guessed that before tackling the ticklish subject of the menu he was measuring the degree of Aunt Dot's temper, because if he tested it too far even the humble boiled eggs might be withdrawn, or hurled into the fire like cricket balls at the stumps. Even so, he was quieter than usual and less inclined to linger at the table, rising to his feet as soon as he had finished eating.

'I'll be off then,' he said lugubriously. 'If that's my tea I've had it, as they say,' adding provocatively as he reached the safety of the doorway, 'Anyways, that'll do till I get somethin' to eat. I've a couple of jobs to see to in the byre before milkin'.'

He winked at me, and I knew that the euphemism of 'a couple of jobs' covered his intention of restoring equanimity with a soothing cigarette, forbidden in the house and generally frowned upon as a waste of money. His first job would be to light the cigarette and the second to smoke it. I smiled back at him, a conspiratorial smile, and watched as he opened the door. But to my surprise he went no further. Aghast at what he saw outside, he slammed the door shut again, then cautiously, as if to confirm his worst fears, opened it a crack and peered out, swearing more vehemently than I had ever heard him swear, even when he shot his own cap off. After the second look he seemed to go to pieces, throwing the door wide open, gesturing wildly at the sky, and in his panic doing what he always did in a crisis – screaming for Aunt Dot, though at first he sounded like someone practising Morse code.

'D-D-D-Dot! D-D-Dot! C-come and look! Quick! Quick, Dot, quickly! Blow me! Now we're for it. Now we've had it! Hell's bells, Dot! Crikey Moses! What do we do?'

She dashed to the door and I to the window. The view from both was depressingly similar. The sky was obliterated by what at first looked like some gigantic dark-skinned prehistoric monster, but which our startled eyes eventually apprehended to be a huge menacing grey balloon, sinking slowly, and threatening to envelop the house. Its approach was accompanied by a loud, unfamiliar hissing sound which turned out to be a flexible steel cable trailing from it and swishing through the long grass of the front meadow. There were ropes dangling too, which must once have held the balloon fast, but now it floated freely at the whim of the wind.

'What is it? Are the Germans coming? Are we being invaded?' cried Aunt Dot.

'No, it's one of ours. It's a barrage balloon,' he said. 'Must've broke loose from its moorin's. Maybe from the coast. I've heard there's quite a lot at the coast.'

I had seen barrage balloons before, but not like this. They were always high in the sky looking small and harmless, not like this menacing monster so close to the ground. This balloon was bigger than the house, in terms of size measuring longer than house and byre together, and taller than the chimney pot. It was formidable.

'She's full of gas and comin' straight for us!' shouted Uncle Matt, as ever applying the female gender to anything unpleasant or problematic. 'If she settles on the roof, the heat from the chimney'll blow her up. And the house.'

Then the breeze lifted the balloon and wafted it lower down the field.

'Oh no! Damn it! She's landin' on the meadow, Dot. That'll flatten the hay. It'll ruin it!'

He and my aunt dithered in nervous agitation outside the door, helpless to prevent the frightful disaster, but moving restlessly to and fro as if activity of any kind might make a difference, might lessen the terrible risks. Then, with a sudden change of wind, the balloon lifted again, now veering in another direction, heading towards the top of the pasture.

'Oh, heck! That's worse! She's headed for the cows!' he yelled. 'She'll land on the cows! We've got to get them out of there, and fast. Everybody help! All hands on deck. Come on, Dot, and you, Emma. And Split! Here, boy, here!'

Without even pausing to close the door we ran, Uncle Matt taking the road and opening the gate, Aunt Dot and I tearing through the meadow, over the stile, and straight down the pasture behind the cows. I lost my fear of the big beasts in my eagerness to save them, and in my greater fear of the balloon. At least, I thought, I could save Beauty. And sure enough, the calves bounded after me, passing through the gate with the first cows to evacuate the field. The rest followed, and at a faster pace than usual. Normally at milking times the herd proceeded with solemn majesty, as slowly and ponderously as a procession of dignitaries. But now with all the rumpus going on around them – with everyone shooing them forward and Uncle Matt yelling 'Hauf, hauf!' at the top of his voice, and Split given his head for once and barking like a mad thing at their heels, and with the frantic shouting and whistling on all sides, and the eerie hiss of the approaching balloon – they scattered in panic. Their big eyes bulged as they loped along, lumpy and wobbling, charging in confusion up the humpy hillocky pasture and jamming the gateway in an undignified scramble, all trying to squeeze through at once. But finally they staggered onto the road, automatically turning left, bound for the byre. Uncle Matt chivvied them on, and when the last one had passed through the congested opening, Aunt Dot closed the gate, looping the chain over the hook in the post in an unconsciously symbolic gesture, as if she could lock out the threatening balloon that now loomed ever nearer.

We breathed again only when the cows appeared to be out of harm's way and we felt brave enough to look back. Just in time. There was a clattering sound as the cable hit the top of the wall, sending ridge stones flying into the pasture, the cable itself swinging around like a wild thing. Then its metal end suddenly caught in the gate, coiling over the wooden bars and locking fast, wedged between the gatepost and the wall. Now the balloon came gently to rest, settling along the path recently occupied by grazing cows, stretching through the middle of the pasture, long and grey and rubbery, like a beached whale.

A little later that evening, as soon as he had finished milking, Uncle Matt rushed down to Thorny Edge to phone the police at Aidensmead and Shiretown, and spent some time, as well as several begrudged coins at tuppence a go, trying to convince them that he had captured a barrage balloon in his pasture. He persisted, however, and the following morning, bright and early, two uniformed policemen called at the house, requesting a cup of tea, which Aunt Dot rather unwillingly supplied, allowing only one ginger biscuit each. They were inclined to linger, showing a marked reluctance to investigate the balloon, but she was keen to see action and gave them short shrift. So finally, having nothing better to do, they took a stroll across to the pasture. They paraded round and round the balloon, inspecting it from every angle while debating the appropriate course of action to take, and after a joint decision that it would be wise to wait for reinforcements, they drove off, not returning until after lunch.

The day had dawned hot and sunny, unusually so, as if for once the Lornhope wind, resting on its laurels, had taken the day off. It was a Saturday and the bush telegraph that operated in Sourhope, despite the shortage of bushes, spread word of the escaped balloon far and wide, so that as the day progressed, the pasture and its environs took on the popularity of Piccadilly Circus. The first to arrive, after the postman had made his delivery to Nettle Head and relayed the news, were Mr and Mrs Phillip and Miss Titchmarsh, all anxious to view the balloon before officialdom removed it. Despite the fine weather, Miss Titchmarsh carried her fat grey umbrella and had to be forcibly restrained from prodding the balloon with its metal spike, but Mrs Phillip cautiously stood well back. She wore a dress as blue as the summer sky, matching her eyes to perfection, and Uncle Matt adjusted his cap, fastened the top button of his shirt to hide an inch of vest, and dashed up the steps to escort the group to the pasture, nodding and gesturing as proudly as a tour guide showing off one of the great wonders of the world. At this stage he had not thought things through and was still taking a proprietorial interest in the barrage balloon. He hung over the gate, waving a nonchalant cigarette at his capture, indicating its finer points, apparently without fear or comprehension of the danger. And he helped me to climb the gate for a better view of this grey monster that sprawled along the pasture, tail towards us, its cotton surface quivering as if it were a live thing that might at any moment break free and fly away. Recklessly adopting his casual attitude, I jerked the gate with my hands and knees, jiggling it to and fro till both the gate chains and the balloon cable rattled.

'That's a big fish you've caught there, Uncle Matt,' I said jokingly. 'See how the skin shivers – like the thing's breathing.'

'It's a sinister-looking object,' was the verdict of Mrs Phillip and, true to form, Uncle Matt agreed wholeheartedly.

'It is. You're right. It's very sinister. Definitely. It worried me like the dickens when it came down, I can tell you, in case it blew the house up. And it took some doin', some real speedy action, bravin' life and limb to get the cattle out in time.'

'You mean – they were in that field, and you had to get to them before the balloon did?' asked Mrs Phillip admiringly.

'Oh yes. Well you have to, don't you? Times like that you don't think about yourself. You just get on with it. Imagine the disaster if the balloon had landed on my cows. I could have lost my whole herd.'

'Even so, you were very brave, Mr Wheatley,' insisted Miss Titchmarsh. 'What a terrible risk to have to take.'

'Brave indeed!' agreed Mrs Phillip, with such warmth that Uncle Matt blushed to the roots of what little hair he had left.

I noticed that he had tossed these modest statements casually into the air, as if he alone had saved the cows, as if he had forgotten the part played by Aunt Dot, not to mention me, not to mention Split, whose crazy barking did more than anything to ginger up the cows' footwork. But I understood why he failed to give credit where it was due, because I could tell that he was trying to impress Mrs Phillip, and I liked her too. She made herself very agreeable, admiring my dress and hair, and I felt almost as disappointed as Uncle Matt when her husband decided to take her home, especially as he had already disappointed me in other respects, his hair having reverted to a colour as grey as the balloon, with no trace of the daring purple I had heard so much about.

We were not, however, short of visitors. As the morning wore on a number of cars and carts brought other onlookers, all curious to see the famed balloon. In the main they crowded into an adjacent field, which conveniently rose to a mound at a higher level so that they could look down as in an amphitheatre on the activities in the pasture. There they relaxed and socialized in a holiday atmosphere, as if they were at an impromptu village fete, whereas in the pasture the faces of authority were serious and the atmosphere tense. Various officials commandeered the pasture, their helmets, trilbies, and tin hats dotted like mushrooms round the balloon, until it seemed to me as I counted the heads that there were more people in the pasture than there had previously been cows. The first two policemen had been joined by reinforcements, both uniformed and plain-clothed. Then came air-raid wardens, the Home Guard, and several unidentified gentlemen looking hot and bothered in navy blue suits. The policemen stationed themselves at intervals, keeping the crowd at bay and guarding the captive balloon, while other officials strutted round the pasture, exuding self-importance, and gathering together from time to time in animated discussion on how best to proceed. They took no account at all of Uncle Matt's helpful suggestions, but virtually ignored him, treating him like the rest of the bystanders, keeping him out of the pasture. His own pasture! So naturally his attitude to the balloon soon changed. No longer proprietorial towards it, he was now vociferously against it, and fiercely against all the hangers-on that it attracted.

Meanwhile, the crowd of spectators steadily increased. By midafternoon there were about sixty people peering over the wall, kept out of the pasture by the police. And fresh faces were constantly arriving. The scene became a noisy and animated one. Some adventurous youths leapt the wall for a closer look, enjoying the thrill of being chased back over it, while smaller boys in short trousers and girls in cotton frocks were held shoulder high for a better view of the spectacular balloon. Men in shirt sleeves stood arguing about how to tackle this curious inflated object, all of them seemingly masters of the art of balloon management, and women in summer dresses and Sunday-best white cardigans delved into capacious bags and brought out lemonade and sandwiches to pass round. So in the heat of the day nothing less than a festive air prevailed in the field, but in the pasture all was not well. No satisfactory agreement could be reached on procedure, and senior officials convened another meeting in a quiet corner, away from the sleeping giant, almost as if they were afraid that it might hear and attempt to defend itself. They decided by a majority vote (though there was some dissention from one awkward warden, known to be of independent thought) to hold fast and await developments, continuing to pursue their present policy of doing nothing, a policy which had so far been very successful.

Then one of the blue-suited brigade had the bright idea of sending for the real experts, whom he referred to as the 'ack-ack, beer-beer lads'. They would know what to do, he said. They knew everything there was to know about balloons. They would take the responsibility. That idea was warmly welcomed by those with no ideas at all, carried unanimously, and put into immediate effect. A police sergeant was despatched to make the necessary phone call, and the crowd rippled with excitement. But nothing happened. On and on we waited in the stifling heat, and the crowd began to lose interest in staring at the stationary balloon, which no longer entertained. 'It doesn't do anything,' fretful children whined. 'It's just boring. Why doesn't it *do* something?' So to relieve the monotony, spectators settled themselves in gossiping groups on the grass, little boys chasing each other over the grassy mound, little girls picking wild flowers, making starry chains from big moon daisies. And through it all, Uncle Matt complained, fulminating with helpless rage.

'They've none of them no business here nohow. That they haven't,' he said, confusing himself with double negatives. 'They need their heads examined and so do the police for lettin' them come. And in their droves as well! My meanin' is – it's not a game, is it? That balloon's as dangerous as a careless match in a gas works. Not to mention,' he added petulantly, 'the fact that it's my land they're tramplin' on and nobody but nobody's asked me.'

At that point we were standing on the upper verge of the road, well back from the pasture, with a clear view of the goings-on in both fields. Though I kept my feelings to myself, I neither shared nor understood my uncle's animosity to spectators, especially when I spotted two familiar faces, Amy and Ida, among the people near the wall at the broad end of the balloon. The day being fine, I had been allowed to wear my favourite green dress in order to visit Ida later that afternoon, and caught up as I now was in the convivial atmosphere, I was secretly eager to join the throng and mingle with the field party. But to my annoyance my determined uncle took firm hold of my shoulders from behind and held me back. Oh how I resented his restraining arm! And oh how wrong I was to doubt his judgement!

'No, Emma. You're not budgin' from here at present. On no account are you to move any nearer. Not with those irresponsible idiots ditherin' about down there. I'm serious now, Emma. Deadly serious. That there balloon's a deadly weapon. It's crammed full of gas, and that's an awful lot of gas by any reckonin'. Even more than there's comin' from the mouths of them so-called experts gassin' away in the pasture, and that's sayin' somethin'. I mean, they've spent hours gettin' nowhere, and wouldn't you think one of them – just one – would know what to do? For goodness' sakes! They're all supposed to be *trained* for emergencies!'

'But couldn't I just say hello to Ida? Please, Uncle Matt? I'll come straight back. I'll only be a minute.'

'No, Emma. Not yet. I want you to have a good look down the pasture there. See that warden with a red shirt and a face to match? The one that's faffin' and fidgetin' as if he had ants in his pants? Well, that's Tom Cattermole and I know him well. He's gettin' edgy, keen to get on with the job, and a man like that in a situation like this is a loose cannon. I can see he's itchin' to get stuck in, right or wrong. He's buzzin' about like a bluebottle round a fish head. And I tell you, girl, whatever he's got in mind, you can bet your bottom dollar it's a bad idea.'

Sure enough, at that point, after once more unsuccessfully demanding instant action from a cautious huddle of officials, Tom Cattermole broke away irritably. Loudly shouting his contempt for everyone to hear and throwing his hands in the air in a defiant gesture, he advanced upon the balloon with the apparent intention of discharging the gas. It was not an action that any right-thinking person would have advised, but the unthinking crowd cheered and applauded, their roaring encouragement acting on the misguided Tom Cattermole as a powerful spur. He became the hero of the hour, the only true man of action in the field. The crowd waved enthusiastically and chanted, 'Cat-ter-mole! Cat-ter-mole!', expecting something interesting to happen at last. And suddenly, for whatever reason – whether from misguided heroism, or from some hopeless sense of time passing to no purpose, or simply from reckless impatience – he flung his jacket and helmet aside and made a rapid desperate lunge at the balloon, leaping onto the tail and scrambling over it, clinging to the undulating surface as a limpet clings to rocks.

He looked very small and ineffectual in his red shirt, sprawled on the sixty-foot mass of streamlined cotton, a tragic-comic figure, as if a crab had scuttled onto a beached whale. A sudden hush fell on the crowd, at once impressed and appalled by his brave but foolhardy deed, as he held on tightly with one hand and with the other groped blindly at the balloon. It was an unforgettable sight, sadly one that has always lived with me. But in that shocking instant of seeing it, I found myself precipitated forward, rapidly propelled across the road and down behind the wall, as Uncle Matt, anticipating catastrophe, acted to save me, pushing my head low in the shelter of his protective shoulders.

For perhaps the split part of a second nothing happened. Then there was a tremendous explosion, deafening and terrible, and poor brave Tom Cattermole was no more. Indeed, there was barely enough left of him to bury, though bits of him mingling with bits of balloon were blown over three fields. Stunned and terrified, we stayed crouched, involuntarily shaking and sobbing, having no will to move. We only raised our frightened eyes when a deathly silence fell, and out of the silence we heard a nervous cough beside us and a voice asking very politely for Mr Wheatley. Only then did we straighten up and turn to see a young policeman with tears running down his blackened face and leaving crooked streaks upon it like rain on a dirty window pane. He addressed my uncle humbly, helmet in hand, not a trace of officialdom left.

'We wondered, sir, if we might bring the casualties to your house for the time being. My sergeant's gone to phone for doctors and ambulances, but they'll take time to travel up here. Would that be all right, sir, with you and your good wife?'

Uncle Matt gazed sorrowfully at him, then slapped him kindly on the shoulder and gave a deep sigh.

'Definitely,' he said. 'Bring them along, lad. Bring them all along. And tell me, what else can I do for you, bonny lad?' And the two turned reluctantly towards the pasture, where a grey cloud of smoke hung in the bright sky like the ghost of the ill-fated balloon.

In acute misery I started to follow them but was once again prevented.

'The pasture's no place for you, Emma. No place for a little girl. You go straight home, pet.'

'But I must look for Ida and Amy. Make sure they're all right.'

'You'll see them soon enough. Maybe too soon. Go home and warn your Aunt Dot that the casualties are comin'. Give her a hand if you can, pet. Helpin' her would be the most useful thing you could do right now.'

I did as bidden, and in a sad steady stream the casualties came. Some were only suffering from shock, some just slightly hurt but in need of tea and sympathy. Others had more serious wounds, complaining of metal embedded in arms or chests, presumably fragments blasted from the metal cable. As the worst cases were carried past on makeshift stretchers, I found that even a cursory glance at them was enough to upset me, but Aunt Dot never flinched. She coped amazingly well, accepting the situation into which circumstances had thrust her with praiseworthy calm and stoicism, revealing a side to her character that I had only glimpsed once, when she dealt so compassionately with Mad Mary. For more than an hour her clinically clean house became a busy hospital, with the worst cases laid carefully in the living room and the rest sitting wherever they could in the kitchen, while she presided like a matron over both wards, doing her best to make all comers comfortable.

Had I been wearing a hat that hot day I would have taken it off to her. Cometh the hour, cometh the man, they say, but in that hour it was the woman who came into her own. She produced spare cushions and pillows, and rugs and blankets, some from our own beds. She tore up a clean sheet for use as cloths and bandages, and organized the more able victims into helpers. She had a reassuring word for everyone, and made endless cups of hot sweet tea. I thought

I was witnessing some sort of metamorphosis whereby she had dramatically changed from a woman who would tolerate neither neighbours nor dirt in her home into a woman who welcomed comparative strangers and transcended petty considerations regarding dirt, and even blood and gore.

But I had other things to think about on that terrible day. With a sinking feeling in my stomach I saw Amy carried into the living room, and though she was still alive, someone had covered her face from view, indicating that her wounds were serious. Blood was seeping onto the cloth, and in fright and trepidation I sought out Ida, and was pleased to find her in the kitchen. But she just stared at me impassively with no sign of recognition. I held her teacup and tried to persuade her to drink, but she made no effort. I could see no sign of injury, but despite the warmth of the afternoon, she felt cold and clammy to the touch and looked very pale. Nor did she respond to anything I said, or contribute a word of her own, or seem aware of anything around her. When the doctor came he diagnosed severe shock, and she and Amy, together with four men with deep wounds from metal splinters, were whisked to Shiretown Hospital in the first ambulance to arrive. Other casualties followed, and less serious patients received treatment from the doctor before being escorted home by the police. Those who could cope for themselves gradually dispersed, and eventually we had the house to ourselves, and with a heavy heart I helped my aunt and uncle to clean up the mess.

'Just think, Emma,' said Uncle Matt thoughtfully, as we worked together, straightening and tidying, sweeping and washing, and scrubbing everything in sight, 'just yesterday at this time we had nothin' to bother us except maybe the disappointment of boiled eggs and burnt toast for tea. Sometimes you don't know when you're well off, and that's a fact. I just wish I could put the clock back. If only we could go back in time to stop the whole damned horror from happenin' – to stop Tom Cattermole before he took that fatal foolhardy leap onto the balloon.'

'Oh, if only we could,' I agreed fervently, thinking that I would have saved Amy and Ida. 'If only we could just go back to this morning, Uncle Matt. That would do.'

I grieved in many ways during the following weeks. It was my first experience of death in a fellow human being, and it shocked and horrified me that Tom Cattermole's life had been snuffed out in an instant, even as I watched. Yet not knowing him as a person, I grieved less for his violent death than I did for the living, for Amy's injuries, for Ida's distress, and if truth be told, for myself – for my loss of friends and my return to loneliness. I missed everything about my visits to Fern Cottage, and I willed my dear friends to get better, desperately wanting them home, wanting to have things as they were again and turn the clock back as Uncle Matt had wished. In the meantime I wrote to my mother, pouring out the gruesome details of the exploding balloon and its sad aftermath, but not forgetting to mention piano lessons, my passport home.

Then one Saturday when I was at a loose end, there being no Fern Cottage to visit, I wandered aimlessly through the kitchen and happened to glance at the calendar. For the first time, having had much on my mind of late, I noticed June's pig, the Large White Yorkshire. It was the biggest, fattest pig so far, so fat that it ballooned, giving me an idea. I quickly found my pencils and changed its colour to grey, increasing and defining its shape and adding a cable and ropes, so that it became a replica of the barrage balloon before the explosion. Events over the past year had been mirrored by my calendar pigs, and now I naïvely aimed to use the pigs to reverse them. By restoring the barrage balloon, albeit on paper, I thought to put the clock back after all, and effect a similar restoration to Amy and Ida. Perhaps then they would indeed get better.

Alas, how often in life it happens that we take casual farewells of close friends not knowing it is for the last time, and later, long to relive that crucial moment and alter the course of events. I never saw Ida again, though I heard she made a complete recovery, if recovery from such a traumatic experience can ever be complete. Nor did I see Amy for many years. Among other injuries, she lost an eye in the explosion, and spent time in hospital, convalesced with relatives, then sold Fern Cottage and moved away. When I met her by chance some thirty years later she seemed the same sweet person – kind, gentle and hospitable. She had never married, and I gathered that the young man who had managed to hang his hat up in her house had married someone else. Her eternal optimism remained, but I reflected sadly that there had been nothing wonderful round the corner for her after all. Only another, harder corner.

For a long time after the accident things were not the same in the valley. People came to terms with the traumatic event in their own individual ways, but for me the tragedy left a deep and lasting impression. From then on, when I walked to and from school or Thorny Edge I always took the longer route via the road. Needless to say, I could never bring myself to set foot in that pasture again.

Chapter 25
Music has Charms?

July came round again and I realized that almost a whole year had passed – a long, long year – since I had first arrived as a stranger in Sourhope. I still ached to be back home with my mother, but at least now in the summer sunshine I could appreciate some fleeting warmth and colour enlivening the valley. Wild flowers abounded everywhere, brightening the verges, encrusting the crevices of quarry and stack yard, and squeezing between the varied grasses of the hayfields. The hay grew so tall that it tickled my chin and swayed in graceful waves in the wind, giving off a wonderful aroma from fragrant herbs, from cicely to meadowsweet and thyme.

Surrounded as I was by such a variety of flowers, it seemed only natural to pick them, and since Aunt Dot could never tolerate flowers in the house, I gradually invented a solitary game in which I made them into playthings, creating small flower people – mainly female, as they wore dresses and were easier to stand upright. Using succulent stems, I stuck stalks through them on which to hang flowery sleeves, heads, skirts and so on, and took great pains in their creation, populating the yard with flower people and arranging them round the garden spring at night. In those first desolate days after Amy and Ida disappeared, somehow it was comforting to be surrounded by people, even if they were only made of flowers and as ephemeral as my other relationships seemed to be at that time. After a few days, however, I became aware of something that excited my mind to strange possibilities. Every morning I found that my creations had mysteriously vanished, leaving not a petal behind, and with the fertile imagination of childhood I drew the conclusion that they had in some magic way come to life and gone off together to a secret destination. Though I should have known better than to mention it, I put my theory to Aunt Dot, and she wrinkled her forehead and clicked her tongue as if I had finally taken total leave of my senses.

'Now I've heard everything!' she declared, giving me a penetrating stare suggesting that her mind was once again turning towards finding me a psychiatrist, so I tactfully apologized and beat a hasty retreat.

'Sorry Aunt Dot,' I said, although not sure what for, and then I tested the theory on Uncle Matt. His reaction was different but equally unhelpful. He gave his cap a thoughtful twirl and eyed me kindly, clearly deciding that under the circumstances of recent events he would humour my childish whims and fancies.

'Disappearin' flower people, eh? Well that's a queer one, Emma. We'll have to get the detectives in. Maybe call in Scotland Yard, eh? Inspector Hornleigh might solve the mystery. It's a beggar, isn't it? It sure is, pet. Uh-huh. So that's the latest, is it, girl? You've fallen out with the hens and now you're talkin' to flower people. My guess is you're missin' Ida's company. Of course you are. I dare bet on it.'

He sounded unconvinced by the disappearing-flower phenomenon, but undaunted, I carried on creating more and more people, searching the fields and banks for unusual plants, and becoming increasingly inventive in my handiwork. Then one morning when I crossed the forecourt earlier than usual, before Uncle Matt had 'mucked out' the byre, as he put it, I noticed my beautiful flower people littering the midden, where they had been thrown in a broken bedraggled heap and now lay wilted and dead. That was the end of that. I made no more. I instantly understood that Aunt Dot's metamorphosis into a kindly saviour on the day of the explosion had been short-lived and that every night after I went to bed she had collected and crushed the intrusive flower people. Like a ruthless dictator, like Hitler in fact, she had exterminated them en masse. As far as she was concerned, life had returned to normal, and she gave no thought to helping me through my loneliness and grief at yet another loss of friends.

So it was that in the absence of other diversions I threw myself into study. When not required to help with 'little jobs' around the house, I sat on the flat-topped garden wall enjoying the wafting smell of hay, with my head buried in books. I knew that studying was an unpopular pastime with my peers, and there was no denying that I was already unpopular in the senior class, but even so I was drawn to reading, an anti-social habit for which I soon found myself ostracized. Even the popularity derived from being known as someone who had been threatened by a Nazi gun was forgotten at such times as when the girls were one volunteer short of a rounders team, yet I still chose stubbornly to stay curled up with a book. Irene, on the other hand, liked being in the thick of things, and though we were still friends and I still ate lunch in her upside-down house, the rest of the time we went our separate ways.

Mr Clout's crash course in neglected subjects ended with lengthy examination papers in English, Maths, and of course Nature Study, and shorter papers in Geography and History. Sadly, through no fault of my own, I got off to a late start in the first exam, and was greeted by an upsetting tirade from Mr Clout before he even heard my excuse. He was inclined to shout first and seek explanations later, at the expense of raising his blood pressure and reducing me to a nervous wreck. As it happened, on that particular day Joe had made a special effort to arrive early and his lorry left Windlestraw in ample time, but when we reached High Nether, only a third of the way to school, we were held up waiting for Mrs Downley. We waited and waited without a sign of her, until finally Joe switched off the engine, leapt from the cab and hurried down the farm track. He returned with an ashen face despite his healthy tan.

'Mrs Downley's dead, Emma. Just down the lonnen there. She's lyin' on the track, poor soul, beside the churns she was pullin'. By heck, it's awful, Emma. It's terrible! That poor, poor woman! Ah'll have ter nip down to the farm and tell her old man, curse the selfish blighter. I'll be held up quite a bit, so ya'd better run. Sorry, lass. Ah'm really sorry.'

I felt terribly sad for Mrs Downley, whose death was the second in my life so soon after the first. At intervals during the day my thoughts returned to her, and I found it difficult to concentrate fully on exam papers. I kept wondering why her husband had treated her so cruelly, using her as a carthorse, and who would haul the milk up to the stand now, and why life in this part of the world seemed so much harsher than at home. Mrs Downley had been the first person I had seen in the valley, and now, in a comparatively short time, like several others, she was gone. But I had no time to dwell on the tragedy just then. I had to run non-stop the rest of the way to school, my short legs flying to beat the clock, covering the ground much faster than I could have managed a year ago, but still not fast enough. It took me about twenty minutes to settle down in class and breathe easily again, but despite this inauspicious start to the exams, on the whole I felt I had acquitted myself quite well. Nevertheless, I was surprised by the results, which Mr Clout announced with his usual pomposity, tweaking his unruly beard, dramatically flourishing his lists of marks, and frequently pausing for effect – a waste of theatrics,

I thought, since his pupils paid him scant attention. But I could sense the tension round me as my name cropped up more than once, and each time, or so it seemed to me, every syllable was deliberately drawn out in one lingering breath, like a mournful wail.

'First English, in which Em-maaah Em-maaah-son is top. Well done, girl! Very well done!' And later, 'History – Em-maaah Em-maaah-son top again. Good work!' And then 'Geography – Em-maaah Em-maaah-son once more. A remarkable achievement, young lady. Yes indeed!'

It came as a positive relief when Irene's brother beat me into second place for Maths, and when Irene achieved top place by a wide margin for Nature Study. Nevertheless, the overall percentage put me just ahead, at the top of the class, instantly increasing my unpopularity tenfold. And to make matters worse, Mr Clout, not as a rule given to praising pupils, extolled my virtues to the lofty ceiling, rubbing all other noses in my success.

'Em-maaah Em-maaah-son has beaten you all and she's only nine! If she puts a little more effort into Nature Study she'll go far. She has immense potential for such a small person, and will in the fullness of time undoubtedly pass for the grammar school. She's already showing you the way, and I suggest you all buck up your ideas and try to be more like her. Yes, indeed! Emulate Em-maaah. That's my advice.'

Disaster! My popularity, though never high on the social scale, now plummeted to the depths. I could sense the hostility like an extra presence in the class. The more he praised me the more it grew, and the more helpless I felt. Not for the first time, I turned to Miss Speedwell, finding sanctuary in her room at playtimes. I longed for the last day of term when I would no longer have to endure Mr Clout's mortifying praise and the growing resentment of the class, which I felt as keenly as a tongue-lashing from Aunt Dot, or as the bitter wind in the school cabbage patch, situated as it was well away from the wall. My only consolation was the absence of Eddie Gormley and his gang, who, now that the hay season had started in earnest, truanted on and off throughout July in order to help in the fields. They contrived to miss the exams, but then to my horror turned up again, large as life, on the last day of term. They were all officially leaving school, and all were in rumbustious high spirits, spending the morning irritating Mr Clout, trying his limited patience, until by lunchtime they were all under threat of punishment by the cat-o'-nine-tails.

'I dislike thrashing pupils on the last day of term,' he said with uncharacteristic benevolence, while at the same time flicking *The Cat* with a cautionary cracking sound against his desk. 'Particularly on the last day of a school career, however misspent and wasted that career has been. But I shan't hesitate to do so if any one of you puts a foot wrong this afternoon. Are you quite clear on that point, Gormley, you numskull?'

Gormley nodded insolently, completely unabashed, and as we all surged out of the room I suddenly felt a hand round my neck and was repulsed by his foul breath on my cheek as he whispered, 'Ah've come back just fer you, Sourpuss. Come ta get ya at last.'

Taken by surprise, I backed against Miss Speedwell's door, cowering from his malicious grimacing face as it leered closely into mine.

'Well, little bitch. I see you're still a sickening little snob,' he hissed, 'and I hear you're a sickening little swot as well.'

It was the last straw, and tired of eating humble pie, tired of being the butt of everyone's insults, I surprised myself by answering back, inspiration coming from copying his style. 'I see you've still got disgusting yellow teeth, and I hear you're a stupid dunce as well,' I retaliated, and he recoiled, his face livid, and raised his fist, plainly rattled that I had dared to stand up to him.

Quickly I turned the door handle and slipped inside the classroom. Irene knew where to collect me when the coast was clear, but I spent an anxious lunch hour worrying. I was sure that Gormley would retaliate, that he would seek me out for further torment, and my mind raced frantically with futile plans. I had almost decided to play truant myself, but as I secretly intended to quit school that day for ever, I needed to clear my possessions from my desk. In the event, however, just as we were returning for the afternoon session, Gormley took matters into his own hands.

Intent on mischief, he and Fletcher climbed the school wall to reach the tower, and rang the bell ten minutes early. Then they dropped back into the yard, innocently resuming a game of football. But Mr Clout had seen Gormley's dive from the wall, and in a flash he dashed into the yard, grabbed him by the scruff of the neck, and shook him like a dusty rug. Interested spectators gathered round, some cheering, some jeering, for which side nobody knew. Then Gormley, apparently no longer regarding himself as a pupil or subject to school rules, dared to defy the headmaster. He wriggled deftly out of Clout's fierce grasp, leaving him flapping his tweeds helplessly, then leapt the wall and fled, running across the fields to freedom, and thankfully out of my life. I gave a heartfelt sigh of relief as he disappeared, and could now concentrate on more agreeable farewells on this day that I assumed would be my last at the school. First I approached Miss Speedwell to thank her for her many kindnesses, without which my year at St Simon's would have been intolerable, and she seemed touched and pleased, but at the same time perplexed.

'*Leaving*, Emma? Are you absolutely sure, dear? Mr Clout never mentioned it. Are you quite positive? There's still a war on, you know.'

A thought struck me: people always mentioned the war in relation to my going home.

'Am I a prisoner of war, miss? I know they put them on farms.'

'No, of course not, Emma. What an odd idea! You poor girl. You must feel very much a stranger here, very unwelcome to think like that.'

'Well anyway, I'll be starting piano lessons soon,' I said, as if that explained everything, and she smiled and pressed my hand.

'That'll be nice, Emma. I hope you do. I hope things turn out just as you wish. Though I'll miss you. Very much. You're a great little girl, and don't let anyone persuade you otherwise. And if by any chance you do come back in September, I'll be delighted to see you again.'

I parted on pleasant terms with my good friend Irene too. I walked home with her part of the way, promising to meet up during the holidays, though I fully expected soon to be gone from Sourhope. And nowadays, since reaching the great age of eleven, Irene had been less keen on my company, tending to regard me as a mere child and herself as almost grown up. As I doubled back, passing the school once more, with my homely satchel slung over my shoulder, I paused for a moment at the wrought-iron gates, recalling my first day there. I gazed at the silent bell tower and the empty yard, just as they had been that very first morning when I felt so jittery and Uncle Matt, just as jittery, had taken me in – in more ways than one.

It all seemed a very long time ago, something that had happened to a different person. I had changed a great deal in that difficult year, becoming independent beyond my years, and graduating in some sort of unseemly haste from a callow infant to a top senior. I felt little wiser but a lot older, as if, like the snakes in the bracken, I had shed several skins and grown new ones to present to the world. With a deep sigh and without looking back I moved on up the road, hoping to be leaving St Simon's for the last time, yet inexplicably sad, not for leaving the school I hated, but for saying goodbye to the child I had been when first delivered to its gates.

When I got home I put my school report on the sideboard, but no one showed any interest. It was a simple missive, a folded paper in a long brown envelope and, when I came to think of it later, just the sort of official-looking document that Uncle Matt shied away from, lest it turned out to be a time-wasting, pencil-licking, form-filling exercise, or even worse, a bill requiring urgent payment. I noticed that he hurried past it, eyes averted; no doubt hoping it would go away. And it did, because by the next morning Aunt Dot had tidied it into a drawer, the drawer that held Uncle Matt's much-thumbed certificate of achievement in milk production. And there the matter might have rested. I knew, however, that Uncle Matt was the one person to derive pleasure from my position in class, and that afternoon, while helping him in the hay, I told him the good news. With Sandy's reluctant cooperation he had managed to cut and turn Todd Tingate's meadow, and now we worked together. With me using a small rake, cut down to size, and him a big fork, we shaped the hay into small kyles.

'By it's grand hay. It is, definitely. Good and dry and sweet,' he said. 'I reckon we could pike this lot tomorrow. What do you think, Emma?' Unable to contain myself any longer, I answered on a different subject, straight to the point without preamble.

'I was top of the class in the exams, Uncle Matt.'

He smiled broadly, almost losing the straw between his teeth that he had been chewing for an hour or more, and gave me a knowing wink.

'Were you now, pet? Top again, eh? Well I'll be blowed! But it's only what I expected, like. After all, you were top at Christmas and you're that bit older now.'

'Yes, but that was just the infant class, Uncle Matt. This time it's the seniors.'

'You don't mean – you're top of the big class?'

'Yes.'

'Are you sure, Emma? I mean ter say – there's big lads in that class,' he pointed out, as usual automatically assuming male superiority. 'Lads of thirteen and fourteen.'

'I know, Uncle Matt. And big girls too,' I answered wryly.

'And you're top of all them?'

'Yes.'

He scratched his scanty whiskers pensively. Then the penny dropped. His blue eyes widened. The straw fell unheeded from his mouth and the hay from his fork.

'But if you're top of that lot, Emma, you're top of the school. My meanin' is – the whole blinkin' school!'

'I suppose so,' I agreed, smiling bashfully.

He stared at me as if Einstein had fallen from the sky and assumed a small girl's form.

'By heck! I mean to say, by heck, Emma! By, but you're a grand scholar. That you are. I knew you were clever, like, but not that clever. I reckon you must be some kind of genius!'

I basked in his praise, desperate to be appreciated by someone for something – anything. But in all fairness, I had to put him right.

'I'm no genius, Uncle Matt. It wouldn't have happened in a normal school. You see, I work hard and some of the others aren't interested, and they have to do farm work early in the morning and late at night. And our ages are all mixed up. And some of the older pupils didn't even take the exams. They just can't wait to leave, so I'd probably be quite ordinary in an ordinary school.'

'Well, I dunno, Emma. I hear what you say, but I don't think you'd ever be ordinary. And say what you like, Emma, you're top of the school. That's somethin', isn't it? That sure is somethin'!'

He stood, work suspended, leaning on his fork, the big prongs stuck fast in the ground and his chin rubbing thoughtfully over the top of the rounded handle as he continued to stare, as if staring hard enough would help him understand – give him X-ray eyes enabling him to see my brain working, like the busy mechanism of a skeleton clock.

'Anyway, Uncle Matt,' I said, embarrassed by such a penetrating stare, 'I left my school report on the sideboard if you want to read it. Though I think Aunt Dot tidied it into the drawer.'

'Ah,' he said, relieved. 'Is that what it was? You've sure put my mind at rest. I thought it looked kinda like a bill, maybe them income tax blighters after my hard-earned money again. And had it been a bill, Emma, I'd want nothin' to do with it just at present. But if it's your school report now – why then I'll definitely have a read of it. Maybe over a cup of tea, to enjoy it to the full, like. Well, Emma, you clever girl! You fair take my breath away. You definitely do!'

'Really, Uncle Matt, it's not me. It's just such a strange school.' But he continued to regard me as some kind of miracle of scholastic achievement, and from time to time I caught him shaking his head and muttering to himself incredulously.

'Top of the school, eh? Only top of the whole blinkin' school! What a girl! Well, I'll be a monkey's uncle!'

He was fond of that expression, and I often wondered where it left me, his niece. Was I the monkey? But I did feel gratified by his pleasure in my achievement, and now I knew full well the strength of his pride in me, like that of father for daughter. For a moment I suffered pangs of guilt thinking of my carefully laid plans to leave him in the lurch, but sorry as I was, and fond of him as I had become, nothing could shake my resolve to go home, to be with my mother. And just as Uncle Matt's affection could momentarily weaken that resolve, so Aunt Dot's apparent indifference strengthened it. She gave every appearance of being less than impressed by my school report, which she had read in private and without comment until pressed for a reaction by my excited uncle.

'Did you know, Dot, that our Emma's top of the school?'

'Yes, I've read the report. It's not bad,' she replied in matter-of-fact tones.

'Not bad? It's miraculous! It's bloomin' incredible at her age! The whole school, you know. Big lads an' all.'

'We-ll – yes,' she said with the air of one conceding a minor point. 'But what a pity she was only second in Maths. Such an important subject! And she isn't top in Nature Study either, despite forever cluttering the place up with flowers. So she could have done better. But there we are. As I say, she's done quite well, and nobody's good at everything. Very few of us anyway.'

'Crikey, Dot! I don't believe I'm hearin' this. She's still top, isn't she? So in my book she's a very clever girl.'

'Clever is as clever does,' answered Aunt Dot primly. 'Clever words butter no parsnips. *Clever* doesn't wash those dishes, or fill those buckets with water, or scrub the kitchen floor. In my experience, *clever* can be too clever for its own good.'

She seemed determined to resist any temptation to praise me, and though Uncle Matt went on to read my school report over and over again, just as he did his milk production certificate, maybe a hundred times, my aunt never referred to it again. Meanwhile, I waited with mounting but suppressed excitement for my mother's arrival, spending my time methodically taking my farewells of the farm, saying goodbye to each group of animals in turn. But once again I ended up disillusioned. All the attention I had lavished on the ungrateful creatures was clearly only returned by cupboard love. The pigs grunted back briefly and then buried their snouts in potato peelings; the hens pecked round my feet as impassively as ever, squawking till I moved out of their way; and Sandy, once he detected a lack of sugar lumps in my hand, soon showed me a clean pair of heels. It was the same story with the sheep and goats and cows, all apparently indifferent as to whether I stayed or went – all, that is, except Beauty, who licked me enough to save me washing my arms and neck for months ahead.

Then finally I said goodbye to the calendar pigs in the kitchen, in particular to the current portrait for July, which brought to a close the year of my stay at Windlestraw. July's pig was unusually petite, a slow-growing variety called the Welsh, who looked as lean and business-like as a pig can look, giving the impression of a porker that is going places. She reminded me in her slight build of the first calendar pig I had treated with my pencils to a facelift – the impeccable Tamworth, a pig so dainty and well-behaved that I had endowed her with some of my own characteristics. I did so again now with Miss July, completing the year's cycle from August to July, and titivating this young pig with golden hair and green eyes. Then I slotted an umbrella through her curly tail, hung a suitcase round her neck, and drew a signpost either side indicating the direction of her journey. Behind her I drew a leaning striped pole labelled Thorny Edge, and in front an attractive green post with a sign for Summer Hill, my real home. Everything was now in place for my departure.

And suddenly my mother was there, bringing the boys with her, and she was all smiles, as if she had planned a secret to please me. I thought I knew the secret. I thought I had planned it myself. So I was in no hurry to hear it. I could savour the moment, though the boys were eager to spill the beans. They had grown taller, and seemed to have grown in common sense too, but in my view there was still room for improvement. I was, however, pleased that they appeared to have accepted my homecoming, and to all intents and purposes were content with it.

'There'll be a surprise for you when we go home,' said Neal. 'Wouldn't you like to know what it is?'

'No thank you,' I replied, knowing the surprise, knowing I was going with them.

'Bet you would really.'

'No.'

'I'll tell you if you like,' said David.

'No, it won't be a surprise if you do, will it? And anyway, I know it already.'

'You can't. It's impossible.'

'Well, we'll see.'

They had arranged to stay for a fortnight, and there followed twelve happy days of working and playing in the hay-scented air, balmy days of picnicking in the sun and talking till late in the lamplight. As the end of the visit drew near I could scarcely contain my excitement. The prospect of going home at last felt like a wonderful dream come true, like a dozen Christmas Eves rolled into one. Then one afternoon a large van pulled up outside and suddenly everyone else became excited too, as if, in some mysterious way, the sight of the van had transmitted my excitement to the whole household. They all rushed outside, noisily laughing and joking, leaving me at a loss.

'It's here!' shouted David. 'The van's here!' And he led the way to the yard, where everyone stood in boisterous anticipation, commenting on the activity round the van.

'What is it, Mum? What's going on?' I asked, anxious to be part of the happy scene.

'It's your surprise, Emma,' she said, giving me a hug, and I began to experience my first twinge of fear that fortnight.

Surely, I thought, I had not overlooked anything? Were there now to be two surprises? Or – a bitter pill to swallow – was this the wrong surprise? After all, it needed no large van to take my small luggage. But as I watched nervously, apprehensively, two burly men with rolled-up sleeves opened the back of the van and got down to business. With a loud clatter they lowered a wooden ramp to the road, and with much grunting and grumbling and shouting of directions, brought out a big, heavy object, hidden under a shiny red dust sheet and held underneath by a substantial sling. They struggled with it to the road and, once clear of the van, laid their cumbersome burden to rest and shouted to Uncle Matt, who was stationed at the top of the steps, exuding an air of importance.

'Right, mate, where do you want it?'

'Down here. Right this way,' said Uncle Matt, indicating with his thumb the steep stone steps leading to the yard. The carriers peered suspiciously over the wall.

'No way! Not on your nelly, mate!' said the nearest, spitting contemptuously with practised accuracy into the targeted rockery.

'No way!' repeated the second. 'Never in a million years!' And without another word, but with one accord, they picked up the sling and began to retreat, returning their delivery back to the van.

Everyone groaned, and Uncle Matt hurried forward, waving a conciliatory hand and speaking forcefully. 'It's all right, man. Come on lads. Don't be daft. You can't take the thing away now. Don't worry. I'll see you all right. I'll see you down the steps. I'll give you a hand an' that. Many hands make light work. Definitely.'

They lowered the bulky load, looking doubtfully at each other, and shrugged, but after further pressing offers of help they picked up the sling and proceeded, staggering at times, with knees sagging, and resting every few seconds to wipe perspiration from their faces onto their shirt sleeves. Finally they turned, manoeuvring downwards, the rear carrier carefully tilting the bulky load, the front carrier feeling his way backwards with tentative feet. Now and then their hidden burden wheezed painfully or made a jangling noise resembling the twanging of harp strings, as it slowly descended under its fluttering gaudy cover, moving jerkily from side to side, like a festive Chinese dragon. I noticed that Uncle Matt, who made a great show of taking some of the weight, grunted enough for three but contributed little, mainly acting as a sort of buffer between load and wall.

'I'll guide you down. No bother!' he said airily. 'Come on lads. Left a bit. Now easy does it. Keep it movin'. Steady as you go.' At this, the rear carrier paused and turned aside to spit at the inoffensive violas.

'Some people are put on this earth to be blinking useless,' he muttered bitterly. 'But they've still got plenty to say for themselves.' His colleague added, 'That's right, plenty. That's dead right,' and they both glowered resentfully at my unperturbed uncle.

Then suddenly, as the load was tipped at full tilt, the covering slipped away, shimmering to the ground like a red silk robe, and amid general cries of acclaim, the much-heralded surprise was revealed to my incredulous and horror-stricken gaze. Indeed, I stared at it with such abhorrence and loathing that it might have been another barrage balloon, or a live dinosaur, or some other terrifying monster. But it was in fact only a piano – large, made of mahogany, and so old-fashioned that it had a pair of swaying candle-holders attached to the front like antlers. In a slow and sinister progression, or so it seemed to me, this mahogany monster crawled threateningly to where I stood, its scrolling brass candle-holders swivelling to and fro, while I remained motionless, rooted to the spot. I could hardly believe my eyes, and was consumed with hatred for the ugly monstrosity. It was only a piano, but to me it symbolized ultimate rejection. Not for a moment had I considered the possibility that a piano would be brought all the way to Sourhope to defeat my escape plans, fastening me there even more securely, like an extra padlock on a prison door. Nor had it occurred to me that my mother would go to such lengths to keep us apart, and I felt stunned, keenly aware of the difference in the way she treated my brothers and myself. My head pounded and I ached with hurt and humiliation. My doom was sealed, I thought. I was condemned to remain in Sourhope, abandoned by my family for ever.

I gazed in abject misery as the piano passed me by, its protruding candle-holders leaning invitingly towards me as if to grasp my hands and gather me in. Then it moved on, candle antlers drooping like a dead deer as it proceeded through the kitchen and turned into the living room. Everyone followed in a joyful cavalcade. Everyone except me. But no one even noticed my absence. As if in a dream, I heard Aunt Dot promising the carriers a nice cup of tea, and the boys arguing about who would be first to show off his prowess on the piano, but nothing could have persuaded me to go inside the house in the company of that frightful mahogany interloper. I could face no one. I had to get away, far away from unfeeling people and the very sight of that hateful, fateful piano. But only when the bizarre procession had disappeared did I stir into action. Then I flew up the steps and ran and ran, my short legs flying as if the hounds of hell were after me, heedless of where I ran or why. By the time the piano had been placed in position and the boys had each hammered out a tune on the keyboard, precluding any possibility of conversation for the assembled adults, I was long gone and out of sight.

I should have run to Thorny Edge, to the comfort and safety of friends, but I had gone beyond logical reasoning, and was not consciously running anywhere, but rather was instinctively running away. I headed for the moors instead, past all the familiar places and on into the unknown – past Dyke Head high above me with its vacant windows staring at the sun, past Todd Tingate's, scattering grazing goats in my wake, and past Moss House, startling sheep in my path into frantic pirouettes. I paused only to catch my breath and then went on running – past Brackenfield, sending hens skittering from the track, and past Nettle Head, where haymakers waved from the meadow. Then on and on over the fell, into the wilderness that was Lornhope.

Despite the warmth of the afternoon in the valley, once I reached the fell the Lornhope wind came out to play, teasing and tormenting like a persistent bully. It blew sharply cold, tearing at my thin summer dress and whipping my hair over my eyes till I could scarcely see, and soon I lost all sense of distance and direction. I disturbed rabbits, who raced against me, and grouse whirred indignantly into the air, screaming their inhospitable cry – 'Go bak! Go bak! Bak, bak, bak!' – a warning I should have heeded but hardly heard. Nor did I stop, but went on running as if competing in a marathon race that I had to win at any price, forcing myself relentlessly onward. I soon lost sight of the tracks and ploughed through the heather, scratching my bare legs and causing thin trickles of blood to bleed into my white socks, but unaware of anything except the need for flight.

Then at last I did stop, suddenly and abruptly, and only just in time. Some sixth sense caused me to look down and I found myself poised on the very edge of the dam, teetering so perilously close that I could see the sheer sides below me shelving steeply into the deep water. Startled, I stepped back. Once in there, with the waters closing over my head, I would never be seen again. Yet somehow I seemed to be drawn magnetically towards the edge, and I wondered – if I drowned, would anyone care? Should I let myself slide into the water, making an end to all my troubles? I had lost all hope and if my mother no longer loved me I felt I would rather die. Then I remembered Uncle Matt's affection, his fatherly pride in all my small successes. At least he would care, I thought, drawing back a little. Then, feeling suddenly tired and defeated, I sank to the ground, slumping wearily to rest on a mossy mound.

Feathered heads popped up inquisitively from the heather, turned to inspect me, then lost interest and went about their business. But I noticed a huge bird soaring overhead, sailing in slow, widening circles, scanning the skyline for supper. It looked big enough to snatch me and carry me off, like the giant bird in the story of Sinbad the Sailor that carried him out of the desolate valley. I curled into a ball in case it spotted me, my eyes tightly shut and my hands clinging desperately to the woody stalks of the heather. Then, ominously, I heard the flap of wings as the big bird swooped, and in sudden fear I squinted skywards. The bird held a writhing creature in its powerful talons and was flying away with it, into the blue and out of sight.

I sighed in relief, sorry for the victim but glad to have escaped, and in that telling moment I knew that though it seemed I had little to live for, I had no wish to die. Yet in the stillness that followed I felt a sense of total isolation, marooned on that desolate moor with no idea of what to do or where to go. I began to cry, still curled in a ball, now cold and shivery, sobbing bitterly into the heather. And after a while, exhausted by exertion and emotion, I fell into a deep sleep.

I have no idea how long I slept, but was woken by the soothing movement of a hand stroking my hair. It was a pleasant sensation, so much so that at first I wondered if I were still asleep and dreaming. Had it all been a dream? The piano? My flight? The bird of prey? I lay peacefully, imagining that it was my mother stroking my hair, as she used to often in the evenings in just that gentle way. I felt warm now, as if I had been covered with a woollen blanket, or an overcoat perhaps. But presently I became aware of a strong smell, vaguely redolent of something or someone that had recently made a big impression on me.

And then a low rasping voice began singing a familiar song, 'Goodnight Sweetheart', in a faltering tuneless croak above my head. I had often listened to that song on the wireless at home before the war, played as a slow, sweet dance tune, but now it was barely recognizable, sounding so strangely tortured that it verged on the macabre. It seemed that the singer was suffering from a sore throat, so strained were her vocal chords, and also from a poor memory because she remembered very few of the words, resorting to filling in the gaps with extra 'Goodnights', to which she gave a curiously sinister emphasis.

Then all at once a twinge of alarm seized me. No longer soothed by the stroking, I tried to focus my brain on the memory of that distinctive voice, that peculiar smell, tried to recall a scene that I suspected I would rather forget. Little by little, and almost against my will, my thoughts returned to dark winter evenings, to a ghoulish presence in the kitchen doorway and glaring eyes watching me like a predatory animal. And then I knew with clear certainty who was holding me, who was stroking my hair, and croaking her weird strangled song. So devastating was the sudden realization that I lay rigid, not daring to move, though I desperately wanted to run, to be magically transported a million miles away. Perhaps, I thought, I would have been better off with the bird of prey, and for a little while I stayed stiff and motionless, conscious, despite the warm covering, of a distinct chill down my spine, too frightened to look up and have my worst fears confirmed.

The stroking and croaking continued, the overpowering smell suffocated my senses, and finally, with a supreme effort, I sat up and forced myself to turn, ever so slowly, ever so reluctantly, and raise my head. Terrified, I looked through wild black hair into the smiling face and glaring eyes of Mad Mary. I stared in horror, unable to breathe. Then, for the first time in my life, I lost consciousness, falling forward in a dead faint and into Mad Mary's lap.

Chapter 26

The Posse

What happened next I learnt later, listening to the story again and again, different versions from different people, and never tiring of hearing it, whichever version it was. Indeed, all the storytellers tired of the tale long before I did.

It seemed that after I ran away and the piano responsible for my sudden departure was installed in the position earmarked for it, Aunt Dot gradually came to the conclusion that it looked all wrong against that particular wall. For some time, however, having fastened her mind firmly on placing it there, she characteristically refused to admit defeat. So, under her precise direction, the carriers shunted the heavy piano back and forth, an inch here, half an inch there, becoming hot and bothered in the process and rapidly losing patience with her perfectionist demands.

'To the right a fraction. No, that's too far. Yes, yes, back a bit. Left a touch. No, too much. What a pity you couldn't get it right the first time.'

By then the carriers, now known to the assembled company as Bert and Fred, were suffering on several counts, as much from exasperation as from perspiration, and Bert, the burlier and more senior of the two, felt compelled to speak up and protest, flicking his striped blue braces with his thumbs as he stuck out both chest and chin belligerently.

'Do ya think, missus,' he asked through clenched teeth, 'do ya think ya could make yer mind up once and fer all, before we collapse in a pool of grease?'

'Yeah, that's right. Collapse in grease,' repeated Fred.

'Won't be long now,' Aunt Dot assured them. 'Then I'll make us all a nice cup of tea. Believe me, I'm ready for one. Now, just move it a teeny bit this way, and that'll be it, I think. Yes, that's as right as it'll ever be. But there's only one other thing. It needs to go closer to the wall. Yes, that's better. Although – no! Oh, dear me, no! Sorry,

but it still looks all wrong. I'm afraid that wall won't do for it. Won't do at all. What a pity you had to put it there. You might have known. After all, you're used to placing pianos.'

At this juncture, Uncle Matt, who had been hanging around in the hope of the promised cup of tea, it being sticky, thirsty weather, sensed trouble ahead, and fearing a major piano move which might involve his physical assistance, decided to make a swift exit.

'Er – um – things to attend to in the byre,' he muttered to no one in particular, and did his famous vanishing act, slipping away to enjoy a peaceful cigarette.

After he left the scene the piano moved around quite a lot more, a nerve-racking procedure entailing heated discussion and strenuous manoeuvring, which he told me later he was very glad to have missed. At length, however, the heavy instrument found its way to an acceptable position, which, by some strange perversity, and to the chagrin of the carriers, turned out to be the very same spot on the very same wall where it had originally come to a standstill. There it was once again positioned and repositioned to Aunt Dot's satisfaction and finally was allowed to rest and settle. But not for long, because the boys, who could hardly wait to pounce on it, each took a turn to play a much-practised tune and, misinterpreting my aunt's polite but lukewarm response as a request for an encore, began to squabble for the monopoly of the keyboard.

By this time the carriers were in rather a truculent mood, and to make amends for their extra trouble Aunt Dot busied herself, with my mother's help, in providing tea, ginger biscuits and drop scones baked on a black griddle over the open fire. The scones were served warm and lightly spread with margarine, which she reserved especially for visitors, and the carriers, now settled comfortably at the table, tucked in appreciatively, noisily smacking their lips. They reasoned that though the topping might only be margarine and not to their refined taste, a fresh scone, even if sprinkled with unidentified black specks, some as big as currants, was a fresh scone, a bit of a treat, and the more that came their way, the merrier.

Everyone being thus occupied with their own affairs, my absence from the social scene was only noticed by my mother, and she gradually became uneasy. So as soon as she could, she sneaked away to look for me, first in the house and then in the outbuildings. On reaching the small byre, she came upon Uncle Matt just inside the door, and broke in on his meditations as he sat cross-legged on a milking stool in a cloud of smoke, looking like a disgruntled gnome. As she approached, however, he demonstrated a splendid reflex action, instantly springing to his feet, quivering with guilt, and then heaving a sigh of relief as he recognized her and relaxed again.

'Oh, it's just you, Ellie. Thank goodness for that! What a shock you gave me. Thought it was Dot at first. I'm snatching a few minutes of peace before I go back to the house.'

'Sorry to disturb you, Matt,' she said sympathetically. 'It's Emma I'm looking for. I thought she might be with you. She's simply disappeared into thin air. You haven't seen her, have you?'

He shook his head, looking puzzled but not yet unduly concerned.

'No, Ellie. Not since the piano arrived. She was definitely in the yard then, so she can't be far. She must be about somewhere. I mean to say, she knows her way around. Emma never gets lost. But I'll help you look, and don't worry, Ellie. My bet is that we'll find her in a jiffy.'

So together they searched the premises, including the wash-house and hayloft, but inexplicably drew a blank. Next Uncle Matt dashed into the house and returned with a pair of binoculars, with which he scanned the countryside for any sign of a small girl. But in vain. Then they both began again, searching all the places they had already thoroughly searched. Meanwhile, the boys continued competing for the piano, both performing at once but playing different tunes, causing discord in more ways than one, because the carriers resented the instrument being played at all.

'We're paid ta deliver pianas, not listen ta them,' pointed out Bert more than once, adding, 'especially when played by incompetent amateurs at close quarters.'

'Very close quarters, and at teatime an' all,' agreed Fred.

Muttering to each other in rebellious undertones, they agreed that enough was enough, and they had already fulfilled their contract beyond the call of duty. They had endured sheer torture on a hot day at the hands of a little woman who was impossible to please, they had moved the piano at least a thousand times, and there the obligation ended. Short on patience, they itched to take action, something along the lines of closing and locking the piano lid, but were restrained from this intention by the indomitable presence of Aunt Dot. Though they dwarfed her in size, they quailed before her steely gaze, that cold, hard glint in her eye that had previously caused both a fractious bull and a Nazi spy to think twice before crossing her. So as long as she remained in the room they were circumspect in voicing criticism. Nevertheless, eventually Bert, who had elected himself spokesman, could not resist airing his views.

'That there piana shouldn't be played until it's tuned proper,' he pointed out, looking round authoritatively, and Fred lent his support.

'That's right. Spot on, Bert. Shouldn't be played.'

'When a piana's travelled and been moved about a bit – and blimey, that one sure has moved about – it has ta be re-tuned.'

'That's right. Re-tuned,' echoed Fred.

'So what you should do, lads, is give the piana a rest,' said Bert, and Fred, determined to maintain a solid front, parroted this advice.

'That's right, lads. Give it a rest.'

Aunt Dot gave no indication of having heard these informed recommendations. Whether she was deafened by the cacophonous performance on the piano, or her mind was elsewhere, or she was privately in agreement with the carriers, she continued grimly griddling scones and making tea, finally managing to drink a cup herself. The boys also ignored the unwelcome advice. Neal tested the carriers' theory by running his fingers up and down the scale of C major three times – a recital to which the carriers listened with their fingers in their ears – and pronounced his verdict.

'Sounds all right to me. Pretty much as always. Tickety-boo in fact.' And with that he redoubled his efforts, rattling away on the top half of the keyboard with a lively rendition of 'Chopsticks' while David occupied the lower octaves, playing a bass version of 'Three Blind Mice', causing the carriers to regard them with growing disapproval.

'That's a terrible racket,' observed Bert tetchily.

'Terrible,' agreed Fred.

'I like a good tune as much as the next man, but that isn't one,' moaned Bert. Just then, however, Aunt Dot popped into the kitchen and, in her absence, matters came to a head. Bert rose from his chair and advanced upon the enthusiastic pianists, towering over them in what David later described as a threatening manner.

'Might I make a suggestion, lads?' he enquired, flexing his muscles and bending his knuckles back and forth till they made a cracking noise. 'Might I suggest that ya put the lid on it? Know what I mean, lads? Right now. If ya know what's good fer ya. All right, lads?'

The boys hesitated, glancing at Fred, who nodded in agreement and added 'Yeah, that's right. Put the lid on it.'

David was not so easily discouraged. His creative instinct,

suppressed during the tedious manoeuvring, made him stubbornly determined to perform.

'Aunt Dot, could you come here for a moment?' he shouted, glaring defiantly at Bert, but the response from the kitchen was disappointing.

'Not just now, boys. I'm busy. Busy, busy, busy. I don't know what's happened to your mother. She's supposed to be helping me. You can come and help if you like. I'll find you a nice little job.'

Taking advantage of his opportunity, but with a cautious glance over his shoulder, Bert closed in, so close that the boys could smell his sweaty shirt. They said afterwards that he was spluttering scone crumbs onto the keyboard and that he had a worrying habit of lifting and extending his shoulder muscles and expanding his chest, giving the impression that he could change shape, growing and swelling upwards and outwards, like a smelly giant. Reluctantly, the boys closed the piano lid as so forcefully advised. Then, seething with righteous indignation, they made a beeline for the door, and only when they reached the safety of the threshold did David recover his fighting spirit and turn around.

'We'll see what my mother has to say about this! And anyway, it's her piano, not yours. And it's not your house either. So there!'

And so it came about that my brothers, who might otherwise have been reluctant conscripts, joined the search for me at an early stage. As soon as they caught up with our mother, their petty piano problems had to be put aside, and Uncle Matt assigned them areas to be combed for clues as to my whereabouts. At first they took the situation lightly, like a game of hide-and-seek, but the longer I remained missing, the more they realized the seriousness of it, especially when Uncle Matt called them over to him and voiced everyone's thoughts.

'This is a waste of time. She's definitely not around here. We'll have to look farther afield. I just don't understand it. She's never gone missing before. She knows the whole valley like the back of her hand. It doesn't make sense to go off like that and not say a word. It's just not like her. Tell you what, Ellie, you let Dot know what's happening and we'll have a quick look in the top lot and down as far as Low Windlestraw, then call back for you. We'll take Split. You never know – he might turn out to be some use for a change.'

Aunt Dot paused in the middle of brewing yet another pot of tea and listened, astonished.

'I've said it before and I'll say it again – Emma's a strange child. Why on earth would she disappear when her piano's finally arrived?

368

She's been looking forward to this day for weeks. Anyway, you hold on a moment and I'll come with you. It won't take me a tick to get ready, and these gentlemen are just leaving.'

Tired of pandering to their insatiable thirst and prodigious appetites, she bestowed her steely glance on Bert and Fred, who gaped back disappointedly. They were sitting pleasantly relaxed, ready to make a day of it. Bert had noticed a fresh plate of scones virtually untouched, and three ginger biscuits going spare. But there was no mistaking Aunt Dot's inhospitable tone.

'As far as we're concerned, missus,' said Bert with an ingratiating smile, 'there's no real hurry. We've finished work for the day.'

'No hurry at all, missus,' echoed Fred.

'Oh, but I'm afraid there is. A very great hurry,' she replied, firmly removing their cups and plates. 'We have urgent business to attend to. A missing child to search for.' And in no time at all they found themselves escorted to the door and hustled out into the yard.

Next she set about dampening the fire, smoothing her hair, and generally pottering about, while my mother waited impatiently, moving restlessly from room to room, unable to stay still for a second, and as she passed from kitchen to living room for the umpteenth time, her attention was caught by the pig calendar, and with a pang she remembered my amusing drawings. She stared, studying July's sow more closely, and suddenly called out in alarm, 'Dot! Oh Dot! Come and have a look at this. Now I understand. It was the piano, Dot. That's what upset her. She never really wanted it. It was only an excuse to go home. See the signposts? See the pig's suitcase? She's leaving Thorny Edge and travelling to Summer Hill. Emma must have thought we were taking her with us. My poor little girl! She's never understood. She must be desperately homesick and desperately hurt. And it's all my fault. I didn't listen. I thought she'd settled down. I'll never forgive myself. Never! And now she's run away and I've lost her.'

'Nonsense!' replied Aunt Dot briskly. 'We'll soon find her. Of course we will. It's just a pity that we hadn't set off sooner. But nobody tells me anything. I'm kept completely in the dark. Anyway, here's Matt with the boys, so we'll be off straight away, and waste no more time.'

As if by right, Split led the way, streaking ahead and then waiting, his nose sniffing the ground as if he imagined himself to be a blood-hound. Oddly he appeared to sense who was missing and be restless for action. A fairly silent search party followed him, and although they didn't know it, the searchers were also following in my foot-steps – first to Todd Tingate's, examining every inch of it, on to Moss House, where they joined by Miss Titchmarsh, and then to Brackenfield, where Uncle Matt entertained strong hopes of finding me.

'Emma was uncommon fond of the hens,' he explained. 'Used to chatter to them all the time.' My mother clutched his arm anxiously.

'Please, Matt. Don't speak of my little girl in the past tense. I can't bear it. I'm worried sick as it is.'

'Sorry, Ellie. Didn't mean it like that. Just thought she'd most likely be here.'

But they found nothing there – nothing but hens toppling over each other to escape the sudden invasion, and a stray sheep that they shooed back onto the fell. Then they set off for Nettle Head, with Split well in front and turning from time to time impatiently, eager to hurry them along. From the high ground behind the farmhouse they could see the land spread out before them, without a sign of an extra inhabitant. Uncle Matt took a quick tour round the house and waved to the Phillips, who were working at the bottom of their front meadow. They were plainly in a rush to finish the hay before milking time, and he decided not to disturb them. Even the comely sight of Mrs Phillip in peach pyjamas could not divert him from his purpose that day.

'There's no point in going on,' he said. 'Emma was always nervous of the fell. So we might as well head back. We'll check our house again and then try t'other way. I reckon she's gone to Thorny Edge to see Irene. Here, Split! Here, boy!'

But Split was already on the fell, wagging his tail in anticipation of being followed, and whining as if trying to convey a message. When called again he crept forward very slowly on his stomach, then stopped, turning his head towards Lornhope and then back to the watching group, whining softly, persuasively, entreating them to follow. Even with the power of words, he could not have been more eloquent.

'Stupid pesky animal!' exclaimed Uncle Matt. 'No point in going further. She'd never risk the fell on her own. Come here, Split! Right now, you daft dog!'

Split whined louder, like a child deprived of a treat. He stood up and wagged his tail, waiting, and then he jerked his head towards the fell, still waiting, licking his jaws. Then he ran some twenty feet up the fell, turned and sat down again facing the bemused group, and gave a low bark as if to say, 'Bear with me. I know what I'm doing. This time I'm right.'

'He couldn't know something that we don't, could he, Matt?' asked my mother, thinking she had interpreted the dog's meaning. 'I'd hate to think of Emma out there on the fell alone. Anything could happen.'

'Shouldn't think so,' said Uncle Matt disparagingly. 'Not him. He knows nothing. He's a mutt. Tell him to go up-by and he'll go down-by. Tell him to do this, he'll do that. Always contrary-wise. Nobody in the valley's saddled with such a stupid collie. He's useless!'

'All the same, he seems so sure, so determined. What do you think, Dot?'

'Well, I think Matt's right. Emma's wary of the fell. I can't imagine her going up there on her own. What would be the point?'

'But it would be dreadful if she has and we walk away. Aren't there swamps on the fell?'

'Well – yes, in places,' agreed Uncle Matt. 'Not that many, like. Over the years I've only been in one swamp. It happened one dark night takin' a shortcut. But I've come across a few shog-bogs in my time, shakin'-bogs that heave up and down when you walk on them, though they're not as dangerous as the swamps. Still – tell you what – best to be sure. You all stay here and I'll have a good look. But chances are the mutt's leading us on one of his wild goose chases.'

He ran up the fell to where Split sat, and the dog instantly retreated another twenty feet, repeating that manoeuvre every time my uncle drew near. They proceeded in this fashion until Uncle Matt came upon a rise in the ground, a hillock providing a good vantage point in every direction. He could see nothing at all untoward, not for miles around. He cursed soundly at being misled once again by the wretched dog, and in a sudden flash of fury rounded on Split, who was still waiting some distance ahead, and shouted at him, loudly, angrily.

'Come here! Come away now! You blinkin' useless idiot!'

Split gave a low growl, like a dog swearing under his breath, and backed up a little. A clash of wills ensued, with my uncle shouting commands and Split constantly flicking his head towards Lornhope and refusing to budge. But sadly Split lost the tussle. Uncle Matt snorted impatiently and then turned and stumped furiously down the fell, marching in step to Split's reproving bark. After a few minutes of consultation the disappointed search party set off for Thorny Edge, my mother constantly stoppping to look back. Split held out alone on the fell for a while, but finally and reluctantly capitulated, now bringing up the rear by the same distance that he had previously kept the lead, as if reined back by an invisible dog strap. His whole demeanour had changed, and he now had a drooping gait and a trailing tail. He epitomized displeasure and disgust, a dog disillusioned with the human race, and in particular with his master, Uncle Matt. Split's heart was no longer in the hunt.

At Windlestraw the group divided, Uncle Matt and the boys taking the field route and the women the road. Despite all my uncle's orders to the contrary, Split elected to follow the women, but he constantly paused to look back towards the fell, his hangdog look letting it be known that he was there under sufferance, only along for the walk.

'Meet you at Bill's place, at Coldstone Mea,' said my uncle. 'Hope one of us has good news by then.'

But both groups arrived at Bill's farm within minutes of each other and with no news at all, except the bad news to tell Bill.

'Oh no! But that's a terrible thing. Terrible. A dreadful thing. What a worry! By heck it is!' he said, genuinely concerned. 'It's a sad, sad day when a child goes missin' and no mistake. But we'll do what we can to help. Ah know how much ya'll be frettin'. Ah do, like.' To everyone's surprise, it was not my mother but Uncle Matt he patted consolingly on the shoulder.

Then his family downed tools and joined the hunt, and so did the occupants of every farm and cottage they passed. Neighbours left whatever they had in hand and hurried to swell the ranks of the search party. The people of the dales, who normally kept themselves to themselves, eking out a lonely and at times solitary existence, could be relied upon to rally round unselfishly should one of their number, even an incomer, find him or herself in trouble. At such times there was a strong community spirit, and so it was that in no time at all the search party grew till it could only be described as a posse, and a sizeable one at that. It seemed that the entire valley was out looking for one little girl – even, from whatever motive no one knew, the yellow-toothed Eddie Gormley.

Dales folk came just as they were and ready for anything, mostly wearing caps or straw hats or knotted handkerchiefs on their heads, and in noticeably casual dress. Collarless shirts and colourful braces were very much in evidence, and women as well as men stepped out in wellingtons or sturdy boots. Several carried sticks to flatten the long summer undergrowth, and others carried curious objects which they simply felt might come in useful – a length of rope, a large meat hook, a whistle, a big torch, though it was still broad daylight. A number brought noisy dogs, who conflicted with Split and added to the prevailing hullabaloo. And one bizarre individual stood out from the crowd, not only because his trousers were tied at waist and ankle to repel invaders, but also because he brandished a voluminous red flag, which he held vertically when stationary as if presenting arms, and waved with spirited abandon whenever there was a forward surge.

What with the flag and the sticks and the dogs and the sheer numbers, which included women and children, it was an impressive array of searchers, at times spreading out to cover a wide territory, at others concentrating on a specific area. So by the time they reached Thorny Edge it could safely be said that not a blade of grass had missed scrutiny or a stone been left unturned. Not a hayrick had been left unexplored, not a barn left uninvestigated, and not a byre left unsniffed by dogs. Of course, once it had been established that not a soul had seen me in the vicinity of Thorny Edge – not even Irene Milburn, on whom all hopes had rested – the zest rather went out of the expedition and the posse began to lose heart and disintegrate. Most of the women and children left for home, as did the easily bored Eddie Gormley. And a splinter group formed to search the river banks and the Elf Holes – just in case.

So it was a smaller and slightly dispirited posse that made its way back to Windlestraw, stopping for a quick cup of tea before tackling the vast and forbidding expanse of the fell. In that brief respite the visiting dogs were tied outside; the flag-bearer furled his flag and propped it beside the fireplace, saluting it ceremoniously; and the rest of the tired team, now mainly men, gave the boot-scraper their undivided attention prior to filing through the kitchen. They entered in a slow procession as they wiped their feet, treading upon the three mats with heavy synchronized steps, as if dancing the hokey-cokey. Once more the sanctity of Aunt Dot's home was invaded, and the invaders stood around, hats off, gulping tea and discussing the next step to be taken in the present emergency, filling my mother with alarm and despondency. She heard them speculate on the slim chances of finding me alive after all this time, and on the unlikelihood of finding me at all before dark, and on the question of whether the police should now be brought in, until she could stand it no longer.

'I'm off to look for her myself,' she confided to Uncle Matt. 'I just can't wait here, drinking tea and doing nothing while my Emma's out there, lost and alone. She's only nine, bless her. My baby. And she could be anywhere. In all kinds of trouble.'

'I'll come with you,' he instantly volunteered. 'But you'd better take a coat, Ellie. It'll be cold on the fell. And I'll take a rug for Emma, for when we find her, like.'

Without further ado they headed for the front door, only to open it to the pleasant aspect of Mrs Phillip, her hand raised ready to knock. She had changed from peach pyjamas into a variegated green dress, and looked, as Uncle Matt happened to notice in passing, as pretty as a picture, even the picture in Mr Clout's study, he thought to himself.

'Oh – er – it's you . . .' he stuttered, stating the obvious and blushing in confusion, and it was his rosy countenance that Mrs Phillip addressed.

'Yes, it's me,' she said with a smile of amusement. 'And thank goodness I've caught you in at last. This is my third visit. But I see you have company. Sorry to interrupt. Are you having a party?'

'Oh no. A search party more like. Little Emma's gone missing,' he said, and she nodded, as if not altogether surprised.

'Ah – I wondered. That's why I'm here. I had to come back.'

'You mean – you've *found* her?' cried my mother, and a tense silence settled on the living room.

'No, but I think I know where she is. I saw her hours ago, running towards Lornhope. Just a distant glimpse of her pink dress as she disappeared onto the fell. I thought she was with you, Mr Wheatley. She's always with you. Then when I caught sight of you all searching behind our house and coming back from the fell without her, I wondered if something was wrong. I came here, but found nobody at home.'

'Thank you. That's what I thought all along. The dog was right,' said my mother, squeezing past as she rushed out of the door, followed closely by Mrs Phillip, followed closely by Uncle Matt, followed at some distance by the rest of the posse.

'How-way lads. Leave everythin'. She's been sighted!' shouted Bill, and they all hurried out, no longer a focused team but scattered in twos and threes, with the flag-bearer grabbing his flag and bolting, running as fast as the awkward pole would allow him to, as he tried to regain his position at the front.

None, however, moved as fast as Split. Though never out of sight, he was always ahead. Uncle Matt told me that he and my mother led the rest but they couldn't catch his dog. Like a black-and-white rocket he hurtled past all competitors, ignoring the usual route along the track, and taking a direct short cut through the meadow, over the burn, and up to Todd Tingate's, where he prowled restlessly to and fro, watching with obvious impatience the slower human progress as if to say, 'Hurry up! I was right all along. Now you know. So hurry, before it's too late!' His heart was back in the chase. Aunt Dot, who determinedly drank her tea down to the last drop before departing, and would have done so even if the ceiling had fallen in, left the house last, finding herself some distance behind the rearguard of rescuers. But she raced down the dene, light and lithe as a gazelle, and soon caught up, passing the mainly portly men with ease.

This time, however, Split was the undoubted leader, sniffing his way and seldom deviating, as if he knew perfectly well what he was about. He led the search party straight past Nettle Head to the vantage point where he had taken his stand against Uncle Matt. And nose to the ground, he started towards Lornhope, but suddenly slowed right down. He was now nervous, now hesitant, his ears pricked and his hackles rising. He paused, momentarily startled, for the weird and unexpected scene that met his bemused gaze made him consider a change of tactics. It seemed that now he was no longer on a simple St Bernard dog mission of rescuing a lost child – at least not exclusively. Ahead of him he could see an eerie apparition, dark and hunched, draped in long black rags that flapped and fluttered in the wind. Then the crouching figure rose from the heather as if about to move forward, briefly suspended in a sombre shape against the sky, looking for all the world like a giant bat.

He crept closer, keeping low and panther-like, till he recognized with surprise the macabre figure as an occasional visitor to Windlestraw. He had confronted the strange creature before and for some reason she always made his hackles rise and his lip curl into an involuntary snarl. His sharp eyes noted that she was clutching a large, filthy cushion clasped tightly to her black coat, and under it dangled a pair of child's legs, all that was immediately visible of the half-hidden body she carried. She swayed slightly, struggling to keep her balance in the wind and bowed down by a burden that was clearly too heavy for her.

Split barked softly, planning his next move. Should he blunder in as his instincts dictated, making as much noise as he could muster and creating mayhem with his usual reckless abandon? Or should he for once hold back, appraising the new situation, awaiting further developments, and allowing time for reinforcements to arrive? Unaccustomed as he was to thinking things out, he soon became restless, and unable to contain himself any longer, he decided on a middle course. He crawled slowly towards the gloomy apparition, trailing a cautious tail, but at the same time ready for action, growling his most menacing growl.

Chapter 27

Reunions and Partings

Just then I would have welcomed the reassuring sound of Split's growl, or that familiar bark, the belligerent charade that promised more than it fulfilled, seldom coming to tooth-and-claw attack. But I heard nothing except the rapid beating of my own heart. I still thought myself alone in the wilds with Mary and was frightened almost out of my wits. During the hours that I later learned had been spent by the search party diligently combing the valley, I had experienced many moments of abject terror. How bitterly did I regret running away from Windlestraw as I lay marooned on the heather, lost and alone! And how much more so when I found myself gazing into Mary's sinister face, though for a while at least I was spared conscious suffering in the blessed oblivion of a dead faint. But when I did regain my senses it was with a shudder of fear, remembering where I was, and why, and with whom.

Curiously, however, my initial reaction was one of claustrophobia, as if Mary had put me inside a foul-smelling bag. In my half-dazed petrified state I failed to realize that she had only covered me with her coat – Uncle Matt's coat, as it happened, though barely recognizable as such. But wrapped closely inside it I felt choked by the overpowering stench of her body and clothes, smelling so strongly of sweat, swamps and cowsheds. Furthermore, I felt utterly helpless in the dark. At first, with a pang of fear, I wondered *why* it was dark. Surely, I thought, I could not have slept that long? Had Mary taken me to one of her lairs? A murky, smelly byre? A gloomy barn? A dark cave? The Elf Holes perhaps? But then I guessed that the darkness was caused by a dark woollen cover she had tucked tightly round me. A blanket? Oh *please no*, not a blanket! At that thought my blood ran cold. For several months after Mary's visit to the farm I had been plagued by a recurring nightmare in which she returned to smother me with a clinging black blanket. I began to panic, filled with horror as I wondered fearfully if that frightful nightmare was about to become a reality.

Then came movement and I saw a chink of light. So it *was* daylight after all! With relief I realized that it was only an old coat that covered me, stifling me, and the cushion that held all Mary's worldly goods was pressing me close to her odorous layers of rags. In an awkward, clumsy way she was carrying me, as she might a stray lamb, clutching the body to her and letting the legs dangle. And she held me with difficulty, grunting from the strain of my leaden weight. She trudged as far as she could at a stretch, then, half-sitting, half-kneeling, allowed herself a short rest, cradling me in her arms and humming tunelessly before struggling to her feet to stagger on, her warm, stale-smelling proximity filling me with repugnance.

But what to do? For a moment, in my terror, my brain felt numb. Then it raced tempestuously with wild and perilous schemes of escape. I pretended to be unconscious still, aiming to take her by surprise, to jerk my body out of her grasp, leap to the ground, and then make a run for it, run like the wind. But I had heard somewhere that mad people have an extraordinary grip, and certainly Mary held me as tightly as any vice, as she staggered resolutely on and on for what seemed like an eternity. My thoughts were in turmoil, searching in vain for a solution, churning out anguished and unanswered questions. Where on earth was she taking me? Would I ever see my family again? My mother? Uncle Matt? Again and again I prayed desperately but silently, 'Oh please, *please*, let me go free. Let me go back to my mother. I'll do anything. Even stay in Sourhope. Yes, even that.'

At times Mary stumbled, uttering sharp cries like a stricken animal, raising my hopes that she would loosen her hold. But on the contrary she tightened it, determined not to drop me, clinging to her cumbersome burden as if she carried a precious object from which she would never be parted. Now she rested more often, sometimes standing, sometimes kneeling, but whenever she paused she wrapped me even more securely, smothering me till I could scarcely breathe. So we journeyed on, a staggering, stumbling, incongruous pair, and all the while I was rigid with fear, utterly trapped within Mad Mary's power. Despite my discomfort I kept still as long as I could, but finally curiosity overcame caution and, desperate for fresh air, I turned slightly, taking the risk of opening the coat and peeping through the gap, terrified of what I might see.

Then I gasped, starting in surprise, wonderful surprise, hardly able to credit my own eyes, intense relief flooding over me. At last I began to understand what was happening and to view the abhorrent Mary

378

in an entirely different light, to appreciate her as I would never have thought possible. For in that brief glimpse I saw daylight in more ways than one. I saw that Lornhope was very much behind us and that Sourhope lay unmistakably ahead. I recognized familiar buildings in the distance, and surely that was Nettle Head below? Then I knew! Then I understood that Mary had no intention of abducting me. Quite the contrary. She was taking me home! She simply thought to care for me as she cared for any lost or injured creature she found, and kept safe, and wrapped warmly, and if possible returned to its natural habitat. I realized then that despite all appearances Mary was far from mad, just generally misunderstood. So, plucking up all my courage, I wriggled in her arms, and as she instinctively tightened her grip, I bravely claimed her attention.

'Mary! Mary, you can put me down now, thank you. I'm fine. I can walk.'

She stopped, letting her coat fall open, and looked down at me, the thick black crustations of dirt on her skin cracking into a smile as she lowered my feet gently to the heather. She tried to speak, and with no lingering thoughts of running away I waited patiently, watching her struggle to force speech from her intensely grimacing face. At last she blurted out three simple words, in strangely strangled tones.

'O-all r-right n-n-nowooh.'

'Yes, thank you, Mary. And thank you very much for carrying me back. You must be exhausted. You've been so kind, Mary. Really very kind,' I managed to say, and that was all, because suddenly Split was upon us, bounding to my rescue.

He had thrown caution to the wind and reverted to norm, charging in regardless and running amok. He leapt at us both, spinning round like a top in the air, snarling and barking fit to scare away a dozen Mad Marys, but his act was all bluff and Mary knew it. For he circled and circled, dodging about like a timid boxer, darting in as ferocious as a hungry wolf, but always backing away again, never staying near enough to harm anyone, especially not himself. He desperately wanted to save me, but to him Mary was like a big black solid shadow, and he was nervous of shadows, even his own.

'Stop that, Split! Stop it, you silly dog!' I shouted. 'That's enough! Mary's my friend!' I looked up to see her pleased expression, a warm smile that gave a hint of beauty under the layer of grime, a glimpse of the dark beauty she had once been.

Split, however, had no time for this ripening friendship and, wilfully disobedient as ever, ignored my instructions, barking and snarling enough to deafen the entire population of the five counties that met on Lornhope. And now we could see Uncle Matt near at hand and three women close behind him, and the rest of the posse trailing after them in a long, straggling line, with the cheerful flag waving in the wind and the rival dogs barking in competition with Split. Turning in alarm, Mary smiled briefly in farewell, clutched her tattered cushion to her side and moved off, while Split yelped fearfully, jumping out of her way. Then, fleet of foot without the burden of me to bear, she fled swiftly up the fell, travelling in the direction of Dyke Head, her long black garments trailing behind her, sweeping the heather.

Perhaps, I thought, she would find shelter in an empty outbuilding, or even in the deserted house itself, with its faded armchairs, dingy bed, and infestation of resident spiders. I wondered if I would ever see her again, and to my surprise no longer felt fear at the prospect. I watched her go, dark and swift as one of the shadows that Split feared, while he gave her rapidly vanishing figure a final warning bark, now feeling safe in asserting his authority. Then he leapt happily at me, in his enthusiasm almost bowling me over. On the horizon Mary paused for a moment, giving me a slow, graceful wave, her silhouette forming an uncanny black shape against the amber evening sky. I waved slowly back. Then she was gone.

And suddenly I was being smothered again, this time by my mother, squeezing the breath out of me and raining kisses on my face and hair. It was a pleasant sensation and I offered no resistance, though I kept my reserve. After a year of being starved of such demonstrations of affection I hardly knew how to cope with a sudden feast. Besides, the sense of rejection had gone deep, and despite my relief at being rescued, somewhere in the hard core of my being lay buried feelings of hurt and resentment.

'Oh, Emma! Emma! Thank God you're all right! Thank God you're safe! I thought I'd lost you!' she cried, tears running down her cheeks. 'It nearly killed me. Don't ever do that to me again.'

Not yet ready to relent, I stood with fingers clenched in fierce determination, and gazed at her accusingly.

'You did lose me. At least you gave me away. You left me up here on my own and took the boys home.'

'Sorry, Emma. I'm so sorry, sweetheart. I'd no idea you felt that way.'

'You didn't want *me*. Just the boys.'

'Oh, that's not true. Is that what you thought? Oh, I'm so sorry, Emma. I meant to keep you safe, and I really believed you'd settled down here. You seemed to be doing well at school and everything. I really didn't know how strongly you felt. I just wanted to protect you from the war.'

'But the boys went home,' I stubbornly pointed out.

'Your aunt Dot didn't want the boys,' she whispered discreetly. 'She wouldn't have them. I wanted to keep you all safe, but she would only take you.'

'Safe!' I exclaimed, scathing in my condemnation. 'Safe! With exploding barrage balloons and Nazi spies! Safe! With guns pushed in my face and people threatening to kill me. Safe! I don't think so, Mum.'

'Oh, my poor girl! I didn't know. I didn't realize.'

'And people hitting me for no good reason. And bullying me at school, and thrashing me with the cat-o'-nine-tails. And scary people wandering about at night – like Mad Mary – though she's all right after all. I ran all the way to the dam and nearly fell in and she brought me back. She carried me all the way. She saved my life.'

'The dam! Oh, my goodness, you could have been drowned. My lovely precious girl! I had no idea. I only thought to protect you. It seemed so quiet up here, and cut off from the war. So peaceful compared with home.'

'Peaceful!' I snorted disparagingly, still on my high horse.

'Well, Emma, what are we to do now? Let's make no more mistakes. Would you like to go back home with us?'

'Of course,' I answered simply.

'But what about the air raids and the bombings?'

'What about them, Mum? You'll be there.'

'All right, that's settled then. We'll go the day after tomorrow.'

'But what'll happen to the piano you've brought?' I enquired, suspicious of such an easy victory.

'Oh, we'll send a van for it and sell it. We don't need two pianos now,' she said, and for the first time that day I smiled, imagining Bert and Fred hauling the heavy piano back up the steps.

There followed an emotional reunion all round, and I wallowed in the unaccustomed wealth of affection being showered on me. Only Uncle Matt seemed strangely troubled, torn between his delight at seeing me and a pressing matter tormenting his mind. Finally, he cleared his throat and put his dilemma into words.

'Emma, my pet, I'm that pleased to see you, bonny lass. I can't tell you how much. I've been worried sick, and it's just grand to set my eyes on your little face. It sure is. But, Emma, did you happen to notice that coat Mary had on? Surely it was my old coat? My lovely old coat, that I've missed an' all. I'd swear to it, Emma. Definitely. I recognized it straight away. That's my coat, I said to myself, and it was. I dare bet good money on it. And my meanin is, Emma, what a state it's in!'

'Yes, you wouldn't want it now, Uncle Matt.'

'Wouldn't I?' he asked doubtfully.

'No, it's filthy and stinking. It smells like the manure heap.'

'Hmm,' he murmured. 'Coats can be dry cleaned.'

'Not that one, Uncle Matt. It's gone too far. It's really too bad. It's horrible! Honestly.'

'Hmm,' he murmured again, clearly unconvinced.

And throughout the walk back to the farm, while everyone else was jubilant, laughing and chatting in relief at a successful outcome to an expedition that they had thought to be doomed, while Split kept leaping round my legs excitedly, and while the red flag waved merrily in front of the cheerful crowd, he remained morose and silent. Although he remembered to offer me the rug, which I declined, having had enough of being treated like a parcel, the thrill of finding me alive and well, though genuine and essential to his well-being, had been temporarily eclipsed by a second, but this time sad, reunion, this one with his lost and much-loved old coat. That had been a brief but painful encounter; one that hammered home the unfortunate fact that though I had been safely returned to the fold, his beloved coat had definitely gone for ever.

It might have helped to cheer him up had Mrs Phillip stayed with us, but she separated from the posse when we reached Nettle Head, leaving him to wallow in his sudden depression. He was, however, quite alone in this morbid mood. Everyone else crowded joyously round me, keen to hold my hand or offer piggybacks. And Elsie and Bill and several other opportunists insisted upon giving me a cuddle. Then we all returned to Windlestraw, where the diligent foot-wipers again filed over the three mats, this time moving with a lighter, nimbler tread, more like the slinky steps of a sand dance. In good heart they settled down to celebrate with whatever was on offer – not exactly the appropriate fatted calf, but the usual tea and ginger biscuits with the addition of chunky corned beef sandwiches spiced with pickled onions. In a party atmosphere I came to know residents of Sourhope whom I had never met before, and, in view of my imminent departure, would probably never meet again. They listened intently as I explained Mad Mary's heroic part in the proceedings, and as my story unfolded it altered the popular perception of Mary to the point where those present, though not impetuously generous by nature, promptly vowed to extend to her the hand of friendship and the gift of hospitality in future.

They were, however, canny, careful folk, not inclined to go overboard. At a distance Mary was a heroine, but meeting her face to face was a different matter, and it had to be said that her pungent smell alone argued strongly against social acceptance. So the sentiment was there but the offer of friendship strictly limited, and the proposed hospitality only extended to the benefactors' outside premises, not to the carefully guarded privacy of their cosy homes.

'She's welcome to a bit o' bread at my back door any time,' said one, setting the tone.

'Aye, same here,' declared another. 'There's always stale bread goin' beggin', and mebbe a chunk o' cheese and sec-like.'

'Or leftovers,' offered a third. 'You know – them bits and pieces that the dogs generally get. Or the pigs. Some o' them scraps'd mebbe be acceptable ta Mary.'

'Aye – or what aboot milk? That's cheap enough and handy, like,' was the final suggestion, winning universal approval and solving the delicate matter once and for all.

I learnt later that from that day on, Mary was able to take her pick of the accommodation in barns and byres for miles around, and mainly lived, so the rumour went, rather like a baby on bread and milk. I would have preferred that they did more for her than that, much more, since there was a strong possibility that she had saved my life. But in one sense it was an appropriate outcome because the woman known as Mad Mary was, as I had been fortunate to discover, still only a child at heart and would remain a child all her life.

So it was that the piano turned out to be my passport home after all. Its surprise arrival set in motion a chain of events that ended happily, for me at any rate. But reflecting later on the outcome of that day, I learnt another of life's difficult lessons as I realized that the major decisions we make, however well meant and apparently exclusive to our own welfare, can have adverse and unforeseen repercussions on others. I was going home at last; no doubt about that.

And deep down I knew it was the right decision. Yet the day before I left Sourhope I sat as usual on top of the five-bar gate leading from the stack yard, thoughtfully surveying the valley for the last time as a resident, and contemplating an insoluble problem.

In the warm sunshine, looking down the shorn meadow where a second crop of wild pansies had sprung to life in colourful drifts, it was difficult to visualize the valley as I had experienced it at other seasons of the year. It was hard to remember the long, harsh days when the cruel Lornhope wind howled like a lonely wolf; or the dark days when rain lashed and soaked, playing on its victims like a fierce spray from a hose; or the winter storms when vindictive snow blizzards blinded the eyes and stole the breath, and icy air froze the very marrow. Young as I was I knew, now that I was finally leaving this savage place of violent contrasts, that part of it would always go with me and part of me would remain behind.

Though I would not have thought it possible, I knew I would miss this lonely valley. I would miss the vast clear canopy of sky and the mysterious shadows moving constantly over the moors, the plaintive cry of the peewit and the joy of walking waist deep in wild flowers. And of course, I would miss the farm. My departure, which had always seemed a clearly defined decision, so simple, so cut and dried, now raised questions that surprised and distressed me, bringing me to the present problem, which in my child's mind, mostly fixed on the here and now, had not existed until that moment.

For when I had gone from Windlestraw, who would take my place? Who would talk to my little old lady hens, or chase the wandering geese back home, or find lost ducks? Who would feed pet lambs, or cuddle Beauty who thought me her mother, or scratch the pigs' backs? Or even improve the pig calendar by colouring character into the bland faces advertising superior pig feed? And most important of all – suddenly of supreme importance – who would look after my Uncle Matt? What would become of him? I knew from his excessive grief over the loss of an old coat that he would miss me more than he could possibly imagine. For one thing I knew he loved me as a daughter, and for another, wherever he went I went, like a second shadow but never a silent one – forever prattling in his receptive ear, forever ready to hear his oracular views on life.

So who would listen now to his words of wisdom, or appreciate his tuneful performance when he serenaded the cows? Who would he seek out after an argument with Aunt Dot, to justify his own viewpoint and put himself in the right? Or complain to when her cooking sank below the acceptable standard of almost edible? There again, who would keep him company as he mended his dry stone walls, or fed the stock, or tramped his land, battling with moles and shooting at rabbits? And who would hold his hand when the going got tough? Or hang on to his arm at the mart on special Tuesdays, climbing high in the arena to spy from a bird's-eye view, looking for possible bargains and rival bidders?

Oh yes, he would miss me, just as I would miss him, and I grieved for him. But I had made my choice and I stood by it. If I had had the use of a giant pair of scales balancing my home and my mother on one side and Sourhope with Uncle Matt on the other, it would have tipped temporarily towards the latter, for I would always retain a deep affection for my complex but essentially lovable uncle. But it would then have rebounded, coming down heavily on the former and settling there for good. No one, not even he, could replace my mother, and I longed to be back home.

Nevertheless, I felt surprisingly and incredibly sad. And suddenly weighed down by a strange sense of guilt and betrayal, I deliberately avoided his company. The very sight of him gave me a twinge of remorse. Then two days later we departed and this time I had no doubt at all that I was on my way. I watched as my clothes and few other belongings were packed and placed with the other luggage in the car boot. Then we all trooped out to the car, but at the door I paused, feeling compelled to say a particular goodbye and thank you to Aunt Dot. After all, whatever our differences, I had been her guest for a whole year. Yet ours had never been a close relationship, and uncertain as to how to proceed, I waited for a sign from her.

'Aunt Dot . . .' I began tentatively, and she answered at once.

'Well cheerio, Emma. Be a good girl,' she said, as if that were the most important thing in life. Then characteristically she added, 'What a pity you didn't tell us you were so desperate to go home before the piano was brought all the way up here. At vast expense to your mother, I might add, and a deal of trouble to everyone else.' And then softening a little, with just a slight tremble of the stiff upper lip, she finished with, 'But never mind, I want you to know, Emma, that you'll always be welcome to come back. Whenever you like. Come for your holidays. All of them if you want.'

I had cracked her brittle defences after all, I thought, and reaching up I gave her a hug, only the second we had ever exchanged, and, surprising myself as well as her, I planted a kiss on her cheek. Her face crumpled and she blew her nose in a business-like manner as I turned to leave, but when I looked back to wave she was herself again, smiling her fixed little smile. At the top of the steps I said goodbye to Split, cuddling him so affectionately that he tried to follow me into the car, but Uncle Matt deftly diverted him, kneeing him in the ribs and shutting the door with a bang as if to show the dog who was boss.

The temperamental Morris jerked into action, spluttering and groaning its way to Thorny Edge as if it too was displeased at my departure, though it travelled more steadily than usual because for once Uncle Matt had nothing to say, no passing comments with which to entertain us. He neither remarked on anyone or anything we passed, nor reminded us, as was his habit, how privileged we were to benefit from his exceptional driving skills. On the contrary, his usual ebullient spirit appeared to have deserted him, leaving him pale and disconcerted. The rapid change of circumstances, depriving him of yet another dear companion in addition to his coat, had been too sudden, too cruel, reducing him to a state of apathetic gloom.

I sat behind him, also silent, torn by mixed emotions. While the boys squabbled over space in the back seat I gazed out of the window at the valley that had become more familiar than home. And as I gazed I thought I glimpsed Split here and there, sprinting through the fields below. From various vantage points I could see a stream-lined black-and-white shape, at first keeping distant pace with the car and then streaking ahead, until finally I felt compelled to speak up.

'I think Split's following us, Uncle Matt. I'm sure I can see him running through the fields.'

'You and your imagination, Emma!' he replied gruffly. 'It'll be the death of you one of these days. You know full well that the pesky dog's at home.'

Rebuffed, I subsided back into silence, but when we reached the bus stop, there stood Split, a self-appointed reception committee, panting excitedly and wagging his tail in a metronomic welcome. Once again I took a sorrowful goodbye of him and then of Uncle Matt, and felt both partings keenly. I had forgotten how much I would miss Split, and as I stroked and cuddled him I knew that for a time at least he would miss me. He gazed at us expectantly, looking like a very bemused dog – aware that something important was happening but unsure of what, though suspicious that he would disapprove if he did know. He kept wagging his tail very slowly, restlessly shifting his paws, and panting in a breathless way as he turned from me to Uncle Matt and back again as if confused and waiting for enlightenment. And Uncle Matt looked as bemused and dejected as the dog as we stood side by side facing the road, the way we had so often stood in the past, expecting the bus to arrive at any moment.

'I sure will miss you, bonny lass,' he said, with indescribable emotion. 'My meanin' is, Emma, I'll just miss you, all the time.'

His eyes blurred in a watery blue agony and I threw my arms around his neck and kissed both cheeks, hugging him tightly.

'I'll miss you too, Uncle Matt. So much! You've been great. Just great! Like the very best of fathers. But I'll come back to see you. Soon as I can. I promise. Cross my heart and hope to die.'

'Dunno, Emma. Won't be the same. Not the same thing at all. I wish you wouldn't go. There's still a war on you know. You could get yourself killed and then where would we be? Anyways, I've got used to your funny little ways, used to having you around an' that. I have, Emma. You're good company. And I think of you as my own daughter. Definitely.'

'I *must* go home, Uncle Matt. I don't belong up here. And I must be with my mother. But I'll be back, and I'll write every week.'

'Reckon that'll have to do then. But things'll never be the same. And there again, after a bit you'll likely forget. Yes, I dare bet my shirt on it.'

'I *never* forget you, Uncle Matt. Nor the times we've had together. I promise,' I said, and I meant it.

'By heck, Emma, life's awful sad,' he said miserably, and I stroked his arm and searched my mind for words of comfort.

'You've still got Mrs Phillip,' I said with a sly smile.

'Oh, dunno about that, Emma. Mebbe not for long. There's talk that they're leavin', an' that. It's rumoured that the climate up here doesn't suit her, and I must say I can't blame her. It's a hard life up here, and not for the likes of her. She's a tender blossom, she is, like an orchid. No, everythin' seems to be changin' for the worse, Emma. There's just no joy left in life.'

'Cheer up, Uncle Matt. Perhaps Mr Clout'll change his mind and sell you his picture,' I suggested, clutching at straws.

'Fat chance!' he replied morosely. 'I offered him the princely sum of three shillings and ninepence – a dashed good price but he wouldn't take it. He just sat there on his dignity, so to speak. 'Sides, I'll have no cause to call on him once you've gone. No, that door's closed an' all now.'

'Well – at least you've still got Aunt Dot,' I reminded him.

'That's true,' he said pensively.

'With that amazing red hair, don't forget.'

'That's right. Have you ever seen such a colour, Emma?'

'Never, Uncle Matt. I always thought it was – well – magic.'

'Magic. That's it. Definitely,' he said hollowly, struggling with conflicting emotions, novel and disturbing.

Just then the red bus drew up and I hesitated, afraid of missing it but reluctant to leave him in such an upset state. But finally I gave him one quick but clinging hug and tore myself away. I boarded the bus last and then rushed to the back seat next to the boys to join them in waving to him as he stood, wretchedly unhappy, between the old Morris and Split, whose tail still wagged very slowly, uncertainly. The two of them looked so bewildered and forlorn that I could hardly bear it. From the height of the bus seat Uncle Matt appeared somehow smaller and not at all like the image that he usually presented to the world, the sprightly, dapper man who could charm the birds off the trees if so minded and take on all comers in pursuit of a bargain.

At that moment he seemed shrunken, his shoulders sagging despondently and arms hanging lifelessly by his sides. He pretended that the sun was in his eyes but made no attempt to shade them, and I could see tears trickling down his cheeks unheeded. He looked simply desolate, and I remembered my own deep feelings of desolation all those months ago when the bus first left me behind. He had consoled me then, but now I could not comfort him in return. Then Split stepped into the breach. Sensing something terribly wrong, he did what he always did and pushed his wet nose comfortingly into Uncle Matt's hand, a kindly gesture that went unnoticed and sadly unappreciated. In a moment, and rather to my relief, the bus moved off, and I waved frantically until the distressed pair disappeared from sight.

'It's so sad, Mum. I can't stand it. It's really too sad to bear,' I said, tears welling in my own eyes, trickling down my own cheeks. 'I feel just awful about Uncle Matt. I don't know how he'll manage without me.'

'Yes, it's very sad, Emma. He'll certainly miss you. I know how much I missed you. It was very hard at first. But it's this wicked war to blame. So much suffering of all kinds. So much pain and loss and grief.'

'I don't know why I should, but somehow I feel to blame,' I sobbed. 'I never wanted to come here and stay here. It wasn't my fault. But I don't like to hurt anyone, and now I think I've gone and broken his heart.'

She laughed, relieving the tension, and put her arm round my shoulders.

'I doubt that, Emma. He'll be upset for a while, but he'll soon get over it. He's a strange man. A bit obsessive in some respects. Always inclined to go to extremes. Look at all the fuss he made over that old coat! And doubtless he has grown fond of you and he'll miss your company, but it's my experience that most men's broken hearts mend in no time. We'll come back to see him and you'll find that I'm right. So don't upset yourself.'

'But are you quite sure he'll be all right?'

'Positive, Emma. Worse things are happening to people every day at present. Much worse. And besides, if I know him, and I think I do, he'll be regaling them in the post office by now, drinking tea and tucking in to home-baked treats in Olive Featherstone's kitchen, with his nose stuck in the *Sporting Man* trying to spot a likely winner. Anyway, pet, you've made your choice and that's that. It's what you wanted and it's all settled. We're on our way now, back to civilization.'

She turned to the window with the thought of home fresh in her mind, home with all its hustle and bustle – its busy crowds and interminable queues, the ominous sound of air-raid sirens, the thunder of anti-aircraft guns and terrifying bombs, and the blackout with searchlights criss-crossing dark, threatening skies. She looked behind her towards the tranquil village of Thorny Edge, still and silent as ever, with its homely old church nestling amid a small cluster of stone houses; and at the surrounding hills of Sourhope, now purple-tinged with heather and bathed in morning sunlight. A passing cloud cast soft shadows over the chequerboard of fields where cattle and sheep grazed peacefully, and a pure white horse galloped through the pasture alongside the road, racing the bus, its silvery tail and mane streaming in the wind – graceful, beautiful.

Lost in admiration, she watched the horse until a sudden twist in the road hid it from view. Then she sighed deeply. 'Or maybe not,' she murmured musingly, half to herself. 'Maybe, after all, we're just leaving civilization.'

I had no interest then in philosophical considerations. Nor could I bring myself to care one way or the other. I snuggled close to her shoulder, thrilling with excitement at what lay ahead – a return to my old familiar life. All was well with my world. War or no war, I was at last on my way home.